COLONIAL
NEW YORK

A HISTORY

A HISTORY OF THE AMERICAN COLONIES
IN THIRTEEN VOLUMES

GENERAL EDITORS:
MILTON M. KLEIN & JACOB E. COOKE

MICHAEL KAMMEN

COLONIAL NEW YORK

A HISTORY

CHARLES SCRIBNER'S SONS, NEW YORK

Copyright © 1975 Charles Scribner's Sons

Library of Congress Cataloging in Publication Data

Kammen, Michael G
  Colonial New York: A History

(A History of the American colonies)
Bibliography: p. 376
Includes index.
  1. New York (State)—History—Colonial period,
ca. 1600-1777. I. Title. II. Series.
F122.K27   974.7'02   75-5693
ISBN 0-684-14325-9

1 3 5 7 9 11 13 15 17 19 C/C 20 18 16 14 12 10 8 6 4 2

Printed in the United States of America

F
122
.K27

THIS BOOK IS INSCRIBED
TO MY COLLEAGUES
IN THE DEPARTMENT OF HISTORY
AT CORNELL UNIVERSITY
1965–1975

CONTENTS

ILLUSTRATIONS

EDITORS'
INTRODUCTION

The American colonies have not lacked their Boswells. Almost from the time of their founding, the English settlements in the New World became the subjects of historical narratives by promoters, politicians, and clergymen. Some, like John Smith's *General History of Virginia*, sought to stir interest in New World colonization. Others, such as Cotton Mather's *Magnalia Christi Americana*, used New England's past as an object lesson to guide its next generation. And others still, like William Smith's *History of the Province of New-York*, aimed at enhancing the colony's reputation in England by explaining its failures and emphasizing its accomplishments. All of these early chroniclers had their shortcomings but no more so than every generation of historians which essayed the same task thereafter. For it is both the strength and the challenge of the historical guild that in each age its practitioners should readdress themselves to the same subjects of inquiry as their predecessors. If the past is prologue, it must be constantly reenacted. The human drama is unchanging, but the audience is always new: its expectations of the past are different, its mood uniquely its own.

The tercentenary of John Smith's history is almost coterminous with the bicentenary of the end of the American colonial era. It is more than appropriate that the two occasions should be observed by a fresh retelling of the story of the colonization of English America not, as in the case of the earliest histories, in self-justification, national exaltation, or moral purgation but as a plain effort to reexamine the past through the lenses of the present.

Apart from the national observance of the bicentennial of American independence, there is ample justification in the era of the 1970s for a modern history of each of the original thirteen colonies. For many of them, there exists no single-volume narrative published in the present century and, for some, none written since those undertaken by contemporaries in the eighteenth century. The standard multivolume histories of the colonial period—those of Herbert L. Osgood, Charles M. Andrews, and Lawrence H. Gipson—are too comprehensive to provide adequate treatment of individual colonies, too political and institutional in emphasis to deal adequately with social, economic, and cultural developments, and too intercolonial and Anglo-American in focus to permit intensive examination of a single colony's distinctive evolution. The most recent of these comprehensive accounts, that of Gipson, was begun as far back as 1936; since then a considerable body of new scholarship has been produced.

The present series, *A History of the American Colonies*, of which Dr. Kammen's volume is part, seeks to synthesize the new research, to treat social, economic, and cultural as well as political developments, and to delineate the broad outlines of each colony's history during the years before independence. No uniformity of organization has been imposed on the authors, although each volume attempts to give some attention to every aspect of the colony's historical development. Each author is a specialist in his own field and has shaped his material to the configuration of the colony about which he writes. While the Revolutionary Era is the terminal point of each volume, the authors have not read the history of the colony backward, as mere preludes to the inevitable movement toward independence and statehood.

Despite their local orientation, the individual volumes, taken together, will provide a collective account that should help us understand the broad foundation on which the future history of the colonies in the new nation was to rest and, at the same time, help clarify that still not completely explained melodrama of 1776 which saw, in John Adams's words, thirteen clocks somewhat amazingly strike as one. In larger perspective, *A History of the American Colonies* seeks to remind today's generation of Americans of its earliest heritage as a contribution to an understanding of its contemporary purpose. The link between past and present is as certain as it is at times indiscernible, for as Michael Kammen has so aptly observed, "the historian is the memory of civilization. A civilization without memory ceases to be civilized. A civilization without history ceases to have identity. Without identity there is no purpose; without purpose civilization will wither." *

Despite its importance, New York has attracted very few historians of its colonial period: a slim volume in the Yale Chronicles series in 1919 and a contemporary history published in 1757 constitute the sole efforts to compress the state's colonial past into a single volume. What deterred historians was the tangled skein of cultural, economic, ethnic, sectional, and political threads that had to be unraveled to understand the complexities of a province more socially diverse than perhaps any other mainland British colony in North America. A common historiographical escape from the challenge was to treat the province's Dutch beginnings as an essay in cultural antiquarianism, however attractively quaint, to disavow any attempt to make sense of the political factionalism and personal rivalries of the years 1664–1763, and then to resume the story when New York joined its sister colonies in the great contest against the mother country. Thus was lost the vital century during which New Yorkers grew to maturity and began to play out their unique experiment in creating community out of social disorder and in converting a Dutch outpost of commerce into a thriving and politically sophisticated English colony.

It is precisely this heretofore neglected century that the author of this volume makes signally comprehensible by his skillful use

---

* Michael Kammen, *People of Paradox* (New York, 1972), 13.

of primary and secondary sources and his remarkable familiarity with the terrain on which the drama was enacted—and those physical remains that remind us of that past. Unlike Carl Becker, who made the prerevolutionary era appear as mere prelude to the War for Independence, Michael Kammen discerns in New York's colonial history those underlying themes which stemmed from its Dutch heritage and were reinforced by its English experience: a persistent attempt to legitimize institutions in a colony launched without a formal charter of government, and a concurrent effort to rear a society on unstable and heterogeneous demographic foundations. How New Yorkers overcame the precarious pluralism with which they began their existence and painfully but persistently adjusted their institutions to their social diversity is revealed in these pages. The experience was not yet complete when New York was thrown into the maelstrom of revolution. Vigorous in opposition between 1763 and 1768, New Yorkers hesitated after that date; but once committed to independence, they became central agents in the grand design that led from colonialism to republicanism. Despite the fragility of its unstable, pluralistic heritage, the colony was able to contribute effectively to the winning of independence. New York's colonial history, viewed in conjunction with the histories of the other twelve colonies, clarifies the meaning of a revolution whose inception, however fortuitous, produced consequences so momentous that they live with us still.

MILTON M. KLEIN
JACOB E. COOKE

PREFACE

It is incredible to think that the most recent biography of early New York appeared in 1919, more than half a century ago. Since that time we have learned a great deal from scholars as well as history buffs about particular aspects of the province's history. We have also learned to ask different sorts of questions about the colonial period generally and to utilize new methods in seeking answers to those questions. It is, therefore, time for a fresh attempt at integrating particulars into a new, cohesive narrative of what occurred in New York between the era of European reconnaissance and the age of American Revolution.

Because the history of settlement along the Hudson River has all sorts of complexities—streaming freshets and unexpected eddies—the reader should be informed at the outset about some of them; for they will, in various ways, be encountered again and again throughout this book. In many respects, provincial New York was simply part of a colonial empire and shared many characteristics in common with its neighbors north and south. Like them it had to develop viable institutions and legitimize the necessary arrangements of its public life. Like them it contained contrary tendencies toward both centralization and localism, as well as tensions between the impulses to freedom and the imperatives of authority. Like them, too, it had ill-defined frontiers, troublesome relations with the Indians, class conflict, and uneven economic development. And like Massachusetts, Pennsylvania, and Virginia, though not adequately noticed by historians, New York was also a cockpit of the Revolution. When the Founding Fathers established a federal government in 1789, it was no accident that they located its seat in New York City.

Nevertheless, New York also remains a colony apart, different both in kind and in degree from all its provincial siblings. It alone among the continental colonies had been conquered by the English and not simply colonized from the outset. It alone became truly bilingual. And it especially became the most polyglot and socially mixed of them all. Hence the problems of pluralism and of attendant instability often seemed more severe in New York than elsewhere. Consequently the gaps between law or expectation on the one side and experience or accommodation on the other were great—with respect to white-Indian relations, the imperial commercial system, procedures for naturalization, suffrage, and divorce. Always the discrepancies between what government wanted people to do and what people actually did were glaring and fraught with signal consequences. No other group of colonists, moreover, may have been quite so pervasively materialistic and intent upon the exclusive quest for creature comforts. Unlike New England, where getting and spending were partially restrained by Puritan inhibitions, and unlike the South, where proto-English elegance became a mitigating ethic of sorts, the Yorkers' materialism was undiluted by divinity, gentility, or propriety. They simply grubbed on: the "Art of getting Money," said one contemporary, was "the only principle of life propagated among the young People."

All of these phenomena—the ones New York shared in common with its neighbors as well as those peculiar to it alone—provide major themes in the chapters that follow. For however much New York may have been sui generis among the English colonies, it was also, I think, a paradigm of what America at large would become in the nineteenth and twentieth centuries: pluralistic, conflict prone, materialistic, and individualistic within certain ill-defined bounds of conformity. The dominant themes in the history of colonial New York as it is narrated here, therefore, will essentially be opposite sides of the same coin: political adjustment to social change in a heterogeneous setting (as in 1683, 1689, or 1766, for example) and social adjustment to political change (as in the years after 1664, 1691, and 1776).

There is one other emphasis that may require some notice and explanation. During the summer of 1972, I tried to fulfill the injunctions of Francis Parkman and Samuel Eliot Morison that the historian ought to see and experience, as much as possible, whatever he writes about. To avoid the ennui and errors of the armchair historian, I traveled up and down both sides of the Hudson River valley, from Tappan to Glens Falls, out and back on Long Island, and through those portions of the interior Iroquois country that had been settled or explored by 1777. With maps and guidebooks and architectural histories in hand, I found that far more of New York's physical heritage has survived than I ever imagined: not merely isolated houses and churches, museums and working farms, but whole villages like Hurley or the charming Huguenot section in New Paltz remain virtually unchanged since their origin more than two centuries ago. In sum, the most exciting sources that I have encountered in researching this book have been the material remains of manors and forts, homes and inns, churches and post roads. Wherever possible, I have tried to convey some sense of these remains; for in them the past perseveres into the future, immortalized so long as we have eyes to see, the curiosity to care, and the patience to preserve our unique heritage.

It is a particular pleasure to acknowledge the debts incurred in preparing this volume. Professor Milton M. Klein invited me to write it in 1967, waited very patiently for the manuscript to develop, and then gave me the benefit of his extraordinary knowledge of colonial New York. He has been a blessing both as editor and friend.

I am obliged to a number of New York specialists for generous permission to read unpublished versions of their work-in-progress: notably Professors Thomas J. Archdeacon of the University of Wisconsin, Milton M. Klein of the University of Tennessee, John M. Murrin of Princeton University, Robert C.

Ritchie of the University of California (San Diego), Bernard Friedman of Indiana University, Edward Countryman of the University of Warwick (England), Hendrik Edelman of Cornell University, and Bruce B. Detlefsen of the New York State Education Department.

Students at Cornell, once again, have been helpful in many ways: through their enthusiasm for the history of colonial New York, their willingness to explore pertinent problems with me, and their own excellent dissertations and honors theses. I am particularly obliged to Mary-Jo McNamara (my research assistant for a year), Douglas S. Greenberg, Langdon G. Wright, Robert G. Smith, David E. Narrett, Robert L. Hampel, and Steve J. Stern for their efforts and for their friendship.

Staff members at a great many institutions have been notably helpful; but I must especially thank those at the Cornell University Libraries, the New-York Historical Society, the New York Public Library, and the Museum of the City of New York. At the New York State Historical Association in Cooperstown, Wendell Tripp has been a cooperative accomplice and a genial host.

Funds for research and travel were made possible by the Colonel Return Jonathan Meigs Fund* at Cornell University and by the National Endowment for the Humanities which

---

* It should be noted that the historic Return Jonathan Meigs (1740–1823) neatly personifies several of the central themes of my story. A Connecticut man, he knowingly passed counterfeit paper money in New York a few years before the American Revolution. Although he was caught, jailed, brought to trial, convicted, and sentenced to be hanged, Connecticut and New York authorities agreed to pardon and release him. When the war began he was "in mercantile pursuits" in Middletown, Connecticut, and the captain of a militia company. In 1775 he distinguished himself at the siege of Boston, then served under Benedict Arnold in the northern assault upon Quebec, was imprisoned there, later exchanged, and returned to the army. During the spring of 1777 he led a spectacularly successful raid against the British and Loyalist regiment at Sag Harbor on eastern Long Island. In 1779 he participated in Anthony Wayne's stunning bayonet attack upon Stony Point along the Hudson. By war's end he had become a respected colonel, and he lived on until 1823 and the ripe age of eighty-two.

awarded me a Senior Fellowship in 1972–73. Mrs. Connie Ingraham and Mrs. Mary H. Mall cheerfully transcribed my crabbed handwriting into clean typescript. Jacob E. Cooke, Carol Kammen, Elsie Kearns, Barbara Wood, and Mary Beth Norton exercised their historical and editorial skills on the book at several stages of its growth. I am very grateful to them all.

August 7, 1974
Ithaca, New York   MICHAEL KAMMEN

COLONIAL
NEW YORK

A HISTORY

1

CARRACKS AND CANOES

In September 1609, *The Half Moon* sailed inquisitively up the Hudson, from the Narrows to the site of modern Albany. Again and again along its way the three-masted carrack encountered canoes filled with Algonkian Indians eager for trade. The natives brought tobacco and maize, oysters and beans, beaver and otter skins, which, wrote Robert Juet, the ship's mate, "wee bought for trifles." The travel-weary Europeans had trinkets and beads, hatchets and knives, to swap for fresh food and furry treasures. Neither side fully trusted the other, and the crew expected "treacherie" at every turn. Certain that the Indians would betray them if given half a chance, the explorers acted accordingly. "Our Master and his Mate determined to trie some of the chiefe men of the Countrey, whether they had any treacherie in them. So they tooke them downe into the Cabbin, and gave them so much Wine and *Aqua vitae,* that they were all merrie. . . . In the end one of them was drunke . . . and that was strange to them; for they could not tell how to take it." So it was, in this autumnal encounter between an eighty-ton carrack and some swift canoes, that two civilizations touched and began to get a taste of each other.

The Half Moon was not, however, the first European vessel to enter the Hudson. In 1524 Giovanni da Verrazano, sailing for the king of France, brought the *Dauphine* into lower New York Bay. Verrazano anchored off the shore of Staten Island at the entrance to the Narrows; but he neither named nor claimed the "very big river, which was deep within the mouth." An unexpected squall forced him to abandon exploration and put to sea. A Portuguese mariner poked into the river a year later; and venturesome French traders, perhaps as early as 1540, descended it from the north in order to trade with the Mahicans and Wappingers. An Englishman may have crossed the Hudson in 1568 during a fabulous overland journey from the Gulf of Mexico to Canada, and Dutch sea traders clearly knew something of the river by 1600. Not until 1609, however, with Henry Hudson's voyage from the mouth to the head of navigation near Albany, was there a full description of the river and, more important, the first stimulus to European colonization along its shores of verdant forest and fertile meadowland.

The Hudson is not very long. Flowing 315 miles from its source, Lake Tear of the Clouds, 4,293 feet high on the southwest slope of Mount Marcy in the Adirondacks, it ranks only seventy-first in length among American rivers. But it is navigable to large vessels for 150 miles, and it is precisely along that stretch that much of our story transpired between 1609 and 1777. The river's drainage area covers 12,200 square miles, and it flows past six separate physiographic sections: the Canadian Shield, the Folded Appalachians, the Catskills, the Hudson Highlands, the New England Upland, and the New Jersey Lowland. Few rivers cut across such geological diversity in so short a span.

Because the river has a moderating influence upon air temperature, its lower valley becomes a kind of chute through which warm air can travel northward. Iona Island, forty-five miles north of the Battery, marks the dividing line, for beyond it the sea breezes do not blow, and therefore southern plants do not grow. The salt line stretches yet another fifteen miles to Newburgh, however, and ocean tides reach all the way to Troy. Except during the spring runoff, downstream currents are not very strong. Consequently a log thrown into the river at Albany would require the better part of a year to reach the ocean. For every eight miles that the log moved downstream, tides would carry it back seven and a half. No wonder the Indians called the Hudson "the-water-that-flows-two-ways"; and no wonder the men in the carracks and canoes were able to catch both salt- and freshwater fish in identical sections of the river.

A European ship, like *The Half Moon*, might come in from the Atlantic with Sandy Hook to port and the East Bank shoals to starboard. Turning north between the banks, it would sail through the Lower Bay, into the Narrows between Brooklyn and Staten Island to the Upper Bay, pass Governor's Island, the tip of Manhattan Island, and then into the principal channel of the river. At this point, where the Holland and Lincoln tunnels are today, the Hudson seemed to an observer in 1625 "for the most part a musket shot wide." Manhattan then was crisscrossed by freshwater brooks and was less regular in coastal outline than it is today. Even more striking from a modern perspective is the fact that newcomers always commented upon the island's wonderful fragrance—the "sweete smells" from its grasses and wild flowers.

Passing the Palisades' sheer cliffs on the port side and Harlem's woods to starboard, a ship would move up to the reach between Dobbs Ferry and Croton-on-Hudson, where the river achieves its greatest breadth at Haverstraw Bay, a span of three miles. Here the Hudson resembles nothing so much as a large snake immediately after gorging itself—a stout and bulky bulge interrupting an otherwise svelte stream. That bulge was indeed bursting: with sea sturgeon, striped bass, shad, herring, menhaden, tomcod, as well as many smaller fish. The riverbanks here spill onto marshy lowlands that rise only a little above sea level.

Then, from Montrose Point on up to Cornwall and Storm King Mountain, the Hudson narrows because the highlands lean diagonally from southwest to northeast, connecting the hills of northern New Jersey with the Taconic Mountains of the New England Upland. Even so, the river's channel remains deep and reliable. "This is a very pleasant place to build a towne on," Juet wrote in 1609, looking at the sites of Garrison and West Point. "The Road is very neere [to the banks], and very good for all winds, save an East North-east wind." For generations to come, "the road" would refer to the ships' channel, for these were waterborne communities. News and crops and furs and people all traveled most easily, almost exclusively, by boat; and water provided mills with power as well as goods with transport. Insofar as the Hudson's water was their life's blood, these early Americans were figuratively bluebloods.

From Newburgh north, through Poughkeepsie, Kingston, Albany, and Schuylerville, the river gradually narrows—like an artery extending farther and farther from the heart—while the valley itself broadens. The Shawangunk Mountains give way to the purplish Catskills and then the Helderberg Hills. Before the lower Adirondack Mountains begin, however, the beautiful Mohawk Valley stretches westward from Albany and Cohoes, like an ancient finger pointing the way for future settlement. West of the Mohawk lies the Great Lakes Plain south of Ontario; west of the Catskills lies the broad but inhospitable Allegheny Plateau; and due north of the Hudson Valley is the dramatic Champlain Valley, stretching up to touch New France. These three regions were not colonized until after the American Revolution. Between 1609 and 1777 they remained the preserve of the Iroquois and their allies, of the *coureurs du bois* and a few spirit-driven missionaries, and of the cold, snowy winters more severe than European colonists cared to cope with.

Projecting eastward from the Hudson's Narrows and Upper Bay, like an elongated crab's claw, lay Long Island, offering its shelter to disaffected New Englanders and its shores to careless, playful whales. Long Island's northern spine, the Manhasset Plateau, rises up to the Harbor Hill Moraine, dips down again, rises once more into the Ronkonkoma Moraine, and then slopes gently down to the Atlantic's sandy beaches, so that a cross section of Long Island resembles the cross section of an airplane's wing. It is the largest island adjoining the United States, extending for 118 miles. Because of its glacial moraine and outwash plains covered with rich soil and because of its warm and humid summers, it was more than ready to yield its abundance to diligent farmers.

Colonial New Yorkers did not, however, fully capitalize on these fine natural resources. No other colony had anything like a Hudson River to facilitate such easy penetration so far into the interior. Yet by the eve of the Revolution in 1775, settlers from

Pennsylvania, Virginia, and Carolina had made much greater advances westward, while New Englanders had filled the Connecticut Valley to a greater degree than Yorkers had peopled the parallel Hudson-Champlain trough. While Manhattan and Albany were firmly established as the terminals for Hudson River traffic, surprisingly little differentiation in function or importance had developed among intermediate points. With the possible exceptions of Schenectady and perhaps Kingston, there were few clues to suggest which villages or river landings would rise above their neighbors in the nineteenth century. Unpredictable Indians, competitive French outposts, and restrictive land policies all combined to keep colonial New York relatively small and underdeveloped.

As New England Puritans crossed Long Island Sound and Dutch Calvinists and French Huguenots built their dorps and forts along the Hudson, they began to sprinkle European place names upon the land. Familiar sounds and words with old associations might make the unfamiliar environment a little more congenial. More important perhaps, bestowing a name indicated possession, or at least created the illusion of possession. So it was that New Netherland became New York in 1664 and Beverwyck became Albany. Some of the early visitors, however, listened to the natives and tried to call places by their time-honored names. If Indians and Europeans used a common nomenclature, they reasoned, it would be easier to negotiate boundaries and land sales.

As it happened, an anonymous English voyager, apparently in 1607, entered the Hudson's mouth, sailed around, conversed with some natives, and then wrote "Mannahata" on his map to the west and "Manahatin" to the east. When Henry Hudson arrived two years later, he likely had a copy of that map; and his log keeper, Juet, wrote that "that side of the river is called Manna-hata." Perhaps these are variants of the tribal name "Mahican," which was sometimes spelled "Manhecan" and sometimes "Manahegan." In any case, the name stuck; accident gave way to acceptance and acceptance to tradition.

In 1614 Adriaen Block sailed his little vessel through the narrow strait east of Manhattan and called it Hellegat ("hell passage") because of the tricky tides. He then circumnavigated Long Island and, discovering its shape, so named it. Going up the Hudson, the Dutch often adapted Indian names to their own tongue, so that Hackensack, Poughkeepsie, and Scheaenhech-stede (which became Schenectady) looked Dutch enough to deceive an Englishman. Breukelyn, Vlissingen (Flushing), and Haerlem, however, were authentic transplants from the old country. Still other place names derived from particular land-owners. Because Jonas Bronck, a Dane, had a large farm just north of Manhattan, people referred to Bronck's River and to "the Broncks," meaning where the Broncks lived—thus, eventually, the Bronx.

Street names evolved more slowly and casually. As late as 1657 New Amsterdam had 120 houses and numerous roads, all without designations more precise or compact than "the path that Burger Jorisson made to go down to the strand." By 1658, however, the notaries began to mention streets by their specific names, and New Amsterdam thereby became the first American city with formally designated streets. The most famous of these began as an Indian trail leading from the north end of Manhattan through the woods to the lower tip where it reached the Hudson. Because the natives brought their beaver skins down it for trade, it became known at first as the "Beaver Path." But with the fort constructed just south of the Beaver Path and with a widening of the road for convenience in trading and gunnery, the people called it by a more likely descriptive name: "Breede Wegh," or "Broad Way." That stuck too. Similarly, Wall Street took its name from the road running just inside the fortification that was built across the island from west to east.

All of these names—Algonkian and English and Dutch—have more to do with modern orthography than with ancient topography; yet long before the seventeenth century there were inhabitants of New York who were none of these nationalities. Until the early 1950s, archaeologists were obliged to be conservative and limit their estimates of New York's prehistory to the period 100–1600. Then the discovery and application of radiocarbon methods of dating revitalized prehistorical studies, so that current understanding stretches back almost eight thousand years, from the Paleo-Indian hunters to the tribal occupants of those canoes in 1609. The last forty-five hundred years of this span are firmly supported by carbon-14 determinations. Our system of classification has thus become much more complex and sophisticated, able to accommodate greater amounts of archaeological data more accurately and flexibly.

Thus we speak of a Paleo-Indian culture to about 5000 B.C., an early archaic (or Lamoka) at about 3500 B.C., a middle archaic at about 2400 B.C., a late archaic to perhaps 1000 B.C., an early Woodland culture to A.D. 400, a second phase of Woodland (or Owasco) culture to 1100, followed by the emergence of Iroquoian and Algonkian cultures right through the coming of the carracks after 1600. What provides the material basis for this periodization? Stone, bone, copper, and antler artifacts—such as fishhooks, knives, needles, whistles, flint points, drills, choppers, scrapers, gouges, adzes, awls, and pestles—as well as pieces of pottery that have survived the assaults of time. Iroquoian ceramics, for example, following their Woodland, or Owasco, prototypes, flourished in central and northern New York and extended westward to northern Ohio as well as southward into Pennsylvania and New Jersey. Typical Iroquois pottery vessels had globular bodies and distinctly separate collars (above the neck) that were rectangulated or castellated.

The makers of these vessels followed a mixed economy of hunting and farming. But the various mountain and highland barriers cut off easy access to the east and west, restricted the resources available to food collectors, and made agriculture a challenge for food producers. Forest covers often being heavily coniferous, soils being stony and unproductive, the Indians located themselves largely in the deciduous or mixed deciduous and coniferous woodlands which provided the foods to sustain deer, turkey, and associated wildlife. Those tribes seeking a more diversified economy were confined to areas of lighter, more fertile soil so that hoe tillage and primitive tools might be workable. Inevitably, then, Europeans and Indians would come into conflict over the choicer agricultural sites.

Ironically, it is precisely this period of protohistorical transition, the later sixteenth and earlier seventeenth centuries, when the material remains ought to gain in density, specificity, and reliability; but in fact they do not. Archaeologists have not been able to locate or identify any of the particular Mahican or Wappinger villages mentioned in written accounts. Most of them have probably been overlaid by European towns and cities. Even relics of what is called the late Woodland culture are scarce along the Hudson, probably because the groups were relatively small in number and highly mobile. As Verrazano wrote in 1524, "They change their habitations from place to place as circumstances of situation and season may require; this is easily done, as they have only to take with them their mats, and they have other houses prepared at once"—a simplification, to be sure, based upon superficial contact but containing a large kernel of truth.

In any case, a great many questions about Hudson Valley prehistory remain to be answered. We do not know when and how the basic gathering economy shifted to include growing corn. Nor can we adequately correlate our archaeological evidence with those descriptions of Indian arts and customs given by explorers and early colonists. We cannot be certain that "late Woodland" artifacts were in fact used by Mahican and Wappinger tribes who met the white men after 1600, though it seems likely; and we cannot establish clear continuities between these Algonkian-speaking tribes and the most permanent inhabitants of the valley—the people of the so-called Vosburg complex—though there are hints at certain sites of direct ancestry.

One of our problems in understanding the early modern history of New York's Indian population from physical remains is that far more settlement sites have been revealed than were actually occupied at any given time. The accompanying figure indicates unfortified villages (a dot) and villages protected by earthworks or stockades (a cross); but at any particular moment, only seventy or eighty of these were actually occupied. Hence it is

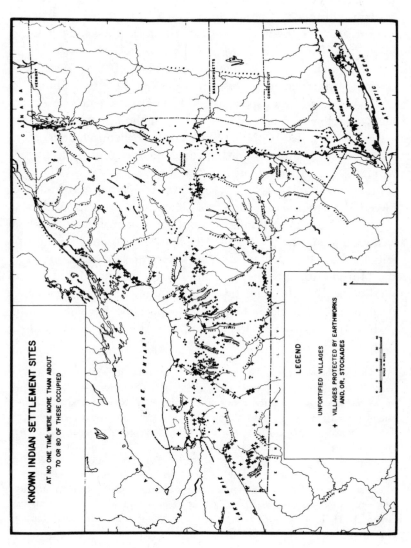

Indian settlement sites in early New York. *From John H. Thompson, ed.,* Geography of New York State *(Syracuse: Syracuse University Press, 1966), 116. Copyright © 1966 by Syracuse University Press. Reprinted by permission of the publisher.*

difficult to estimate population figures and harder still to trace the mobility and stability patterns of particular tribes. Another problem arises from the rapidity of the acculturation process, by which Stone Age skills and implements were replaced with European devices during the quarter-century after initial contact. It is often impossible to know who used a particular artifact—European, Indian, or both—who occupied a particular site, or whether the vestiges of a battle indicate a fight between whites and Indians, or between Mohawks and Mahicans.

Still, much is known about the Indians of New York. Two distinct groups emerged historically after the first millennium A.D. Members of one spoke related dialects classified as Algonkian, and they settled predominantly in the eastern part of the state (as well as in New England and Pennsylvania). The Algonkians, comprising Mahicans, Delawares, Wappingers, Montauks, and many others, dominated for several hundred years after 1000. In about 1300, however, hunger and hostilities forced the Iroquoian Indians of the mid-Mississippi Valley to seek new hunting grounds.* Small groups pushing north and eastward along the Ohio and Allegheny rivers spawned the Erie tribe and subsequently from it the Seneca and Cayuga, then later the Huron tribe, and from it the Onondaga, the Mohawk, and finally the Oneida. The time and manner of their emergence remain conjectural, but by 1570—perhaps even a century earlier—these tribes had coalesced into the League of the Five Nations.

---

* There is strong disagreement among archaeologists and ethnohistorians over this matter of migration. On the basis of recent field work, some archaeologists insist upon the continuous evolution, in situ, of Iroquois Indians out of the earlier Woodland cultures of the Finger Lakes area (see James A. Tuck, *Onondaga Iroquois Prehistory: A Study in Settlement Archaeology* [Syracuse, 1971], xi, 19–21). Even these archaeologists, however, are obliged to admit significant breaks in the chronology of their continuum, and their conclusions are based upon a tiny sampling of sites. Until much more archaeological evidence emerges, I will have to follow the migration theory; it does not ignore artifacts, but it also draws upon anthropological and written materials (see George E. Hyde, *Indians of the Woodlands from Prehistoric Times to 1725* [Norman, Okla., 1962], 12–16, 25–26, 85).

The league's purpose, paradoxically, was to achieve peace through preparedness and militance. According to legend, Deganawidah, a deified figure of Huron-Mohawk extraction, and Hiawatha, a disciple, conceived and completed the league. By tradition the Mohawks first took up the covenant chain, followed in order by each successive neighbor to the west: Oneida, Onondaga, Cayuga, and Seneca. Through this alliance they hoped to achieve permanent peace among themselves and to defend against their common enemies from a position of strength. There may initially have been a genuine Iroquois ideal of universal peace; but if so, the ideal was undermined by the Five Nations' strong sense of tribal superiority: over both the Algonkians to the east and the nonleague Iroquois to the west and south (Huron, Neutral, Erie, Petun, and Susquehannock). With the passage of time, ideals of universal peace became less conspicuous than the bloody process of conquering outsiders and absorbing them into the league's longhouse.

The league was governed by a council of forty-nine sachems. These offices corresponded with an equal number already in existence among the Five Nations at the time the league was formed. Because the several nations had different numbers of sachems, and because the Mohawk, Onondaga, and Seneca remained more powerful than the other two, the unequal numbers were perpetuated in council. The discrepancy mattered little in practical terms, however, because each nation spoke with only one voice and had but one vote. Although the three more powerful members had special responsibility for the conduct of war and relations with other tribes, the league's administrative structure had so many checks and balances built in that none of the three, alone or together, could easily abuse its power.*

As strong as their sense of territoriality must have been, and as complex as their political organization may have been, it is the

---

* From time to time American statesmen, such as Franklin and Jefferson, as well as romantic historians, have suggested Iroquois paternity for the federal system of government created in 1787. There is no persuasive evidence for this claim.

social structure of the Iroquois that seems ultimately most important, and their sense of kinship most determinative. Their societies were matriarchal and matrilineal—a logical measure when one realizes that their men were often away on long hunting trips, were prematurely killed by enemies, and were somewhat casual about entering and dissolving marriages. Older women were deferred to, settled most disputes, and exerted considerable authority in choosing sachems. All real property, both land and housing, belonged formally to the women; compensation for a woman's life required twice as much wampum as for a man's; and Indian children took their mother's names.

The social and economic roles of the sexes, moreover, were carefully defined and divided. Men were hunters while women were cultivators. Men were much more nomadic, whereas women were comparatively sedentary. Men were allowed, even expected, to philander, while women might be wanton only under certain circumstances. Kinship patterns imposed standards of honor and vengeance. In the event of a murder, the persons most immediately affected might be women—a mother, wife, or sister—who could demand either the torture and death of the murderer or the adoption of a captive to take the deceased person's place. Even so, though women might demand revenge and determine the fate of captives, men were responsible for bringing back scalps or prisoners. Participating in a war party became a challenge to manliness, a rite of passage for the young brave, so that failure to participate would bring animus against the youth and onus upon his family.

Each tribe consisted of families or groups of families called clans. The Mohawks, for example, comprised three clans: Turtle, Bear, and Wolf. Because youngsters were required to marry outside their own clan, the village of any given clan included men from other clans. Language, tradition, and customary practices provided a sense of cohesion within the tribes. Each clan and village had its governing council. The latter, in turn, sent representatives—nominated by the older women of privileged clans—to the tribal council. The braves, however, reserved to themselves the choice of chiefs to lead them in battle.

Indian men prided themselves upon their skills as woodsmen, warriors, hunters, and trappers. Yet these skills were exercised to a surprising degree in seasonal patterns, and they dovetailed with the economic roles played by the women. After the Midwinter Festival, for example, toward the end of February when sap had begun to rise in the trees, most families left their villages to camp near groves of sugar maples. For weeks the women were preoccupied with making sugar while the men helped as well as hunted and hoped to trap small fur-bearing animals for the peltry trade. After the spring thaw, men, women, and children all participated in fishing expeditions, with spears and weirs, whatever was appropriate to their locale and the kind of fish then running. In April and May, while the womenfolk planted corn, squash, beans, and tobacco, men and boys repaired older dwellings or built new ones—thereby giving rise to their Corn-Planting Ceremony and Strawberry Festival.

Summer was a time for sociability, for the renewal of friendships and alliances, for politics and diplomacy. Autumn brought the harvest and the Green Corn Festival, a time for naming children born since the midwinter ceremony, for singing chants, for performing the Thanksgiving Dance, and for holding the Bowl Game, a sacred play of chance in which each team tried to win all of 102 beans. Late fall and winter was the time for hunting and fighting, forays against neighboring tribes, and forages for deer, elk, bear, otter, marten, and beaver. So it was that seasonal change separated the sexes and then brought them together again in rhythms of necessity, society, and occasional austerity.

An Owasco-Iroquois village which has recently been restored on Owasco Lake conveys a vivid sense of Indian communal life between the eleventh and sixteenth centuries. It is 300 feet long (about 50 feet less than its archaeological prototype), 120 feet wide, and surrounded by a "palisade" made up of more than fourteen hundred graceful sapling poles. They are bound together (to a height of 4 feet) by vinelike willow withes. Although the "palisade" towers some 15 feet in height, its primary function was not defensive but rather the exclusion of animal pests— bears, wolves, raccoons, skunks, and porcupines—from the village.

Within there are two longhouses, representing different phases of Owasco and Iroquois development. Each would have housed about 120 persons. The framework is made of sapling poles placed in two rows and bent overhead to form arches. Horizontal cross poles support the sheets of elm bark that cover the framework. Slender saplings hold the bark in place externally. Inside, a row of poles extends along the sides, joined to the walls by cross poles. This construction adds strength to the longhouse and also provides for upper and lower sleeping bunks along each interior side. Openings in the roof allowed the smoke from cooking fires to escape, and on those fires, kettles of corn soup simmered almost continuously.

The village contains in addition a small lodge for the medicine man and his patients, storage pits for winter supplies of fruits and vegetables, bark troughs for storing pottery clay in a moist condition, racks for drying and smoking fish, as well as other racks for stretching and tanning skins. A large grinding stone is centrally placed for sharpening and polishing tools; a lookout tree stands tall and alert to aid in the search for wandering game; a life-giving stream cuts diagonally across the village; corn grows in long, narrow plots just inside the "palisade" wall on one side; and an area for games of skill and children's play is set aside on the other. A burial ground was located some three hundred feet east of the village.

Amid all this communal activity, however, the Indians pursued an ideal of self-fulfilling autonomy and personal responsibility. A man strove to be disciplined, impervious to privation and pain, an adequate provider, and a reliable protector. A warrior wanted a skin "seven thumbs thick" in order to be oblivious to gossip, scurrility, and social pressure; hence the well-known mask of stoicism and the less-known emphasis upon the literal interpretation of dreams. Dreams were omens of bad things to be avoided or revelations of wishes to be fulfilled. In either case, dreams were to be taken seriously, to be acted upon in order to preserve one's autonomy. The most frequently reported dreams came from pubescent youths leaving the shelter of childhood; from warriors worried by the prospect of capture and torture; and from the old or the sick, who faced the prospect of death. Their dreams prompted proleptic measures and the satisfaction of covert desires. The sick dreamer required special dances or rites. The lustful dreamer required the *andacwander* rite: sexual intercourse between partners who were not husband and wife. The anxious dreamer required the *ohgiwe* ceremony to relieve his troubled soul about a deceased relative or friend.

Iroquois therapy and therapists, then, allowed for wish fulfillment even at the expense of the privacy of others and tried to channel aggression away from destructive ends, either externally toward outsiders or internally in harmless ways. The effectiveness of the League of the Five Nations, for example, in restraining the revenge process *among* its members may have been partially responsible for the Iroquois' ferocity in chastening enemies without. As a distinguished anthropologist has suggested, "The Iroquois reputation for pertinacity and ruthlessness in fighting with their external enemies may be regarded as an indirect consequence of the blocking of the blood feud among the participating members of the League. The *pax Iroquois* resulted in the displacement of revenge motivations outward, onto surrounding peoples, Indian and European alike." *

---

* Anthony F. C. Wallace, *The Death and Rebirth of the Seneca* (New York, 1969), 46–47. Wallace's observation invites comparison with one historian's hypothesis concerning the relative absence of conflict *within* families in 17th-century Plymouth Colony and the considerable amount of litigation between families: "The family had to maintain a smooth kind of operational equilibrium; basic disruptions and discontinuities must be avoided at all costs. What this probably meant in practice was a strong unconscious restraint on the expression of hostile impulses against the members of one's own household. . . . But it seems that *occasions* for abrasive contact must have been there aplenty, and the anger that resulted had to find some outlet in behavior. This is the point at which the field of neighborly relations derives a real, if somewhat sinister, significance." (John

So it happened that the League of Peace became an agent of destruction, and the Iroquois became the most feared and hated warriors among all their brethren east of the Mississippi River. Their rise to power in the later sixteenth and throughout the seventeenth century ran exactly parallel to the rise of England and the Netherlands, so that their mutual contacts along the Hudson and the Mohawk were in some respects the confrontations of political equals. They were not technologically equal, to be sure, and their cultural traditions were vastly different. But all three had come of age contemporaneously, all three were commercially oriented, and they were in similar stages of self-awareness as political societies. During the 1600s, the Iroquois, the English, and the Dutch were beginning to challenge the hegemony of Algonkian, French, and Spanish power. All three would succeed eventually, but in part their commercial victories would extend them administratively beyond anything imaginable in 1609. Trade begat dominion; dominion begat political troubles and, ultimately, decline.

Once the Indians had been exposed to European trade goods, guns, and liquor, they began to covet them and to collect furs exclusively as a cash crop desirable to the Europeans. This obsession with fur collecting brought a concomitant emphasis upon older tribal preoccupations with hunting and fighting at the expense of settled agriculture and handicrafts. Within less than a generation the Iroquois exhausted the game in their own territory. In order to secure furs elsewhere they engaged in widespread warfare and the conquest of commercial sources. Between 1640 and 1685 they dominated tribes over a huge territory, from Hudson's Bay to the Carolinas, from the Mississippi to the fringes of European settlement. Their purpose was simply to gain control of the entire fur trade, to replace other hunters or else force them to sell their pelts to themselves as middlemen. In the process the Iroquois dispersed or decimated such rivals (and kinsmen) as the Hurons, despite French efforts to prevent them.

Demos, *A Little Commonwealth: Family Life in Plymouth Colony* [New York, 1970], 50.) In terms of their human imperatives and psychic energies, 17th-century colonists and Indians were perhaps not so very different.

Simultaneously, so long as the European settlers in New York failed to find a staple agricultural crop, such as tobacco or sugar, they needed the Indians as trappers and traders, for pelts became New York's nearest approximation to a staple. The Indians of New York were therefore tolerated and accommodated longer than those in any other colony, were respected diplomatically to a greater degree than anywhere else, and lived in a symbiotic relationship with Europeans: independent yet dependent, proud but envious, fierce despite visible signs of acculturation and deterioration.

The coming of the carracks after 1609 simply aggravated the Indians' penchant for rivalry and conflict. Those spots where Algonkian and Iroquoian hunters overlapped were friction points likely to produce a conflagration at any time. Even Algonkians on opposite banks of the Hudson had coexisted only tenuously for years. "Almost all those who live on the west side, are enemies of those on the east," wrote Johannes De Laet, a director of the West India Company, in 1625, "and cultivate more intercourse and friendship with our countrymen than the latter." In short, the various Indian tribes sought alliances with the Europeans in opposition to their indigenous enemies. In so doing they traded short-term advantage for long-run destruction.

In 1624, for example, hostilities began between Mohawks and Mahicans living along the upper reaches of the Hudson. The conflict, which amounted to a protracted, seasonal war, lasted at least four years and resulted in the Mahicans being driven east of the river, thereby setting the stage for the close relationship between Mohawks and Dutch in the Albany area—a relationship that would endure throughout the colonial period. European traders hoped to have friendly relations with as many separate tribes as possible in order to maximize competition and minimize wholesale prices. Conversely, the Indians hoped to trade with more than one European group at any given time. Hence the skirmishing and shifting of tribal campfires in one area after another along the Hudson. Hence, too, the pattern of compromise that slowly emerged: in reality the Indian tribes would normally be allied to and trade with only one European power at a time. More ambitious (or devious) relationships usually proved highly unstable and therefore unprofitable.

Dutch attitudes toward the Indians, generally, were conditioned by the relative freedom and tolerance prevalent in the Netherlands during the first half of the seventeenth century. Life there had been secularized and commercialized to a greater degree than anywhere else in Europe. Toleration was less an article of faith, however, than a matter of convenience. "Live and let live" seemed to be the Dutch scheme. Not that they were free of racial prejudice or failed to view the Indians as morally and culturally inferior—they did; miscegenation in New Netherland was uncommon, and intermarriage virtually unknown. Nevertheless, the few offspring of Dutch-Indian liaisons seem to have been accepted into the Dutch community so long as they were raised in the Reformed church as Dutch children.

Despite a certain commitment, in theory, to missionary activity, Dutch efforts cannot be called strenuous, and the results were pathetic. Only two ministers made any real attempt to work with the Indians of New Netherland, and they seem not to have made a single convert. The one lad who learned to read Dutch and understand the liturgy became an alcoholic and did more harm than good among his brethren. Reformed Calvinism lacked the ritual and symbolism of French Catholicism. Dominies were only permitted to baptize those adult Indians (or their children) who could demonstrate a genuine conversion experience based upon adequate education and understanding. The French Jesuits, by contrast, would baptize almost any Indian upon request—and many did so without even being asked!

The Dutch usually tried to be fair about land titles. They recognized the Indians' prior ownership and therefore the legal necessity of buying the land (after 1652 under governmental supervision). The practice kept land prices low, eliminated speculation, and lessened the chance of fraud and pressure tactics by greedy settlers. Though fraudulent purchases did occur, they were not common; and prices were proportioned to the supply and values of the day. Problems, therefore, arose not from dishonesty so much as from misunderstanding based upon different notions of land ownership and proper sale. In the Indians' cosmology, land could not really be bought or sold. It belonged to the tribe or clan as a community resource for the use of all its members in perpetuity. Transactions that the Dutch considered final were regarded by the Algonkians as partial payment for temporary use, subject to subsequent cancellation and retrocession. As white population spread and land values rose, the Indians often insisted upon further payment. The Dutch misunderstood the reasons for these demands and reacted harshly, often with hostility.

All this leads one to ask: What cultural baggage did the Dutch burghers bring with them to New Netherland? What assumptions did they make about commerce, religion, politics, and society? To understand those assumptions requires some knowledge of the Dutch Republic during the first quarter of the seventeenth century. To generalize about the Dutch "character" is a risky business, of course, because the seven northern provinces alone contained considerable diversity, not to mention the ten southern provinces, which remained Spanish, Catholic, and subsequently became Belgium. Nevertheless, impressions stimulate generalizations and perceptions of national culture—as well as exceptions to those generalizations.

The Dutch seem, from their humor and conversation, to have been at once delicate and blunt, cosmopolitan yet parochial. The qualities associated with Erasmus are also those attributed to the Dutch during their era of colonization: humane, tolerant, moderate, latitudinarian, but most of all, bourgeois. Calvinism, capitalism, and materialism seem to have been the ignition, engine, and fuel for the northern Netherlands during the seventeenth century. Descartes, who spent much of his life in Holland, wrote that "in this great town [Amsterdam] where apart from myself there dwells no one who is not engaged in trade, everyone is so much out for his own advantage that I should be able to live my whole life here without ever meeting a mortal being." Half a century after Descartes, Daniel Defoe wrote a concise, classic description of the economic function of the Netherlands: "The Dutch must be understood as they really are, the Middle Persons in Trade, the Factors and Brokers of Europe. . . . They *buy* to *sell* again, *take* in to *send* out, and the greatest Part of their vast Commerce consists in being supply'd from All Parts of the World, that they may supply All the World again."

Even before the States of Holland formally renounced their allegiance to Philip II of Spain in 1581, and even before the Truce of 1609 ended forty years of war between Spain and the northern provinces, there had been a steady secularization of economic behavior in the Netherlands, a loosening of traditional restrictions upon economic activity, and a tendency to treat business matters as ethically neutral. Calvinism undoubtedly played a major role in Dutch commercial expansion, as historians have often stressed; but equally important—perhaps more so—were two factors in tandem: love of gain among the merchant class, combined with the threat of unemployment and hunger for many of the seafaring community at home.

During the final decades of the sixteenth century, Amsterdam underwent a phenomenal phase of economic growth. Wealthy entrepreneurs and skilled artisans migrated into the northern provinces from the south. Their activity stimulated a marked increase in industrial production, which in turn required new markets. As a result, Dutch maritime activity spread beyond the Baltic, the Mediterranean, and the Levant to Africa, the Orient, and the Western Hemisphere.

By 1648, when the Treaty of Münster ended eighty years of intermittent warfare between Spain and the Low Countries and when Peter Stuyvesant began his stewardship of New Netherland, the Netherlands had become the greatest trading nation in the world. Dutch commercial outposts and fortified factories were scattered from Archangel in Russia to Recife in Brazil, and from New Amsterdam to Nagasaki. The seaports of Holland and Zeeland had provided most of the energy behind these thrusts. Consequently their leading merchants and shipowners gained control of the republic, ruling it as a burgher oligarchy. They dominated the town councils and provincial states in their own image for their own interests. When there were conflicts between

Holland and Zeeland and the agricultural provinces (Utrecht, Gelderland, Overijssel, Groningen, and Friesland), the two maritime centers usually won out, so long as they agreed and cooperated.

Each of the seven provincial states stood as a sovereign unit. In Holland the regents of eighteen towns nominated delegations to the ruling body, and one additional delegation represented the nobility at large. Each town might send as large a delegation as it liked, but each had only one vote. In other provinces the landowning farmers and nobility exercised a larger share of influence. But even where the commercial oligarchs were not as dominant as in the maritime provinces, they enjoyed a measure of power because of their economic importance. The urban magistrates were elected by municipal councils, while rural and judicial posts were filled through the provincial states. In consequence the Dutch Republic was governed by an oligarchy of some ten thousand persons, largely from the upper middle class, who monopolized most of the important provincial and municipal offices.

There was not much in the way of a centralized government for the Dutch Republic as a whole. An awkwardly constituted States-General, which met at The Hague, served as a national administrative body, responsible for foreign policy in particular; but it could not function effectively when provincial interests conflicted. If deadlock or crisis occurred, some powerful figure or group had to offer leadership or impose order through sheer charisma, persuasion, or both. The two most obvious agencies of authority were the House of Orange and the province of Holland, the latter really coextensive with the town of Amsterdam in terms of political power. Even the princes of Orange, however, were greatly influenced by the outlook and interests of the burgher-oligarchs, with whom they cooperated in the work of government and whose support was necessary to the maintenance of their own position.

So it came to pass, during the first half of the seventeenth century, that Amsterdam replaced Antwerp as the commercial capital of Europe; that the Dutch navy achieved the reputation of being the best in the Atlantic; and that the Dutch army became a well-paid, well-led, and well-disciplined force to be reckoned with. Interminable wars were accompanied by a steady increase in Dutch overseas trade, especially after 1590. The Hollanders and Zeelanders worked their ships more thriftily than their competitors and so were able to offer lower freight rates. In turn, this maritime commerce gave the town councils and the regent class greater economic and political power than anyone might have imagined a few years before. The Netherlands by 1609, then, when a truce was negotiated with Spain, were feeling expansive and looking for new opportunities overseas—hence Henry Hudson's quest for the Northwest Passage to the Orient, which led instead to the founding of Dutch outposts along the river he explored.

2

COMMERCE AND COLONIZATION

Dutch commercial rivalry with England became intense by the middle of the seventeenth century, and it ultimately led to the English conquest of New Netherland in 1664. Consequently, it has often been assumed that their rivalry also shaped the foremost features of North American commerce and colonization by Dutch merchants from the very outset of the century. Not quite so. Anglo-Dutch competition was keen, to be sure; and it sharpened in 1609–10 when Henry Hudson, a subject of King James I, signed a contract with the Dutch East India Company to seek a northeasterly route to the Orient. Nevertheless, the Dutch and English nations were both Protestant, relatively small, and cautiously feeling their way in foreign affairs in the early 1600s. They had more in common with each other than they did with the two superpowers of the day, Spain and France: both Catholic, imperious, and hungering to swallow up smaller neighbors. The Dutch bestowed their bitterest hatred upon the Spanish. By more than mere accident, the brief truce between Spain and the northern Netherlands (1609–21) coincided exactly with Henry Hudson's great voyage of discovery in 1609 and the chartering of the Dutch West India Company in 1621. These two events, more than any others, made possible the settlement of New Netherland, and they occurred because of the Dutch desire to best their former Iberian overlords.

The Dutch *East* India Company had been established in 1602 in order to reduce the savage competition among smaller firms operating out of Holland and Zeeland. Their rivalries tended to increase purchase prices in Asia and lower retail prices in Europe—both quite senseless and needless from the merchants' point of view. So the new composite corporation, capitalized at almost six and one-half million florins, came into being with six regional chambers located where the smaller pioneer companies had been. It made a fetish of efficient operations in order to undercut competitors from other nations. Hence its desire to find a secret shortcut to the East and the decision of its Amsterdam Chamber to hire Henry Hudson to do so on its behalf.

Sailing for the Muscovy Company of England in 1607 and 1608, Hudson had established his credentials as a navigator and explorer: courageous, knowledgeable, and imaginative. Early in 1609 he outfitted *De Halve Maen*, a three-masted ship of about eighty tons, sixty-three feet from stem to stern, seventeen and one-half feet in the beam, with a depth of little more than six feet in the hold. If she was small, she nonetheless carried more canvas than most of her contemporaries and presented a higher aspect because of improved hull design and proper ballasting. Her lines foreshadowed the functional design of future sailing craft, with sides slanted inward to break the force of heavy lateral seas. Although the bow and stern were rounded, the vessel was flat bottomed, a characteristic that permitted it to enter shallow waters during ebb tide for repair work on the hull. The helmsman would have stood under his special shelter behind the mizzenmast, steering the vessel with the "whip-staff" connected to the tiller below deck; Hudson himself would have stood upon the quarterdeck, especially at the sight or smell of land, while the crew of less than twenty gathered at the rail.

The Half Moon set sail from Amsterdam, leaving the Zuider Zee on April 6. For more than a month she went to the north and east, doubling up and around the Norwegian coast, but not so far as Nova Zembla. Hudson "found the sea as full of ice as he had found it the preceeding year, so that he lost the hope of effecting anything during the season." Therefore he abandoned his plan (and his instructions) and instead sailed west in search of the elusive Northwest Passage. His course then went from the Faroe

Islands north of Britain to "Newfound Land" and then south along the coast, passing Maine, Cape Cod, Virginia, back up to Delaware Bay, and finally, in September, up the great river that now bears his name. The tale of Hudson's reconnoiter up the river has been told in chapter one. What remains to be related is the political and commercial response to news of his achievement.

His mixed and mutinous crew, both English and Dutch, did not relish the return to Holland, so they put in at Devonshire, England, for the winter, anticipating the chance of yet another search for the Northwest Passage as soon as weather permitted. The company felt differently, however, and ordered Hudson and his crew to return as soon as possible. Meanwhile, news of their adventures had reached the ears of James I, who, not wishing to see the Dutch benefit by his subject's skills, ordered Hudson and the other Englishmen on board not to leave England but to serve their own country instead. Eventually, in 1610, the ship and crew received permission to complete their voyage. Only then "did the directors obtain such favorable reports of the countries discovered by Hudson, that in their opinion these were a full compensation for their disappointment in their principal aim, the passage to India by the north." Hudson's fourth and final voyage, undertaken for prominent London merchants later in 1610, led to the dramatic discovery of Hudson's Bay, but also to the explorer's tragic death in Arctic wastes at the hands of his treacherous crew.

Although the directors of the Dutch East India Company were pleased with the prospects opened by Hudson's voyage, they were then too busy with their profitable trade to Muscovy, via Archangel, to take immediate advantage of new opportunities. But because of the Truce of 1609, Dutch merchantmen now sailed under the protection of the law of nations; and in 1611 they began to visit the "River Mauritius"—as they called the Hudson—to explore, make contact with the natives, and trade for furs. In 1613 Adriaen Block built the first Dutch ship of North American timber, a sixteen-ton yacht called the *Restless*. With it he circumnavigated Long Island, followed the New England shore to Cape Cod, and gave his own name to Block

Island. Soon thereafter, a trading post, called Fort Nassau, was established on Castle Island, just below the site of Albany. By 1614 the Hudson seemed to beckon to commercial exploitation.

Because the four most interested groups of Dutch merchants believed that a monopoly would furnish the best way to stimulate profitable trade with this area, they coaxed the States-General into passing an ordinance protecting their rights and excluding others. It provided that "whosoever shall from this time forward discover any new passages, havens, lands, or places, shall have the exclusive right of navigating to the same for four voyages." Thirteen merchants established their privileges under this ordinance, drafted a map based upon Block's explorations, and requested a charter from the States-General. They obtained it in October 1614, called themselves the New Netherland Company, and received a monopoly to make four voyages in three years. A substantial profit on these fur-trading voyages caused a lively competition when the grant expired in 1618. Although the company hoped for a renewal of its charter, other merchants exerted enough pressure to keep the commerce open until 1621, when the Dutch West India Company received its mammoth *Octroy*, or charter, and extensive privileges.

In 1621, also, the twelve-year truce with Spain came to an end. Passionate Calvinists and ardent nationalists in the Dutch Republic urged renewal of hostilities against their bitter enemy. They wanted to compete more fully with Spanish commerce and constrain the sinister spread of Catholicism. Once again a chartered company with political responsibilities as well as commercial privileges seemed the proper device. So the West India Company received its charter on June 3, 1621, modeled in many respects upon its East India counterpart. It secured a monopoly of all Dutch trade and navigation with the Americas and West Africa, the authority to maintain naval and military forces, the right to make war and peace with indigenous powers, as well as the power to exercise judicial and administrative functions. Equally important, it had the responsibility to "advance the peopling of those fruitful and unsettled parts." Whether this was a mandate for full-scale colonization or merely an incidental piece of contemporary rhetoric is still disputed among American historians, but upon one's interpretation of that ambiguity rests one's assessment of whether New Netherland was ultimately a slow success or a commercial failure.

Although the charter clearly envisioned the possibility of colonization in suitable regions, the company's primary thrust was to be an offensive one against Iberian imperialism. Very shortly the company tried to conquer chunks of Portuguese Brazil, even though the military costs far outreached any profits obtained from sugar and other exports drawn from South American possessions. It is fair to say, therefore, that the company's initial impulse was primarily political and military. It received support and came into being because it might accomplish in commercial garb (with private financing) what the state could not have achieved on its own. It might strengthen the States-General in international affairs while enriching the urban merchants and prosperous burghers. Only gradually, during the later 1620s and 1630s, would these priorities of politics over plantations and commerce over colonization be brought more nearly into balance.

The company had a governing board of nineteen directors: eight from Amsterdam, four from Zeeland, two from each of the other three chambers, and one nominated by the States-General. During the early years of company operations, most of these men felt a greater commitment to commercial extraction and anti-Spanish maneuvering than to the transplanting of Dutch society. More important to our story, most of them were far more intrigued by prospects in Guinea on the African coast, in Guiana on the South American coast, and in the Caribbean than by New Netherland. They could not grow exotic spices in North America, nor exploit an indigenous labor force, nor find fantastic mines. Sandwiched between Jamestown's settlement southward and the Pilgrims in New England, New Netherland's location did not even provide much of a chance to tweak the Spanish snout. The expanse of land stretching from the Delaware to the Connecticut rivers offered only furs, timber, and perhaps agricultural support for settlements more favorably situated. None of these commodities were contemptible; but neither were they high priorities. Accordingly, from the outset New Netherland was relegated to a supporting role in the West India Company's scheme of things. Its position was slow to change, vulnerable to chance, and, when the crisis of 1664 came, expendable by choice.

The company did not actually begin to operate until two years after receiving its charter. Its subscription lists were kept open until October 31, 1623, and private trading was permitted in the area covered by its patent until July 1, 1622. Thereafter the economic opportunities for private initiative would be formally foreclosed for more than six years, gradually accommodated in 1629, and major concessions were subsequently made in 1639. Meanwhile, responsibility for developing New Netherland's potential devolved upon a committee of the Amsterdam Chamber of the company. These "Commissioners for New Netherland" —notably Albert Coenraets Burgh, Samuel Godyn, Johannes De Laet, Kiliaen van Rensselaer, Cars Bicker, and Commer Spranges—were wealthy merchants, and in the years to come they did not hesitate to use their official positions for private gain. Thus entrepreneurship and individual interest were not totally stifled after 1623: they were made selective, discriminatory, and often clandestine. At the very beginning of North American settlement, then, public designs and private needs became so intertwined that never again would either be distinguishable as a separate entity or definable as a higher imperative.

The New Netherland Company's enduring contribution in the years 1614–18 had been the establishment of a year-round trading post at Castle Island (Fort Nassau). In 1624 the Dutch West India Company reestablished that post as Fort Orange (now Albany), augmenting it the following year with additional personnel. In 1625 it also made plans for the first permanent settlement on Manhattan Island, plans that came to fruition the next year with completion of a fort and removal of scattered Walloon families from Fort Orange and the Delaware River to the centralized location of New Amsterdam at the lower tip of Manhattan. At this point, by the autumn of 1626, one can say that the seed of New York—city and colony—had permanently been planted. The factual sequence of events between 1624 and 1626 has never been agreed upon and remains controversial, but certain salient developments can be established.

In April of 1624, the *Nieu Nederlandt,* commanded by Cornelis Jacobsen May of Hoorn, carried thirty families of immigrants to the ship's namesake. Most of these firstcomers were French-speaking Protestants from the southern Netherlands, called Walloons. Upon arrival, eighteen of the families were sent upriver to construct Fort Orange; a smaller group went south to Burlington Island in the Delaware, another to the Connecticut River; and a few remained at the mouth of the Hudson on Noten (Governor's) Island. In 1625 the company sent several supply ships, three others called *Horse, Cow,* and *Sheep* with 105 head of livestock, another yacht with forty-two more immigrants, and an engineer named Cryn Fredericksen to design a fort and town of ambitious proportions. Willem Verhulst succeeded May as commissary, or director, of New Netherland; and in 1626 he gathered the scattered bands of people and animals together, first at Noten Island, and then at New Amsterdam. Thereafter the company's outposts on the Delaware and Connecticut rivers would be maintained by lonely seasonal traders. Leading members of the company who happened to be present in the "colony," as settlers or on shipboard, were to serve the director as an advisory council. There would never be many; hence the director always held enormous political authority in his grasp.

The commissioners in Amsterdam envisoned a company establishment consisting of resident traders, clerks, artisans, soldiers, bookkeepers, and farmers—all employees of the company, all working only for its increase and not for personal gain beyond their meager salaries. Their presence throughout the year would help to organize and regularize the fur trade. It could thereby be conducted during the winter months, when most fur-bearing animals were caught; the employees were accordingly instructed to cultivate two things: good relations with the Indians and enough provisions to be agriculturally autonomous. The commissioners did not expect to send supplies from home after 1626. Although New Amsterdam never suffered a "starving time," as Jamestown and Plymouth did, it became self-sustaining more slowly than the Amsterdam Chamber expected and remained an economic disappointment throughout the thirty-eight years of Dutch control.

Manhattan Island, which quickly became the colony's nucleus, seemed to offer the brightest prospects. Like Boston, Newport, and Charleston, other colonial towns established later along the eastern seaboard, it was an island-peninsula: sheltered from the ocean and the worst winter weather, more easily defended, and accessible to the primary means of transportation: water. It was centrally located between the Albany and Delaware outposts, larger than Noten Island (fully twenty-two thousand acres); and it already had some cleared land, or "flatts." By September of 1626 Manhattan had been purchased from the Indians* for sixty florins worth of merchandise, Fort Amsterdam had been staked out, and thirty houses of tree bark and a stone countinghouse had been constructed. Some of the settlers had also begun to clear and plant fields for the company farms, or *bouweries.*

Between 1626 and 1628, the company added little to its investment in the frail colony of some 270 souls. It sent few people and less livestock. In fact, once the company's commitment to provision the colonists for two years had expired, scant provisions were sent at all; therefore officials in New Netherland had to sell trading goods to the settlers so that they could barter with the Indians for food. In retrospect, the Amsterdam Chamber seems to have been very shortsighted; but its members apparently believed that the people, animals, and tools sent over in 1624–25 were an adequate basis for small-scale colonization and self-sufficiency. Until those minor schemes reached fruition, there was no point putting more money into the mouth of the Hudson.

---

* Not by Peter Minuit, as myth would have it, but by Willem Verhulst, his predecessor, who was banished from the colony in the fall of 1626 for diverting company goods to his own use. Minuit did, however, purchase Staten Island for "duffels, kettles, axes, hoes, wampum, drilling awls, Jews harps, and diverse other small wares."

By 1628 and 1629, the nineteen directors began to reassess their expectations and future prospects for New Netherland. Periodic review of the colony's accounts left them dissatisfied. Agricultural production was disappointing, timber was being obtained at an uneconomically high cost, and the fur trade—the outpost's fundamental *raison d'être*—was growing more slowly than were their greedy hopes. We have from Johannes De Laet, an early director and historian of the company, the following figures:

Year	Export		Value (in florins)
	Beavers	Otters	
1624	4,000	700	27,125
1625	5,295	436	35,825
1626	7,258	857	45,050
1627	7,520	370	56,420
1628	6,951	734	61,075

Clearly the value of each pelt increased annually; but the absolute yield fluctuated, and so the rate of growth must have seemed meager. The value of goods imported to the colony over the same period came to 110,895 florins, a little less than half the value of the furs exported. What is not known is whether the amount spent on merchandise and the overhead costs of transatlantic trade left the company much profit or none at all.

In any case the directors seem to have been disappointed, because by 1628 they decided not to make a further investment in New Netherland. Instead, their diminishing funds were directed into more lucrative prospects. What of their infant colony on the Hudson? Would it simply be abandoned? No, not quite. In June of 1629 the so-called board of Nineteen authorized the *Vryheden*: "freedoms and exemptions for the patroons, masters or private persons who will plant any colonies in, and send cattle to New Netherland." In short, the directors hoped that individual initiative would achieve what a public corporation had not: a flourishing colony flowing with florins, furs, and people. But their innovation did not open New Netherland to individuals indiscriminately. Rather, it provided special opportunities for major stockholders who had been investors since 1623, and it was largely a concession to Kiliaen van Rensselaer and his faction who had been advocating serious colonization from the very beginning.

A qualified entrepreneur who brought fifty persons to New Netherland and settled them there would become a patroon—literally, "patron"—and receive a grant of land either four leagues (eighteen miles) along one bank of the Hudson or two leagues along both sides. No limit was placed upon lateral expansion. Within his subcolony the patroon would exercise judicial and administrative powers, though judgments exceeding fifty florins in value could be appealed to the company, and the patroon's governmental instructions were subject to changes in company regulations. The patroons were also entitled to trade from Newfoundland to Florida, so long as they paid a 5 percent commission to the company. Most important, and most ambiguous, was the patroons' limited access to the fur trade. They could trade for furs only "where the Company has no agent" and had to pay an export duty of one guilder* for every beaver or otter skin.

Opponents of the patroonship system complained bitterly that it gave the grantees a chance to cut into the company's fur trade

---

* Although the laws and ordinances of New Netherland apparently recognized only wampum and beaver skins as official currency, their value was expressed in guilders and stivers. On occasion, actual coin guilders passed as payment. Values were also stated in florins, and we know that Peter Stuyvesant fixed the value of pieces of eight (i.e., eight reals of silver coined into one "piece") at three florins per piece (estimated in 1893 as worth about $1.20 in value). Consequently many light pieces of eight, forbidden in Amsterdam, were brought to the colony where they depreciated about 50 percent. After the conquest in 1664, no immediate alteration of the currency occurred, only a statement of English equivalents. Governor Nicolls issued this order in February 1665: "The Payments for goods imported shall be paid as formerly in Bever Pay at 8 guilders or 13 sh. 4d. [shillings and pence] a Bever. All tobacco shall pay 2 pence a pound English weight in wampum, which is 1½ penny Sterling, or in Bever at 8 sh. a pound."

and that the *Vryheden* had been obtained by fraudulent means. In fact, however, the patroons' access to the fur trade, licit or illicit, was quite limited; there is no firm evidence of fraud; the patroonship proposals received extensive scrutiny between February and June 1629; it would not have been possible to push a prejudicial measure through the company's diverse directorship; and the *Vryheden* was subsequently legitimized as having been properly obtained.

Proper or improper, few people other than Van Rensselaer and his associates leaped to take advantage of the Charter of Freedoms and Exemptions. Given the accumulated experience of the years 1623–29, New Netherland seemed an area of high risk and low prospects. Other investment opportunities must have seemed far more alluring in 1629 and the early 1630s. Only Van Rensselaer's faction had contacts—friends and relatives—already established along the Hudson to facilitate quick profits from patroonships and related projects. Van Rensselaer himself seems to have had his eye on long-term development. He alone was willing and able to bear the heavy expense of initial investment, and his "Rensselaerswyck" was the only Dutch patroonship to enjoy any measure of success. Others were established in the 1630s but were stillborn. Michael Pauw received one in 1630 (Pavonia) that included Staten Island, Hoboken, and Jersey City; but in 1636, with no profits whatever and much anguish instead, he and others sold their patroonships back to the company.

Although it never produced great wealth during its founder's lifetime, Rensselaerswyck functioned viably throughout the Dutch period and subsequently paid good dividends to the "American" Van Rensselaers.* The first tenants came in 1630, and by 1646 some 216 had been dispatched; many withdrew at the termination of their contracts. The patroon experimented

---

* "I should not like to have my people get too wise and figure out their master's profit," Kiliaen wrote in 1639, "especially in matters in which they themselves are somewhat interested." (A. J. F. van Laer, ed., *Van Rensselaer Bowier Manuscripts* [Albany, 1908], 430.)

with various sorts of administration: government by three resident commissioners; management by a single official with limited powers; and finally, in 1648, control by a director. The manorial court established in 1634 was patterned after proto-types then in use on manors in the Netherlands.

Turning from patroonships in particular to land tenure in general, historians have found that Dutch patterns of tenure added sufficient variety to the land system of provincial New York to render it probably more diverse than that of any other colony. The charter of 1629 provided for smaller grants to private individuals who were less opulent than the patroons; and in the long run these proved to be far more important in New Netherland's history. Persons who would settle in the colony at their own expense, or in the service of Dutch sponsors, might be granted outright as much land as they could improve. Unfortu-nately, the company's terms were comparatively ungenerous and the Dutch middle classes so disinclined to emigrate that few settlers were attracted during the 1630s. Only after the States-General exerted pressure in 1638 did more land become avail-able. A year later the director and his council were instructed to provide colonists from the Netherlands, or from friendly states, with as much land as they could cultivate. It would remain their property in perpetuity, for as long as they occupied it, subject to the eventual payment of a quitrent: one-tenth of the produce of the soil "as well as of the increase of all sorts of cattle." This form of tenure, a modified feudal relationship, was known as "free and common socage."

The new Charter of Freedoms and Exemptions that appeared in 1640 added significantly to these terms. It offered two hundred acres of land to anyone who brought five adult immigrants with him, and it promised local self-government. Villages or towns that developed would be governed by "magistrates and ministers of justice" nominated by themselves and selected from a pool "of the best qualified" by the director and his council. Only after these and other inducements of 1639/40 were publicized did the colony really begin to achieve a respectable rate of growth by

The seal of New Netherland. Designed in Holland, it was adopted by the Dutch West India Company on December 28, 1630, and sent to New Amsterdam to be used on the legal documents of the colony. The beaver against a shield is enclosed by wampum. The crest of an earl's crown signified that the territory was a province of the Netherlands. *The Museum of the City of New York. From* Album of New Netherland *by Maud Esther Dilliard (Twayne Publishers, 1963).*

attracting numbers of settlers. They were led to understand, though, that land patents from the director only conferred a right of dominion *after* Indian titles had been properly extinguished in one way or another. Too often, however, rapacious individuals negotiated with the Indians directly, deceived them, or dragged them into the director's presence to have deeds officially "sanctioned" in speedy transactions. Finally, in 1652 Peter Stuyvesant and his associates had to forbid the purchase of Indian lands by private individuals (or the conveyance of lands so purchased) without prior consent from the commissioners or director.

The company reserved Manhattan Island for its own purposes and development, so that ordinarily the various land offers to immigrants did not apply to it. Householders on the island held their lots or farms from the company by permission or by lease but without formal designations, and they seem to have located their buildings pretty much at random. Inevitably there arose the awkward distinction between those colonists who were merely employees of the company, those who were autonomous inhabitants, and those in the former category who, after six years of service, passed over into the latter. Employees included captains of the company ships, the director, commissaries at the several forts, traders, clerks, soldiers, craftsmen, and what were called "hired farmers." All of them had some sort of contract and were assured of daily subsistence and a salary. They all were at the service of the company and equally proscribed from private gain from their labors. In exchange for security they sacrificed prospects of personal prosperity. Once his contract had expired, an employee could remain in New Netherland as a free colonist. Nonemployees, referred to as "colonists and other free persons," were largely farmers. They enjoyed the opportunity of participating in the fur trade by trapping or bartering but suffered the disadvantages of great personal and commercial risk: no daily subsistence and no fixed salary.

These two different statuses developed because the company had to take people on whatever terms it could get them, for it confronted, early on, a congeries of problems concerning the recruitment of labor. It had to select suitable immigrants, induce them to go, motivate them to work productively as company servants, and seduce them into staying—none of which was easy because unemployment in the northern Netherlands was never so severe as to compel industrial and agricultural workers to emigrate in large numbers. Wages were low and working hours long, but an industrious fellow could usually make ends meet in the familiar surroundings of his fatherland. Why, therefore, risk death by ocean disaster, crop failure, or Indian massacre?

In consequence, immigrants were wooed from communities all over western and northern Europe, so that New Netherland, from the start, developed as the most heterogeneous of all North American colonies in its social composition. Father Isaac Jogues reported in 1644 that "there may well be four or five hundred men of different sects and nations; the Director General told me that there were persons there of eighteen different languages." Understandably Dominie Megapolensis feared that the colony "would soon become a Babel of Confusion." Jogues's figure of eighteen does seem a little high, and the dominie did have a vested interest in protecting the special position of the Dutch Reformed church; still, there was an essential truth to their claims. Of the eighty-two emigrants who came to Rensselaers-wyck during its first decade (1630–39), thirty-two, or nearly 40 percent, came from England, Norway, and various German principalities.

For various reasons, the Dutch West India Company had serious handicaps in recruiting settlers. In addition to the relative prosperity and high employment in the Netherlands, there were few religious groups who felt persecuted there, like the Puritans in England. Nor were there significant numbers of younger sons of burgher "aristocrats" for whom New Netherland offered vocational opportunities. Nor were the political privileges proffered to potential settlers particularly attractive. The *coloniërs* had to "fulfill and follow the commands of the Company, already given to them or yet to be given, as also to receive from the aforementioned Company all orders on the matter of their government and justice." At first there was even some ambiguity on the question of whether they enjoyed the basic civil rights and protections afforded citizens at home. After 1625 those rights were assured on paper, but the gossip circulated that government in New Netherland was more dictatorial and less participatory than in Holland or Zeeland. So people shied away, on the whole, and population growth was slow in the colony: there were perhaps 270 persons in 1628, 300 in 1630, 500 in 1640, and less than 9,000 by the time of the conquest in 1664. By contrast, the population figures for Virginia and New England in 1664 were about 40,000 and 50,000 respectively.*

Perhaps it was this rapid growth of population in New England that caused some Puritans to migrate southward onto Long Island. In June 1640, a group of colonists from the Massachusetts Bay town of Lynn landed west of Montauk and founded Southampton, the first English settlement in New York. Within a few years other New Englanders had started East Hampton nearby and Southold on the north shore. Today, two fine relics of the late 1640s survive to tell the tale of primitive life in the salt air: the so-called Old House in Cutchogue, a medieval, framed box with steep roofline, substantial central chimney, and windows with small, leaded panes in diamond shapes; and the Halsey Homestead in Southampton, a classic English saltbox with weathered shingles, broad floorboards, and great oak beams supporting the ceiling of the sitting room. Here in 1649. a group of Connecticut Indians attacked the tiny settlement and massacred Phoebe Halsey, the wife of Thomas. Her ghost is said to hover still over the house and its charming herb garden.

These Puritans had none of our modern devices to help them clear the dense woods of eastern Long Island—only the ax, the grubbing hook, the hoe, and fire. Communities "fired" the woodlands in their immediate localities. Then individuals set to work clearing away trees and underbrush from their own farms, and it was very tough work. "The trees are usually felled from

---

* At the end of the century, Virginia and Massachusetts each had close to 60,000 persons, while New York still had under 20,000.

the stump, cut up and burnt in the fields, except such as are suitable for buildings, for pallissades, posts and rails," wrote the colony's secretary in 1650. "In most lands is found a certain root called Red Wortel, which must before ploughing be extirpated with a hoe, expressly made for that purpose."

Within a few years the broader section of the Montauk peninsula, nearly enclosed by surf, was populated by livestock belonging to the East Hampton villagers. In addition to cattle, small flocks of sheep were raised for their wool, and goats grazed casually among them. Neither became very abundant, however, because of the hungry wolves and wildcats nearby. Swine, on the other hand, seemed to flourish. Long-legged, swift razorbacks lived on the myriad nuts that fell from trees and became critically important to the pioneer economy. "The hogs, after having picked up their food for months in the woods, are crammed with corn in the fall; when fat they are killed and furnish a very hard and clean pork; a good article for the husbandman who gradually and in time begins to purchase horses and cows with the produce of his grain and the increase of his hogs."

Isolated from real markets, the earliest farmers had to supply their families with food and clothing from their own resources. They divided their time, therefore, between raising animals and crops, the pastoral and agricultural aspects of rural life. The critical bridge between both, in many ways, was the ox. No soil could be tilled and no crops could be raised without this slow, powerful beast to pull the plow and cart. Like sheep and swine, oxen could forage for themselves and could be eaten if necessary. The horse was much less useful, by comparison, and less versatile in those early, primitive days. Only later would new conditions give the swifter and more intelligent horse an opportunity to demonstrate its superiority. For much more than the first generation, oxen remained the most significant source of farm power.

Even more important than livestock, New Englanders brought to Long Island their autonomous churches, town meetings, and communal land systems. All three presupposed organic com-

munities with close, neighborly settlement; and although the
ideal became ever more elusive with the passage of time, New
Englanders felt that the ideal and its attendant conditions were
altogether lacking within the Dutch communities of the Hudson
River valley. Therein lay the start of strongly felt differences
between Dutch and English settlers in colonial New York. The
Dutch did not ordinarily migrate in groups. Dutch farmers might
try to place their landholdings along the water, and they sought
defensive shelter at the nearest fortified place; but they had no
social imperative nagging them to settle in concentrated clusters.
In early New Netherland, unlike in New England, Dutch
pioneers did not often insist upon communal privileges and
rights. Instead the company tried to bring scattered individuals
into social units, and in 1640 it formally began to encourage
town settlement. Yet no Dutch town was chartered until
Breuckelen gained that status in 1646—two decades after
colonization began—and only nine Dutch towns were eventually
incorporated in all.

To the Puritans on Long Island, moreover, the privileges of a
Dutch town did not seem very valuable. They were rooted in the
company's wish for military security and efficient administration
but gave the individual few political advantages other than
dealing with local, rather than remote, officials. No town
meeting was contemplated, and the decisions of the *schepens*, or
local magistrates, were only provisional until they had been
ratified by the director and his council. Nor did the *schepens* make
land assignments. The Dutch had common meadows, but the
colony's government controlled their extent and use. Nor did the
Dutch establish a college where clergy of familiar stock and
persuasion might be trained. Their ministers had to be obtained
from Holland where there was a proper jurisdictional body, the
Classis, to ordain them. From the 1640s onward, then, Dutch
remonstrants repeatedly wrote with envy of the colonists in New
England, "where the People have an election every year and
have power to make a change in case of improper behavior, and
that they therefore say is the bridle of their great men."

The colony's early directors seemed most especially to need

some sort of bridle upon their authoritarian tendencies. May and Verhulst each served for less than a year (1624–26), and neither had been regarded as particularly reliable. Then came the coarse and ambitious Peter Minuit, who made a real effort to encourage economic development and opened trade relations with the colonists at Plymouth. In 1631 the company recalled and dismissed him, though he later appeared on the Delaware in 1637 as founder and governor of New Sweden. His successor, Bastiaen Jansen Krol, was a man of some skill and sagacity; but he lasted only a year. Wouter van Twiller was merely a clerk in the company's service when he was appointed director in 1633. Disliked by most of the Dutch settlers, he kept his financial accounts poorly and neglected to report regularly to Amsterdam. In 1638 the company replaced him with Willem Kieft, the most dictatorial of all the early directors, a foolish martinet responsible for the Indian massacre of 1643. Colonists complained about him bitterly to the States-General, and in 1646 he was finally removed. In sum, the quality of leadership during New Netherland's first two decades left much to be desired.

Given such quarrelsome executives, whose petulant personalities set the tone for public life, it should not be surprising that the early inhabitants generally were a litigious lot. In part their problem arose from the fact that grounds of legitimacy in the civil sector were only tenuously defined. New Netherland lacked its own code of laws. Although Roman-Dutch law supposedly obtained, the court administered justice capriciously so far as the populace could see. There were virtually no lawyers in the proper notarial sense, and cases were tried publicly but without juries. Although decisions could theoretically be appealed to the Amsterdam Chamber, distance, time, and expense rendered such a recourse almost meaningless. Civil suits—for debt or trespass— were most frequent; but there were also criminal prosecutions on charges of theft, assault, adultery, slander, and occasionally murder. Between April 1638 and April 1639, for example, the court heard some fifty civil suits and forty-three criminal cases, twenty-eight on complaints of slander. In a community of less than two thousand souls, that was a lot of litigation.

The spiritual life of those souls did not especially concern the company, for not until 1628 did it provide them with a minister: Dominie Jonas Michaëlius. Instead it sent a *ziekentrooster,* or comforter of the sick, to look after their religious needs in 1624, and then a replacement in 1626. Bastiaen Krol and Jan Huygens were not supposed to administer the sacrament of the Lord's Supper, or baptize, or marry people. But because the company could not send an ordained minister at the outset, the comforters were finally given permission to baptize, marry, and preach— provided that they studied the traditional rites with scrupulous care and only read sermons from approved volumes written by Reformed theologians. In addition to offering prayers on appropriate occasions, reading from Scripture, catechizing children, and consoling the sick, the comforters commonly served in secular positions in order to keep body and soul together. Huygens, for example, was also the company's storekeeper in New Amsterdam.

At first they held religious services in private homes, or outdoors if weather permitted. In 1626, when a mill was built for grinding bark used in tanning hides, a large room on the second floor served to accommodate the New Amsterdam congregation. Reformed services were held in the mill until 1633, when a proper church and parsonage were finally erected. Dominie Bogardus arrived that year to replace Michaëlius, and he remained until 1647. Throughout these first two decades the colony had only one Reformed *predikant* and one *ziekentrooster.* By contrast the company sent seven comforters to the West Indies in 1640, and the East India Company sent out fourteen that year. These figures convey some sense of New Netherland's relative unimportance in the Dutch Republic's overseas priorities.

Often the schoolmaster of New Amsterdam doubled as comforter of the sick, and not without some logic. Morning and afternoon school sessions opened and closed with prayer. Twice each week the schoolmaster instructed his pupils in the common prayers and in the Heidelberg Catechism. School books were full of references to biblical history and Reformed theology, so that pedagogical duties might very well overlap with religious instruction and spiritual activities.

By the early 1640s, however, procuring a sufficient complement of *ziekentroosters* for New Netherland was one of the company's more minuscule problems. A ruinous war in Brazil, huge sums spent on privateering expeditions, and general maladministration had brought the company into a serious decline. The Nineteen had always been slow to make policy decisions, and the various chambers had been equally sluggish in administering them. Though technically branches of a single firm, the chambers had begun to behave like business rivals; most of them, for example, maintained their own factors in Amsterdam. Because of the frequent turnover in directors, company policy tended to vacillate with a pendulumlike motion as various factions alternated in power.

This general decline could not help but have an adverse effect upon New Netherland, which was facing its own problems in any case. During the 1630s, a decade of economic stagnation for the colony, private individuals and company clerks smuggled and embezzled furs with impunity. An official audit in 1644 revealed that New Netherland had produced only some fifty to seventy thousand guilders annually but had cost the company more than five hundred and fifty thousand guilders. In 1644 the company desperately needed one million guilders in order to meet immediate demands, and it clearly was not going to be rescued by the struggling Hudson settlements. Hence New Netherland became the lowest of priorities, more vulnerable than ever to English political pressure from the northeast and more irritable than ever because of Swedish commercial pressure from the southwest. Swedes and Finns on the Delaware threatened Dutch fur-trading interests in that area; and with immigrants coming into New Netherland from Massachusetts, Connecticut, and New Haven colonies during the 1640s, the English camel had pushed its nose well into the Dutch tent long before 1664.

What had caused these Puritans of various persuasions to leave the more enviable conditions of New England for fragile New

Netherland? In part they were pushed by religious disputes and land hunger, but they were also pulled by the liberalized conditions of settlement that the West India Company offered after 1638. In that year the controversies between patroons and company directors came to a head. The latter proposed a scheme for colonization that apparently would have thrown the colony's commerce fully open to private enterprise. The patroons as well as the States-General objected to some particulars; but early in 1639 all persons were permitted to ship goods to New Netherland, to trade directly with the Indians, and to export furs to Europe on their own accounts. They were obliged only to pay a duty on goods taken in or out of the province.

Then, in the summer of 1640, yet another concession surfaced. The company issued a new Charter of Freedoms and Exemptions. It cut the size of potential patroonships but created the rank of "master or colonist" for persons who settled five adults in New Netherland; and it confirmed the open privilege to trade for peltry, subject to a 10 percent export charge. Through increased population, customs duties, and enlarging the sphere of its trading operations, the company hoped to cancel its perennial deficit in New Netherland as well as strengthen the settlement against foreign pressures from north and south.

To some degree it succeeded. Between 1638 and 1643 the colony's population doubled, from under one thousand to nearly two thousand. But part of that increase turned out to be transient, for two reasons: first, because some of the immigrants tended to return to their places of origin as soon as they had made some sort of profit; second, and more important, because Director Kieft drove the colony into a bloody war with all of its Indian neighbors between 1641 and 1645, a war that left New Netherland exhausted—physically, economically, and emotionally.

How did it come about? Because the company's charter had originally envisioned commerce rather than colonization as the primary goal, it had not given the company any formal land patent. Ownership remained with the Indians, and their separate titles had to be extinguished by purchase or treaty or both. Most transactions during the 1620s and 1630s were executed in good faith, involved relatively small sections of land, and often left the natives in de facto occupation for years after the sale. But beginning in 1638 the amounts purchased grew in size—in 1639 Kieft bought most of modern Queens from the Rockaway Indians, and in 1640 he completed the Dutch holdings in Brooklyn—and there were colonists eager to bring the land under immediate cultivation. At this point relations between the races began seriously to deteriorate. In addition to disputes over simple landownership, daily quarrels arose over all sorts of things: Indian dogs (really semidomesticated wolves) that killed European livestock and poultry; European livestock that wandered into the Indians' unfenced cornfields, eating and trampling with equal abandon; and last, but hardly least, Kieft's foolish attempt to tax the Indians in order to help recover the costs of fortification and maintenance of a military force—expenditures made necessary by the Indians' hostility, of course.

In the summer of 1641, scattered Indian raids on outlying Dutch *bouweries* brought from Kieft an overreaction that led to four years of intermittent warfare punctuated by truces in 1642 and 1643, but also by savage attacks on both sides. Between April and August of 1645, a series of peace treaties was negotiated, not only with the Indians of Long Island, Westchester, and northeastern New Jersey, but also with the Mohawks and Mahicans up at Fort Orange. Both sides pledged to keep the peace and resolve all grievances through negotiations between the director and several sachems. Prompt justice was promised in case of murders involving both parties. The Indians agreed not to bring weapons near the houses on Manhattan, and the Dutch pledged not to go armed near any Indian dwelling without due warning.

Almost a thousand Indians were killed between 1640 and 1645—population losses that could never be recovered—whereas demographic growth among the Dutch was rapid after the war ended and Kieft was replaced by Peter Stuyvesant. Kieft's policy of intimidating the Indians by brutality and devastation, however, failed; for the neighboring tribes remained a threat to outlying colonists for years to come. From then on the Indian

word for the Dutch—*Swannekens,* "people of the salt water"—
would be preceded by an adjective: "villainous *Swannekens.*"

Meanwhile, Kieft's war had political implications for the
Dutch as well. At the outset of hostilities in 1641, he had met
with the heads of all white families in order to inform them of his
policy and secure their consent. Soon thereafter the commonalty
elected a committee of twelve to deal with Kieft. They disagreed
with him on many occasions, and in 1642 he dissolved them. In
1643, however, he sought advice and support once again and
chose a panel of eight who were subject to popular veto.
Eventually the eight men also opposed Kieft on many matters
and even wrote long letters to the Amsterdam Chamber complaining of his suicidal policies. The Eight seem themselves to
have been ambivalent about critical matters of public policy:
they damned the director for starting the war, yet also complained that he failed to prosecute it fully. What matters,
ultimately, is that political consciousness and participation first
developed in response to Indian problems and military decisions.
The company listened to the Eight and in December 1644
decided to recall Kieft and demand a justification of his
administration.

In the spring of 1645, Peter Stuyvesant was selected to replace
Kieft, but two years passed before the colony's last Dutch
director actually arrived on the scene. The delay was caused by
financial fights within the company. During this period of
transition, New Amsterdam appeared a straggling village of
some one thousand people living in 150 to 200 houses. The
church remained unfinished, the fort was weak, and the muddy
streets stank with excrement from pigsties and privies. Only the
thirty-five taverns seem to have been flourishing. The hinterland
consisted of perhaps fifty *bouweries* on Manhattan, Long Island,
and Pavonia (now Jersey City). Isaac Jogues has left us a
thumbnail sketch of Rensselaerswyck, filtered here through the
lenses of Francis Parkman:

The centre of this rude little settlement was Fort Orange, a miserable
structure of logs, standing on a spot now within the limits of the city of

Albany. It contained several houses and other buildings; and behind it was a small church, recently erected, and serving as the abode of the pastor, Dominie Megapolensis. . . . Some twenty-five or thirty houses, roughly built of boards and roofed with thatch, were scattered at intervals on or near the borders of the Hudson, above and below the fort. Their inhabitants, about a hundred in number, were for the most part rude Dutch farmers, tenants of Van Rensselaer, the patroon, or lord of the manor. They raised wheat, of which they made beer, and oats, with which they fed their numerous horses. They traded, too, with Indians, who profited greatly by the competition among them, receiving guns, knives, axes, kettles, cloth, and beads, at moderate rates, in exchange for their furs.*

This was New Netherland after two decades of settlement: several months' sail from Amsterdam, with fully four months not uncommon. The voyage home was easier—one to two months—because of the favorable westerlies. The company had pursued a series of seemingly contradictory policies, vacillating between colonization as a priority and the simple preservation of its fur monopoly. Between 1624 and 1628 the company made almost no concessions to its colonists. From 1628 until 1631 it opened the possibility of patroonships and just as quickly fell under the influence of directors who stressed the need for short-term profits. The patroons fell into disfavor and were mostly bought out. But little economic growth occurred anyway, so that the 1630s were years of regression. In 1639–40 the company committed itself to a policy of colonization through agricultural development; and once Kieft's insane policy of intimidating the Indians had ended in 1645, the planting of institutional roots and social growth became possible. That was the story of Stuyvesant's years, 1647–64.

---

* Francis Parkman, *The Jesuits in North America*, in S. E. Morison, ed., *The Parkman Reader* (Boston, 1955), 162–63.

3

THE STAMP OF PETER STUYVESANT

Some fifteen men tried to govern New Netherland and New York during the course of the seventeenth century. They were not, on the whole, an impressive lot. A considerable number, including Minuit, Van Twiller, Kieft, Lovelace in 1673, and Andros in 1680, were recalled in disgrace and required to defend themselves against charges of maladministration. Several of them, certainly, did serve as scapegoats for the sins of others or for circumstances beyond anyone's control. But by and large, the early governors were not especially able. The exceptions were Stuyvesant, Nicolls, and Dongan. Stuyvesant ruled for seventeen years—the longest tenure of any governor in the history of colonial New York—and he most certainly left his stamp upon the province.

He is best remembered, perhaps, for his peg leg embroidered with silver bands, the legacy of his first military adventure. In 1644 he had led an assault upon St. Martin in the Caribbean, where a cannonball from the Spanish fort crushed his right leg, which subsequently was amputated. (The unsuccessful siege had to be abandoned after twenty-eight days.) Although the one surviving portrait of Stuyvesant, done from life in about 1660, does not display his famous stump, it does show a strong face, high forehead, long nose, light moustache, an extra chin, and florid cheeks. He is wearing armor plate upon his shoulders, a saffron sash across his chest, and a wide, starched, white collar spreading around his neck. His expression is benign but aloof, alert and ready to bully anyone rash enough to disagree with him.

His contemporaries have left us a clear characterization of the man: strong willed and stubborn, a staunch Calvinist who prided himself upon his piety and culture, a vigilant executive loyal to the West India Company, a man of integrity and courage, a shrewd diplomat working against great disadvantages, a soldier who never shirked from battle but nevertheless lost most of his big ones. It is not quite true that history forgets its losers. Stuyvesant was a loser; but he was also dramatic, self-confident, and often quite clever—so he has been remembered. One of his subjects wrote in 1651: "Our great Muscovy Duke goes on as usual. . . . He proceeds no longer by words or writings, but by arrests and stripes [i.e., whippings]."

When Stuyvesant arrived in 1647, he recognized what one writer has aptly called "the system of organized disorder which had been so characteristic of the West India Company from its very beginning." All too soon the director general found himself the focal point of a cluster of unbalanced and contradictory interests. He fought with the colonists over imposts and taxes, political participation, private morality, the administration of justice, and land purchases from the Indians. He fought with the company over the matter of religious toleration, with the Classis of Amsterdam over the need for a schoolmaster and the behavior of the clergy, with the Rensselaerswyck patroonship over control of the fur trade in the Albany area, and with the company and the States-General over matters of judicial administration. Since the latter two could not themselves agree upon the proper treatment of high company officials, the geometry of conflict got steadily more complex. The colonists and the States-General, for example, fought with Stuyvesant and the company over trading regulations and ultimate control of the province; but the populace and director teamed up against the company over the

Peter Stuyvesant (1592–1672), governor of New York, in about 1660.
Artist unknown. *Courtesy of The New-York Historical Society, New York City.*

matter of funds for building a church and keeping it repaired. There were a great many crosscutting stresses—more, ultimately, than the frail colony could contain or withstand.

Many of these stresses seemed to arise from jurisdictional conflicts, and on the surface of things they did. But deep down, at the root of the matter, were two tangled problems: the lack of legitimacy in public institutions and excessive pluralism in political society. Neither of these problems was unique or peculiar to New Netherland; both occurred in varying degrees in all of the colonies. But they seemed to aggravate each other in unusual measure in New Netherland and elicited endless complaints from contemporaries. Late in 1651, for example, the magistrates of Gravesend (an English settlement on the southern tip of Brooklyn) wrote directly to the Amsterdam Chamber of the company, which had exclusive management of the colony from 1645 onward. The magistrates, oddly enough, were opposed to popular self-government. They acknowledged

that the frequent changing a government, or the power of electing a Governor among ourselves, which some among us, as we understand, aim at, would be our ruin and destruction by reason of our factions and various opinions, inasmuch as many among us being unwilling to subject themselves to any sort of government, mild or strong, it must, on that account, be compulsory or by force, until the Governor's authority be well confirmed; for such persons will not only despise, scorn or disobey authority, and by their evil example drag other persons along, whereby the laws would be powerless, but every one would desire to do what would please and gratify himself.

In concluding their lament and appeal, these magistrates returned once again to the dilemma of establishing legitimacy in a newfound land: " 'Tis not with us as in our Fatherland, or as in Kingdoms and Republics which are established and settled by long and well experienced laws and fundamentals, best agreeing with the condition of the people. But in our little body, made up of divers members, namely, folks of different nations, many things occur in the laying of a foundation for which there are no rules nor examples, and, therefore, must be fixed at the discretion of a well experienced Governor." *

So it happened that certain political imperatives seemed to arise inevitably from the circumstances of unstable pluralism. But not all of the interests involved saw these imperatives in the same light. Consider, for example, the problems that arose from the presence of English communities on western Long Island, lying close by Manhattan. George Baxter, the English secretary of New Netherland, wrote a petition in 1653 in which he envisioned lasting harmony between the two language groups as well as between the governed and their government. For a model he pointed sensibly to the "government of the Netherlands, made up of various nations from divers quarters of the globe." The company's directors, however, did not share his vision of a peaceable kingdom on the Hudson, and later in 1653 they instructed Stuyvesant accordingly: "Unfortunately we take a different view, because the people of *Hempstead* and *Flushing* have actually not only not prevented the raising of the Parliament's flag by some English free-booter, but also permitted it to be done; an example, which induces us not to trust to any of that nation residing under our jurisdiction. Their immigrating and having favors granted to them must therefore be restricted henceforth, that we may not nourish serpents in our bosom, who finally might devour our hearts."

Strong words—but even then the Amsterdam Chamber had not mentioned all of its misgivings. More than merely a kind of fifth column, some of the English towns set a bad example for their Dutch neighbors by demanding local government and a voice in the central system of power. It is fair to say, in fact, that the tension between provincial authority and local autonomy underlay the politics of Stuyvesant's regime more than any other issue. Dutch towns, as a rule, were granted local government later than English towns and on less favorable terms. Apart from New Amsterdam, the English tended to form village communities earlier than the Dutch did, and therefore they required

---

* See E. B. O'Callaghan, ed., *Documents Relative to the Colonial History of the State of New-York*, II (Albany, 1858), 155, 156.

self-control at an earlier stage. Moreover, they brought from New England certain assumptions about the value of self-government and added that "it is much more necessary that they have it under the *Dutch* (whose lawes they know not nor understand their language and the way and manner of their exerciseing this their sole power)."

As strangers the English felt more keenly the need to protect their local privileges, and as immigrant communities they were in a better position to exert pressure and bargain with the director general and his council for advantageous terms of settlement. The Dutch, by contrast, came largely as individuals and continued to see the company as their guardian even after they had gathered into scattered villages.* Throughout Stuyvesant's regime the towns sought ever greater autonomy, with the English communities patterning their requests upon the New England example and the Dutch communities pushing theirs on the basis of their Long Island counterparts. What Gravesend got in 1645, Breuckelen got in 1646. What Hempstead got in 1646, Beverwyck (Albany) achieved in 1652. What Newtown got in 1652, Midwout (Flatbush) received in 1653. And so it went with patents, charters, and municipal privileges.

The principal officials in a Dutch town were the *schout* and the *schepens*. The latter, an alderman or magistrate of sorts, exercised both administrative and judicial functions. In addition to jurisdiction over petty criminal offenses, the *schepens* had authority similar to that of the New England selectman. He could advise the director and council to pass orders concerning roads, the enclosure of lands, and the regulation of churches and schools. In certain cases he could even make and enforce orders without the director's consent. The *schout* corresponded to a modern prosecuting attorney, though at times he served as a sheriff and at others he presided over the court. Most signif-

---

* This significant sentence appeared in the company's instructions to the director and council in 1645: "They shall endeavor as much as possible, that the colonists settle themselves with a certain number of families in some of the most suitable places, in the manner of villages, towns and hamlets, as the English are in the habit of doing, who thereby live more securely."

icantly, however, charters granted to the Dutch towns made no provision for popular participation. They established nothing like the New England town meeting, and all local ordinances eventually had to be approved by the director and his council after they had been passed by the local court. Unlike Massachusetts Bay, where civil rights were contingent upon church membership, voting and officeholding in Dutch towns depended simply upon landownership. Even then, Dutch towns used the suffrage much less than the English towns in New Netherland, following instead the closed-corporation system of communities in Holland (where new officials were nominated by incumbents), and final choice lay with the director.

There were, of course, certain basic similarities as well. Both sorts of towns followed the same system of appeals to the director and council. Both were required, especially after 1656, to build forts and fortify their villages. Both owed allegiance to the West India Company and the States-General. Both, after a period of years, had to pay taxes to the company. And both were given the freedom of public worship for adherents of Reformed Christianity.

The governmental evolution of New Amsterdam is a case apart. Until 1649 the inhabitants made no demands for local control distinct from the powers of company officials. In that year, however, an indigenous group called the Nine Men sent the States-General an appeal depicting their "very poor and most low condition" and asking for redress including a "suitable municipal government." They sent their petition and a remonstrance against Stuyvesant's government to Holland in care of three agents. The States-General investigated their appeal and after much delay pressured the company to make various reforms. In April 1652, it directed Stuyvesant to "erect there a Court of Justice formed, as much as possible, after the custom of this city [Amsterdam]." The court, or "Burgher Government," would include a *schout*, two *burgomasters* (or comayors), and five *schepens*es chosen from among the "honest and respectable" persons of the settlement. When Stuyvesant got around to implementing this directive in February 1653, he appointed the town officials himself rather than permit popular elections. Not until 1656 were these magistrates allowed the privilege of nominating a double number from among whom the director would select their successors.

Soon thereafter Stuyvesant introduced yet another measure designed to keep control in the tight grasp of an elite: he established the greater and lesser burgher rights. The former went to those who had held, or whose ancestors had held, high civil, military, or ecclesiastical offices in the city or who could purchase the right for fifty guilders. The second class included all those born in the city, or who had been residents for eighteen months, or who kept shop and paid twenty guilders. Only those who held the great burgher right were eligible for municipal office. Thereby the oligarchical arrangements of old Amsterdam would be perpetuated, and heredity would mean more than merit in the distribution of power.

There is some risk, however, in assuming that oligarchy or autocracy are ipso facto defective forms of government. Stuyvesant may have been autocratic, but he was neither inefficient nor unconcerned. He assumed that what was good for the company was good for the colony (though not always vice versa), and he administered reforms with gusto: he revised fencing laws to reduce property damage from footloose livestock, built Manhattan's first pier, appointed official surveyors, made stringent fire laws, enforced those against the sale of liquor to the Indians, insisted that Indians be paid promptly for services rendered, levied an excise on imported spirits in order to fund repairs on the fort, demonetized damaged wampum, cracked down on smuggling, and required everyone to attend Sunday services. Not all of these measures were popular, but all were promulgated with the public good in view.

Stuyvesant's desire to strengthen the colony while restoring the company also caused his head-on collision with the big patroonship at Rensselaerswyck. Within that private expanse, a village had grown up around Fort Orange called the Fuyck. Fearing that the patroon would eventually be able to monopolize the northern fur trade, Stuyvesant seized the Fuyck for direct company control. He named it Beverwyck (i.e., Beavertown, later Albany), and established there an inferior court of justice. The patroon's court continued to have jurisdiction over his tenants, but the new one had concurrent voice over company subjects within its boundaries. Much of the new court's business concerned the distribution of land entrusted to its jurisdiction and the regulation of Indian commerce. Thereafter the Beverwyck traders set out to monopolize the northern fur trade, to the utter frustration of the patroon and his tenants. Though Stuyvesant tried to be solicitous of the Van Rensselaers personally, he could not resist the pressure of local merchants or the company's economic demands.

In New Amsterdam the confrontation between private enterprise and public authority became even more complicated. Officials there, whether independent burghers or company men, promulgated a series of regulations designed to supervise virtually every phase of economic life. The States-General, however, while imposing duties on the colony's overseas commerce, objected to any internal regulations that were liable to restrain the optimum rate of economic growth. Stuyvesant's administration sought to control the production and sale of alcoholic beverages—both to raise revenue and to inhibit excessive inebriation (a major problem in the colony). No one who brewed beer could retail it as well. Price schedules were set repeatedly for beer and wine. Beer could not be brewed or stored without an official permit. Tavern hours were controlled by law, and so forth.

An ordinance of 1649 required "that the bakers, who henceforth make it a business to bake for sale, are to bake from clean wheat or clean rye as it comes from the mill, a loaf weighing 8, 4 or 2 pounds at the prices which the Honorable Court shall from time to time fix according to the price and arrival of grain." Many bakers tried to circumvent the various restrictions by baking only the most expensive types of bread. Similarly, since New Amsterdam faced periodic meat shortages, regulations were adopted to conserve the supply and raise a little money as well—through hog and cattle fairs, "free markets," and the need for "slaughtering permits."

Thus a resident of New Amsterdam could pursue almost no

form of economic activity without regulation or supervision. The company's directors, and the Amsterdam Chamber in particular, wished to see consumers protected from fraudulent practices. But they consistently opposed restraints upon individual initiative and freedom of trade—restraints that they feared might make New Netherland less attractive to immigrants and less conducive to economic growth. They considered price controls "impracticable" and the regulation of wages imprudent: "lowering and fixing the pay of the journeymen carpenters, masons etc." would "give rise to great dissatisfaction and troubles . . . among the journeymen." Again and again authorities in Amsterdam warned subordinates in Manhattan to minimize their interference with individual enterprise. "It is better to proceed in this matter with modesty," they wrote, "that commerce, just at present threatened by many dangers, may not be discouraged and people disgusted with it, which apparently would cause a depopulation of the country and deprive us of the means to bring emigrants over there."

It is paradoxical that the Amsterdam officials opposed local monopolies while they themselves enjoyed the largest monopoly of all, at least on paper. In reality, however, the company had relinquished its monopoly of trade in 1647 and thereafter insisted that economic freedom was the *sine qua non* of economic growth. Meanwhile, the director and council in New Amsterdam argued that local monopolies awarded to individuals provided a method of raising revenue as well as a means of ensuring the availability of certain services and products. So as fast as Stuyvesant awarded monopolies—"one to establish an ashery, one to make tiles and bricks, and the third to put up salt works"—the directors disallowed them and ordered him to give no more.

By the time Stuyvesant's administration began, the West India Company was already in precarious financial circumstances. Because it did not have the funds with which to subsidize a major colonial enterprise, it expected its settlers to do for themselves what could not be done for them. After 1644 it ceased to maintain its own traders in New Netherland, and after 1650 it no longer sold goods directly to the colonists. It hoped to reduce its overhead expenses overseas and to shift from a policy of direct commercial participation to one of governmental regulation. New Netherland became less and less important in its overall scheme—at best a breadbasket for provisioning Brazil and the Caribbean colonies. Toward achieving this end the company recommended in 1647 that slave labor in New Netherland "be more extensively cultivated than it has hitherto been, because the agricultural laborers who are conveyed thither at great expense to the colonies, sooner or later apply themselves to trade, and neglect agriculture altogether."

There had been a labor shortage from the very outset. Consequently the company sponsored—reluctantly it would appear—the importation of African slaves, beginning in 1626 with the first "parcel" of eleven. Demand intensified during the 1640s and 1650s and slave shipments became larger and more regular, so that by 1664 there may have been as many as seven hundred blacks in a population of perhaps eight thousand. They worked as agricultural laborers on company farms or on public buildings and military projects for which free workers were unavailable. Even after 1640, when white laborers became more abundant, slavery seemed to be the most economical source of labor. One could buy a "seasoned" slave from the West Indies for just about the same amount it would cost to hire a free wage worker for one year.

The white colonists discovered early that blacks imported directly from Africa were especially rebellious and difficult to control in a system of forced labor; hence a preference developed for slaves who had already been worked at the Dutch colony of Curaçao for a period of "seasoning." The brutal plantation experience there introduced them to European values, taught them what their white masters expected, and reduced their will to resist. The enslaved Africans underwent a harrowing series of psychological shocks—if they survived at all—and yet (small comfort) the institution of slavery in New Netherland seems to have been more benign than in any of the other North American colonies. Slaves had the same status as whites in the courts and they could testify in cases involving free whites. During Kieft's ill-conceived Indian war, the slaves even received arms and helped to defend the Dutch.

The West India Company had intended to monopolize the slave trade to New Netherland, but pressure from individual settlers and the rise of illegal importations forced the company to open the trade in 1648. Even so, it remained the largest importer and owner of slaves in the colony. Because it became too expensive to maintain a large supply of slaves for intermittent use, the company developed a status of "half-freedom" for purposes of economic efficiency. Settlers were eager to hire the blacks for blocks of time, the slaves enjoyed a greater degree of autonomy if not freedom, and no one worried about theoretical inconsistencies.

From this arrangement a significant number of free blacks emerged, and no discriminatory legislation restricted their activities. They could own white indentured servants and intermarry if they subscribed to Reformed Protestantism. There must have been some social prejudice against persons of color; but it was more casual than overt, and the bias owed as much to their non-Christian condition as it did to their racial characteristics. Only at the end of the Dutch period does slavery seem to have emerged as an explicit instrument of racial control. "As to baptisms," one minister wrote in 1664, "the negroes occasionally request that we should baptize their children, but we have refused to do so, partly on account of their lack of knowledge and of faith, and partly because of the worldly and perverse aims on the part of said negroes. They wanted nothing else than to deliver their children from bodily slavery, without striving for piety and Christian virtues."

Clearly the Dutch Reformed church did not restrain its members or even its ministers from using slave labor. In 1644, however, the Classis of Amsterdam declared that slave owners were "responsible for instructing their Negroes in the Christian Religion and that time should be provided for all Negroes to assemble in a suitable place in order to receive instruction from a catechist." Little progress seems to have been made in this direction, and twenty years later Dominie Selyns informed the

Classis that "this has borne but little fruit among the elder [black] people who have no faculty of comprehension; but there is some hope for the youth who have improved reasonably well."

Relatively few blacks became members of the Dutch Reformed church; a handful were baptized each year, and occasional marriages occurred. One barrier to proselytizing arose because many Europeans presumed that a Christian and his children could not be kept in slavery, nor could children born to a Christian. A memorandum sent by some of the colonists to the States-General in 1649 asserted that several black children whose parents had been freed because of long service to the company were kept as slaves, "though it is contrary to the laws of every people that any one born to a free Christian mother should be a slave and be compelled to remain in servitude." There were other obstacles as well, such as denominational regulations about baptism. As a rule only children of communicants could be baptized, and the church frequently specified that an adult could not simply be baptized with the hope that he would subsequently become a church member. Prospective adult converts had to be given the "full treatment" immediately. In short, the whole business of baptism and church membership went round and round in a vicious circle and did more to keep the races apart than to bring them to mutual Christian understanding.

That should not in any way be surprising, however, because the greatest resistance to religious toleration and social pluralism in New Netherland came from the resident ministers of the Dutch Reformed church. The most prominent among these was Dominie Johannes Megapolensis, whose ministry spanned the years 1642–70, seven of them at Rensselaerswyck and twenty-one in New Amsterdam. He deserves most of the credit for establishing the Dutch church on a strong foundation and much of the blame for the persecution of Lutherans, Jews, Quakers, and other sects seeking a haven in the colony. The son of Catholic parents, he converted to Reformed Protestantism in 1626 at the age of twenty-three—whereupon his family disinherited him. During his pastorate at Rensselaerswyck he made some effort to communicate with the neighboring Indians, but his cultural myopia kept the contact minimal. "This nation has a very difficult language," he wrote in 1644, "and it costs me great pains to learn it, so as to be able to speak and preach in it fluently. There is no Christian here who understands the language thoroughly; those who have lived here long can use a kind of jargon just sufficient to carry on trade with it, but they do not understand the fundamentals of the language. I am making a vocabulary of the Mahakuaas' language, and when I am among them I ask them how things are called; but as they are very stupid, I sometimes cannot make them understand what I want." Megapolensis criticized the Indians for their slovenly dress, failure to bathe, immorality, and cruelty toward their enemies. It is no wonder that the dominie failed to convert a single "heathen" during his seven years among them.

His relations with other denominations were complicated by rivalry, outright hostility, and accusations of heresy. Although the first article of Stuyvesant's commission prohibited "any other than the Reformed doctrine," restrictions upon religious freedom applied to public worship, not private conventicles. By 1650, moreover, the company directors had decided to stimulate colonization by liberalizing the limitations upon other denominations. Megapolensis and his fellow clergy fought this tendency and received full support from the Classis of Amsterdam, which wrote in 1656, "Let us then—we here in this country and you there—employ all diligence to frustrate all such plans, that the wolves may be warded off from the tender lambs of Christ." So it happened that they contested, with varying degrees of success, the Lutherans' attempt to bring a pastor to New Amsterdam, the preaching of Quakers and Anabaptists after 1652, and the mere presence of Jews from 1654. As Megapolensis wrote to the Classis in 1655, "For as we have here Papists, Mennonites and Lutherans among the Dutch; also many Puritans or Independents, and many Atheists and various other servants of Baal among the English under this Government, who conceal themselves under the name of Christians; it would create a still greater confusion, if the obstinate and immovable Jews came to settle here." *

Ultimately, however, the dominies could not prevail, for the necessities of population growth, of bulwarks for defense against English or Indian neighbors, and of commercial profits proved to be overwhelming. The company directors summed it up simply in a letter sent to Stuyvesant in 1663:

Your last letter informed us that you had banished from the Province and sent hither by ship a certain Quaker, John Bowne by name: although we heartily desire, that these and other sectarians remained away from there, yet as they do not, we doubt very much, whether we can proceed against them rigorously without diminishing the population and stopping immigration, which must be favored at a so tender stage of the country's existence. You may therefore shut your eyes, at least not force people's consciences, but allow every one to have his own belief, as long as he behaves quietly and legally, gives no offence to his neighbors and does not oppose the government.†

The authorities in Amsterdam had by this time heard many other compelling reasons for making ad hoc concessions to heterogeneity—some of them practical, some of them ideological. In 1652, for example, the New Amsterdam Consistory requested the services of a pastor able to preach in English as well as Dutch. They got just that in Dominie Samuel Drisius, who occasionally gave the Word in French to the colony's Walloons. In 1657, on the other hand, thirty-one residents of Flushing (in Queens) sent a remonstrance home with a different emphasis: "The law of love, peace and liberty in the States," they said, "extends to Jews, Turks, and Egyptians, as they are considered the sons of Adam, which is the glory of the outward state of Holland."

Inevitably the colony's composition grew ever more diverse—

---

* The Jewish immigrants, refugees from Brazil, were required to live in a ghetto. They were instructed to build their houses "close together in a convenient place on one or the other side of New Amsterdam."

† Hugh Hastings, comp., *Ecclesiastical Records: State of New York*, I (Albany, 1901), 530.

by 1660 Huguenots had begun to settle around New Paltz in Ulster County—and an anxious Stuyvesant perceived the consequences in political terms. He informed the directors in 1661 that "the *English* and *French* colonies are continued and populated by their own nation and countrymen and consequently bound together more firmly and united, while your Honors' colonies in New-Netherland are only gradually and slowly peopled by the scrapings of all sorts of nationalities (few excepted), who consequently have the least interest in the welfare and maintenance of the commonwealth." Stuyvesant did not simply fear pluralism per se; he feared the attendant instabilities and lack of cohesion that seemed socially impolitic as well as uncongenial to the creation of political society.

He also knew that New Netherland's liberal immigration policies made it attractive to the worst elements in Europe's changing population. Alcohol taken in excess troubled many of the early American colonies: good water was not always available, primitive conditions were depressing, the trade in slaves and molasses helped to stimulate the production of rum, and liquor was usually in supply for sale to the Indians. Even so, all accounts seem to suggest that the rate of per capita consumption was higher in New Netherland than in any other mainland colony and was particularly noticeable in prominent men: Van Twiller had been an alcoholic, and Dominie Bogardus, some said, could not serve communion without spilling the wine because he usually had the shakes. No wonder Stuyvesant's first reform upon arrival in 1647 was to close all the bars at nine o'clock and impose strong penalties for Sunday drinking and knife fighting. He also had to contend with reckless driving in New Amsterdam; men drove their wagons and carts too fast, thereby endangering pedestrians, especially women and children. The director therefore ordered all drivers to get off their wagons and lead their horses along every street with the exception of Broadway. There they could ride, because it was wide, but slowly.

Sexual promiscuity also seems to have been a problem, particularly between European men and Indian women. After

Arent Van Curler complained to Kiliaen van Rensselaer about improprieties at the patroonship, his lordship printed a pamphlet listing possible offenses and appropriate punishments. Anyone caught having sexual intercourse with "heathen women and girls" would have to pay "the first time a fine of 25 guilders," 50 if the female became pregnant, and 100 if she gave birth. Cornelis van Tienhoven, the colony's secretary for many years, was notorious for his lechery—and success—with Indian women.* His enemies reported that "he has run about as an Indian, with a little covering and a small patch in front, from lust after the prostitutes to whom he has always been mightily inclined." We have no reports from his friends; but, then, he seems to have had few other than Stuyvesant, Elizabeth van Hooghvelt (whom he seduced and abandoned), and Rachel, his widow (after his hat and cane were found floating on the river in 1656). He was neither mourned nor missed.

If organized crime and vice were not yet serious problems in New Netherland, the maintenance of public order was. Tavern brawls were commonplace and sailors ashore were disorderly. In 1658 Stuyvesant established the "Rattle Watch," the beginnings of New York City's police, consisting of nine men who would serve as a patrol designed "to pursue, attack and capture . . . pirates and vagabonds" as well as arrest "robbers or others who would wish to inflict injury and damage." As a warning the watchmen would carry a "rattle," really a wooden, hinged-clapper device, for sounding the alarm. The most ominous warning to potential wrongdoers, however, effected with grim irony, was the tarred corpse occasionally left hanging from the public gibbet, known to all as the "field-bishop." Fortunately, unjust executions by the magistrates were rare in New Netherland.

---

* When Dominie Jonas Michaëlius looked around for an American novelty to send a friend in Hoorn who happened to be a director of the company, he selected the phallic amulet worn by Indian women along the Hudson and explained that they were "two small bones, which the savage women here wear around their bodies as tassels and ornaments, and of which they are quite proud. These are the small bones of the copulatory organs of the male beavers, one end of which comes above the scrotum and then goes further on along the coles."

Fire, however, posed an enormous problem to persons as well as property. In 1648 Stuyvesant appointed four fire wardens to inspect the flimsy chimneys on thatched-roof houses, and he demanded a penalty of three guilders for every dirty chimney. With the proceeds he established a fund for the purchase of leather buckets locally as well as hooks and ladders from Holland for fire fighting. Because of the repeated fires, plus the replacement of older structures with newer ones, precious little from the Dutch period has survived. One incredible exception is the oldest house in New York State, built between 1638 and 1640, which stands in East Flatbush with a wonderfully swaybacked roof. In 1655 it became the home of Pieter Claessen, an aspiring citizen and sometime superintendent on one of the company's farms; it was occupied by his descendants until 1969 when the family donated the two-story frame structure to the city. It has now been declared an official site by the Preservation Commission and is being restored.*

Thanks to the Museum of the City of New York, we do have a superbly detailed reconstruction of New Amsterdam in 1661: a town of some three hundred buildings and thirteen hundred inhabitants. As we stand high on one of the bastions of Fort Amsterdam—its earthwork walls in poor condition—a church, barracks, and Stuyvesant's office lie beneath us. Looking down to the end of the island where there is a cluster of small homes, we see what looks to be that menacing gibbet. In fact it is a tall crane used to load and unload cargoes and to careen ships to be caulked. A few yards away there is a shorter piece of scaffolding which is, indeed, the city gallows. The Blue Dove Tavern, facing Pearl Street, is a favorite haunt for the Rattle Watchers.

Looking south, we see small ferries passing back and forth to Staaten Eylandt and Noten (Governor's) Eylandt. Just on shore

---

* Historical archaeology is just beginning to fight the ubiquitous bulldozer and uncover landmarks of colonial New York. In 1970 archaeologists and historians unearthed fragments of what may have been New York's first City Hall, or *Stadthuis* (1653–99), as well as the Dutch stockade built at Kingston under Stuyvesant's supervision in 1658. (It lasted into the 18th century.) Both of these are wonderful finds and offer much promise to future diggers. (See *The New York Times*, May 30, July 28, Aug. 20, 1970.)

a large, grassy plot serves as the common bleaching ground, where housewives spread their newly laundered linens to dry in the sun. Turning left and east a little, we notice the office of Jacques Cortelyou, a surveyor who has recently made a complete survey of the town. We are facing Long Island now, and here in the East River is the anchorage for seagoing vessels. The little weighhouse on the pier has importance beyond its size, for everything that enters or leaves the port must have the stamp of the company's weighmaster. The beach perpendicular to the pier serves as a marketplace; and along the street above it there are various warehouses, one owned by the company. The tallest roof here belongs to Director Stuyvesant's town house, which the English later called Whitehall.

Turning to the north and east, we see the home and shop of Frederick Philipse (carpenter, architect, and contractor for the company), the brewery of Oloff Van Cortlandt, and the Wooden Horse Tavern of Philip Geraerdy. Across the main canal, which cuts halfway into the island, there is City Hall: the governmental center of the colony as well as of the city. It has meeting rooms, courtrooms, and the town jail with a bell in its cupola to mark the passing hours and, with three solemn strokes, to signal the reading of official proclamations from the steps of City Hall.

To the north are the main canal and its branch. They provide easier access to the market area, as well as mooring for small boats. Like the windmill, the stepped gables, and domestic gardens, the canal is a reminder of Holland; and like the ones at home, it smells. Near the end of the canal stands the poorhouse, overseen by deacons of the Dutch church. Broadway, lined with small homes, reaches out to the wall where village ends and farms begin. By 1661 many settlers were moving out beyond the wall to less crowded locations. West of Broadway there are company gardens, carefully tended to provide fruits and vegetables for the seventy-five or so who are directly employed by the West India Company. In among the vegetables there are fine flower gardens, yet another reminder of home.

West toward the Hudson, or North River, is the burying ground tucked between the homes of Dirck Wiggerts and

Hendrick Van Dyck, homes built with bricks that had been used as ballast on the voyage out. Along Broadway, coming down the island's west side, our eyes are caught by the big house of Martin Cregier, captain of the Burgher Guard (or militia). Looking west, with the Palisades distant across the river, there are mooring areas for small craft and the big windmill built in 1642 for grinding grain into flour. Next to the mill there is a steep path, called the Beaver's Path, which runs down to the riverbank. This was the way into town for ships' sailors, visitors from Pavonia and Communipaw across the river, and Indians arriving by canoe.

Relations between New Netherland and those neighboring Indians deteriorated seriously during the middle and later 1650s; but it must be realized that "the Indians" were not some monolithic entity that always acted as a unit. Treaty relationships with the Dutch were tribal and highly individualized. The Mohawks, for example, negotiated quite separately from the other Iroquois tribes, sometimes against the others' interests, even to the point of seeking Dutch help for hostilities against the Onondaga. Just as the Dutch during the 1620s had tried to exploit hostilities between Mohawks and Mahicans to their own advantage, the Mohawks moved in the 1650s and 1660s to profit from conflicts between New Netherland on the one hand and New England and New Sweden on the other. "If the boundaries are once settled between us and our neighbors," wrote Stuyvesant, "then the daily quarrels, bickerings, jealousies, and claims shall be avoided from either side and a good understanding and correspondence established; these pernicious wars between the Maquaes and the Northern savages would then soon be settled and brought to an end and all the savages could be made to submit or at least to deliberate, when they see the Christians united and drawing a line to keep the barbarians in submission or at least quiet."

Christian unity proved to be chimerical, however, and in 1655 the Amsterdam Chamber decided to eliminate Swedish competition along the Delaware. So they sent a small force to supplement Stuyvesant's own, and he led the whole—more than six hundred men in seven ships—down to New Sweden where he handily captured tiny Fort Casimir and the larger Fort Christina. New Sweden thereupon became New Amstel, an outpost of New Netherland for another decade, just as it had been at the very first phase of Dutch colonization.

Meanwhile, no sooner had Stuyvesant left New Amsterdam for that successful expedition than the Mahicans, Pachamis, Esopus, and Hackensack Indians made a surprise attack upon Manhattan—touched off by a trivial episode in Hendrick Van Dyck's peach orchard. On the night of September 15, these Indians, to revenge the murder of a squaw, made a shambles of many Dutch homes but did a minimum of personal injury. Instead of an eye for an eye, they smashed furniture, ripped up bedclothes, and ransacked homes. They then broke open beer and brandy barrels, drank themselves into a stupor, and a truce was arranged. Stuyvesant hurried back from the Delaware as quickly as he could and found that the "Peach War" had spread to the far settlements. Massacres and kidnappings occurred, Dutch outposts on the Jersey side were burned and pillaged, fifty colonists were killed, twenty-eight farms were destroyed, five hundred head of cattle died or strayed, and thousands of bushels of corn were burned. The Indians seem to have lost some sixty men in the fighting.

Stuyvesant moved vigorously to shore up the city's pathetic defenses, negotiated the release of prisoners, and forbade new farms to be started in isolated areas. No longer would Indians be allowed to stay overnight in the city or to enter it carrying arms. Anyone who sold liquor to them would be punished bodily, and drunken Indians were to be imprisoned until they confessed where they had obtained their drinks. The measures worked, and Manhattan never had another Indian raid. But Esopus (Kingston) did in 1659, undergoing a twenty-three-day siege that Stuyvesant had to come upriver to break.* Hostilities with the

---

* There is good evidence that Dutch settlers provoked the fight: first by supplying the Indians with liquor, and second by firing on them while they were carousing among themselves.

Esopus Indians burst out once more in 1663 and were terminated by a treaty in May 1664. Once again the Dutch required the cession of more Indian land; once again the River Indians had to capitulate, and they ceased thereafter to be a serious threat along the lower Hudson.

One of the ironies that developed from these Dutch dealings with other Europeans and Indians in the New World arose from the need to legitimize authority and impress the enemy. At home in the Dutch Republic the burgher-oligarchs stressed their republican ideology and strongly insisted to the House of Orange that they, and not the *stadholders*, were the real rulers. Since Indians could not be expected to understand the political complexities of the northern Netherlands, however, and since overseas diplomacy occurred in a context of competing potentates, Maurice of Nassau achieved in North America a status he was never accorded at home: "Our beloved Lord and Master, The Prince." To help Stuyvesant struggle through the intricacies of intercolonial protocol, his colony was even designated as a *graafschap*, or countship!

It did him little good, though, in dealing with New England's heads of state. They knew just how precariously the Dutch colony was planted. In the 1640s New Netherland had virtually been willing to mortgage itself to New England in exchange for military assistance against the Indians. English settlers began to infiltrate the colony on a permanent basis and upon favorable terms, including freedom of religion. Lion Gardiner, an English engineer who had served in the Dutch Republic and had a Dutch wife, simply took possession of an island he called the Isle of Wight (now Gardiner's Island); Brian Newton, an Englishman, commanded the military forces of New Netherland in 1647; and Stuyvesant's two negotiators at Hartford in 1650 were English expatriates. In sum, the English were more than simply an upstart element within. They were a sizable community who happened to have sworn nominal allegiance to the Dutch government.

Anglo-Dutch conflict over their respective territorial claims in the New World complicated matters still more. Based upon

Henry Hudson's explorations, the Dutch claimed all land between the fortieth and fifty-fourth degrees of north latitude (subsequently extended southward), although the States-General had not actually designated any boundaries when it created New Netherland in the 1620s. England, meanwhile, insisted that it had historic title to the territory between thirty-four and forty-eight degrees. Though Plymouth's governor, William Bradford, was himself willing to ignore the obvious overlap, he warned the Dutch that if the home governments did not settle the controversy, it would be "harder and with more difficulty obtained hereafter, and perhaps not without blows."

His prediction ultimately proved correct, but it was forestalled in 1650 when Stuyvesant negotiated a successful treaty with the New England colonies. The demographic growth of New England, especially during the 1640s, had spilled Puritans of various sorts into several areas claimed by the Dutch, along the Connecticut River valley and across to Long Island. Aware of his inferior position in terms of population and military strength, Stuyvesant agreed to a boundary line on Long Island running southward from the western edge of Oyster Bay and on the mainland twenty miles northward from Greenwich. He thereby surrendered no land that was actually under New Netherland's jurisdiction or occupied by Dutchmen, and he had at least persuaded the New England colonies to delineate explicitly the extremities of their territory—hopefully the best way to check an expansion that had been under way for almost three decades. Lesser points of dispute were either compromised at Hartford or postponed for future discussion.

Although the States-General finally ratified the treaty in 1656—stalling during the Anglo-Dutch naval war of 1652–54— the New England Confederation, cleverly, never submitted the treaty to England. It would be easier to violate if it remained merely an agreement among colonies; so it did, and so it would be. In 1663 Stuyvesant went to Boston to seek renewed acceptance of the Hartford Treaty; but John Winthrop, Jr., and other Puritan leaders cited their recent grant of Connecticut from Charles II and contemptuously renounced all previous agreements with New Netherland. Stuyvesant must have known when he left Boston for New Amsterdam that time and numbers favored New England. He knew now that David De Vries had been wrong when he wrote of the sand crabs of New Netherland that "their claws display the same colors as the flag of our Prince, orange, white, and blue, thus showing plainly enough that it is our destiny to people and to hold this country." They had not peopled it sufficiently, and their destiny lay elsewhere.

The economic and diplomatic circumstances are simple enough. England had for a long time been eager to challenge the United Provinces' commercial and maritime supremacy. The Anglo-Dutch war of 1652–54 clearly demonstrated Holland's vulnerability and the value of her trade. Numerous Dutch infringements of England's Navigation Act (1651) only increased antagonisms and led to bitter laments such as this petition given to Cromwell in 1658 by more than one hundred ship captains: "The Dutch eat us out of our trade at home and abroad; they refuse to sell us a hogshead of water to refresh us at sea, and call us 'English Dogs,' which doth much grieve our English spirits. They will not sail with us, but shoot at us, and by indirect courses bring their goods into our ports, which wrongs not only us but you in your customs." By 1663 the Anglo-Dutch trade rivalry along the African coast had grown intense, and the English believed that violations of the new Navigation Act (1660) were largely caused by the presence of a Dutch colony midway between Maryland and New England. Consequently the Council for Foreign Plantations welcomed any English claim to New Netherland, however contrived; and by the early months of 1664 war rumors filled the air on both sides of the channel.

In March 1664, without any reference to Dutch claims or earlier English grants, Charles II gave to his brother, James Duke of York, quite a gift. It comprised parts of Maine, all of Long Island, Martha's Vineyard, Nantucket, "together also with . . . Hudson's River and all the land from the west side of the Connectecutte River to the East side of De la Ware Bay." James, who also happened to be the Lord High Admiral of England, immediately organized a fleet of four warships under the

command of Colonel Richard Nicolls. By the end of May the
ships were en route. They stopped briefly in New England to
refurbish and confer. On August 26, Nicolls's flagship, the *Guinea*,
came around Coney Island and anchored at Gravesend Bay, just
below the Narrows.

Stuyvesant sent a messenger to ask the visitors their business.
Nicolls replied that "in his Majestie's Name I do demand the
Towne, Scituate upon the Island commonly knowne by the
Name of Manhatoes with all the forts thereunto belonging."
Stuyvesant fumed and sputtered, then he sent a reply reviewing
the legitimacy of Dutch claims. Nicolls did not even respond in
writing. He simply told Stuyvesant's messengers that after
forty-eight hours his ships would approach New Amsterdam.

City officials accepted the inevitable more readily than their
director. The fort was in a weakened condition. Their grain
supply was as severely limited as their firepower. Once they
learned that Nicolls's terms were magnanimous, they aroused the
entire populace to pressure Stuyvesant into a bloodless surrender.
Dominie Megapolensis talked earnestly with Stuyvesant on a
parapet of the fort, then took his arm and led him away from the
gunner, who, lighted match in hand, had been awaiting the
director's order to fire. The director gave no order, and two
English ships sailed past the fort, past the silent burghers on
shore. Since the ships had the city within range of their guns, all
was over but the signing; that came on September 8, a Monday
morning. A few hours later the Dutch soldiers marched out of
Fort Amsterdam, down the Beaver Path, and boarded the *Gideon*.
Nicolls marched in at the head of his troops and promptly sent
the news of victory to Massachusetts. He signed his letter "ffrom
New Yorke upon the Island of the Manhatoes."

4

THE ANGLO-DUTCH
PROPRIETARY

Historians have long regarded the year 1664 as pivotal in New York's history—the most significant, perhaps, between 1609 and 1776. The colony did, after all, change hands and colors, just as the claws of the Atlantic sand crab—ordinarily orange, blue, and white—become imperial red when captured and boiled. New Netherland did pass from a Dutch company's property to an English duke's proprietary; and there were inhabitants who changed their coloration more willingly and less painfully than the sand crab. Carel van Brugge, for example, became Charles Bridge; and doughty Dutch farmers began to adopt surnames, following the English custom. Pieter Claessen had been so named simply because his father's name was Claes (Nicholas); but soon after the conquest of 1664 he became Pieter Claessen Wyckoff. The phenomenon, copied from the English, was not uncommon.

Despite the discontinuities and very real changes that occurred after the conquest, however, too much has been made of them. Only in a formal, constitutional sense did New York become an English colony in 1664; in many important respects, the province remained predominantly Dutch for yet another generation. In the coming decades, New York would be less attractive to English immigrants than New England, Pennsylvania, or the southern colonies;* and quitrents, that traditional English quid-

---

* It is equally true, however, that few immigrants came from Holland in the century and a quarter after 1664.

dity between tenant and landlord, were not properly established in New York until the last fifteen years of the seventeenth century. Anglicization, in short, did not occur on a large and permanent scale until after 1691, and then only gradually.

It is ironic, therefore, to look at the letter sent soon after the conquest by the *burgomasters* and *schepens* of New Amsterdam. Writing to the Duke of York, they offered obedience to him and to his governor, and predicted that under Nicolls New York would "bloom and grow like the Cedars of Lebanon." We do not know whether their prophecy was merely wishful thinking or pure pandering, but in either case they were simply wrong. The reasons New York did not "bloom and grow" have to do with its peculiar circumstances, with the Duke's policies, his personnel, and with the lingering tenacity of Dutch legacies to an English proprietary.

The English phoenix that arose from Dutch ashes in 1664 did indeed have handsome plumage and was truly unique, but it would not be ready to fly for some time. It was unique because it alone among the continental colonies of British North America had not originally been settled by Englishmen, and all sorts of consequences derived from the simple fact of conquest. Its plumage was only superficially gorgeous because of its outrageous extent. In addition to the towns at the western end of Long Island and the areas along the Hudson and Delaware rivers—the settled extent of New Netherland—New York by then included the rest of Long Island, all of what became New Jersey, an ill-defined stretch along the western side of the Delaware, the western half of Connecticut, eastern Maine extending northward to the St. Lawrence, and all the islands (except Block Island) from Cape Cod to Cape May—a gaudy grant, but unrealistic, and very soon reduced. At least the territory of New York was precisely defined—New Netherland never had been; but its boundaries were wildly disproportionate to the paucity of people and ability to govern, and thereby threw up awkward obstacles to populating, cultivating, and defending the province.

New York would never be larger, nor more vulnerable, nor more resented by its inhabitants within and neighbors without than in 1664. Immediately and inevitably, the phoenix began to lose some of its feathers. In 1665 the Duke of York awarded New Jersey to a proprietary group headed by Lords Berkeley and Carteret. In 1667 Governor Nicolls and his fellow commissioners restored the western half of Connecticut to its eastern alter ego, and the lands along the western bank of the Delaware soon became the object of a long dispute with Lord Baltimore and his Maryland settlement.

By giving away all the land lying between the Hudson and Delaware rivers, the Duke left his subjects feeling "cooped up" (Governor Thomas Dongan's phrase) between New England and New Jersey and competitive with them for immigrants and economic growth. The remote settlements beyond the Delaware were a military liability, as they had been for the Swedes and Peter Stuyvesant. As for upper Maine and the New England islands, they were about as useful as dead limbs on a tree and knots on its trunk: quite visible, but uncongenial to active growth. They added to administrative costs, produced almost no revenue, and brought New York into conflict with Massachusetts as well as France. "It's a very hard thing upon mee," Dongan complained, "coming over hither in troublesome times, finding noe Revenue established & yet having three Garrisons to look after . . . & finding such contest between the Government of Canada, and this about the Bever Trade, the Inland-Country & the Indians. . . ."

Equally important, the population of New York was less English and more diverse than that of any other British possession. This complex consideration dictated many of the terms of surrender in 1664 as well as the informal constitution that followed. According to the Articles of Capitulation, the States-General of Holland and the Dutch West India Company were assured of their property rights (farms and houses) in the province; and the inhabitants, regardless of nationality, would remain as "free denizens." They would continue to enjoy their lands, houses, goods, and ships unmolested. Freedom of conscience, patterns of inheritance, contractual obligations, and the choice of magistrates would at least temporarily "be determined according to the manner of the Dutch." Direct commercial intercourse with Holland, however, could continue for only six months after the surrender.

The charter that Charles II had given to his brother James in March 1664 was the briefest and most hastily executed of all the seventeenth-century colonial charters, as well as the only one ever issued in behalf of a member of the royal family and to one who was also heir to the throne. It allowed him all of the traditional proprietary rights and imposed the fewest restrictions upon his powers. He could control all appointments, make all laws and ordinances (so long as they conformed to those of England), and determine all judicial matters, criminal and civil, except in cases of appeal to the king. He had complete command over trade and could set the customs duties, regulate land grants, and decide all measures in case of attack. The usual provision for a representative assembly was not included, nor was the proprietor's customary oath of fealty. Instead the inhabitants of New York would declare their allegiance directly to the king, and all writs would be issued in his name. When James became king in 1685, therefore, the transition from dukedom to royal colony would necessitate only small adjustments.

In practice, the Duke's relationship to his proprietary was an ambiguous one characterized by authoritarian permissiveness. On paper his powers were enormous, and he yielded concessions only grudgingly and slowly. He dared to deny his subjects such vital privileges as representation while seeking to maximize his revenues from them. Nevertheless, his absolutism was tempered by absenteeship—he never visited New York—and he exercised little personal influence or direction over it. The Dutch were not whipped into line, were given considerable latitude, and readily recaptured the colony in 1673 on account of its neglected defenses. Administration was entrusted to a series of governors with similar origins: staunch royalist backgrounds, military training and experience, as well as proven loyalty to superiors.

Colonel Richard Nicolls (1624–72) had followed the Duke into exile during Cromwell's regime, served in the French army under James's command, and in 1664 fulfilled a threefold mission on behalf of his master: conquest of New Netherland, leadership of a commission to investigate conditions in New England, and gubernatorial responsibility for the transition from Dutch to English government in New York—a difficult task that he executed with considerable skill. He appointed a provincial secretary and four councillors, one of them to be collector and receiver general. With his Council he would regulate the colony's fiscal affairs, establish courts, settle boundary disputes between towns or neighbors, renew land patents, adjudicate problems of land tenure, supervise Indian relations, provide for defense, and regulate military affairs.

Nicolls is best known, however, for writing and promulgating the so-called Duke's Laws, a code designed primarily for residents of Long Island and Westchester. The laws were approved at a meeting in March 1665, called by Nicolls for this exclusive purpose and attended by thirty-four delegates from seventeen towns: thirteen English and four Dutch. The laws themselves are in many ways indicative of the pluralistic complexities that Nicolls faced, of the start toward anglicization at this time, and of the residual tenacity of Dutch ways.

Nicolls's code has often been noted as the first compilation of English laws in colonial New York. In reality he drew upon English, Dutch, and New England precedents; but he also omitted some of the most crucial characteristics of the New England codes known to him. He made no provision for an elected assembly, no provision for town meetings as part of the local administrative system (substituting an elective council and board of overseers), no provision for freemanship as it was understood in New England, and no provision for a public school system like that of Massachusetts. Deferring to the Dutch experience in New Netherland, however, he provided for religious toleration as well as the complicated system of partial retirement and double nomination of local officials.

Finally, by altering in certain critical ways the Dutch and New England practices known to him, Nicolls created regulations unfamiliar to either nationality, such as the compulsory renewal of all former land and town grants and surrender of the old deeds and patents. Not only did this law invalidate all former grants; by requiring new surveys and fees to pay for new patents, it also became a touchstone of discontent and political agitation. In addition, Nicolls altered the necessary requirements for suffrage. Since the traditional bases of town and provincial freemanship had been abandoned, some other test of citizenship had to be established. The code, however, was vague and ambiguous on this matter; and practice would vary from one locality to another. In general, the possession of land in freehold tenure seems to have been required for voting on local matters; but there was no specification of the size of freehold required, and in militia elections all soldiers could vote irrespective of their property holdings.

In many ways, then, the Duke's Laws left New York with a problem of provincial legitimacy because the precise nature and extent of Nicolls's code was not fully manifest. That would remain the case, in varying degrees, all the way to 1752 when the colony's laws were finally and fully codified by William Livingston and William Smith, Jr., and 1761 when a full doctrine of the binding force of the common law in New York emerged. In short, almost an entire century elapsed, 1665 to 1761, before New Yorkers knew with assurance the contours of their legal system. Significantly, although the Duke's Laws were drafted especially for the English settlers of Long Island and were formally approved by them, Long Islanders became the severest critics of Nicolls's code and carped continually between 1665 and 1683 about the curtailment of their political privileges and the imposition of taxes without popular consent.

From the beginning Nicolls had promised to the Long Island towns freedoms and immunities equal to, if not greater than, those enjoyed in New England. Although he failed to make good that pledge, he ruled rather fairly despite his arbitrary powers. In clashes between English and Dutch demands, he tried to be a conciliator and arbitrator. Samuel Maverick, who had worked with Nicolls on the royal commission, remarked reasonably that "by his prudent management of affairs [Nicolls] kept persons of different judgments and of diverse nations in peace and quietness, dureing a time when a great part of the world was in warrs."

Within a few years, however, he grew weary of being a buffer and of being buffeted, and asked to be replaced. His successor, Colonel Francis Lovelace (1621–75), came from an identical background: a strongly royalist family. He had served under Charles I in the civil war, in exile on the Continent with Charles II, and in France as a soldier during the 1650s. Because Lovelace had visited Virginia between 1650 and 1652 and had some knowledge of the colonies, James rewarded his loyalty by appointing him to succeed Nicolls in April 1667. He arrived eleven months later and worked with Nicolls through the summer of 1668 in order to effect a smooth transition. His instructions directed him to continue Nicolls's policies, and like his predecessor he was a reasonably conscientious and tolerant man. Cautious in what he undertook, he conducted his business either unilaterally by fiat, in conjunction with his councillors, through the High Court of Assizes, or by commissions under his appointment and control.

The most pressing external problems that arose during his administration, 1668–73, concerned Indian relations, boundary disputes, insurrection in the Delaware country, rebellion in New Jersey, and the danger of Dutch reconquest during wartime. Internally, Lovelace concerned himself with improving ferriage, roads, and means of communication; regulating trade and extending commerce; promoting indigenous shipbuilding; encouraging diversity and toleration of religious sects; and establishing new villages and townships. Between 1668 and 1672, Fisher's Island (north of Montauk in Long Island Sound) was granted to John Winthrop, Jr.; Fordham Manor went to John Archer; Tisbury (on Martha's Vineyard) was awarded to Thomas Mayhew; and Prudence Island (in Narragansett Bay) was given to John Paine. Along with Nicolls's gift of Pelham to Thomas Pell and Shelter Island to the Sylvester family in 1666, these manors continued the patroonship precedent of generous grants to potential political allies. Whatever may have been gained politically, however, was overwhelmingly sacrificed in arrested economic growth. It would take four decades, or more, before that lesson could be fully appreciated.

The conquest of 1664 undermined the legitimacy of Rensselaerswyck and challenged the patroon's territorial and political privileges. The magistrates of Beverwyck hurried to Manhattan in order to get from Nicolls a set of "articles" for the town, newly named Albany, confirming all of its prior rights, customs, and monopoly of the fur trade. The Van Rensselaers, meanwhile, had to get directly from the Duke a confirmation of their domain, an arrangement that was gradually worked out between 1664 and 1683. The patroon retained his economic privileges but lost the prerogative of having his own court. He sat on the Albany court and could also nominate other members, thereby exerting direct and indirect influence. But his domain became a subdivision of the county government, responsible to its jurisdiction and institutions. What must be emphasized, then, is that New York's government was centralized constitutionally and politically but decentralized in significant respects: socially, economically, and juridically. Local government of a representative and elected nature existed in much of the colony long before representative government was established at the provincial level (1683). This meant that local government would be more immediate and important to ordinary people than central government, that local attachments and parochialism would be encouraged, and that stresses would often arise between local and provincial officials.

The very terms of Dutch capitulation in 1664 had included three separate sets of articles: for New Amsterdam and its environs, for settlements along the upper Hudson, and for the Delaware territories. Similar in many respects, they differed in detail. The realities of social and geographical heterogeneity obliged Nicolls to adapt political organization to the predominant ethnic and interest groups in each area. Yet no area was fully discrete, and imperatives in each were influenced by events in the others. While the establishment of English ideas and institutions on Long Island was retarded by Nicolls's sensitivity

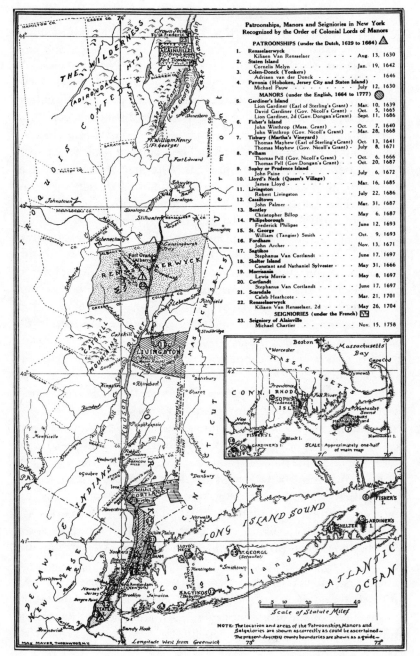

A map of colonial New York showing the patroonships, manors, and seigniories. *From Alexander C. Flick, ed.,* History of the State of New York, II *(New York: Columbia University Press, 1933), endpaper. By permission of the publisher.*

to Dutch practices, anglicization among the Dutch was augmented by pressure from the Duke as well as from English
settlers on Long Island.

Cognizant of New Netherland's diversity, Nicolls helped to
perpetuate it. Particularly between 1664 and 1676, New York's
governmental arrangements were adapted to pluralistic realities
and thereby accentuated them. Nicolls established a county of
Yorkshire, comprised of three "ridings": Long Island, Staten
Island, and the Bronx peninsula. The Court of Assizes set up in
1665 to be a legislative and judicial body had only Yorkshire as
its jurisdiction, and its laws were not enforced in the rest of the
colony. The Hudson River communities enjoyed considerable
continuity with their pre-1664 situations, received no official civil
government until 1673, and derived their actual authority from
military officers instructed by the governor. In town and county
government the Dutch practice of double nomination endured,
the judicial powers of constables and overseers had Dutch
derivations, the county system on the Delaware developed from
Dutch custom, and features of Dutch land tenure persisted on the
patroon estates. Not until 1669–73 did Lovelace try to introduce
English institutions to Esopus.

New York City had a government prescribed for its own
peculiar polyglot circumstances. By June 1665, the old Dutch
forms were superseded by titles appropriate to an English
corporation, some Dutch personnel were set aside to make room
for English patronage, and the English jury system—trial by
twelve of one's peers—was established. Even so, of the seven new
officers governing New York City, four were Dutch, suggesting
that labels and titles changed more dramatically than did
personnel. Thomas Willett, the first mayor of New York City,
although British by birth, had lived in Leyden, Holland, spoke
Dutch, had owned property and traded in New Amsterdam, and
enjoyed friendly relations with Stuyvesant and his circle of
officials. Cornelius Steenwyck, who served as mayor from 1668
until 1670 and again in 1683–84, had settled in New Amsterdam
in 1651, became a prominent merchant, and used his position as
mayor to obtain important benefits for the Dutch. From 1676

until 1691, most of the city's mayors were of Dutch descent. One of them, Stephanus Van Cortlandt (1677–78), was the first mayor actually born in the New World.

The Duke's Laws did not apply to Manhattan until 1674, almost a decade after their passage, and they did not affect the colony as a whole until 1676. It is noteworthy, too, that all Dutch land titles were not only renewed by Nicolls in 1664, but also in 1674 after the States-General surrendered the colony a second time. Nicolls and Lovelace both took pains to pacify the indigenous Dutch elite: by modifying the meaning of the loyalty oath required of them, by appointing English magistrates who were acceptable to the Dutch, by allowing the Dutch Reformed church to enjoy a privileged position in parishes with a majority of Dutch inhabitants, and by allowing Dutch schools to continue pretty much as before.

Throughout most of the proprietary period, Dutch inhabitants made a serious effort to suppress their internal differences in favor of a united front. They did not accept the implications of conquest passively, as has often been asserted, and they would not be reconciled to anglicization for another generation—in part because only after 1691 would their political, religious, and property rights seem fully secure, and in part because social assimilation through intermarriage and acculturation took time and could not be hurried. Only gradually would deputies report to Nicolls that "there is good correspondence between the English and Dutch [on Long Island]; and to keep it the closer, sixteen (ten Dutch and six English) have had a constant meetting at each others houses in turnes, twice every week in winter, and now in summer once; they meet at six at night and part about eight or nine." When Captain Brodhead and his soldiers imprisoned several townsmen in Kingston for such trivialities as celebrating Christmas in the Dutch rather than in the English manner, the tensions that arose led to beatings, armed riots, and homicide. Nicolls could only calm Kingston by suspending Brodhead.

Similarly, Nicolls's attempt to change the name of Haarlem to Lancaster did not take; nor did his desire to have Long Island become Yorkshire. Instead, the tributary streams feeding the Hudson continued to be called "kills"; distances along the river that could be seen point to point remained "reaches"; a farmhouse was still a "*bouwhuys*"; and the celebration of Whitsuntide continued to be "Pinkster," even for English colonists four generations later. *Bouweries* and *stoops* and *cookies* and *waffles* and *coleslaw* and *boss* (the Dutch is *baas*) all passed directly into general usage, part of the common parlance of an eclectic society. The borrowing back and forth should occasion no surprise, however, because Dutch and English are in fact sister languages. Both originated in proto-Germanic and developed as variants of Low German (i.e., spoken by people in the low country). Logically, therefore, there are many cognate words and shared phrases that cannot be translated directly into any other language, at least not without ludicrous results.*

English	Dutch
book	*boek*
day	*dag*
give	*geven*
pepper	*peper*
sleep	*slapen*
swan	*swan*
water	*water*
now and then	*nu en dan*
it speaks for itself	*het spreekt vanzelf*
through thick and thin	*door dik en dun*

---

* Despite the many similarities and linguistic affinities, I have come to feel that over the past century industrious editors and translators have inadvertently caused the Dutch and English periods to be fused, conflated, or homogenized—use the verb of your choice. Owing to the extraordinary diligence of Edmund B. O'Callaghan, Henry C. Murphy, Jonathan Pearson, Berthold Fernow, A. J. F. van Laer, and others, virtually every document from the Dutch period has been translated into English. The consequent accessibility has been a boon to American scholars; but it has also given the unfortunate impressions of greater continuity, earlier anglicization, and less residual Dutch impact than was actually the case in colonial New York.

So it was also in the realm of religion. The Classis of Amsterdam encouraged the Reverends Drisius and Megapolensis to resist the introduction of English liturgy into the Dutch Reformed church. They resisted with considerable success, and their denomination spread as the colony expanded. In 1664 there were eleven Dutch Reformed congregations in New York, by 1701 there were twenty-nine, and by 1740 there were sixty-five.

When Nicholas van Rensselaer arrived in New York in 1675, he brought a letter from the Duke of York to Governor Andros directing him to assist Van Rensselaer in obtaining a place in a Dutch church. Andros complied and the Duke's client became a junior colleague of Dominie Schaets in Albany. When word got out that Van Rensselaer had been ordained by the Anglican Bishop of Old Sarum rather than by the Classis of Amsterdam, however, the furies quite literally broke loose. Dominie Van Niewenhuysen of New York City sent his church elders up to Albany to forbid Van Rensselaer to conduct baptismal services. The hybrid cleric won this first skirmish in 1675, but during the next three years he was fought with hammer and tong by orthodox Calvinists led by Jacob Leisler and Jacob Milborne. The particular controversy ended in 1678 with Van Rensselaer's death; but the bitter consequences lingered on, for the alignment between 1676 and 1678 had pitted Leisler and his supporters against Philip Schuyler, Stephanus Van Cortlandt, and very possibly Robert Livingston. That alignment simmered for a heated decade and then, in 1689, boiled over.

The public situation of religious groups in New York after 1664 remained ambiguous for several decades and has been labeled by one authority as "an establishment without a name." The Duke's Laws prescribed that churches capable of accommodating two hundred people be built in suitable and accessible localities. The householders of each parish were to choose eight men to act as overseers, with responsibility for making and proportioning the assessments needed for the building and repair of churches, the wants of the poor, maintenance of the ministry, and management of parish affairs. No minister would be permitted to officiate in New York unless he brought testimonials to the governor attesting to ordination by a bishop in England or by virtue of some foreign prince of the "Reformed religion." The ministers of each parish were required to preach every Sunday, to pray for the royal family, and to administer the Lord's Supper at least once a year in each church. Sundays were not to be profaned by "travellers," laborers, or "vicious persons," and no congregation was to be disturbed during the time of prayer, preaching, or divine service.

In essence, the Duke's Laws established a nondenominational state church—a necessary hybrid born of social pluralism. Churches would be supported by levies made upon inhabitants of the parish, and the state would define conditions for the ministry. Only Protestant ministers would be recognized; they would be inducted by the governor, and their duties would be prescribed much more explicitly than during the Dutch regime. Although the majority in any town could establish a public church, Nicolls ensured that other congregations would also be permitted to conduct their own services. The instructions given to Governor Andros in 1674 directed him to "permit all persons of what Religion soever, quietly to inhabitt within the precincts of your jurisdiccon, without giving them any disturbance or disquiet whatsoever, for or by reason of their differing opinions in matters of Religion; Provided they give no disturbance to the publique peace, nor doe molest or disquiet others in the free exercise of their religion." Andros remained faithful to his charge and in 1678 reported to London that "there are Religions of all sorts, one church of England, Several Presbiterians & Independents, Quakers & Anabaptists of Severall sects, some Jews but presbiterians & Independents most numerous & Substantiall."

Consequently, reports began to waft back to the Old World, like vapors from a bubbling broth, that New York had its particular freedoms and attractions. In May of 1669, for example, Samuel Maverick wrote from Fort James to Sampson Bond, an English clergyman:

I shall only informe you what is allowed, and may be expected to be enjoyed by the Inhabitants, within his Royall Highnes his territories heare.

Ecclesiasticall liberties are, 1, Liberty of conscience to all, provided they raise not fundamentalls in religion, nor disturbe the publique peace. 2, Cerimonies may be used or omitted. 3, The Booke of Common Prayer may be made use of or not.

Civill liberties are,—All freeholders, not scandalous in theire lives & conversations, are capable to vote att the election of officers, military and civill, in theire severall towneshipps.

Although Bond did decide to emigrate, he chose New England rather than New York. Others, however, especially Huguenots and Scots, began to arrive in the later 1660s and 1670s. Their presence accentuated the diversity of a colony already notable for its heterogeneity. By 1680 foreign visitors to the province encountered a touch of nativism and suspicion of strangers. Jasper Danckaerts, a Dutch sectarian of the Labadist persuasion, recorded in his diary (January 29, 1680) that he and his companion were required to appear before the mayor of New York City "and give our names and further information as to our doings and condition, as all strangers now and henceforth, whether men or women, must do."

When Danckaerts and Sluyter decided to visit Albany a few months later, they learned that "this could not be done without the special permission of the governor." Eventually Andros allowed them a passport, they went, and Danckaerts made these interesting observations about the upriver Dutch: "As these people live in the interior of the country somewhat nearer the Indians, they are more wild and untamed, reckless, unrestrained, haughty, and more addicted to misusing the blessed name of God and to cursing and swearing."

Danckaerts found certain marked similarities among the people of particular localities within New York, and that discovery (and others like it) should cause us to qualify carefully what we mean when we speak of pluralism in colonial New York. The province as a whole, and New York City in microcosm, did indeed contain stunning diversity. But the regional living units, scattered villages along the Hudson River and Long Island, were individually much more homogeneous and hostile to strangers and change. In brief, the province contained unities within diversity, like the various orchards comprising a fruit farm.

✧ ✧ ✧

Dutch strength in the Atlantic world started to decline after 1645 with the beginning of the rebellion in Pernambuco, Brazil. The Dutch lost Angola and Benguela in 1648 and were expelled from Brazil in 1654. The ultimate causes of their expulsion were not very different from the reasons for their loss of New Netherland a decade later: too few Dutch colonists settled in family units, too many foreign nationals of marginal allegiance (Portuguese in Brazil, English in New York), and inadequate provisions for defense. Nevertheless, in 1673 the States-General made one last desperate attempt to regain a foothold.

The third Anglo-Dutch war erupted in the spring of 1672. The next year a substantial Dutch fleet plundered English shipping in the Caribbean, then along the Chesapeake coast, and finally arrived at New York to besiege the still-defenseless colony. With Lovelace away at Hartford visiting Governor Winthrop, twenty-three vessels carrying sixteen hundred men looked frightening to Lovelace's subordinate, Captain Manning. Meanwhile some inhabitants cheerfully visited the Dutch fleet offshore in order to assure the commanders that Fort James was indeed dilapidated. When Manning sent a message inquiring why the Dutch came "in such a hostile manner," Admiral Cornelis Evertsen, Jr., answered that they had come to take what "was theyr owne, and theyr owne they would have." When Manning asked to see Evertsen's commission, he replied that it was in the barrel of his cannon and that the English would see it soon enough if they did not surrender the fort. The next day they exchanged broadsides for four hours while Anthony Colve landed six hundred men on the west side of Manhattan. Some four hundred armed Dutch burghers encouraged them to storm the citadel, whereupon Manning raised a flag of truce, surrendering the fort and New York. On July 30, 1673, Dutch colors fluttered once again over the city.

When Lovelace finally returned to New York he was arrested for debt, stripped of his property, and ordered to leave the colony. In 1674 his estate was seized for debt by the Duke of York; he was eventually imprisoned in the Tower and died in

1675. Meanwhile, for more than a year the province became New Netherland once more, the city became New Orange, Albany was called Willemstadt, and Kingston was Swanenburg. A provisional government consisted of a five-man advisory council of war which appointed Colve to be governor general. Local government and oaths of allegiance reverted to their status of before 1664, but ecclesiastical arrangements remained liberal. Finally, some attention was paid at last to the city's defenses and police.

From month to month the local English and New Englanders made noises about forcefully recapturing New Netherland, but English political ineptitude combined with colonial particularism to prevent that from happening. Factionalism and mutual jealousy stood in the way of concerted action by the four New England governments; but in October 1674, they achieved their goal bloodlessly. Charles II and the States-General signed a treaty at Westminster whereby the Dutch relinquished all title to New York forever. Surrounded by English colonies, unattractive to immigrants, New Netherland had little value and low prospects so far as the States-General could see.

Peace was then proclaimed from the City Hall and English rule restored—with resentment but without violence. The fort, lacking adequate arms and ammunition and enough men garrisoned and trained to defend it, stood as little more than a symbol of possession. It was barely ironic, therefore, when the fort proved to be defenseless even against colonial hogs after 1674. They ran freely through the city, rooted about the earthworks, undermined the palisades, and exposed the interior. Most of the locals had long acknowledged that their fort was fit for little more than a pigpen.

Changes began to come more rapidly after 1673. Peter Stuyvesant had died the year before and was buried in the chapel he constructed a decade earlier upon his own land (since supplanted by the Episcopal Church of St. Marks-in-the-Bowery). The Duke of York replaced Lovelace with Edmund Andros, like his predecessors an arch royalist and a military man, accustomed to obedience from inferiors and subordination to superiors. Determined to watch and control his colony much more closely after 1674, James made Andros the instrument of supervision. In addition, James constituted his secretary, treasurer, auditor and receiver general, attorney and solicitor general as a small board of commissioners to advise him upon matters of law and policy. Fearing that failure to procure any income from his proprietary was the result of carelessness and fraud, he eventually sent over John Lewen as a personal auditor to investigate economic conditions in New York.

In 1675 changes also began to occur, at last, in the provisions made for public health in New York. Inhabitants had increasingly been "casting filth before their houses." Consequently the mayor and Council warned them of their responsibility for cleaning the streets every Saturday and chided them also about obstructing the streets with wagons, carts, sleds, timbers, "dirt, mucke, or stones." In 1675, too, the city fathers decided to abandon and fill the canal. It had become impossible to keep clean; it stank worse than ever and provided a breeding place for pests. Individual householders along its banks were held responsible for filling it in with stones and paving it level with the street. Although these precautions did not prevent the virulent smallpox epidemic of 1679, they did mark the beginning of some attention to public health in a gradually crowding community.

The most graphic measure of change between Nicolls's administration and that of Andros, however, may be seen by comparing the report each man submitted to London: Nicolls in 1669, Andros in 1678. Both stressed the presence of liberty of conscience, both suggested that laws made for the colony were in conformity with those of England, and both dealt with taxes and duties on commodities. But there the similarities cease. Andros's report spelled out in much greater detail the organization and functions of government. Nicolls's report emphasized the need to grant privileges in order to attract immigrants and specified free fishing and fowling, as well as free trade in furs. Andros was silent on these matters. Nicolls was much more concerned than Andros with obtaining land from the Indians and conditions of land tenure, management, and cultivation. By contrast, the objects of greatest concern to Andros received no mention at all in Nicolls's report: defense (the militia, forts, and privateers), intercolonial relations (trade, judicial proceedings, and boundaries), and economic development (places for trading, urban growth, the merchant class, personal wealth, obstacles and stimuli to commerce).

In short, as New York began to mature, its priorities shifted somewhat from attracting people to regulating them, from acquiring land to maximizing its yield, from stabilizing group relations to stimulating economic growth. New York would never, throughout its colonial history, be adequately populated; but the appeals and inducements would become less anxious than those of publicist Daniel Denton in 1670: "I may say, and say truly, that if there be any terrestrial happiness to be had by people of all ranks, especially of an inferior rank, it must certainly be here."

The Dutch claimed that there were 6,000 inhabitants in 1673; there may have been as many as 10,000 in 1680 and 15,000 by 1685. New York City seems to have had about 1,470 persons in 1665, only a handful of them English (of 254 individuals listed for taxation, only 16 had English names). By 1676 the city had grown to more than 2,200 persons (and of 302 taxables, 115 seem to have been English). Between 1665 and 1676, moreover, the proportion of persons falling into the higher tax brackets increased as a commercial elite began to establish itself. By contrast, Albany's population in 1679 must have been more than 1,000; two-thirds of the taxables fell into the two lowest brackets, and very few English names appeared. Albany remained more homogeneous in nationality and less hierarchical economically. By 1683 the population of Long Island exceeded 5,500; there were still five Dutch towns, but twelve English villages as well; and Southampton was the third-ranking community in the colony, with some 680 people.

The fact is obvious, yet too often ignored, that roughly half of all these people were females. Because women in Holland had been treated more generously at law than elsewhere in Europe— they could own property, make contracts, participate in business

Ashwood armchair with a Carver-type back, made in New York during the later seventeenth century. *The Metropolitan Museum of Art, Rogers Fund, 1941.*

A stained gumwood fireplace wall, with Dutch tiles, from a farmhouse (known as the Benjamin Hasbrouck house) in High Falls, Ulster County, built in 1752. *The Metropolitan Museum of Art, Rogers Fund, 1933.*

An iron fireback made in New York in 1768. *The Metropolitan Museum of Art, anonymous gift, 1944.*

in their own right, and leave their dowry to whomever they wished—Dutch women in New Netherland and early New York were "emancipated" to a greater degree than women in the other colonies.* Even so, most of the women in New York at this time were still *"goede vrouwen,"* devoted (or chained, according to one's perspective) to hearth and home. The hearth, quite literally, was the repository of their vital skills and devices: the copper kettle with its brass handle, a "hearthcat" to support the kettle, the copper skillet with its iron handle, the *doofpot* in which coals were kept alive overnight, the iron shovel and fire tongs, the pair of andirons supporting a long spit, and the cast-iron fireback—inscribed with *"Hollandia Pro Patria"* and the lion of the Netherlands holding seven arrows to represent the seven provinces.

With their resources and skills, women would roast a haunch of venison, tender, fat, and spicy; or a dry but flavorful wild turkey; or a fatty wild goose. They would prepare the mutton and even occasionally a raccoon with its porklike flavor. With their children they gathered plentiful peaches in September, abundant apples in October, and made quantities of cider. If they lived along the lower Hudson and Long Island, they might also help to gather oysters—some almost a foot in length—pickle them for export in small casks, and burn the shells into lime. They would participate in the transformation of wild grapes into jelly, the cultivation of melons, and the consumption of rum. A bride's world was fattening and busy, but no more vulnerable to taunts than that of her husband. In 1678, for example, anonymous pranksters in Albany caused the usual stir by hanging beaver testicles attached to a bladder from a tree in front of the home of a new bridegroom.

As Jasper Danckaerts discovered in 1680, isolated inhabitants of the interior were "more wild and untamed" than the urbanites of New York City. Likewise the farmers of Long Island: "the

---

* For cases involving property disputes, seduction and breach of promise, divorce, rape, and witchcraft, see Victor H. Paltsits, ed., *Minutes of the Executive Council of the Province of New York: Administration of Francis Lovelace, 1668–1673* (Albany, 1910), I, 240–323, 327–36; II, 390–97, 751, 789–90.

boors, who talked foully and otherwise . . . even without speaking a word about God or spiritual matters. It was all about houses, and cattle, and swine, and grain." Communications were slow during much of the seventeenth century, and they were largely dependent upon water. The Dutch were not ambitious road builders. They opened roads from their farms to the rivers—the Croton in Westchester; Wappinger Creek in Dutchess; Stockport and Kinderhook creeks in Columbia; the Claverack, the Rondout, and the Catskill—but they were slow to start roads from south to north and depended heavily upon the Hudson despite its unreliability. Here is one typical traveler's account:

We went on board the boat, and immediately got under sail, with a favorable but light wind, and by evening arrived at the entrance of the Highlands. [Next day] The wind was ahead, but it was calm. When the tide began to fall, we tacked, or rather drifted along, but with little progress. We passed through the Highlands however, and came to anchor by the time the ebb was spent. The weather was very rainy. [Next day] The wind was still contrary, and blew hard, therefore we tacked, but in consequence of our being very heavily laden we advanced but little. [Next day] At daylight the tide served, but the wind was still ahead, though steady. We continued tacking with considerable progress, and at ten o'clock arrived before the city of New York, where we struck upon a rock. The water was falling, and we therefore immediately carried out an anchor, and wore the yacht off. A slight breeze soon afterward sprang up, and took us to the city.

During his term as governor, Lovelace began to make some effort to improve the efficiency of travel and communications. Early in 1669 he ordered the construction of a proper road between New York City and Harlem and, later that year, the establishment of better ferry service at Spuyten Duyvil. Most important, on January 22, 1673, he inaugurated regular overland mail service to Boston by sending the first courier from the fort at Bowling Green. For half a century to come, the mail would be carried only by riders (and delivered, as a rule, in less than a week); mail coaches did not appear until around 1730. Envelopes did not exist, of course, until the 1840s. Instead, letters were folded three times in each direction, tucked in, sealed with wax or a sticker, and addressed on the outside.

For much of the seventeenth century, however, letters and mail were relatively unimportant, much less so than in our own time because these were in many respects preliterate societies. Lovelace did not succeed in his attempt to introduce a printing press to the province—he wanted to publish a catechism for the Indians—and printing did not actually begin in New York until 1693. The point, then, and it could (in terms of its implications) turn out to be the most meaningful generalization one can make about early New York, is that this was an aural culture: one in which the spoken word had greater import than the written word, one in which what people heard mattered more than what they read.

What were the components and consequences of this aural culture? Proclamations, commissions, instructions (and the Riot Act), were read aloud, usually from the steps of City Hall. As Governor Nicolls instructed magistrates in all the Long Island and Westchester towns in 1664, "I do require you to assemble your Inhabitants and read this Letter to them." The reading of a proclamation, in fact, was more nearly a public proceeding than the formal meeting of governor and Council, which occurred in private and went unreported.*

Because of the absence of political journalism, people were often more candid at the conference table, in the courtroom, and at the community meeting than they are today. Where discourse went unrecorded, people were more likely to say what they

---

* See, for example, the "Narrative and Remonstrance of the Deputys assembled at Hempsteed, in March, 1664/5": "We were convened, being deputys chosen by the several towns in a Generall Assembly held at Hempsteed, where his Majesty's aforesaid patent was first *read,* and a commission from his Royal Highness the Duke of Yorke, empowering and investing the aforesaid Col. Richard Nicolls, with authority to put the contents of the said patent into practice and execution, who *declared* unto us. . . . We appointed a Committee to attend the Governor for his resolution. . . . We received answer by our deputies [orally, not in writing]. . . . In conclusion the Governor *told* us." [Italics mine.]

meant and to mean what they said. In consequence, too, people listened more carefully, and there was greater concern about "whosoever shall Reproach or Defame any person or Persons . . . or whosoever hereafter shall any wayse Detract or speake against any of the Deputies" (Court of Assizes, 1666).

In this aural culture, there was also an emphasis upon immediacy and the authoritative voice, and an aversion to extensive written exchanges. In 1671, when the Long Island towns sent Lovelace a protest against taxation, he replied that "in regard of the distance of place & the avoyding all *prolixity* which would inevitably ensue should theise disputes be managed by wryting," he was sending commissioners to deal with them directly in order "to begett a true understanding" between them. In a culture of public recitation, points had to be made succinctly and sequentially. Speaking to the gathering at Hempstead, Nicolls remarked that arguments of a committee from Connecticut were "too long here to be recited." In those days, of course, men voted orally, and the swearing of a public oath had more than symbolic significance. An oath involved a binding public commitment, a rendering of integrity before temporal listeners as well as the Ultimate Auditor.

An aural culture provided the inevitable context for communities of limited literacy. Although we do not have precise figures, it has been estimated that 60 percent of the Dutch women in New York (1660s) were illiterate, with a slightly lower figure among the men. Where many people could not read and most could do little more than sign their names, listening became queen among the senses, essential to survival. Given the regularity of bell ringing and chimes, the constant presence of town criers and Rattle Watchmen, early New York was not far removed from Johan Huizinga's description of humming and buzzing in late medieval towns: "The contrast between silence and sound, darkness and light, like that between summer and winter, was more strongly marked than it is in our lives."

New York City was like many a late medieval town in yet another respect. It was petit bourgeois to an extent that seemed to anticipate (but invert) Adam Smith's famous injunction of

1776: "To found a great empire for the sole purpose of raising up a people of customers, may at first sight appear a project fit only for a nation of shopkeepers." * In this case the colonial town seems to have been as crowded with shopkeepers as it was with customers. "He had a small shop," Danckaerts observed of Arnoldus de la Grange in 1679, "as almost all the people here have, who gain their living by trade, namely, in tobacco and liquors, thread and pins and other knick-knacks." A month later the same visitor felt compelled to remark "that the people in this city . . . are almost all traders in small articles." It should not surprise anyone, therefore, that the first merchants' exchange in America was established for New York City by Governor Lovelace. A city of shopkeepers was well begun.

Economic individualism encourages political tenacity (as well as stinginess), and by 1680 Governor Andros found that he had a tax revolt on his hands. The Duke of York's principal interest in New York hinged upon revenue derived from taxes—specifically, duties on imports and exports. The customs rates that had been promulgated on a three-year basis in 1677 expired, and by inadvertence they were not promptly renewed. When William Dyre, the collector of customs, tried to execute his office irrespective of the lapse (by impounding the goods of merchants), the populace rose up in wrath, tried him, and sent him "home" a prisoner. He was exonerated in England, of course; but his case, coupled with the constant grumbling of Long Island towns about being "inslav'd under an Arbitrary Power," caused the Duke to contemplate major political concessions for his proprietary.

James recalled Andros early in 1681, and Lieutenant Anthony Brockholls, his successor, reported late in the year that New York's government was "wholly overthrown, and in the greatest confusion and disorder possible." Disaffection throughout Long Island rekindled the desire there for annexation to Connecticut and spread rapidly up the Hudson to such villages as Kingston. The Duke chided Brockholls for failing to make at least a temporary renewal of the customs rates; and John Lewen, the

---

* Adam Smith, *Wealth of Nations*, II, bk. iv, chap. 7.

Duke's special "Agent and Servant" in New York, indicated to his master that there were serious derelictions, and probably fraud, going on in the colony.

James knew, by 1682, that alterations would have to be made. The changes he chose initiated nine years of tumultuous transition: from ducal proprietary (1683–85) to royal colony (1685–87) to incorporation within the Dominion of New England (1688–89) to control by an alliance of merchants and disaffected politicians (1689–91) to re-establishment of the royal colony on new foundations (1691). Change begat change; and when the commotion of transition had finished, New York entered a different era. Between 1683 and 1691, New York molted its exoskeleton half a dozen times, like an immature crayfish during its first phase of life.

5

POLITICS AND THE PERILS
OF INSTABILITY

Between 1665 and 1682 a penumbra of protest had spread
gradually over New York, merely darkening in some areas,
menacing in others. The sources of protest varied from one time,
place, and issue to another; but the common denominators, the
heaviest portion of that penumbra, were plain enough: lack of a
provincial assembly and the accompanying sense of arbitrary
government; an omnipresence of economic monopolies and
privileges for special interests; resentment of taxation and the
collection of customs duties.

In consequence, a series of serious shifts began to occur in
1683: changes in the colony's constitutional arrangements, in its
economic circumstances, and in its relationship to the world
without—the French and Indians, neighboring colonies, and
government at "home." These changes and attendant frustrations only served to deepen the voices of discontent between 1683
and 1688 and foretold the fiercest perils of instability for the
period 1689–91. Just as protracted rainstorms precede a hurri-
cane, so the politics of unrest preceded rebellion. Skies darkened,
spirits were dampened, and inhabitants expected the worst.
Their very fears, it turned out, hurried the whirlwind along and
made it all the more tumultuous.

The man chosen by the Duke of York in 1682 to set his colony
straight was cast in the same mold as his predecessors. Thomas

Dongan, like Nicolls, Lovelace, and Andros, was a soldier, royalist, and devoted follower of the Stuarts' fortunes. The younger son of an Irish baronet, he had served in France under Louis XIV and in Tangier as lieutenant governor under the English flag. A Roman Catholic, like his patron, Dongan was tolerant in religious matters during his regime; indeed, it was the last comfortable time for Catholics in New York for many years to come. His Catholicism, however, was carefully tempered by his English nationalism and genuine concern for the colony. When he perceived a rising amount of activity by French Jesuits among the Iroquois and learned that the Jesuits' influence was more political than spiritual, Dongan protested vigorously to De la Barre, the Governor of Canada, and subsequently to De la Barre's successor, the Marquis de Denonville.

Although Dongan received his commission in September 1682, he did not arrive in New York until August 1683. A gubernatorial time lag of eleven months was not at all uncommon in colonial New York—with Kieft and Lovelace it had been ten months, for example, and with George Clinton it was twenty-seven months (1741–43)—but over and over again these delays contributed to discontinuity, public anxiety, and "lame duck" problems for the predecessor. Certainly that was the case in 1682–83. Dongan had barely stepped off the boat before the people of East Hampton assailed him with a petition citing all the arguments for a colonial legislature. This time, however, their persistence was rewarded, for Dongan's instructions (issued in January 1683) at last ordered him to call for elections to an assembly:

You are also with advice of my Council with all convenient speed after your arrival there, in my name to issue out Writs or warrants of Summons to the several Sheriffs or other proper Officers in every part of your said government, wherein you shall express that I have thought fit that there shall be a General Assembly of all the Freeholders, by the persons who they shall choose to represent them in order to consult with yourself and the said Council what laws are fit and necessary to be made and established . . . and you shall issue out the said Writ or Summons at least thirty days before the time appointed for the meeting of the said Assembly. . . . And when the said Assembly so elected shall be met at the time and place directed, you shall let them know that for the future it is my resolution that the said General Assembly shall have free liberty to consult and debate among themselves all matters as shall be apprehended proper to be established for laws for the good government of the said Colony . . . and that if such laws shall be propounded as shall appear to me to be for the manifest good of the Country in general and not prejudicial to me, I will assent unto and confirm them.

So far, so generous, and unexceptionable as well. But particular provisions made the Duke's position very clear: "I also authorize you to adjourn or dissolve [it] as you shall see reason and cause." Then came the crux of the matter:

I do further direct you not to pass any law upon any occasion whatsoever for raising any public revenue, unless express mention be made therein that the same is levied and granted unto me. . . . And you are as much as in you lyeth to take effectual care that there may be a constant establishment for raising of money sufficient to support and maintain the charge of the government of those parts both civil and military . . . and are not to suffer any public money whatsoever to be issued or disposed of otherwise than by a warrant under your hand. . . . And you are not to pass any laws . . . whereby my revenue may be remitted, lessened or impaired, without my especial leave or commands therein.*

Several of the Duke's advisers had persuaded him in 1681–82 that the only way to make New York peaceful and productive would be to allow his settlers a legislature, which all the other English colonies already had. He agreed to do so on condition that the provincials be willing to support the government as well as pay back the arrears accumulated since the controversy began. "I seeke the common good and protection of that countrey and the increase of their trade," he insisted, "before my advantages to myselfe in the matter." Precious few took his protestation at face value.

---

* For Dongan's instructions, see Charles Z. Lincoln, ed., *State of New York: Messages from the Governors,* I (Albany, 1909), 6–8.

In any case, Dongan followed directions, and on October 17, 1683, New York's first legislative Assembly met at Fort James. The impatient Long Islanders sent six deputies, two from each "riding"; New York City (including Harlem) sent four; Kingston and Albany had two each; and Staten Island, Schenectady, Martha's Vineyard and Nantucket together, one each. Pemaquid, on the coast of Maine, failed to send a delegate, though it could have. Of the seventeen, most had been directly elected by freeholders. In New York City, Schenectady, and Pemaquid, however, sheriffs were to *appoint* freeholders, who in turn would elect their representatives. Although a majority of the first assemblymen must have been Dutch, it would appear that the seven or eight Englishmen present seized the initiative, for the most famous product of this legislature—which also comprised a Council of six appointed members as well as the governor—was distinctly an English document.

The Charter of Libertyes and Priviledges was drafted as a frame of government designed to protect the colonists' liberty, property, and opportunity to assent to their laws and taxes. The charter rescaled representation in the Assembly by county— Dongan and the Assembly had just divided New York into twelve counties: New York (Manhattan) and Richmond (Staten Island); Kings, Queens, and Suffolk on Long Island; Orange and Ulster up the west bank of the Hudson; Westchester and Dutchess opposite; Albany to the north on both sides; Cornwall County in Maine; and Duke's, comprising the two islands in New England—giving four to New York City, three to Albany, and two to each of the rest. This reorganized body would forever be "the Supreame and only Legislative power under his Royall Highnesse." Bills approved by the Assembly would become laws and remain in force until vetoed by the Duke or else repealed.

Whoever wrote this charter—and their identities are un- known—took special pains to provide for individual liberties. They insisted that the right to vote for representatives be ensured to the freeholders and freemen of any corporation and defined a freeholder as anyone who qualified under English law. The authors took the article guaranteeing liberty of person directly from Magna Charta: "THAT Noe freeman shall be taken and imprisoned or be disseized of his Freehold of Libertye or Free Customes or be outlawed or Exiled or any other wayes destroyed nor shall be passed upon adjudged or condemned But by the Lawfull Judgment of his peers and by the Law of this province." From the famous Petition of Right (1628) they adapted a paragraph protecting New Yorkers against taxation without representation, and they devoted the longest single section to providing liberty of conscience for all Christians.

In addition to these and other protections of personal liberty, the charter included advanced parliamentary privileges for the legislature—a guarantee of triennial meetings, control over the time of their sessions, the power to set qualifications for their own members, protection from arrest while on Assembly business— and on the very day the charter was agreed upon, the lower house implicitly asserted its right to originate money bills, in imitation of the House of Commons. The Assembly worded its first revenue act in such a way that the "Representatives" of the province of New York, with the advice and consent of the governor and Council, gave and granted to the Duke the "Dutyes and Customes hereafter Specified."

Despite its apparent liberalism, the charter was acceptable to Dongan's Council of six and to the governor himself. Perhaps Dongan would have been favorably disposed anyway; but his affirmation must have been encouraged by one of the Assembly's first acts: a law presenting him with a gilded income, equal to a penny on the pound for all real and personal property belonging to inhabitants of New York. After Dongan's approval, the Charter of Libertyes was published (by voice) at City Hall on October 31, 1683, the "Inhabitants having notice by sound of Trumpet." A year later, after James's commissioners suggested a few amendments concerning customs, the duke had it signed, sealed, and ready for return to New York. It never got there, however.

By late 1684 and early 1685, Charles II had begun to contemplate imperial reorganization and closer control over his American possessions. This was not the time for liberal charters to be awarded; hence the delay. After Charles died in February 1685 and James became king, the Lords of Trade decided to reappraise New York's charter. The resulting "Observations" pointed out that the document gave New Yorkers rights and privileges greater than those enjoyed by any other group of colonists—a dangerous precedent. Supreme legislative authority should not be so vaguely invested in the governor, Council, and "People" met in general assembly. The governor should not be so dependent upon his Council. And the insistence upon triennial legislatures in New York would put a greater obligation on that government than "ever agreed to in any other Plantation." Moreover, might not such an assurance seriously "abridge the Acts of Parliament that may be made concerning New York"?

After considering these queries, King James reversed the decision he had made five months earlier as Duke of York. On March 3, 1685, he did "not think fitt to confirm the same" and instead decided that the government of New York should be "assimilated to the Constitution that shall be agreed on for New England, to which it is adjoining." Not until May 1686, however, a delay of nineteen months since James's original assent, did he send Dongan new instructions explicitly declaring the charter to be "disallowed . . . and made void." In September Dongan read the heartbreaking repeal (as well as his new commission and instructions) to his Council but not to the whole legislature, which had last convened in October 1685. The charter Assembly never met again.

The Assembly's actions during its brief lifetime of three sessions, however, do serve as an index to its paramount concerns. It first passed laws providing for naturalization of foreigners, establishing courts of justice, preventing willful perjury, providing for municipal taxation and support of the poor, preventing fraud in the conveyance of lands, and imposing penalties for letting pigs run loose and bounties for the destruction of wolves. It passed thirty-one more laws at its second session in October 1684: authorizing persons twenty-one years of age to convey lands and persons fourteen years of age to choose their own guardians; regulating the practice of medicine and surgery, the qualifications of brewers, the election of constables, the punishment of runaway servants, the purchase of Indian lands, marriage procedures, orphans, burials, real estate actions, relations between masters and slaves, servants, laborers, and apprentices; concerning the militia, cattle, cornfields, and fences; encouraging trade and navigation; providing compensation to judges; and confirming various decisions by former courts.

Meanwhile, in these same hopeful years between 1683 and 1686, Dongan granted liberal charters to New York City and Albany. The city's charter became operative in 1684 and divided the municipality into six wards; each would elect an assistant and an alderman. The six assistants meeting with the appointed mayor and recorder and with the alderman would constitute a common council with full power to make laws, orders, and ordinances not contrary to the laws of England and the colony. In July 1686, Albany received a charter of incorporation providing for appointees and the election of city officials similar to those of New York City.

What may have been most significant about these municipal charters, however, was not the officialdom for which they provided but the particular privileges they awarded to each community. One of Dongan's instructions in 1683 had directed him to consult with his Council whether it would be expedient if New York City were granted "immunities and priviledges" that exceeded those enjoyed elsewhere in the colony. When James became king in 1685, the city officials sent him salutations, congratulations, and hopes for such special concessions as would help it to "flourish and encrease" the royal revenue. Ever since 1670, New York City's merchants had held an exclusive monopoly over the Hudson River carrying trade, a cause of dependence and resentment in Albany. In 1678 the city received a monopoly over the export trade as well; in 1680 it got the flour-milling monopoly; and in 1684 it became the sole port of entry for the province (thereby diminishing Southampton on Long Island). Albany's charter of 1686 conveyed the right to sole conduct of the Indian trade, an important franchise and one desperately needed to compensate for New York City's exclusive port privileges. Schenectady had been Albany's main competitor for the fur trade, and its residents at least got the right to make commercial transactions in Albany. Even so, bitter complaints were made because the fur trade was essentially controlled by just twenty or thirty men.

The whole problem of economic privileges and exclusive monopolies became highly political and sensitive during the 1680s. Because local artisans and entrepreneurs resented competition from other towns and villages, they sought governmental assistance. Albany levied a special tax on people who came there only when the Indians brought their pelts. In certain Long Island towns, resident coopers received protection against the competition of Boston barrel makers. And Huntington jealously prohibited "any person . . . of any other town upon this Island" to fish or go whaling within its jurisdiction.

Inevitably, all of those diverse people whose interests were affected adversely by these monopolies grew increasingly restive. Long Islanders were especially provoked because in many cases they would have preferred to trade in Connecticut and Boston among Puritan contacts rather than with strangers in New York City. Farmers who had to send their grain there to be milled and packed, regardless of where they lived, were enraged; they hated to be so much at the mercy of merchants, millers, and bakers. And it infuriated the Albany traders that their furs had to be reshipped when they reached New York City.

In short, there were many who did not oppose monopolies per se but only those monopolies that affected particular interests invidiously. There were also those small farmers and traders whose economic well-being was adversely affected by any and all grants of exclusive privilege. Monopolies may have been justified, in part, by mercantilist theory and more palpably by the need to make private entrepreneurs more venturesome in order to encourage economic growth. But they were despised by all who failed to benefit from them. Not surprisingly, violations and smuggling became a way of life for these people—"pious lawbreaking," they called it.

Andros and Dongan received constant complaints from Albany and Long Island about New York City's port monopoly. For a brief period, beginning in 1684, the Long Island towns received port privileges of their own. All ships leaving their harbors had to post a one-hundred-pound bond against their engaging in illegal trade. Dongan stationed revenue officers at Southampton, Southold, and East Hampton in order to enforce this and other regulations. In 1687, significantly enough, when the people of central and eastern Long Island (Suffolk County) sought more ports and fewer revenue officers, they asked Jacob Leisler to present their petition. Neither side could be satisfied with the status quo. City merchants resented the competition, continuous smuggling, and expense of extra officials. Long Islanders hated the high duties. When Dongan decided to close Long Island's ports in 1687 and station ships there to prevent violations of the Navigation Acts, he had begun to sow the harvest of disaffection. His successors would reap a whirlwind.

The same sort of fierce competition occurred among the artisans and laborers, except that the extension of exclusive privileges within the lower orders of society was fraught with more ambiguity. In 1674 the public carters of New York City complained in a petition to the city court "that there were some who intruded in that employment" and subsequently that the brewers, bakers, and others had been "setting day Laborers, on worke to carry up their corne and other things, which of right apperteynes to them." Did guilds or unions have the right to control their special services in a particular locality? And did they have the right to go on strike in seeking redress? No one knew for certain, and labor unrest grew apace. The first criminal prosecution for a strike occurred in New York City in 1677. The prosecution stressed contempt rather than conspiracy, and the Common Council dismissed twelve carmen (teamsters) "for not obeying the Command and Doing their Dutyes as becomes them in their Places."

The first prosecution in the history of New York City that rested fully on grounds of criminal combination occurred in 1680. The twenty-three coopers of the city "subscribed a paper of combination" to sell their casks only in accordance with rates set

Gumwood highboy made for the Mitchell family of Port Washington, Long Island, at the close of the seventeenth century. *The Metropolitan Museum of Art, Rogers Fund, 1936.*

by their membership. This cooperation in order to set prices (rather than demand higher wages) would have been criminal according to English law at this time, so the coopers were fined fifty shillings for "the church or pious uses." In 1684 the fifteen carmen of New York City were successfully prosecuted for refusing to obey city regulations concerning their guild. A year later, when the porters became recalcitrant, they petitioned that a committee be appointed to investigate the rates and regulations pertaining to their guild. Soon after that they refused to comply with the Common Council's regulations concerning the cording of wood and were dismissed from service.

In sum, the status of guilds and the privileges of laboring men were not very clearly defined at this time; but, in general, it would seem that while guilds might enjoy monopolies, the government could also regulate them for the "common weal." By contrast, it was not at all clear whether other forms of favoritism would also be made to serve the public interest, and such special privileges spurred resentment among the unfavored. Between 1685 and 1687, for example, Dongan awarded four generous manors to private individuals: Lloyd's Neck (north of Hunting-ton, L.I.) to James Lloyd; the massive Livingston Manor (upriver on the eastern side) to Robert Livingston; Cassiltown to John Palmer and Bentley Manor to Christopher Billop, both on Staten Island.

In 1685 Dongan issued a patent creating the Manor of Rensselaerswyck, a patent quite different from the original charter of 1629. Legitimized by James II, it provided for the first time a clear and valid title to the whole domain (excluding Albany). For these extensive lands the owners would be required to pay an annual quitrent of fifty bushels of good winter wheat—considerably less than the former requirement. Despite these generous economic terms, however, the new patent was, intentionally, only a land grant. The Van Rensselaer family lost its political privileges in the city of Albany, notably that powerful participation in town government that had been enjoyed ever since 1665. After half a century as the touchstone of conflict, the domain reverted to its original conception as a private venture, albeit more agricultural than commercial. Albany would be an independent entity, and the newly created county government would attend to the needs of the inhabitants of Rensselaerswyck. Although the patroon's political powers had receded, his agrarian rights remained valuable. Because of the vastness of his landed monopoly, the peculiar forms of landholding introduced for its development, and the permanently agricultural character of its economy, a landed aristocracy did dominate in that locality and endured well into the nineteenth century.

More far-reaching than the new patent for Rensselaerswyck, however, was Dongan's decision to recall the land patents issued by Andros and replace them with new ones requiring higher quitrents. Dongan pressured the towns into capitulating by threatening to buy from the Indians those lands within the townships that had never been purchased previously, and subsequently to resell them to strangers. Rather than lose their homogeneity and internal control, the towns accepted Dongan's offer of new patents that would include the disputed lands. Although English communities on Long Island were the most sensitive to this strategy, Kingston and other Hudson River towns were subjected to it as well.

Additional factors aggravated these causes of discontent. Although Dongan's instructions of 1686 killed the Charter of Libertyes and curtailed the Assembly, they nevertheless insisted that taxes voted by the Assembly should remain and that thereafter the taxing power be given to the governor and his Council. This policy reversal stimulated two immediate protests: on Staten Island and in Jamaica (Queens). Although these outbursts were localized and contained for the moment, citizens remained nervous about rising taxes and their diminishing ability to pay.

Specie, or hard money, had long been scarce. Taxes were customarily paid in produce. Therefore a continuous struggle went on over valuation of the sorts of produce to be accepted in payment. The farmers, of course, maintained that certain agricultural products were unfairly devalued while their taxable property was excessively overvalued. No wonder Dongan declared, early in 1688, that "when I come to New York to impose another tax on the people I am afraid they will desert the province." Within a few months, however, he demanded a new levy of £2,556, an odious tax that would be particularly denounced a year later by Jacob Leisler.

All of these discontents grew steadily stronger in New York throughout the 1680s and called attention to the colony's slow rate of economic and demographic growth. Certain broad-gauge historical factors were partially responsible: land policies of the Dutch West India Company and of the Duke of York had discouraged freehold farming; the lack of representative government placed taxation beyond the citizens' control; New York's pivotal location in the Anglo-French rivalry for North America made it more dangerous for settlers than some of its neighbors. But the colony's diversity created additional difficulties arising from conflicting regional interests. New York City had become a trading center and insisted upon economic monopolies to facilitate its growth. The Albany area depended upon farming and the fur trade, resented the city's monopolies, and demanded a looser relationship with the French and Iroquois than the governor could tolerate. Long Island's economy revolved around foodstuffs, livestock, and whale oil. It was oriented much more toward New England than toward the rest of New York, and it found the Navigation Acts a great hardship in consequence. The Delaware settlements comprised small tobacco plantations, and after 1681 they were drawn increasingly toward Pennsylvania's economic orbit.

In sum, New York's subeconomies were more often competitive than complementary. Here, for example, is an excerpt from the statement presented on April 6, 1684, to the governor by New York City, seeking a monopoly of flour milling:

This Citty being the Matropolys of the Province hath from tyme to tyme been the Mayne Supporte thereof the flowerishing or Decay of which Doth Influence all its Parts. . . .

That the Manufacture of flower and Bread . . . hath been and is the

cheif Supporte of the trade . . . and if used and Practiced in Other
Parts of the Province must of necessity Lessen Our Trade and
Consequently the number of the Inhabitants Imployed Therein.

All Other Parts of the Province have Some Perticular Advantage and
way of Liveing, As Long Island by Husbendry and Whaleing, Esopus
being the fatt of the Land by Tillage, Albany by Indian Trade and
husbandry, this Citty noe Other Advantage Or Way of Liveing but by
Traffique and Dependance are one Another Cheifly upheld by the
Manufacture of flower and Bread.

To us Itt is Evident That had all Parts of the Province Equall Liberty
to make flower and Bread noe Parte thereof would be Advantaged
thereby, but the trade Soe Dispersed that it would be much Impared if
not wholy Loste. . . .

Soe that the Establishing the makeing of flower and Bread in this
Citty Only takes nothing from Other Parts of the Province, but if
Removed or Admitted in Other Parts, will be the Apparent Ruine and
Decay of the Same. . . .*

If geographic and demographic diversity posed economic
problems for New York's white population, political pluralism
remained no less significant for its Indian inhabitants. Different
Indian tribes had made independent alliances with the Dutch
and English, and on occasion one group of Iroquois would even
seek the help of Europeans against a neighboring group of
Iroquois. Moreover, the various clusters of tribes had diverse sorts
of relationships with the provincial government. The Hudson
River Indians had become subjects of the Duke, while the
Iroquois had not. Although allied with New York politically, and
partially dependent on it economically, they insisted repeatedly
that they were "free" and required the officials to call them
"brethren." Thus the governors issued commands to the River
Indians, negotiated agreements with the Iroquois, and dealt with
the Susquehannocks through their masters, the Iroquois.

The Five Nations, meanwhile, demanded that independent
Indian tribes outside of New York's jurisdiction ally themselves

---

* Herbert L. Osgood, ed., *Minutes of the Common Council of the City of New York,
1675–1776* (New York, 1905), I, 149–50.

directly with them, irrespective of the actions and requirements of the colonial government. The Iroquois made raids upon Mohegans in Connecticut and Piscataways in Maryland, for example, in order to enforce their demands. From time to time they made overtures to Indians under French hegemony, thereby gaining allies and subordinates. During the second half of the seventeenth century, the Iroquois constantly compelled their myrmidons to furnish them with warriors. When the tributaries felt that their self-interest was at stake, they participated with some enthusiasm; otherwise they begged off, or became hard to find. In some circumstances the governors of New York and Pennsylvania were able to compel tributary obedience to Anglo-Iroquois imperatives and in others persuaded the Indians to abandon their demands. In 1672, for example, the Mohawks complained at Albany of being harassed by the Mahicans of the Hudson Valley area. The English commander at Albany promised to make every effort to keep the Mahicans peaceful.

By the end of the 1670s, the so-called Covenant Chain had been formed, a political and diplomatic arrangement—defined by metaphors as much as by treaties—designed to stabilize Indian relations within what are now New York, New Jersey, Pennsylvania, and Delaware. It also facilitated English penetration into vast regions then claimed by France. So far as the English were concerned, Covenant Chain Indians were legally subject to their sovereignty—whether they knew it or not. The Indians, however, "conceived the Chain as an organization of peers, unequal in power and status, but equal in the right of each to govern itself." As Francis Jennings has remarked, "instead of the Chain's being part of the British Empire, the Empire's colonies were part of the Chain."

Relations between the English and the Indians were initially not very different from Dutch-Indian relations before 1664. A few policy changes occurred because the River Indians became less and less threatening and because the English were more eager than their predecessors had been to extend their jurisdiction inland. The English did little to modify traditional practice concerning traffic in arms. They maintained the same discrimination in favor of the Five Nations, and at Kingston the trade continued to enjoy legal advantages as a necessary stimulant to the fur trade. For a full generation after 1664, the English were no more able than the Dutch had been to convert Indians to Christianity. Except for Albany, the government's only formal action was to restrain Indians from performing their own religious rites, on the grounds that doing so disturbed the peace.

As Anglo-French rivalry began to deepen during the 1680s, however, New York's traditional Indian policies began to change. More than any of his predecessors, Dongan sought to win control over the interior—western New York, the Great Lakes area, and the Ohio Valley—for England. He hoped to substitute New York's influence for that of the French in this region, and he intended to use the Iroquois as well as the Albany fur trade as major factors in an aggressive foreign policy. He enjoyed the full support of Albany's traders and magistrates, and he was encouraged by an autonomous thrust in Iroquois behavior early in the 1680s: the Five Nations first attacked their western neighbors—the Illinois, Ottawa, and Miami—and then began depredations against the French for giving support to the western Indians.

Dongan's tactics were straightforward enough. He wooed the Iroquois with presents and a series of congenial conferences. He tried to make new alliances where there had previously been hostility or neutrality. He sought to have boundaries defined more precisely than they had been and made the colony's defenses more reliable than before. Finally, in 1684, he ordered the Duke of York's coat of arms to be displayed at all of the Iroquois "castles" as a symbol of English sovereignty. Dongan thereby hoped to establish himself as the acknowledged protector of the Iroquois. Somewhat surprisingly, they seemed to accept. "Wee have putt our selves under the great Sachim Charles that lives over the great lake," said the Onondaga and Cayuga; and they presented two dressed deerskins to be sent to the king "that he may write upon them, and putt a great Redd Seale to them." The Mohawks, Oneidas, and Senecas were more restrained in their professions; but they, too, declared their allegiance to the

English. In return they expected military support against French attack and unrestricted arms for use against the western Indians.

In reality, however, the Iroquois maintained a shrewd independence. They continued to allow "Onontio," their name for the governors of Canada, to call them his children while they reaffirmed their own freedom of action. "We are born free," they declared to La Barre in 1684. "We neither depend on Yonnondio [the French governor] nor Corlaer [the English governor]. We may go where we please, and carry with us whom we please, and buy and sell what we please." Although they conceded "Corlaer's" jurisdiction in order to have his support against the French, they never allowed their concessions and promises at Albany to prevent them from acting as their vital interests required.

Meanwhile, late in 1686, England and France made a treaty of friendship and neutrality. Designed to clarify various disputes concerning their colonial possessions from Hudson's Bay to the West Indies, it barely mentioned the Iroquois problem, requiring only "that the officers of neither king shall molest the subjects of the other in establishing their respective colonies or carrying on commerce and navigation." Along with many other issues that colonial governors had been unable to resolve, the problem of jurisdiction over the Five Nations was put off for arbitration in Europe. Both governors received copies of the treaty in June 1687. While Dongan informed his French counterpart, the Marquis de Denonville, that he would respect the agreement, the French governor went ahead with plans for an invasion of the Seneca country in western New York.

Denonville arrived at Irondequoit Bay on June 30 with three thousand French regulars, Canadian militia, and Indian warriors. The Seneca retreated to the south and east, behind the marshy terrain of Lakes Seneca and Cayuga. The expedition burned their villages, took formal possession of the region, and then returned to the strategic mouth of the Niagara River, where they built a long-sought fort. In August, Denonville left a garrison of one hundred men at the fort and returned to Montreal. Although Dongan had given the Five Nations a great deal of verbal encouragement, he provided minimal military support (some ammunition plus a handful of Algonkian warriors), and many of the Iroquois resented the inadequacy of their English ally in time of need. From the latter part of 1687 onward, anti-French feeling among the Iroquois began to abate.

By the fall and winter of 1687, reports flowed into New York that the French were preparing another attack, and that this time Albany itself would be an object if the English continued to provide Indians with firearms. Rumor had it that the French had made fifteen hundred pairs of snowshoes. Dongan, therefore, alerted Albany and Schenectady, ordered Indian scouts to patrol the northern approaches, provisioned the area for a winter's siege, and prepared (with 350 troops) to spend the winter at Albany himself. He even wrote Denonville to demand reparation for trading goods seized on the lakes, the release of Iroquois prisoners held by the French, and abandonment of the new fort at Niagara. Those rumors of a winter attack proved, in the end, to be false; but they deepened the bitterness of Anglo-French antagonism, increased the Iroquois' bargaining position between the two powers, and, most of all, frayed the ragged nerves of New York's settlers even more than political instability and economic depression had already done.

When Dongan returned to New York City in March 1688, his most pressing problem was neither diplomatic nor military, but rather fiscal. In 1687, because of the impact of French and Indian unrest upon the fur trade, New York's provincial revenue had fallen to three thousand pounds. The winter of 1687–88 added heavy military expenses at Albany plus the cost of maintaining forts in the Indian country. Dongan's requests to Virginia, Maryland, Pennsylvania, and the Jerseys for defense money met with meager results: five hundred pounds grudgingly given by the governor of Virginia after the House of Burgesses rejected two appeals for an appropriation. When the home government refused to assume any responsibility for Dongan's military obligations, the only recourse left to him was an increase in provincial taxes—a burden the citizens of New York and Long Island could ill afford in 1688. As indices of prolonged depression, the assessed value of real and personal property in New York City had declined from one hundred thousand pounds in 1676 to seventy-five thousand pounds in 1685. Simultaneously the price of wheat, an important product in a grain economy, had fallen from four shillings sixpence a bushel in 1680 to three shillings in 1688.

The years 1688–89 were momentous ones in Anglo-American history. In New York they marked the culmination of a discontented decade and a severe loss of confidence in the very ligaments of public order and personal security. Contemporaries certainly seemed to believe that they were living through a period of unusual stress and instability. In 1681 the City Council of New York accused John Lewen, the Duke's agent, of causing "Greate Disorders and Confusion." Long Island soon became the scene of frequent tumults "tending to the Breach of the peace, Disorder of the Government And Contempt of the Authority Established." In Kingston there were "undue and Unlawfull Meetings of people without Authority," as well as "Disorders and Troubles" growing out of opposition to taxation.

What had been welling up for a generation in New York—between 1664 and 1688, but with special intensity since 1685—was a collective outburst of anxiety and anti-authoritarianism: anxiety over the menace of Catholics, an influx of Quakers, and Indians in particular; the hostility of Dutch against English, Long Island interests against ducal domination, Albany autonomy against New York City privileges, and farmers against favored merchants. Pluralism, once again, became the matrix of uncontrollable instability. Dongan made particular note of it in his report to the Lords of Trade early in 1687: "New York has first a Chaplain belonging to the Fort of the Church of England; secondly a Dutch Calvinist, thirdly a French Calvinist, fourthly a Dutch Lutheran—Here bee not many of the Church of England; few Roman Catholicks; abundance of Quakers preachers men and women especially; Singing Quakers; Ranting Quakers; Sabbatarians; Antisabbatarians; Some Anabaptists; some Independents; some Jews; in short of all sorts of opinions there are some, and the most part, of none at all."

The Duke of York as well as Governors Brockholls and Dongan all being Roman Catholic, the 1680s were a relatively favorable period for their coreligionists in the province. Major Jarvis Baxter, commander of the garrison at Albany, as well as Ensign Bartholomew Russell at the fort in New York and Matthew Plowman, customs collector of the port, were also Catholics. A Jesuit school appeared in New York City at this time, and, not surprisingly, the colony's Catholic population increased. Their presence incited the "antipapist" bigotry of Jacob Leisler and other ardent Calvinists, for whom Romanism was one of the major evils to be extirpated in 1689.

The growing membership of religious minorities during the 1680s, however heretical, was ultimately less problematic, perhaps, than the ethnic proliferation that threatened to engulf the traditional Dutch majority. They had long since seen their political power ebb away; but now their commercial hegemony seemed to be threatened as well. In November 1683, "An Act for naturalizing all those of forreigne Nations at present inhabiting within this province and professing Christianity" declared "that all and Every person and persons forreigners of what nation soever . . . that at any time hereafter shall come and arrive within the said province with an entent to become his Majestyes subjects . . . may be naturalized by act of Assembly and from thenceforth shall in all respects be accounted deemed and Esteemed as his Majesties Naturall borne Subjects, and shall have and Enjoy all such priviledges freedoms and immunityes within this province as other his Majestyes Subjects have and Enjoy."

In sum, by the 1680s New York had already become a multifarious society. But among the many nationalities present, two in particular competed for commercial and political power. As the English presence came increasingly to threaten the Dutch, a situation emerged that has been well described for a different setting by a Dutch scholar: "In a dual society . . . one of the two prevailing social systems, as a matter of fact always the most advanced, will have been imported from abroad and have gained its existence in the new environment without being able to oust or to assimilate the divergent social system that has grown up there, with the result that neither of them becomes general and characteristic for that society as a whole." * The older Dutch merchants feared a further decline in their fortunes, an apprehension all the more bitter because it came after real gains had been made in the 1660s and 1670s. They envied and resented those English newcomers whose superior connections enabled them to supplant the established traders or create alternative channels of trade.

In times of stress and insecurity, moreover, New York's varied composition made it especially vulnerable to rumors of conspiracy within, attack from without, or, worst of all, a deadly combination of the two. Imagine the reaction, then, when New Yorkers learned in 1688 that their colony (as well as New Jersey) had been annexed, by royal fiat, to the Dominion of New England (a megacolony created by James II two years before). Imagine the anxiety in August 1688 when Edmund Andros returned to New York as archgovernor of the dominion, thereby supplanting Dongan, who had been recalled. Even Francis Nicholson, who served as Andros's deputy governor in New York, later testified "how fatall it hath been to this city and the Province of New York for to be annexed to that of Boston, which if it had continued would have occasioned the totall ruin of the Inhabitants of said Province." Jacob Leisler and his cohorts were outraged when New York's public records were carted off to Boston, because doing so hindered the transaction of commercial affairs. In 1692 the New York City Council remarked upon "that unhappy Annexation to New England whereby our Traffique not only drooped, but all that was dear and valuable amongst us wholly destroy'd."

Imagine, also, the consternation in April and May 1689 when

---

* J. H. Boeke, *Economics and Economic Policy of Dual Societies as Exemplified by Indonesia* (Haarlem, 1953), 4.

a rumor reached the city that one thousand French and Indians were preparing a murderous attack upon Albany. Even though a sloop subsequently came downriver with news that the rumor was false, the Provincial Council discovered that it "could not so easily beat it out of the peoples minds, being so possest with jealousyes and feares of being sold, betrayed . . . that it was almost impossible to do any thing that would please them." In an aural society, and in an era of hearsay as well as heresy, rumors did not seem scurrilous. They were simply the ordinary way in which most people acquired information concerning public affairs. And in an aural society still without a printing press, it was especially risky to be a revolutionary leader because one had to reveal himself in order to propagate his cause. One could not rely upon pseudonymous essays and anonymous broadsides.

Jacob Leisler, however, had never sought to conceal his identity and discontent. The son of a German Calvinist pastor, he had come to New Amsterdam in 1660 as a twenty-year-old soldier. In 1663 he married the widow of a wealthy merchant; and through her capital and connections he became prosperous, prominent, and privy to some of the leading families in New York, among them the Bayards, Van Cortlandts, and Loocker-mans. Although he became a militia captain, his connections were largely with the older Dutch elite, not with the new Anglo-Dutch establishment. He remained a contentious man of substance on the periphery of power, and he found himself even more marginal when the Dominion government devoured New York in 1688.

Although Leisler eventually assumed leadership of the rebellion in 1689, he does not appear to have initiated it. When news reached New England that James II had been overthrown in England and that William and Mary had seized the day, Bostonians arose in April 1689 to imprison Governor Andros and declare the Dominion defunct. That demise, combined with the story of probable French invasion, caused New York to reach a frenzy of excitement in mid-May. The towns on eastern Long Island, which had been planning to send a statement of grievances to England anyway, rose in revolt against the authority of Lieutenant Governor Nicholson, and they were soon joined by towns in Queens and Westchester counties. They turned out appointees of the central government and elected others to replace them. On May 31 the New York City militia seized the fort in order to "save" the colony, and on June 8 Jacob Leisler was commissioned as captain of the fort. Two months later he became commander in chief of the province. During these summer months the significant upheaval involved an effort by prominent older settlers, supported especially by the Dutch populace, to displace the insecure, newly emerged Anglo-Dutch elite. Although the rebels identified themselves politically (and expediently) with English whiggery; their program, such as it was, sought a restoration of traditional corporate liberties for communities rather than an enlargement of personal liberties for individuals and social groups.

When Nicholson fled New York for England in order to submit his complaint against the rebels, he left the colony controlled by Leislerians: a de facto government lacking legitimacy. Leisler wrote to Massachusetts, Connecticut, and Maryland for advice—all three colonies were now themselves ruled by revolutionary regimes—and he received favorable, flattering replies. He proclaimed William and Mary to be Their Majesties, in New York City on June 22* and in Albany (which Leisler could not yet control) on July 1. Late in June he also sent a circular letter to all of the provincial towns asking them to elect delegates to a governmental committee that would meet in New York City. Nine towns responded, and their delegates deliberated until August 15, issuing orders, discussing finances, and finally, on the last day, discoursing about their grievances. This convention then appointed a ten-man committee of safety, with Leisler in charge, empowered to act upon legal, administrative, and military matters. They imprisoned opposition leaders and drove others into exile.

---

* Because the proclamation had to be "published" orally, Leisler did so twice: once in front of the fort and again at City Hall "up town." In Albany the king and queen were vocally proclaimed twice also, in Dutch and in English.

Eventually, the Privy Council got around to proclaiming Their Majesties in New York; and William, through his secretary of state, sent Nicholson a letter of authorization that empowered him to control the government and maintain the welfare of the king's subjects there. Conveniently, however, Nicholson had left, and the order was addressed alternatively "in his absence to such as for the time being take care for Preserving the Peace and administering the Lawes of our said Province in New York in America." When the documents finally arrived in December, Leisler intercepted (or accepted) them himself, and interpreted them as applying to him in Nicholson's absence. He had been "preserving the peace," albeit an armed peace enforced by his militia; and from that moment until March 1691, he regarded himself as the legitimate head of a constitutional government.

On February 20, 1690, Leisler issued writs for electing members to an assembly. His summons would almost seem to be an ultimatum: "Elect and make choice of two proper and fit persons to repair forthwith to this city, empowering them as your representatives to consult, debate and conclude all such matters and things as shall be thought necessary for the supply of this government in this present conjuncture, of which you are not to fail, as you will answer the same at your peril." Surprisingly, there was no response to this decree; whether the reason was apathy or fear of treason and subsequent retribution we do not know.

Leisler issued new writs on April 8, and this time an assembly was elected. It met on April 22 at the home of Leisler's son-in-law, Robert Walters, and enacted several pieces of legislation: a tax of threepence in every pound for general public purposes, and the freedom for all inhabitants "to bolt [flour] and bake and to transport where they please" so that "the one place should have no more privileges than the other." Leisler, as governor, subsequently prorogued this session summarily. When the Assembly convened again on September 15, 1690, it reenacted the tax imposition—an effort to equalize the tax burden— provided for the election of local assessors and collectors, punished persons refusing to serve under Leisler's commissions, prohibited the departure of anyone from the colony without Leisler's consent, and regulated the transportation of property.

In a complex and qualified way, it may be said that Leisler's Rebellion drew largely upon Dutch support. Except for his son-in-law, Jacob Milborne, and Samuel Edsall (Milborne's former father-in-law), all of Leisler's close associates were Dutch. Some of his supporters at large, certainly, must have been English, French, and various other nationalities; but the majority were Dutch. Leisler's chief antagonist, Nicholas Bayard, insisted that the insurgents were simply "a parcel of ignorant and innocent people, almost none but of the Dutch nation." Nevertheless, this rebellion did not aim at a formal restoration of Dutch rule in the manner of 1673; it was in many respects a spontaneous rising of frustrated burghers supported by Long Islanders with political and economic grievances of long duration.

The town of Albany, however, the largest Dutch community in the colony, opposed Leisler. Although the Albanians disliked Andros's Dominion regime, they distrusted Leisler and hoped to preserve their autonomy. Their leaders, such as Peter Schuyler and Robert Livingston, knew Leisler to be a tactless hothead, and they feared that disruption of their delicate personal relationship with the Iroquois would bring disaster to their town. They feared, too, the loss of their monopoly over the fur trade. So they called their own convention of prominent citizens and decided to go it alone until word came from England.

On November 8, 1689, Milborne marched a militia unit up to Albany's gates and requested the town's capitulation. He did not get it; and fearing attack by the Albanians and Mohawks combined, he withdrew to New York City after eight futile days. In December the Albany Convention also refused to yield to Captain Joachim Staats, Leisler's remaining representative in Albany. The commander in chief seemed stymied as 1690 began, but very soon an unforeseen disaster strengthened his hand. On February 9, a band of two hundred French and Indian marauders, down from Montreal, entered the unguarded gates of

Schenectady at night, massacred sixty-two people, carried off twenty-seven more, and set fire to the village. The pathetic survivors fled to Albany, where the people fell into a panic of apprehension.

Leisler then resolved that Albany must not be left autonomous. Alone it could not resist a concerted French attack, and its loss would endanger the rest of the colony southward. In March he tried again; and this time, fearing another attack by the French, Albany accepted his authority. Leisler appointed three commissioners, including Milborne, to control the town. He soon demonstrated his genuine concern for the safety of New York's northern settlements. In April he called for an intercolonial conference to meet at New York in order to discuss the French menace. Massachusetts, Plymouth, and Connecticut responded, and the latter actually dispatched troops for the defense of Albany. The soldiers soon became weary of Milborne, smallpox, and dysentery, lost interest in intercolonial cooperation, and went home. In late July and early August, Leisler joined New England's military expedition against Montreal and Quebec, but that turned out to be an abortive attempt.

With respect to local and provincial affairs, Leisler's regime demonstrated considerable capacity for public administration. It organized a government and raised funds, issued commissions, created courts, suppressed riots, appointed military officers, created a commission that sat as a court of vice-admiralty, and sent agents to England. These were not wildly lawless years, and the wheels of government did not cease turning.

Leisler realized, however, that his tenure would inevitably be short—though he must have been dismayed at the abruptness with which it ended: in jail and on the gallows. King William had appointed a new governor for New York in January 1690, though characteristically for the colonial scene, Henry Sloughter did not arrive at his station until fourteen months later, on the evening of March 19, 1691. He "published" his commission by having it read before a public gathering and demanded surrender of the fort. Three times Leisler refused, claiming that it was contrary to military rules to give up a fort after dark. Later, this refusal became the basis for charging Leisler with treason. The next morning Leisler did surrender the fort, was immediately arrested, along with nine others, and was charged with treason and murder.

Their trial lasted from March 31 until April 17. Two men were acquitted, but eight were convicted and sentenced to die. Ignorance of English law, politics, and political thought had essentially led the Leislerians into serious errors of judgment. Their trial, while technically fair, was heavily weighted against them because of their unfamiliarity with English law and their opponents' overwhelming desire for revenge. Leisler and Milborne refused to answer the indictment against them, claiming that the court lacked legitimate jurisdiction. On May 16, Sloughter executed the order that Leisler and Milborne be hanged "by the Neck and being Alive their bodys be Cutt downe to the Earth and Their Bowells be taken out and they being Alive, burnt before their faces; that their heads shall be struck off and their Bodys Cutt in four parts." The other six rebels were reprieved and eventually, in 1694, pardoned by the crown.

As Leisler had become increasingly domineering and demagogic, his initial coalition of supporters began to be dissipated. The towns in Queens County had repudiated his claims and accused him of tyranny. Merchants in Manhattan had begun to send petitions against him to England. The colony of Connecticut withdrew its support, and the cost of maintaining adequate defenses—Anglo-French war resumed in May 1689—became an enormous burden for the colony's depressed economy. There remained, to be sure, a loyal core of Leislerians. They maintained the "martyrdom" of their leaders as a political issue for more than a decade, and in 1695 they obtained a parliamentary act clearing the names of Leisler and Milborne and restoring their estates to their proper heirs. The rebel leaders lingered on in provincial memory for fully a generation, and they remained as controversial in death as they had been in life.

The years between 1683 and 1691 were determinative ones in many ways for New York. Both the memory and the reality of factionalism lingered on, so that instability became one of the least attractive aspects of public life in the province. As Cadwallader Colden recalled in his reflections upon the "great Animosities, which continued many Years": "Each Party, as they were at different times favoured by several Governors, opposed all the Measures taken by the other, while each of them were by Turns in Credit with the People or the Governor, and sometimes even prosecuted each other to Death. The publick Measures were by these Means perpetually fluctuating, and often one Day contradictory to what they were the Day before." This incessant instability, coupled with the colony's excess of pluralism and its peculiar land system, made it unattractive to immigrants for years to come. It remained underpopulated and underdeveloped, so that the most significant phenomenon of the coming decades may well have been an internal development: the dynamics of anglicization.

6

ANGLICIZATION AND
SOCIAL CHANGE

The two decades after Leisler's Rebellion have most commonly been discussed in terms of enduring battles between Leislerians and anti-Leislerians. Those tensions, though visible and vexing, were nevertheless not the most significant phenomena of these two decades, nor even the most pressing problem in public affairs, as we shall soon see. What was most significant, and irrevocable, about the years 1691–1710 was that the discontinuities between new English institutions and older Dutch domination began to be more evident than the accustomed persistence of Dutch legacies and development. In a word, anglicization became widespread: in the arrangements of public life throughout the province, and socially in all areas except for the upper Hudson Valley.

It is ironic, perhaps, that pervasive anglicization first occurred under the aegis of a Dutchman, William III. But the irony only indicates that monarchs meant less than the inner dynamics of social change. Just as the Dutch in New York had largely retained their identity under the English proprietary, 1664–85, so they would start to lose it under the Prince of Orange who ruled Great Britain after 1688.

The phenomenon of anglicization may be seen most immediately in the establishment of a new judicial system in 1691 and the reception of English common law thereafter. There was nothing gradual or evolutionary about the appearance of English common law in New York. It supplanted the Roman-Dutch civil law on a broad scale in the years after 1691: a remarkable transformation in a relatively brief period of time. The Judiciary Act of 1691 established for the first time the Supreme Court of Judicature and in so doing provided a perfect opportunity to eliminate precedents based upon local law, substituting instead a legal system deriving its procedures from the English common law. In addition, the act set up courts "for the Ease and benefitt of each respective Citty Town and County within this Province" and explicitly acknowledged that they were empowered to function in the same way "as all or any of the said Judges of the severall Courts of the Kings Bench, Comon Pleas & Exchequer in England Legally doe."

Concomitantly, the first phases of development and acceptance of a legal profession—marked by special learning, a sense of public service within the context of the common law, and a rise in social status—occurred in New York between 1691 and 1709. By the latter year lawyers formed an informal bar association, the first in North America, in order to regulate legal fees. Even so, attorneys had never been popular and would be regarded with suspicion for some time to come.* In order to understand the rapidity and significance of what transpired between 1691 and 1710, we must look more closely at the nonuse of attornies in seventeenth-century New York.

In 1647 New Netherland had obviated the need for lawyers by utilizing councils comprising three arbitrators to settle disputes. Fees for legal services of any kind were carefully restricted after 1658, with free services provided for the poor. Hostility toward lawyers continued during the proprietary period. According to the Duke's Laws, anyone "indicted and proved and Judged a

---

* See Governor Bellomont's letter to the Treasury Lords, Sept. 8, 1699: "There was not such a parcel of wild knaves and Jacobites as those that practised the law in the province of New York, not one of them a barrister, one was a dancing master, another a glover, a third . . . condemned to be hanged in Scotland for blasphemy and burning the bible. . . ." *Calendar of Treasury Papers, 1697–1701/2* (London, 1871), 327.

common Barrator" would be fined or imprisoned. In 1677 the Provincial Council decided that attorneys were not "thought to be useful to plead in Courts."

Through most of the seventeenth century, public officials such as notaries, secretaries, and clerks had handled much of the legal work done by attornies in England. Under the Duke's Laws, moreover, specific procedures had been designed to reduce dependency upon lawyers: the concept of agency whereby more skillful persons were ethically obliged to assist the less fortunate, and the concept of attorney-in-fact whereby any person could have his legal needs fulfilled by a public magistrate on an ad hoc basis. Individuals appeared in court, if necessary, under a civil system that gave judges much greater authority in matters of fact and law than would have been the case under the common-law system in England.

Nor had juries been used in New Netherland. Litigants simply appeared before the magistrates, who exercised both the fact-finding and the judicial functions. Judges played a more active role in the Roman-Dutch system and commonly handed down decisions without the litigants having benefit of counsel. Arbitration, which had been important in New Netherland, remained so in the proprietary period after 1664 and received explicit institutionalization in the Duke's Laws. In addition, the underlying emphasis of Dutch civil law also continued: cases were still decided on the basis of general, theoretical rules of justice rather than according to empirical, historical precedents of the common law.

All of this, of course, fit appropriately with the circumstances of an aural, largely preliterate society. The law was a matter of simple ethics and justice rather than written precedents; hence the adequacy of ad hoc practitioners rather than full-time lawyers. The colonists, moreover, were court goers because judicial sessions provided diversion from daily routines. One need not be fully literate to understand what was going on: one need only listen. Everyman, in consequence, may well have been more familiar with the law than his counterpart today.

Court records from the 1660s, 1670s, and 1680s reveal a

relative ignorance of (or indifference to) the English common law, in addition to a general lack of precision or sophistication in handling legal documents. After 1691, however, especially with the Supreme Court of Judicature newly established, the process of indictment came to be properly understood and widely used. By the end of the century, its employment compared favorably with English practice: certain identification of persons, time, and place; precision about the nature of the offense; and the proper phraseology are all present. Between 1699 and 1707, moreover, New York adopted the customary English practice of using the writ of habeas corpus in defense of personal liberty. During these same years, also, English laws and traditions of inheritance began to supplant earlier Dutch practices, even among the landed elite of the Hudson Valley.

Not surprisingly, then, by the first decade of the eighteenth century, practitioners trained in English law had emerged and gained control over the administration of justice. Between 1700 and 1712 the number of trained lawyers in New York almost doubled as against the number present between 1664 and 1699. Growth in population and commerce increased the demand as well as the need for regularity and predictability in the law. As property was acquired and its acquisition became widespread, people felt a stronger need to have it protected by law. In consequence there was a marked improvement in the quality of colonial justice, at least as measured by English standards. Those cases which occurred between 1701 and 1709 (and which are fully reported) indicate that New York's attorneys worked carefully according to British standards. And why not? Most acquired their legal education in the same way as their counterparts in England; and many, indeed, were themselves trained in England: John Palmer, Thomas Rudyard, George Farewell, Matthias Nicolls, John Tuder, Nicholas Bayard, John Bridges, and Sampson Broughton. In two short decades, 1691–1709, New York had newly modeled a bench and a bar along English lines.

During these same years the nature of citizenship in New York City acquired its proper English meaning and implications. In order to vote, or to hold office, or to practice a trade, or to carry on any business, one had to be a freeman. One became a freeman through birth, apprenticeship, or redemption (purchasing the right). Citizens by dint of birth paid an enrollment fee, as recorded by New York's Common Council in 1691, 1702, and 1707. In 1694 the same body established regulations for achieving citizenship through apprenticeship and in 1707 added fines to penalize noncompliance. "Att the Expiration of the Indentures," read the order, repeated in 1695, 1697, 1701, 1702, 1706, 1707, 1711, and 1712, "the said Apprentice Shall be made Free of the Said City by his Said Master if he have well and truely Served him." Between 1707 and 1711, New York's laws governing apprenticeship in general were brought into closer compliance with England's.

Those who obtained citizenship by purchase were usually foreigners (or "strangers"), and New York's regulations for them distinguished between the "Merchant Trader or Shop-Keeper" and the "Handicraft man" or artisan. In 1691 their respective fees for admission to freemanship were established at three pounds, twelve shillings, and one pound, four shillings. After 1702 they were reduced to twenty and six shillings apiece. That same year, however, a city ordinance also ordered that those who "are poor and not able to purchase Their Freedoms be made Freemen of this Citty Gratis," a concession occasionally repeated thereafter. In some cases all fees were remitted; in others the applicants achieved freemanship by "paying the Fees of their Certificates only." Early in 1695 a city ordinance declared "that an Oath be drawn up & Administered to all Such as Shall be made Free or are Already Free According to the Usage & Practice of Corporations in England." *

All of these procedures and regulations had their origins in medieval precedents derived from fourteenth- and fifteenth-century London. During the ducal period of New York's history,

---

* The earliest oath of a New York City freeman to survive in its entirety dates from Mar. 28, 1707. In phraseology and content it is strikingly similar to the standard oath used in 14th-century London.

however, when English administrative forms were first introduced, violations and aberrations were commonplace. Strangers passed as freemen and tried to engage in business without first obtaining legal permission. Promptly upon royal reestablishment, therefore, efforts were made to enforce traditional English practices respecting citizenship. "All the Inhabitants of this Citty," said an order of May 9, 1691, "that Shall bee Warned by Mr. Thomas Clarke to produce their ffreedoms to Retaile or use any handicraft trade within this Citty are hereby Required to Satisfie the Said Clarke [clerk] in their ffreedoms or give Sattisfaction to the Mayor of the Citty within fourteen dayes time after Such Demand made by Mr. Clarke upon fforfeiture of Twenty Shillings." By the beginning of the eighteenth century, colonial New York had reproduced and attempted to enforce inherited English methods of acquiring the franchise and trade privileges, taking the oath of citizenship, as well as the traditional duty of "being in Scott and Lot" (paying taxes for municipal expenses).

Equally indicative of anglicization in this period was the beginning of public printing in New York. As recently as 1686 Governor Dongan's instructions had included the following prohibition: "And for as much as great inconvenience may arise by the liberty of printing within our province of New York, you are to provide by all necessary Orders that noe person keep any press for printing, nor that any book, pamphlet or other matters whatsoever bee printed without your special leave & license first obtained." King James II knew the political uses and implications of the press and sought to stifle the devices of opposition. By 1693, however, Governor Fletcher wanted a narrative (hence public praise) of his current defense measures in print, so the colony finally got a public printer in order to satisfy an executive's ego.

William Bradford, who received the appointment in April 1693, had first set up his press in Philadelphia eight years earlier. A Quaker in Pennsylvania, he became an Anglican soon after his arrival in New York, serving as a vestryman of Trinity Church between 1703 and 1710. The quality of his printing was not especially good, for he had inferior equipment and seems to have been indifferent to good typographic appearance. Nevertheless, he continued as crown printer in New York until 1742—almost half a century of service to the colony.

Bradford's early publications are especially revealing, both as indexes of anglicization and as indications that an aural culture would soon be giving way to a literate one in which the written word would mean much more than it ever had before. In 1694 he printed *The Laws & Acts of the General Assembly . . . in Divers Sessions* (since 1691), the first collection of New York's legislation. A year later he printed *A Journal of the House of Representatives for His Majesty's Province of New York*, the earliest publication of the proceedings of any legislative body in the English colonies. In 1698 Bradford printed two very significant titles: one by Francis Daniel Pastorius called *A New Primmer, or Methodical Directions to Attain the True Spelling, Reading & Writing of English*; the other by Bradford himself, entitled *The Secretary's Guide, Or, Young Man's Companion . . . Containing 1st. The Grounds of Spelling, Reading and Writing True English*, which went through numerous printings.

Between 1693 and 1710 Bradford kept extremely busy, publishing 250 titles, an average of almost 14 each year. His gradual success must have been a cause as well as a consequence of the steady growth of literacy in early New York, for the rate of illiteracy among adult white males in the colony may have dropped by as much as 50 percent between 1698 and 1746.*

Literacy was still sufficiently limited in the late seventeenth century that a skillful scrivener could hope to make his way quickly in public life. Robert Livingston, founder of a New York "dynasty," knew English and Dutch with equal proficiency and had had countinghouse experience in Rotterdam. Hence he began his career as clerk to the general court of Albany County,

---

* My estimate is based upon percentages of military personnel able to sign their names (or only make their marks) on petitions and pay receipts in those years. I found 79 percent illiteracy in 1698, 40 percent in 1746. My samplings are sufficient to be suggestive, but not conclusive. Between 1732 and 1741, Bradford's final decade as printer, his average output rose to more than 20 items per year.

Robert Livingston (1654–1728), politician and entrepreneur, ca. 1718. Portrait attributed to the *Aetatis Sue* limner. *Abby Aldrich Rockefeller Folk Art Collection. By permission of Henry H. Livingston.*

and subsequently as secretary to the commissioners for Indian affairs. In 1695 the crown gave him the latter position, an influential one, for life. A year later Governor Fletcher remarked that Livingston had "made a considerable fortune . . . never disbursing sixpence, but with the expectation of twelve, his beginning being a little Bookkeeper, he has screwed himself into one of the most considerable estates in the province." Livingston was a literate man in a society just verging on literacy. A knowledge of numbers and letters meant power, and Robert made the most of his.

Education and standards of measure* also began to be anglicized during these decades. Livingston was of Scots descent, for example, and his wife, Alida, was Dutch. All four of their sons, however, received Anglo-American rather than Dutch-American educations: the first at English and Latin schools in New London (Connecticut), New York, and London; the second in English and French at New Rochelle; the third at Edinburgh and London, where he was the first native New Yorker to enter the Inns of Court (1706–10); and the fourth at Northampton (Massachusetts) under Solomon Stoddard. In 1713 the Reverend John Sharpe left to the city a collection of English and Latin books "towards laying the Foundation of a Publick Library at New-York in America." These eventually contributed to the core of the New York Society Library.

Equally important at this time were the first efforts made to plant a strong Anglican presence in New York. Two enthusiastic partisans, Governor Benjamin Fletcher and Colonel Caleb Heathcote, both of whom hoped to see the Church of England established throughout the province, arrived in 1692. Although they did not succeed entirely, they were instrumental in obtaining the Ministry Act of 1693, which provided the church with public support in four counties: New York, Richmond,

---

* Although the English regained permanent control of New York in 1674, they made no attempt to standardize weights and measures until 1703, when the Assembly passed "an Act to bring the weights and measures of this place, which hitherto have been according to the Standard of Holland, to that of England." Thereafter *schepels* and *morgens* were supplanted by pecks and acres.

Queens, and Westchester. When they met with resistance from the Assembly in 1692, Fletcher rebuked the legislators with this admonition: "There are none of you, but that are big with the privileges of Englishmen and Magna Charta, which is your right; and the same law doth provide for the Religion of the Church of England, against Sabbath breaking and other profanity." The privileges of Englishmen, he argued, required the spiritual obligations of Englishmen. So partial establishment was won, "the most that could be got at that time," Lewis Morris later wrote, "for had more been attempted, the Assembly had seen through the artifice, the most of them being Dissenters, and all had been lost."

As it happened the Anglicans and the assemblymen could not agree upon the proper meaning of "a good sufficient Protestant Minister," so the act of 1693 soon became a bone of contentious interpretation. The governor had an advantage, however, because he believed that he had the power to validate the ordination of any clergyman, and he soon made it clear that only those in Anglican orders would receive his approval. Even so, Anglican clerics would be in short supply for some while to come, so that surrogates had to be accepted; and the act of 1693 also provided "that all former agreements made with Ministers throughout this Province shall continue and remain in their full force."

According to Fletcher's interpretation of the law, all persons in the four lower counties had to contribute to the Church of England's support. He and his successors also assumed that only Anglican clergy were entitled to public maintenance.* Governor Cornbury insisted upon regarding the Church of England as fully established, and he tried between 1702 and 1708 to install its clergymen in the pulpits of unwilling congregations. Although he did not always succeed, he did intimidate some Dutch schoolmasters into applying for their licenses from him, thereby acknowledging, at least partially, jurisdiction by the English civil

---

* In 1697, Fletcher gave to Trinity Church a charter that took for granted that the act of 1693 had established the Church of England.

government over an arm of the Dutch Reformed church. In 1710, moreover, Bradford printed *The Book of Common-Prayer, and Administration of the Sacraments*, the first American edition of the standard Anglican prayerbook.

Most of all, anglicization occurred at this time because New York became more fully integrated into the British imperial scheme of government. Between 1692 and 1694 the governor of New York served as chief executive of Pennsylvania as well; from 1698 until 1701 his jurisdiction included Massachusetts and New Hampshire, too; and from 1702 until 1738 he was also governor of New Jersey.* In addition, Fletcher was nominally, at least, the militia commander of the Jersies, Connecticut, and Rhode Island, an indication that Whitehall was coming to see New York as the fulcrum of imperial defense. In 1684, the first intercolonial Indian conference, attended by Virginia, Maryland, Massachusetts, and New York, had been held at Albany. Others took place there in 1694 and 1700, with New Jersey, Pennsylvania, and Connecticut also among the participants.

New York politicians learned increasingly during the 1690s that their orbit of authority was not self-contained, that ultimate decision-making power lay in England, and that transatlantic connections would have to be cultivated in order to achieve partisan goals. In 1692 John Povey became the colony's agent, or lobbyist, in England; his appointment was the first recorded public expenditure for maintaining a regular provincial agent. (Earlier agents had been sent, in 1687–90, on an ad hoc basis for special missions to serve factional ends.) After 1691 a certain attitude became commonplace among provincial politicians with serious aspirations, expressed typically in a remark by James Graham to Robert Livingston in 1692: "You will now doe well to use your Interest at home." How often that phrase would be repeated thereafter!

---

* In Feb. 1692, Benjamin Fletcher's commission contained a clause empowering him to unite East and West Jersey with New York. Dr. Daniel Coxe appeared before the Privy Council on behalf of the Jersies, however, and "after a long Debate" succeeded in delaying the loss of New Jersey's autonomy for another decade.

Still another form of anglicization in the realm of government and politics can be found in the way that Britain became rapidly the measure of things-as-they-ought-to-be, or else a convenient rationale for undesirable circumstances in New York. When the Assembly complained in 1693 "that the taxes and impositions are heavy," Governor Fletcher replied that "it is not harder with us than with our brethren in England. . . . We must therefore bear it with cheerfulness and patience." When some provincials lamented in 1699 "that England should put a limitation on their trade," Governor Bellomont responded with acerbic contempt. "How extravagant and wild is this notion. Does not England put a restriction on its own trade in some cases?" Bellomont's rhetorical bewilderment then led him to explicate in full the colony's constitutional position: "This Province is subject to the Crown of England, and it is its greatest glory and happiness that it is so, for by that means the people are entitled to the protection of the Crown, and are under the best constitution of laws, and that in fellowship with the best and bravest people in the world, the people of England; and they must be obedient to English laws; it is their duty and interest so to be." *

In 1691, even before Leisler had gone to the gallows, New York began to take shape as a regular royal colony—the shape and role it would have until 1776. The new Assembly met early in April, chose James Graham (who had been associated with Andros) as its Speaker, and passed legislation for "Quieting and Setling" the recent disorders. It established the government's revenue, confirmed earlier land grants and patents, provided for a provincial militia, set up a system of courts, approved a table of fees for public services, and declared "what are the Rights and Priviledges of their Majesties Subjects inhabiting within their Province of New York." Although the governor and king both retained a veto power over the Assembly's bills, all laws would be effective until royal disapproval occurred, which could easily be

---

* The quotations from Fletcher and Bellomont will be found in Lincoln, ed., *Messages from the Governors*, I, 37, 79, 80. For Cornbury's lengthy reiteration of the same theme in 1702, see ibid., 100.

delayed for a long time by accident or by design.* The
assemblymen insisted upon having annual rather than triennial
meetings and claimed for themselves a variety of parliamentary
privileges: deciding when to meet and adjourn, determining their
members' qualifications, and being immune to arrest while
attending sessions.

Governor Sloughter died in the summer of 1691, only a few
months after setting up the new government. The Council
appointed Major Richard Ingoldesby to replace him on an
interim basis; and he, like his predecessor as well as his successor,
Benjamin Fletcher (1692–97), sided strongly with the anti-Leislerians. All of them pursued vindictive policies, tried to keep
Leislerian partisans out of the Assembly, and generally served to
heighten old animosities rather than diminish them. Fletcher
ingratiated himself with the Bayard-Van Cortlandt-Nichols-Phil-
ipse faction by granting great chunks of valuable land, including
five new manors: Philipsborough and St. George in 1693 to
Frederick Philipse and William "Tangier" Smith; Sagtikos,
Cortlandt, and Morrisania in 1697 to Stephanus Van Cortlandt
and Lewis Morris. Virtually no quitrents were collected. All
military purchasing and contracting went to the anti-Leislerians,
as did most political patronage—so much so that the colony's
salary list quickly grew disproportionate to provincial income.

In return Fletcher sought bribes and excessive perquisites,
mulcted the customs service of thousands of pounds, overlooked
flagrant trade with pirates so long as he got his share in tolls, and
collected personal tribute from the Indian traders at Albany.
One critic wrote in 1695:

To recount all his arts of squeezing money both out of the publick and
private purses would make a volume instead of a letter. . . . He takes a
particular delight in having presents made to him, declaring he looks
upon 'em as marks of their esteem of him, and he keeps a catalogue of
the persons who show that good manners, as men most worthy of his
favour. This knack has found employment for our silversmiths and

---

* Not until 1696 did the Lords of Trade and William disallow the Assembly's
declaration of rights because of several "large and doubtful expressions" that
differentiated New York from all other colonial governments.

furnish'd his Excellency with more plate (besides variety of other things) than all our former Governours ever received. Such clowns as dont practice this good breeding, fall under his frowns, or a haughty glance of his eye at least, if they don't feel the weight of his hands. . . . Some Officers he makes his favourites who are his tools and pimp to his frauds upon the publick.

Happily, Fletcher was finally recalled and was replaced in 1698 by Richard Coote, Lord Bellomont in the Irish peerage. He found the colony in wretched condition: impoverished and bitterly factionalized. He carried out the reversal of the convictions and attainders that had been perpetrated upon the Leislerians, set aside a day of fasting and humiliation designed to quiet the "heats and differences" between groups, tried to reform the colony's corrupt administration, apply sound principles of public management to colonial affairs, and suppress illicit trade. He called immediately for a new Assembly and had Bradford print a broadside "commanding Sheriffs to take effectual care that there be a free and fair election of members." Because of his sympathetic support, the Leislerians enjoyed four more years of power, 1698–1702, but never again thereafter. Bellomont seemed unaware of how precarious the colony's economy was. It declined steadily between 1694 and 1701, so that New York was absolutely insolvent by 1701–2. Bellomont's strong sense of integrity was undermined by a mean temper, a tactless instinct to vilify his opponents, a tendency toward poor judgment of people, and a proclivity to alienate potential allies unnecessarily.

The enduring animosities between Leislerians and anti-Leislerians—or "Black People" and "White People," as they were then labeled *—have, if anything, been overstressed by historians of this period. The animosities were important, to be sure, but they were neither so clear-cut, nor consistent, nor determinative as we have traditionally believed. There was, for one thing, fluctuation in their ranks. Power within the Leislerian group

---

* See *Collections of the New-York Historical Society for the Year 1868* (New York, 1868), 425; and O'Callaghan, ed., *Documents Relative to the Colonial History of New-York*, IV, 1071.

shifted after 1695 from small merchants and artisans in the New
York City area to country yeomen and gentry. Abraham De
Peyster, one of the foremost Leislerians by 1698, may have been
the second-richest person in New York City. Several leading
figures, such as Van Cortlandt and Livingston, shifted their
allegiances back and forth as expediency required. To many,
ideology meant less than opportunity.

More importantly, however, any reading of the extensive
documents for the two decades after 1691 will reveal that
political factionalism was only the third most pressing public
issue of the day, discussed less often than physical security and
fiscal responsibility. These, indeed, were the two matters mentioned first and second in almost every governor's communications with the Assembly. The pattern is almost monotonous:

I hope therefore you will take effectual care to make such suitable
provision for the securing the frontiers that the seat of the war may
continue remote from us. [Ingoldesby, 1692]

We . . . pray that your Majesties will graciously be pleased, either by
sending us a sufficient force and supplies from England, or by your
Majesties special and direct orders to the several adjacent Colonies, to
assist us in the defence of this important Place. [Assembly, 1692]

A small regular fortification of stone [at Albany], furnished with such
ordnance and stores of war as their Majesties have sent hither with me,
will defend us and all their Majesties' provinces and colonies on this
main. [Fletcher, 1693]

The chief matters you are called together for are two; the first is the
defence of the frontiers and of our Indians. . . . The other matter fit for
your consideration is the debts of the government, occasioned by the
many unforeseen occurrences and accidents in this time of war.
[Fletcher, 1695]

I must recommend to you the care of recruiting his Majesty's companies
at May next (when the term of those enlisted by your act determines),
otherwise it will be impossible to cover the out plantations; those
farmers will remove and leave the country waste, the consequence of
that will be the desolation of the city, which must then become a
garrison. [Fletcher, 1697]

Secure but this [colony], and you secure all the English Colonies, not only against the French, but also against any insurrections or rebellions against the Crown of England. . . . A 1000 men regular troops here and a 4th rate man of War at Boston and a 5th rate here at New Yorke would secure all the English plantations on this continent firm in their allegiance to the Crown, as long as the world lasts. [Bellomont, 1699]

The first thing which I earnestly recommend to the care of you, Gentlemen of the House of Representatives, is the providing for the defence of the city and port of New York, which seem to me to be much exposed; and likewise for the defence of our frontier, which I have found in a much worse condition than I could have imagined. [Cornbury, 1702] *

One reason for the primacy of defense in legislative and executive deliberations was the series of Anglo-French wars waged, primarily in Europe, between 1689–97 and 1702–13. As long as they lasted, New York remained the most vulnerable of all the English colonies and the most impoverished on account of defense appropriations. The first book ever printed in the colony was by Nicholas Bayard and Charles Lodwick, *A Narrative of an Attempt Made by the French of Canada Upon the Mohaques Country Being Indians Under the Protection of . . . New York* (1693), and it emphasized the single most dominant theme in the first two decades of provincial printing: defense.† There were published acts to raise money to pay volunteers for frontier reinforcement, proclamations warning the people to erect beacons as signals of an approaching French fleet, broadsides against soldiers and sailors deserting, bounties encouraging enlistment, journals of expeditions to Albany, rewards for the destruction of enemies

---

* See Lincoln, ed., *Messages from the Governors*, 27–31, 35, 52, 57, 65, 71, 88, 98–99, 103, 105, 107–8, 112–15, 120; O'Callaghan, ed., *Documents Relative to the Colonial History of New-York*, IV, 505.

† See Charles Evans, comp., *American Bibliography: A Chronological Dictionary of All Books, Pamphlets and Periodical Publications Printed in the United States of America from the Genesis of Printing in 1639 Down to and Including the Year 1820*, 14 vols. (Chicago, 1903–59), I, nos. 632, 666, 667, 672, 674, 676, 734, 743, 761–63, 768, 769, 807, 844, 944, 1139, 1415, 1522. Subsequent notes will also refer to Roger P. Bristol, *Supplement to Charles Evans' American Bibliography*, 2 vols. (Charlottesville, 1970–71).

found nearby, directives that all men take the oath of allegiance, queries concerning the construction of forts, and so forth. These were tense times, and security, not factionalism, was the paramount concern in public life.

In point of fact, New York's involvement in both King William's War and Queen Anne's War was relatively small; and the reasons for this inactivity are revealing, especially since the province had much at stake. The traditional explanation is simply that powerful Albany fur traders feared that war would disrupt their commerce with the Indians and French. So they lobbied successfully for inactivity or neutrality. Actually, the truth is more complicated. The Albany group believed that an intercolonial force, supported by the British fleet, could make a successful expedition against Canada, but that until such an expedition was ready, costly local skirmishes ought to be avoided. New York's fortifications were so weak that to provoke the possibility of premature French and Indian counterattacks seemed foolish. New Yorkers were tired of ineffectual but expensive frontier raids and preferred a position of "prudent defense." The Iroquois, moreover, wanted peace, or at least neutrality, so as to be able to trade with both sides. The French, in turn, were willing to forego attacks on New York in order not to antagonize the Five Nations.

By 1708, however, English authorities at home decided not to allow a futile defensive policy to continue any longer; hence the intercolonial Canadian expeditions of 1709 and 1711, both of which failed. New York cooperated in each, lost financially from them, and thereafter lapsed once again into inactivity. When Governor Hunter arrived in 1710, he found the usual—poor defenses and no money—so he had to be content with "a precarious security, under a suspicious neutrality." War weariness, French willingness to abstain from attacks on New York, Iroquois neutrality, provincial factionalism, and misappropriated military funds all added up, by 1711, to a virtual tradition of inaction. The English government contributed, too, because it did not provide a governor between 1691 and 1709 who could reconcile colonial and imperial interests. Nor would it contribute significantly to colonial defense measures. The regulars garrisoned in New York were so ragged, so disreputable, and so poorly fed that they mutinied in October 1700, just two days after the Assembly had passed a mutiny act! New York, in sum, was in no condition to seek engagement in foreign adventures at this time.

"The Trade of Albany is chiefly Beaver," the Reverend John Miller remarked in 1695. "Formerly it may have been to the value of £10,000 a year, but is now decay'd, by reason of Warr between our Indians and the French." The population of Albany declined as well: from 662 men in 1689 to 382 in 1697; from a total population of 2,016 in 1689 to 1,449 in 1697. Bellomont took a census of the entire province in 1698 and recorded 18,067 persons, more than a quarter of them in New York City. By 1703 the total population had risen to 20,748, and by 1712 the rate of increase had begun to climb. Census figures are missing for five counties in 1712, so we cannot make an aggregate comparison. But whereas New York, Kings, Richmond, Westchester, and Orange counties contained 9,069 persons in 1703, they contained 12,286 in 1712, a gain of 3,217. The largest increase came in New York City (1,404), but there was substantial growth in Westchester and Staten Island as well (857 and 775 respectively).

In the five counties for which we have returns in both 1703 and 1712, the rate of increase among blacks and whites remained almost identical: 26 or 27 percent. (There were 7,767 "Christians" in 1703, 10,511 in 1712; 1,301 slaves in 1703, 1,775 in 1712.) Otherwise the proportionate composition of New York's population began to shift significantly at the end of the seventeenth century, not only in terms of national origin, but also with respect to the impact of the growing numbers of English upon all the rest. In March 1687, Governor Dongan informed the Lords of Trade that not even twenty English families had immigrated to the colony in seven years past. Dutch and French had been coming, however, especially French Protestants after revocation of the Edict of Nantes in 1685. Many of them remained in New York City; but the most memorable made their mark upriver at New Paltz, where they built sturdy stone houses along the Wallkill River. Using native limestone and fieldstone, with mortar of clay and straw, they constructed walls two feet thick.

The homes they established between 1692 and 1712 still stand and are a delight to visit along "Huguenot Street": the Hugo Freer house (1693–1720) with its wooden gutter troughs; the Abraham Hasbrouck house (1694–1712) with its steep roof and three stout chimneys; the Louis Bevier house (1698) with its original handblown glass windowpanes, its cellar kitchen, and its unusual subcellar; and the Jean Hasbrouck house (1694–1712) with its enormous loft for storing grain and its huge beehive chimney made of imported bricks. The earliest Walloons had come here, in the shadow of the Shawangunk Mountains, in 1677; they purchased land from the Indians and began to farm the land in common, governed by "The Duzine," a council made up of representatives from each of the twelve original families. Their ethnic identity endures to this day. (The French in New York City, by contrast, seem to have been anglicized by the mid-1720s, when a bitter dispute disrupted their congregation.)

From this same period we also have a few samples of English and Dutch architecture that have survived. In Setauket, Long Island, for example, halfway out on the north shore, there stands a substantial English "saltbox" farmhouse, built about the year 1700. Its interesting features include unusually high ceilings, heavy exposed framing, great fireplaces with unusual smoke channels, and early paneling. It is owned and exhibited today by the Society for the Preservation of Long Island Antiquities, has been modestly decorated with late Jacobean and Williamite period furnishings, and has been carefully reshingled—roof and walls—with wooden wedge shingles.

Up the Hudson there are a number of important Dutch legacies from this period: Madam Brett's lacy-shingled homestead in Beacon, built in 1709, subsequently a resting place for Washington, Lafayette, and Von Steuben; Jan Mabie's steep-roofed stone house, built about 1700 in what is now Schenectady County, the oldest surviving house in the Mohawk Valley; the Knickerbacker family mansion in Schaghticoke (twenty-five

miles northeast of Albany), built after 1709 by Johannes
Harmense Knickerbacker with boards from his own sawmill; and
the charming Old Dutch Church of Sleepy Hollow (now in
North Tarrytown) built between 1685 and 1697 by Frederick
Philipse for the small congregation living on Philipsburg Manor
(he had two hundred tenant farmers in 1702). Its walls are more
than two feet thick, built from local stone except for flat yellow
bricks brought from Holland to outline the windows and door.
The structure is gambrel roofed and octagonal in the rear. A
small but graceful tower surmounts it, and within still hangs the
embossed bell, cast to order in Holland in 1685.

Several of the finest residential buildings from that era are still
called "forts" on account of their security arrangements against
Indian attack. Fort Crailo, a Van Rensselaer country house of
brick on the east bank of the Hudson, opposite Albany in what is
now the town of Rensselaer, has two full stories and a gambrel
roof. The main part of the structure is typical of its time in
having two rooms with a hall between on each floor. Two
funnel-shaped openings in the west wall were designed for
defense by musketry; hence it is "Fort" Crailo. Similar openings
may be found in the Van Cortlandt manor house at Croton and
at "The Old Fort," or Daniel DuBois house, in New Paltz. The
latter, built in 1705 to supplant a log palisade, fulfilled one of the
terms of the Huguenots' patent, which required that they build
"a place of Retreat and Safeguard upon Occasion." Fortunately,
the Huguenots remained on good terms with their Indian
neighbors and never needed to use the gun holes in the stone wall
nearest the street.*

Many of the early Dutch homes still standing throughout the
Hudson Valley contain furnishings characteristic of the very
early eighteenth century: a great *kas,* or cupboard, with decora-
tive paneling and great ball feet; oak armchairs and walnut
benches; a simple gate-leg table, or possibly even a more elegant

---

* For a useful discussion of the "fort-idea" in residential architecture, see
Helen Wilkinson Reynolds, *Dutch Houses in the Hudson Valley before 1776* (New
York, 1929), 31, 50, 52, 110, 113.

A *kas* of painted oak and gumwood made in the Dutch style in New York, ca. 1720. Because most homes in colonial New York lacked closets, the *kas* was an indispensable piece of furniture: a multipurpose wardrobe, closet, and chest of drawers. *Kas*es were made with loving care and were passed along from generation to generation. *The Metropolitan Museum of Art, Rogers Fund, 1909.*

stretcher table, walnut with ash and rosewood inlay; ash and beech side chairs; a Friesland wall clock; a delft pitcher; Dutch tiles; a brass sweetmeat box and candlesticks; pewter beakers; and, if Father Time has been especially kind, a tall cedar secretary, often close to six feet high, inlaid with beech and walnut. One can almost sniff the crullers, the cookies, and the coleslaw.

There were, at this time, some people of Dutch descent who did make a strong effort to preserve their national identity. Some even migrated northward from the New York City area to places upriver where it would be easier to maintain those traditions. But for many the task seemed hopeless, and to others inexpedient. Schuyler, De Peyster, Van Rensselaer, and Van Brugh daughters all married Livingstons, subsuming their names while preserving family fortunes.

After 1691 the Dutch Reformed church was bitterly split into pro- and anti-Leislerian factions, thereby weakening the church as an agency of ethnic cohesion. An excerpt from a letter to the Classis of Amsterdam, sent by certain New Yorkers in 1698, tells the tale: "Those who had been most bitter in these affairs, were elected to fill all the Church-offices. Thereby the people came to abhor the public services of religion, so that only about one tenth enjoyed the celebration of the Lord's Supper. And some to this day . . . have never resumed the celebration of the same." Some clergymen were boycotted by their congregations, and many others shifted their affiliation from the Dutch church to others. Three dominies complained to the Classis of Amsterdam in 1692 that "we ministers, possessing no power . . . are treated with scorn, and paid in insults, and deprived of what is justly our dues, receiving no salary worth mentioning." The next year Reverend Dellius reported "the daily decay of my churches by the constant removal of inhabitants, both rich and poor."

Between 1693 and 1696 the Dutch Reformed ministers in New York received no communications from their superiors in Amsterdam and became apprehensive that all of their local privileges and status might be withdrawn. Therefore they petitioned Governor Fletcher for a charter of incorporation that would guarantee them their positions and property. He accommodated them in 1696 with a charter that remained unchanged until 1784. It confirmed the consistory's authority to fill its own pulpits; to buy, sell, and hold property; to lévy rates on members to support the clergy and church; and generally to manage its own affairs so long as it offered allegiance to Great Britain and paid an annual fee. (A year later the Anglican church in New York City received a similar charter for an annual fee of one peppercorn.) The Dutch Reformed church thereby became "semiestablished," alongside the Church of England (which had risen from about thirty people attending services in 1679 to more than ninety-five families in 1695), which caused many of the Dutch clergy to see some sort of correspondence in mutual interests—a misleading delusion in the long run. By mid-century a decaying knowledge of Dutch undermined the liturgy, pews stood empty on Sunday, and angry pamphleteers harangued the faithful clergy.

At the close of the seventeenth century, New York's social development still was beset by consequences of unstable pluralism. Even contemporary perceptions of the problem were fraught with prejudice. Here are just two examples:

Our chiefest unhappyness here is too great a mixture of nations, and English the least part; the French Protestants have in the late King's reign resorted here in great numbers proportionably to the other nation's inhabitants. The Dutch, generally the most frugall and laborious and consequently the richest; whereas most of the English are the contrary, especially the trading part. [Charles Lodwick, 1692]

As to their religion, they are very much divided; few of them intelligent and sincere, but the most part ignorant and conceited, fickle and regardless. As to their wealth and disposition thereto, the Dutch are rich and sparing; the English neither very rich, nor too great husbands; the French are poor, and therefore forced to be penurious. As to their way of trade and dealing, they are all generally cunning and crafty, but many of them not so just to their words as they should be. [John Miller, 1695] *

---

* Charles Lodwick's fascinating letter, May 20, 1692, to two members of the Royal Society in London, appears in *Collections of the New-York Historical Society*,

These were years of Anglican condescension, of Anglo-Dutch tension, and of strong anti-Catholicism in New York. More than ever before the province almost seemed to be divided into three discrete segments, each with its own character: heterogeneous New York City, truly a social hodgepodge; predominantly English Long Island, still resentful; and the heavily Dutch Hudson Valley, more isolated and slower to change.

Yet change was relentlessly beginning to overtake all three sections, although at different rates of speed, varying not only by region but according to individual institutions and processes as well. Between 1689 and 1709 the Assembly started to acquire power over local functions at the expense of counties and towns. Town meetings became less frequent. By 1700 some met only once a year, and local officials in certain areas were reduced to being mere caretakers. Local government in 1710 may have enjoyed less vitality than it had half a century earlier. A slow centralization of authority became evident under Governors Fletcher, Bellomont, and Cornbury: executive, legislative, and judicial centralization. While Leislerians and anti-Leislerians were competing for power at the provincial level, many others tried desperately to evade civic responsibilities at the local level. Town records reveal increasing examples of men who refused to serve as constables, clerks, and fence menders. Efforts to enforce governmental participation were not always successful, nor were attempts to regularize the residential requirements for citizenship. In 1702 an ordinance insisted that voters and officeholders in New York City must live in the ward where they voted (or which they represented) and be a freeholder or freeman.

Economic changes of consequence were also evident during the first decade of the eighteenth century. In 1696, forty square-rigged vessels, sixty-two sloops, and as many boats were entered at the New York customhouse. In 1700 Bellomont

---

2d Ser., II (New York, 1849), 243–50; John Miller's *Description of the Province and City of New York . . . in the Year 1695*, first published in 1843, is reprinted in Cornell Jaray, ed., *Historic Chronicles of New Amsterdam, Colonial New York and Early Long Island*, 1st Ser. (Port Washington, N.Y., [1968]). The quotation is on p. 31.

reported that forty-three topsail vessels and eighty-one sloops belonged to the port of New York. Eight years later Cornbury found only twenty-eight of both. What could possibly have caused such a dramatic decline? Wartime losses, in part; but principally the Boston carriers had simply driven New York's merchant marine from their own port. New Englanders offered lower rates and thereby dominated New York commerce between 1702 and 1709. Very few vessels entered New York directly from Europe during these years, resulting in a disastrous diminution of direct trade with ports of market or supply. Exports from the port of New York in 1706 had fallen to one-sixth of what they were in 1700. The value of imports from London was only 40 percent of what it had been in 1700.

The decay in shipping may serve as an index of overall economic decline in these years. Specie virtually disappeared from the port of New York, partly because of European remittances required by the unfavorable balance of trade and partly because of the steady drain to Boston merchants. The problem got so serious that in 1709 the exportation of specie was prohibited. New York's merchants had built up enormous debts in London, and their economic gloom affected artisans, shopkeepers, and farmers as well. Although the province had no income to speak of, the Assembly neither renewed the customs rates in 1708 nor sought any other form of revenue. Instead the assemblymen kept trying to fulfill their campaign promise that new taxes would not be levied. By 1710, fiscal irresponsibility had just about brought the colony to complete ruin.

On the brighter side, some attention to road building and physical mobility began to awaken in this period. During King William's War, 1689–97, provincials discovered how very difficult it was to move even small bodies of troops from one place to another inland. With the Hudson River frozen for so much of the winter, sailing vessels had no value for transportation then, and the few rudimentary roads were worthless for deploying troops. Tree stumps were strewn across even the better paths, and new routes had to be improvised constantly as wagons and horsemen churned spring mud into ghastly bogs of muck.

In 1703 the Assembly finally decided to take some action and passed the first major highway legislation for "Laying out, Regulateing, Clearing and preserving Publick Comon highways thro' out this Colony." It ordered a road at least four rods wide to be laid out through New York and Westchester counties to Connecticut (what became the Boston Post Road) and another stretching out Long Island as far as East Hampton. Two others were projected for the Hudson River counties: one running up the east bank through Westchester, Dutchess, and Albany (today's Route 9) and the other up the west bank from Orange through Ulster and Albany counties.

The legislators recognized that better highways (or *any* highways) might facilitate commerce, and they provided for roads "to such Convenient Landing Places in each respective Town & Village where their respective Scituacons will afford and require it for the better & easier Transportacon of goods and the Commodious passing of Travellers as Direct and Convenient as the Circumstances of Place will admit." The 1703 law also declared that road repairs would be the responsibility of those persons through whose lands the roads ran and designated highway commissioners in each county with wide discretionary powers in administering the local road systems. The commissioners could, for example, require the demolition of fences or enclosures, or conversely, they could permit the construction of "swinging gates" where one highway led to another or to river landings. In 1705 the act was extended for another three years, and in 1708 the Assembly clarified some earlier obscurities by defining more precisely, for instance, what it meant by "clearing" the highways (cutting brush, removing stones, trimming off branches that overhung the road, etc.). Any eligible person who neglected or refused to perform highway labor might suffer a public sale of his properties. By 1708 the colony had started to attend to communications.

In consequence, it began to receive more visitors by land than it had before. Late in 1704, for example, Madam Sarah Kemble Knight, a gentlewoman from Boston, traveled by horse through New England, down into Rye, then to New Rochelle, and finally

to New York City, where she stayed from December 8 until the
21st. Her impressions are valuable as well as charming.

The Cittie of New York is a pleasant, well compacted place, situated
on a Commodius River wch is a fine harbour for shipping. The
Buildings Brick Generaly, very stately and high, though not altogether
like ours in Boston. The Bricks in some of the Houses are of divers
Coullers and laid in Checkers, being glazed look very agreeable. The
inside of them are neat to admiration, the wooden work, for only the
walls are plasterd, and the Sumers and Gist [beams and joints] are
plained and kept very white scowr'd as so is all the partitions if made of
Bords. The fire places have no Jambs (as ours have) But the Backs run
flush with the walls, and the Hearth is of Tyles and is as farr out into
the Room at the Ends as before the fire, wch is Generally Five foot in the
Low'r rooms, and the peice over where the mantle tree should be is
made as ours with Joyners work, and as I suppose is fasten'd to iron
rodds inside. The House where the Vendue [public sale] was, had
Chimney Corners like ours, and they and the hearths were laid wth the
finest tile that I ever see, and the stair cases laid all with white tile
which is ever clean, and so are the walls of the Kitchen wch had a Brick
floor. . . .

They are Generaly of the Church of England and have a New
England Gentleman for their minister, and a very fine church set out
with all Customary requsites. There are also a Dutch and Divers
Conventicles as they call them, viz. Baptist, Quakers, &c. They are not
strict in keeping the Sabbath as in Boston and other places where I had
bin, But seem to deal with great exactness as farr as I see or Deall with.
They are sociable to one another and Curteos and Civill to strangers
and fare well in their houses. The English go very fasheonable in their
dress. But the Dutch, especially the middling sort, differ from our
women, in their habitt go loose, wear French muches wch are like a
Capp and a head band in one, leaving their ears bare, which are sett
out wth Jewells of a large size and many in number. And their fingers
hoop't with Rings, some with large stones in them of many Coullers as
were their pendants in their ears, which You should see very old women
wear as well as Young.

They have Vendues very frequently and make their Earnings very
well by them, for they treat with good Liquor Liberally, and the
Customers Drink as Liberally and Generally pay for't as well, by
paying for that which they Bidd up Briskly for, after the sack has gone

plentifully about, tho' sometimes good penny worths are got there. Their Diversions in the Winter is Riding Sleys about three or four Miles out of Town, where they have Houses of entertainment at a place called the Bowery, and some go to friends Houses who handsomely treat them.*

Materialism and alcoholism—Madam Knight was hardly the first to notice. " 'Tis in this country a common thing," Reverend Miller remarked, "even for the meanest persons, so soon as the bounty of God has furnished them with a plentiful crop, to turn what they can as soon as may be into money, and that money into drink." Miller went on to observe that shopkeepers in New York got at least 100 percent markup on English goods, often 200, 300, and sometimes even 400 percent. Profiteering, piracy, high living, swearing, fornication, and adultery all were much noticed and, therefore, presumably prevalent. "There are many couples live together without ever being married in any manner of way; many of whom, after they have lived some years so, quarrel, and, thereupon separating, take unto themselves . . . new companions." Even when couples married, complained Miller, "enjoyment precedes the marriage."

In Lord Bellomont's opening speech before the Assembly in 1699, he commented upon the "great marks of irreligion and immorality in this place, and I take it to proceed from a long habit of breaking the laws, which has introduced licentious and dissolute living." Despite Bellomont's own unwitting collusion with the famous Captain Kidd, the privateer-turned-pirate who received his royal commission through Bellomont's intercession, despite the venality of Fletcher and corruption of Cornbury, all three governors kept publishing and reprinting pronouncements concerned with private vice and public morality. There were various acts "for restraining and punishing privateers and pyrates," proclamations against cursing and violating the Sabbath, and broadsides because of "our sins and immoralities and prophaneness." There was also the second protest against slavery

---

* Perry Miller and Thomas H. Johnson, eds., *The Puritans* (New York, 1938), 441–42.

ever printed in America (1693), a six-page *Exhortation* prepared by Quakers, as well as Fletcher's broadside soliciting contributions to redeem Christians from slavery in Morocco. Finally, there were ordinances regulating abuses in standards of measurement and Cornbury's proclamations against air pollution: "sundry persons," it seems, had been burning great quantities of dead oysters and oyster shells, causing considerable smoke and nauseous odors.*

It is curious, of course, that this passion for public rectitude and civil order reached its peak during Cornbury's regime, for he was despised by contemporaries as the most venal of all the colonial governors. He gave away great chunks of real estate to his favorites, including a patent for thirty thousand acres astride the Mohawk Valley, the huge Kayaderosseras patent where the Hudson and Mohawk rivers meet (eight hundred thousand acres), and the Hardenbergh tract south of Albany, larger than the entire colony of Connecticut. He favored the Anglicans unfairly and illegally. Worst of all, he made public appearances in the elegant costumes of his cousin, Queen Anne. A transvestite governor was more than most New Yorkers could bear, and they still commented upon Cornbury's behavior many decades later. "It was not uncommon for him to dress himself in a woman's habit," wrote William Smith, Jr., in 1756, "and then to patrole the fort in which he resided. Such freaks of low humour exposed him to the universal contempt of the people." †

---

* See Evans, comp., *American Bibliography*, I, nos. 636, 663, 664, 668, 669, 842, 843, 1088, 1089, 1090, 1141.

† One wonders whether Cornbury's antics would have been allowed to anyone other than the royal governor. At the court of Fort Orange and Beverwyck in 1654, "Abraham Crabaat, for having last Shrove Tuesday walked along the street in woman's clothes, is, although it is the first time and he offers the excuse that he did not know that he was doing wrong, condemned to pay a fine of six guilders for the benefit of the poor, with costs, to be paid immediately, provided that if he, Crabaat, or any one else shall hereafter undertake to do this again, he shall be arbitrarily punished as an example to others." *Minutes of the Court* (Albany, 1920), I, 118.

bury's administration, though he was not always a willing accomplice. From time to time he informed the Assembly "of the usage and custom of the Parliament of England." In its turn, however, the young Assembly began to claim for itself privileges recently acquired by the House of Commons. It rejected efforts by the Council to amend money bills, and in 1705 it won permission from the crown to appoint a treasurer who would control the disbursement of special funds outside the routine support of government. By 1707 it was actively seeking control over the expenditure of all tax revenues and insisting that it was the proper guardian of the "liberties and properties" of New Yorkers "and those rights they mean to be that natural and civil liberty, so often claimed, declared and confirmed, by the English laws, and which they conceive every free Englishman is entitled to."

In 1707 Cornbury sought to strengthen the Anglican grip on New York by denying a local preacher's license to Francis Makemie, a distinguished Scottish Dissenter who had recently been elected moderator of the Philadelphia presbytery. Makemie had been invited to preach in both the Dutch and French Reformed churches. When Cornbury said nay, Makemie conducted services in a private home "in as publick a manner as possible," whereupon Cornbury had him arrested, incarcerated for forty-six days, released on March 11, and remanded for trial on June 3, 1707. If Makemie had left the colony and agreed never again to preach within Cornbury's jurisdiction, the governor would have dropped the charges. Makemie, however, was determined to make of his *cause célèbre* a precedent for all dissenters; so he stood trial and won the case. His three lawyers (who were Anglicans) pleaded, and the jury agreed, that Cornbury's royal instructions* gave him the right to control only

---

* This aspect of the episode reveals how unclear the nature of public authority still remained in colonial New York and suggests how difficult it was to define legitimacy there. When Makemie first came before Cornbury he defiantly declared, "Your instructions are no law to me," and his lawyers contended that a royal governor's official instructions did not have the force of law.

Anglican priests. All Trinitarian clergymen, except Roman Catholics, were entitled to toleration so long as they went about their business peaceably.

The implications and consequences of this trial are noteworthy. First, the presiding judge observed that it was the first such trial for religious persecution in all of the American colonies, a statement that requires qualification but reveals its importance in the eyes of contemporaries. Second, although the jury found Makemie not guilty, the court imposed upon him the entire costs of his trial and imprisonment. This injustice so enraged the citizenry of New York that in 1708 the Assembly passed an act making it illegal to assess an innocent party for expenses. Third, Makemie's victory made explicit the limitations upon Anglican hegemony in heterogeneous America. And fourth, Cornbury's tyrannical behavior in the affair led to his recall to England and imprisonment.

In other respects, however, these were not such bonny years for the Reformed churches of New York. The Society for the Propagation of the Gospel (S.P.G.), a missionary arm of the Church of England, was established in 1701 and promptly began aggressive activities in the colonies. The society intended to convert Indians and blacks, establish Anglican churches where there were none, strengthen those that were weak, and publish and distribute Anglican prayer books in languages other than English. On the whole, it got a good reception in New York. Several French Reformed congregations went over, en bloc, to Church of England worship, and the society was vigorous wherever Dutch pastorates were unfilled and poorly served or where there was dissension.

As it happened, the Dutch Reformed churches of New York suffered considerable dissension, especially after 1706, and the consequences could only serve to weaken them. A bitter quarrel between 1706 and 1713 involved several pastors, congregations in Schenectady and Long Island, the Classis of Amsterdam, and Cornbury. In 1709 a fierce quarrel occurred in Kings County over the rights of two dominies to hold the livings there. The controversy extended over years and eventually caused some of the Dutch Reformed adherents in Kings and Queens to shift allegiances to Anglicanism. In 1709, also, a Presbyterian clergyman from New England wrote that Dominie Du Bois, pastor of the Dutch Reformed church in New York City, had invited him to preach there, "for most of his Dutch congregation understand English. . . . The church was [as] full as it could hold . . . of English, French and Dutch."

If these evidences of social change were quite apparent by 1709 and 1710, so, too, were economic and political shifts that augured well for a new era. The provincial economy, so depressed between 1694 and 1708, started a slow climb upward thereafter. The prices obtained for meat commodities began to rise in 1708 and those for flour and wheat in 1710, though a really marked increase did not occur until 1713. Scottish and German immigration began to be visible after 1708, which helped to populate the rural areas and stimulate certain aspects of economic growth.

In politics the center of gravity, or critical relationship, moved from the governor and Council to governor and Assembly. Anti-Catholic feeling and family alliances became less determinative in public affairs after 1705 and diminished somewhat as sources of tension. In 1709–10 a major redistribution of political power seems to have occurred, suggested by the unusually high rate of turnover in Assembly seats. In the 1709 elections, twelve new men were chosen for the twenty-two seats, and the following year nine men were elected who had not been members in 1709. For a short period under Council President Richard Ingoldesby, 1709–10, the Assembly gained effective control over the colony. It passed appropriation bills which placed monies directly in the hands of a provincial treasurer and specified the particular purposes for which they were to be spent. All fiscal officers, whether royal or provincial, became accountable to the lower house.

Between 1710 and 1712 the new governor, Robert Hunter, and Whitehall put a stop to such aggressiveness, insisted upon the necessity of parliamentary legislation for colonial finance, and greater consolidation of American government into a more centralized administration dependent upon the crown. Whitehall would have its way for several decades longer; but by 1710 precedents had been established and political opportunities created that would not be forgotten in New York. In the 1730s they recurred, with long-term constitutional consequences. Meanwhile, the most significant developments would occur in the realm of economic growth.

7

ECONOMIC GROWTH AND PROBLEMS
OF INTERGROUP RELATIONS

By the second decade of the eighteenth century, basic commercial patterns had developed in colonial New York that would shape its economic destiny for several generations to come. Before about 1712, the rates at which trade multiplied, production increased, agriculture improved, and population grew were varied, erratic, and uncertain. A depression that began in the 1670s had carried over into the 1680s; and thereafter the Leislerian brouhaha in politics, the Anglo-French wars, and the hovering presence of French privateers, as well as French competition in the fur trade, all served to curtail the potential for full economic activity. With the cessation of war in 1713, however, New York entered its first major period of concentrated commercial growth. This phase lasted (with ups and downs) for almost two decades; and it had profound implications for the colony's labor force, Indian relations, political activity, and provincial attitudes—both public and private.

What were some of the signs of economic change and growth? Between 1714 and 1717 the number of ships clearing the port of New York each year averaged 64 vessels and 4,330 tons annually, a rapid rise over earlier years. By 1721 the average had leaped to 215 ships a year totaling some 7,464 tons. By that time New York City had developed an extensive trade with the British West Indies, captured from Boston and British carriers a considerable share of the Chesapeake tobacco trade, and secured as well a sizable portion of Rhode Island's commerce. Between 1708 and 1715 there was an increase of 150 percent in the number of locally owned vessels, and this renewed flow of capital into shipping would inevitably be beneficial to local artisans. An index of New York's imports from Great Britain, based upon the average yearly imports of 1715–19 (a period of surge) as unit 100, suggests a rate of growth that was strong overall if not consistently steady on a year-to-year basis.*

Year	New York's imports	% Change from previous year in N.Y. imports
1720	69.2	− 33.6
1721	93.9	+ 35.7
1722	106.3	+ 13.3
1723	98.1	− 7.8
1724	116.6	+ 18.9
1725	130.7	+ 12.1
1726	157.0	+ 20.1
1727	124.8	− 20.5
1728	151.0	+ 21.0
1729	119.8	− 20.7
1730	119.1	− .6
1731	122.3	+ 2.7
1732	121.3	− .9
1733	121.1	− .2
1734	151.2	+ 25.0
1735	148.7	− 1.7
1736	159.1	+ 7.0
1737	232.8	+ 46.3
1738	246.8	+ 6.0

There are still other indications that New York's economy began to pass from frail infancy into vigorous adolescence at this time. After 1701 wampum ceased to be used any longer as a

* These figures are adapted from charts found in Richard A. Lester, *Monetary Experiments: Early American and Recent Scandinavian* (Princeton, 1939), 76, 121.

medium in the colony, and in 1709 the provincial government issued paper currency for the first time—an expedient that increased the amount of money in circulation and thereby added fluidity to the commercial life of New York. The invention of the schooner (in Gloucester, Massachusetts) in 1713 stimulated an embryonic shipbuilding industry, leading in 1728, for example, to establishment of the excellent Walton family shipyards of New York. Wholesale prices in New York City rose steadily between 1721 and 1727, shooting up dramatically in 1729–30.

Yet another consequence of economic growth in these decades was that the port of New York achieved commercial autonomy and ceased to be a satellite of Boston. Until about 1710, sailings between Boston and England were so much more regular than from New York that merchants from the latter port carried out many of their commercial transactions with Europe through Boston. Bills of exchange drawn in New York on England were commonly handled by Boston merchants. New York's governors, therefore, paid expenses drawn against the crown by making bills payable to New York merchants; the latter then endorsed them to Bostonians, who in turn sent them to London for collection. By this process, as Curtis Nettels has written, "the New York trader settled his account with Boston merchants for European and other goods, and the latter received the means of purchasing in England."

There had been, in consequence, inevitable sources of friction between New Yorkers and New Englanders. One arose because the citizens of Southold, Southampton, and East Hampton on Long Island preferred to sell their whale products and buy manufactured goods in Boston. New York's merchants thereby lost both a market for their wares and a means of making payment for English goods. A second problem arose because Boston merchants carried hard specie away from New York, cut some of the silver from the coins, and sent back the clipped pieces to pay for grain in New York. The Massachusetts men refused to buy processed flour, moreover, but insisted upon taking raw grain to Boston and making their own flour. They would then undersell New York flour in the British West Indies and obtain most of the coin available there. Had it not been for the trade with Dutch Surinam and Curaçao, New York would have obtained no hard specie at all.

Under Governor Hunter the Assembly began to take measures to alleviate those problems. In 1713 he secured the enactment of special duties upon European goods, rum, and wine when imported from another colony. Acts passed in May 1715 provided a 5 percent duty on English products imported through Boston. All Massachusetts ships importing directly to New York from the West Indies would have to pay a duty of three shillings per ton. Wine, distilled liquor, and cocoa were to cost twice as much when coming from Boston as when shipped directly from the place of original production. The New England trade was thereby taxed one way or another, whether the goods came straight from the Caribbean or indirectly through Boston. Hence Long Islanders complained bitterly about Assembly policies that seemed discriminatory against their interests. Samuel Mulford's appeal to the Assembly in 1714, arising from the seizure of twelve ships trading directly between Long Island and New England, many of which had been forced to pay fines, embodied the Long Islanders' complaints:

Our vessels being thus carried and drove away, we have not Vessels to carry the Growth of the Countrey to a Market; nor bring us such Goods as we wanted: And if any come from *New York* with Vessels and Goods, and the People would deal with them, the Trader would set the Price on his Goods, and also on what the People had of the Growth of the Countrey: And if the People would have sent their Effects to *New York* to have got Money to have paid their Taxes, or bought goods, they were denied to have Fraight carried to *New York*, or Goods brought from thence in their Vessels: so that they were Compelled to take what they were proffered or keep their Goods by them. *Southold* people being much Oppressed, as they informed me: Wheat then selling at *Boston Five Shillings* and *Six-pence* per bushel, and at *New York* but *Three Shillings and Four-pence;* they had not liberty to carry or send it to *Boston:* Nor any Vessel suffer'd to come at them from thence; and not coming to them from New York, their Wheat and Grain lay by them, until the Vermin Eat and Spoil'd it; and they were much Impoverished thereby.

Robert Hunter (1666–1734), governor of New York, in about 1720,
Portrait attributed to Sir Godfrey Kneller. *Courtesy of The New-York
Historical Society, New York City.*

Being persuasive and influential, Mulford had to be expelled by the Assembly before the revenue acts of 1715 could be passed.

In addition to competition from Boston, New York had also suffered from the rapid rise of Philadelphia as a port. Until about 1685, New York City had been the mart for Pennsylvania, West New Jersey, and the Delaware counties. But by 1687 Governor Dongan complained that his colony was losing the Delaware River tobacco trade to Philadelphia and that Pennsylvania had begun to cut into New York's domination of the northern fur trade. Cornbury later insisted that prospective immigrants preferred Pennsylvania because there were no trade duties there. In any case, by the close of the seventeenth century the volume of Pennsylvania's trade virtually equaled that of New York, and the newcomer colony bought very little from its older neighbor. After 1713, however, New York kept pace with Philadelphia in commercial growth and in certain years even maintained an edge in the rivalry. In the year following June 1715, for example, seven vessels brought goods from Philadelphia to New York, while six carried shipments in return. Of these six vessels, New Yorkers owned five as against one owned in Pennsylvania. New York imported wine, rum, linseed oil, rice, pitch, tar, beef, and pork—all in small amounts; and sent flaxseed, furs, iron, staves, cordage, and chocolate—in larger quantities. Each sent European manufactures to the other, but New York enjoyed much the more favorable balance of trade: its exports exceeded its imports.

Similarly, between 1715 and 1717, twenty-four vessels carried goods from New York to Virginia, and twenty of these were owned at New York. Of sixteen vessels making the return voyage, New York merchants owned fourteen. They also controlled the distribution of English-made goods. In 1715, for example, twelve New York vessels took such goods to the tobacco area, but only one brought that type of consignment in return. Consequently New York began to enjoy a favorable balance of trade with the Chesapeake, and hard money appeared in Virginia's list of exports.

New York desperately needed that margin over its neighboring colonies and with the Caribbean, because its balance of trade with Great Britain became less and less favorable with the passage of time. Just as the impressive growth of New York's imports between 1715 and 1740 serves as a useful measure of economic growth, so the widening gap between imports and exports also serves to demonstrate the increasing complexity and necessity of New York's commercial involvement with other colonies. While imports more than doubled over a quarter-century, the exports that New York sent "home" rose by only two-tenths of 1 percent. The colony came to depend upon its coastal trade, its carrying fees in transatlantic commerce, and especially upon its Caribbean markets.

Not surprisingly under the circumstances, New York's economy in the early eighteenth century began to be gradually anglicized, just as its politics and society had been ever since the 1690s. English birth or parentage became a positive advantage to aspiring city merchants, since extensive contacts in Britain were vital for commercial success in establishing relationships with reliable factors and obtaining adequate credit. By 1720 many of the richer citizens in New York were of English stock, while those of Dutch descent tended to be in the second rank so far as wealth was concerned.

A particular turning point for the entrepreneurial spirit in New York seems to have occurred in 1710; that year marked the beginning of a series of attempts, both personal and collaborative, to stimulate economic progress. Since the fur trade had been diminishing in volume, the search for a new staple got seriously under way in 1710, and the first declared object of that search became naval stores. At the same time, efforts were also made to expand the volume of manufacturing, augment the Hudson River carrying trade, and increase the colony's laboring population. Many city merchants, moreover, seem to have contracted a speculative fever in the winter of 1710–11. Silver, said Secretary George Clarke in March, "is scarcer to be met with if possible than truth and honesty." Robert Livingston had owned property in New York City since 1693, but only in December 1709 did he apply for and receive the right to engage in business there. The

Trade between Great Britain and New York
(in thousands of British pounds sterling)*

Year	Imports of New York	Exports of New York
1715	54.6	21.3
1716	52.2	22.0
1717	44.1	24.5
1718	63.0	27.3
1719	56.4	19.6
1720	37.4	16.8
1721	50.7	15.9
1722	57.5	20.1
1723	53.0	28.0
1724	63.0	21.2
1725	70.7	25.0
1726	84.9	38.3
1727	67.5	31.6
1728	81.6	21.1
1729	64.8	15.8
1730	64.4	8.7
1731	66.1	20.8
1732	65.5	9.4
1733	65.4	11.6
1734	81.8	15.3
1735	80.4	14.2
1736	86.0	17.9
1737	125.8	16.8
1738	133.4	16.2
1739	106.1	18.5
1740	118.8	21.5

timing is significant, because in 1710 Livingston's interest in provincial politics diminished as the scope of his commercial activities broadened.

---

* These figures are drawn from Richard A. Lester, "Currency Issues to Overcome Depressions in Delaware, New Jersey, New York and Maryland, 1715-1737," *Journal of Political Economy*, XLVII (1939), 203.

During Caleb Heathcote's term as mayor of New York, 1711–13, the city undertook a series of improvements designed to facilitate commercial expansion: a large bridge by the custom-house was completed, henceforth convenient for landing and shipping merchandise; the market building at the foot of Broad Street was repaired and a new one set up near the north end; Broadway was graded; and a better location was established for hiring and selling slaves. Heathcote had an abundance of schemes for entrepreneurial improvement. As he wrote to the earl of Oxford late in 1712, "I am ashamed at my being so oft troublesome to your Lordship. . . . The Occassion of It at this time is, my being not so full, & particular, in my fformer Letters relating to the Pitch & Tar designe, as I have since thought was needful."

Although naval stores eventually emerged as significant products in eighteenth-century New York, they never became a staple. Flour did instead and was well established in that role by the early 1730s. Meanwhile sugar refining also got started. There had been a refinery as early as 1689; a short-lived monopoly on refining sugar was awarded in 1725; and in 1729 the Bayard family erected, close to City Hall on Wall Street, a large building in which they worked at what they called "the mystery of sugar refining." In 1728 the Walton family established excellent shipyards; and just a few years earlier Charles Crommelin founded the Holland Trading Company, which for years conducted an extensive and lucrative business between New York and Amsterdam.

In 1723, commerce in colonial New York became the subject of an extended memorandum prepared for London officials by Cadwallader Colden, then surveyor general of the province. His report is so comprehensive and judicious as to justify including a lengthy excerpt here:

The Trade of New York is chiefly to Britain and the British Plantations in the West Indies: besides which we have our Wines from Madeira and a considerable Trade with Curacoa; some with Surinam & some little private Trade with the French Islands—The Trade to the

West Indies is wholly to the advantage of this Province the Balance being every where in our favor so that we have money remitted from every place we trade with, but cheifly from Curacoa and Jamaica, these places taking off great quantitys of Flower for the Spanish Trade. . . . But whatever advantages we have by the West India Trade we are so hard put to it to make even with England, that the money imported for the West Indies seldom continues six months in the Province, before it is remitted for England The Current Cash being wholly in the Paper Bills of this Province & a few Lyon Dollars

In the time of the last war [1702-13] when the great scarcity of Provisions happened in France, we had a very profitable Trade with Lisbon for wheat, by which several have made estates but that Trade was of no long duration, for the Distance made the carriage so chargeable, being the Ships were obliged to return empty, that the Trade could not be carried on any Longer without Loss, after wheat fell to its usual Price, tho the Wheat of America, be of greater value there than the European, and we can not hope for a return of this Trade unless such a general scarcity of Provisions happens over Europe as did then

The Staple Commodity of the Province is Flower & Bread which is sent to all Parts of the West Indies we are allowed to trade with, Besides Wheat, Pipe Staves & a little Bees Wax to Madeira, We send likewise a considerable quantity of Pork, Bacon, Hogshead Staves, some Beef Butter & a few Candles to the West Indies. The great Bulk of our commoditys in proportion to their value, is the reason we can not Trade directly to the Spanish Coast as they do from the West Indies it being necessary to employ armed vessels to prevent Injuries from the Spaniards & Pirates, but we sometimes send vessels into the Bays of Campechie & Honduras, to purchase Logwood & we have it imported from thence frequently by Strangers. This commodity is entirely exported again for England

Several of our Neighbours upon the continent can not well subsist without our assistance as to Provisions for we yearly send Wheat & Flower to Boston & Road Island as well as to South Carolina tho in any great quantity Pensylvania only rivals us in our Trade to the West Indies, but they have not that Credit in their Manufactures that this Province has

Besides our Trade by Sea this Province has a very considerable inland Trade with the Indians for Beaver other Furrs and Peltry & with the French of Canada for Beaver. all which are purchased with

English Commodity except a small quantity of Rum. As this Trade is very profitable to England, so this Province has a more considerable share in it than any other in His Matys Dominions and is the only Province that can Rival and I believe out do the French, being the most advantagiously situated for this Trade of any part of America. . . .

There is not any where a richer soil for producing Hemp than in many places in this Province—Such Land as has every year borne grain for above fifty years together without dunging in which I believe this excells all the other Provinces in North America—Our barren Sandy Lands bear great quantitys of Pitch pine for Tar, The Northern parts of the Province large white Pines for Masts; & for iron we have great plenty of that Oar in many places close by the Bank of the River where Ships of 3[00] or 430 Tons may lay their sides the ground every where covered with wood for the Furnace and no want of Water Streams any where for the Forge.*

Colden's account emphasized the colony's dependence upon foreign trade and the centrality of wheat and flour as export commodities. It was no accident that Marbletown's official seal, devised early in the eighteenth century for the Ulster County farming community, displayed two deer and three sheaves of wheat engraved upon a silver shield. Colden's report also makes clear the great necessity to New York of West Indian and non-British trade. Some representative shipping figures of tonnage cleared at the port of New York between June 24, 1715, and June 24, 1718, highlight that fact:†

Destination	Tonnage
Great Britain	4,382
British continental colonies	4,234
Newfoundland	395
British islands (West Indies, etc.)	8,776
Madeira, Africa, etc.	1,395
Non-British colonies	2,595
Europe	615

* O'Callaghan, ed., *Documents Relative to the Colonial History of New-York*, V, 685–88.

† From James Truslow Adams, *History of the Town of Southampton* (Bridgehampton, N.Y., 1918), 143.

These and other available figures should also serve to demolish one of the oldest myths about colonial commerce: the myth of a neatly triangular trading pattern. Whether one examines maritime traffic with the Caribbean, with the Atlantic coastal colonies, with Europe, or with Africa, one finds a heavy predominance of bilateral rather than geometric voyages. Between 1715 and 1765, fully 80 percent of all vessels trading to and from New York engaged in trade with only one regional area. New York benefited, moreover, from competition between various communities of English merchants. During this same half-century of 1715–65, for example, London and Bristol vied for control of the New York market, a battle that Bristol began to lose during the 1730s.

As London merchants became ever more dominant in the transatlantic trade, they often became active participants in the decision-making process with colonial businessmen, investing profits with them in joint ventures and linking them with alternative spheres of business activity. Samuel Storke's relationships with his American correspondents, for instance, were not simply those of a passive creditor (the customary view of colonial trade from an American perspective) but rather reveal a high degree of cooperation and interaction in matters of entrepreneurial initiative, credit, and investment. Most of the credit extended by Storke resulted not from some eager greed by New York merchants (and a subsequent tendency to fall behind in paying for imports), but instead from Storke's own initiative in sending consignments to colonial customers. Shipping records for the port of New York also reveal that goods of European rather than English origin comprised the largest percentage of shipments to the colony from both London and Bristol. The notorious navigation system did not protect British manufactures so much as it sheltered an extensive reexport trade.

What we do not get from Colden's detailed report, however, is a sense of the periodicity of New York's commerce or of its regional variations and local needs. We are aware of long-term shifts in export production—furs, "peltry oile," and cattle became less important after 1700; wheat, corn, and lumber became more so—but less sensitive to the seasonal ebb and flow of commercial life. Investment in privateering, for example, peaked in 1712–13, the last years of Queen Anne's War, and again briefly in 1719–20. But on the whole, the two decades after 1713 were quiet ones for privateering, a potentially lucrative source of profits that would boom again at mid-century.

There were periodic laments about lulls in commerce. "The General Complaint here is a Consumption of Trade," wrote George Clarke's private secretary in September 1721, "& your Office is not without a taste of the unhappy effect of a Languishing Commerce, business being so dull that I have not for this Six Days or more cleared a vessel or taken any money in the Office." Or, in March 1724, when Isaac Bobin reported that "we have had two very dead quarters for business . . . but hope it will be brisker." On the whole, however, these were flush years, especially for the newer industries. Soon after 1715, for instance, New York began to import tobacco for conversion into snuff— made by grinding and flavoring dried tobacco leaf—a trade that enjoyed extraordinary activity between 1720 and 1734, with peak years particularly in 1722, 1725, and 1726.

Shifting our attention to localities outside of New York City will help to give a sense of regional differentiation in the colony's first phase of concerted economic growth. On eastern Long Island, for example, whaling began to develop in the early eighteenth century. That industry, in turn, stimulated the business of barrel making for whale oil containers: four thousand were manufactured on Long Island in 1707 alone. By 1711 the Assembly decided to place a tax upon whales taken—an impost that would be politically controversial for a decade—and after 1712 Sag Harbor began to be settled. By mid-century it had become the most important port on eastern Long Island and subsequently commanded a romantic role in the history of American whaling and seafaring.

Caleb Heathcote, who became the wealthiest man of his time in Westchester County, started out with some family money brought from England in the 1690s, inherited New York City properties from a cousin in 1710, and still later inherited ten thousand pounds from his brother William. Meanwhile, he engaged in trade as a merchant and contractor, built gristmills, a leatherworking shop, a fulling mill, a linseed oil mill, and a sawmill; raised flax and hemp; speculated in real estate; and became the collector of Westchester County taxes, a lucrative post.

Adolph Philipse inherited a sizable fortune from his father, Frederick, who began as Peter Stuyvesant's carpenter, married a rich widow, bought Westchester land, operated ships, dabbled in the slave trade, and died in 1702 with some ninety thousand acres of the fertile Hudson Valley in his possession. All of these enterprises flourished under Adolph's supervision between 1702 and 1745, when he retired at the ripe age of eighty. During these years his tenant population grew from two hundred to eleven hundred and his slaves numbered twenty-three or so, a substantial group by standards of New York or the northern colonies generally. His tenants and slaves brought barley, wheat, and corn to his mills along the Pocantico River. He added bolting equipment to the gristmill operation, as well as a coopering shop for the production of barrel staves. Some of his flour went straight to New York City as it came from the mill; some was shipped to foreign ports, and much of it went to a bakery built at the Upper Mills (in today's North Tarrytown) for the preparation of ship biscuits—a firm and dry kind of hardtack that could withstand dampness at sea for an extremely long time before molding. Philipse shipped these in large quantity to New York City's maritime markets. By 1720, his prosperity blooming, Philipse doubled the size of his father's manor house, added a dairy room on the lowest level, a new kitchen, a second parlor, two new bedrooms, and an office overlooking the mill for his overseer. These were fat years for this diligent scion of inherited Dutch guilders and acres.

When the Anglo-French conflict called Queen Anne's War ended in 1713, the population of Albany County could safely expand and did so with several significant consequences. First, a

A mahogany tall case clock (96 inches high) made in New York during the second quarter of the eighteenth century. Each corner of the brass clockface is mounted with a spandrel cast in the design of a peacock amid foliage and scrolls. This clock was owned by Philip van Rensselaer of Cherry Hill, an Albany merchant. *Collection Albany Institute of History and Art.*

real estate boom developed, particularly in the decade after 1717. Second, as the area became settled and as new farms were cleared and planted, grain and lumber emerged from a subsidiary to a dominant role in the upriver economy. Third, as the locus of the fur trade moved westward, Albany merchants sought alternative and supplementary means of paying for imports, which meant increasing involvement in the West India trade. Since the Albanians imported especially from Amsterdam, it was logical and advantageous to send flour, butter, and unprocessed grain to the Dutch islands where they could obtain bills of exchange acceptable in Holland. Between 1725 and 1730, for example, Barent Sanders of Albany had seven correspondents on the six islands of Surinam, Curaçao, Jamaica, Barbados, St. Thomas, and Antigua.

During the 1720s, two Van Schaicks began shipping masts downriver. In 1726 a chocolate mill for processing cocoa appeared in Albany. The brick trade was encouraged by kiln construction in 1727. And in 1729 the first mill appeared *inside* the city limits of Albany. In 1711 there had been only thirteen sloops anchored there; by 1744 there were at least twenty-four of fifty tons burden (or more) which commuted regularly to New York City. The fur trade remained a matter of some significance; but as settlement spread, the Indians retreated northward and westward. By the 1730s and 1740s, therefore, William Johnson on the Mohawk and John Henry Lydius on the upper Hudson supplanted Albany's fur traders as determinative agents with large stakes in the peltry exchange. By 1730, when Oswego replaced Albany as the center of fur trading, Albany merchants adjusted to the loss of their monopoly by forming partnerships with erstwhile rivals in Schenectady and by diversification.

The likes of Adolph Philipse, Caleb Heathcote, and Robert Livingston were lucky to have obtained most of their broad acres before 1710. By that time much of the choicest land along the Hudson had been snapped up by greedy politicians and speculators, so the next two decades brought a comparative lull in New York's customary game of land grabbing. In 1708–9, the crown decided to regrant certain lands it had previously appropriated;

but more important, the ministry then issued instructions designed to prevent exorbitant land grants from being made in the future. New York's governors were sharply criticized for bestowing lavish gifts of forest, with no requirement of adequate quitrents and no obligation to improve or cultivate the land. Henceforth these *quid pro quos* would be attended to, the wildly inconsistent land policies of several decades past would begin to be regularized. They led gradually to augmented immigration, demographic growth, and the spread of settlement through the interior.*

The first large-scale attempt at artificial seeding of the population began in 1708, 1709, and principally 1710, when Governors Lovelace and Hunter brought with them from England more than two thousand Palatines. These hapless refugees from religious oppression and Louis XIV's wartime ravages in the Rhineland had fled to England, found neither work nor comfort there, and so became pawns in a royal scheme to populate the upper Hudson and Mohawk valleys, serving as a buffer against the French and Indians while producing naval stores from New York's pine forests. Hunter and his Council decided to locate them along the Schoharie River on land that had, unknown to them, already reverted to Mohawk Indian ownership back in Bellomont's time. Hence Hunter had to go to Albany, repurchase the land, and promise Chief Hendrick that thereafter no lands would "be bought in a clandestine manner in private from any Drunken Idle Indians."

Soon afterward, however, Hunter discovered that this stretch of land was not really suitable "for the design in hand." It had few sizable pine trees and inadequate access to navigable water. He then acquired four thousand acres from Robert Livingston on the east side of the Hudson, plus an ungranted tract of two

---

* Nevertheless, management of New York's land system did not improve efficiently or immediately after 1710. Governor Hunter (1710–19) appreciated the need for cordial relations with the landed interest in order to obtain provincial revenue; and Augustine Graham, his surveyor general, left no materials on which even to base a rent roll of the crown's domain in New York. Casualness and corruption remained commonplace.

thousand more on the west side; and here the "poor Palatines" finally settled in five small townships. Almost immediately, though, a long and disastrous dispute developed between them and Hunter. Preparing pitch pines to produce turpentine, resin, tar, and pitch was unfamiliar, distasteful work to them. They had to work, moreover, in supervised gangs. Many of their children, especially those orphaned during the stormy Atlantic crossing (470 Palatines died from a group of about 2,800), were apprenticed in Albany and other places far from the new townships, and many believed that Hunter and others had conspired to deny them their promised freeholds along the Schoharie. In 1711 they refused to work and demanded relocation. When they became mutinous, Hunter had to send sixty soldiers from Albany to disarm them. For a brief while his firmness prevailed, and some naval stores were produced. All too soon, however, Hunter's funds ran out, his credit collapsed, and the Tory ministry in London lost interest in the project. By 1712 the governor had to inform the disheartened Palatines to fend for themselves as well as they could; so they scattered in diaspora through central New York and Pennsylvania.

Other ethnic groups arrived under less tragic circumstances and had, perhaps, more permanent impact upon the colony. French Huguenots continued to come, leaving their legacy through such conspicuous families as the De Lanceys. Even more significant was the discontinuous influx of Scots and Scots-Irish. Richard Nicolls, the first English governor, was descended from Scots gentry; his master, the Duke of York, made an unsuccessful attempt to send Scottish immigrants in 1669; and Covenanters came from the Lowlands between 1660 and 1688. But the major waves washed up later: Jacobites from the Highlands, especially those transported after the abortive uprisings in 1715 and 1745; Scots-Irish Presbyterians from Ulster after 1717; and officers and men discharged from Highland regiments that had served in America, especially after 1763.

By 1720 Scotsmen and Ulstermen had penetrated into the two lower counties along the west bank of the Hudson. During the next decade they formed Presbyterian congregations at Goshen,

Bethlehem, and Monroe in Orange County and at Wallkill in Ulster County. Their numbers included Charles Clinton, an Ulster Scot who sired a distinguished American line that included De Witt Clinton. Local place names, moreover, serve as a permanent reminder of their pioneer efforts: Fort Montgomery, Campbell Hall, Burnside, Glen Spey, Ireland Corners, Glasco, New Scotland, and Selkirk. The process of anglicization in eighteenth-century New York thus began to take on a special Scottish hue, as did the provincial officialdom dominated by such figures as Robert Livingston, Robert Hunter, Cadwallader Colden, Archibald Kennedy, James Alexander, and Goldsborough Banyar.

Despite the immigration of these Scots, Palatines, and Huguenots, however, New York remained one of the less attractive Edens in eighteenth-century America. The landed class enjoyed a great deal of economic and political power. Its members preferred to lease their lands rather than sell, so would-be yeoman farmers readily chose Pennsylvania and other colonies to the south where tracts could be purchased outright. Although it is true that tenants on patented (as opposed to manorial) estates could pay cash rents and avoid supervision by the landlord as well as awkward feudal clauses requiring special services, they suffered nevertheless from many kinds of discrimination. The laws of real property protected and perpetuated the landlords' privileges. The law of inheritance prohibited the division of real property and required that estates pass intact to eldest sons. And the Assembly, comprised largely of substantial landowners, was quick to enact legislation that would reinforce insecure titles for fellow property owners. "What man will be such a fool," Bellomont asked in 1700, "as to become a base tenant to Mr. Delius, Colonel Schuyler, Mr. Livingston . . . when, for crossing Hudson's River that man can for a song purchase a good freehold in the Jersey's?" That rhetorical query would be put again and again in decades to come.

During the first half of the eighteenth century, therefore, New York lagged behind the other colonies in population growth. By 1756 it had some 97,000 persons, as compared with 220,000 in

Pennsylvania, which had been initially colonized two generations after its northern neighbor. Considering New York's
demographic history in and of itself, however, it is noteworthy
that the population more than doubled during the years that
comprised its first really generative period of economic growth.
Overall population grew from 18,067 in 1698 to 40,564 in 1723
and then moved more gradually to 73,348 by 1749. We have
significantly detailed figures from censuses taken in 1723, 1731,
1737, 1746, and 1749:

Year:	1723	1731	1737	1746 *	1749
White persons					
Men	9,083	14,610	17,393	13,922	16,898
Women	8,763	11,529	17,518	12,816	15,789
Boys†	8,500	10,243	8,347	12,938	15,457
Girls	8,047	6,673	8,238	12,806	14,612
Total	34,393	43,055	51,496	52,482	62,756
Black persons					
Men	2,186	2,932	3,551	2,893	3,317
Women	1,810	1,853	2,714	2,034	2,656
Boys	1,178	1,402	1,397	1,964	2,379
Girls	997	1,044	1,279	2,216	2,240
Total	6,171	7,231	8,941	9,107	10,592
Total of all persons	40,564	50,286	60,437	61,589	73,348

* The 1746 census does not include statistics for Albany County. Because of
the danger from French and Indians in that area, figures could not be gathered
in the countryside. It should also be noted that there are no census statistics for
the free Indians, so that this chart is not a full profile of the provincial
population. All of these data have been adapted from the much fuller (but not
entirely reliable) tables in Evarts B. Greene and Virginia D. Harrington,
American Population before the Federal Census of 1790 (New York, 1932), 96–100.

† The distinguishing age for children is unspecified in the census of 1723. It is
10 and under in 1731 and 1737, 15 and under in 1746 and 1749. The ages
selected for purposes of differentiation, as well as the shift that occurred after
the 1730s, is revealing, both about the changing threshold of the work force as
well as the attitudes of the census takers toward adolescence and the potential
age for useful employment.

One of the most significant shifts in New York's population during the first quarter of the eighteenth century concerns the number and proportion of black people. The census of 1703 reported 18,282 whites and 2,383 blacks, which means that as the century began blacks comprised more than 11 percent of the colony's population. By 1723, however, the proportion had jumped above 15 percent, and it hovered very close to that figure through mid-century. By 1771 the ratio had slipped back to 11 percent, which suggests that the most rapid growth in New York's black population occurred during the second, third, and fourth decades of the century. It comes as no surprise, therefore, that a slave market was established in New York City by 1711—the Common Council directed that slaves for hire should stand at the Wall Street market house so that inhabitants would know where to find them—and that after 1732 a duty was imposed upon the importation of slaves: forty shillings per slave from Africa, four shillings on any other. The slave trade had come to be a lucrative business as well as a considerable social problem, as will be seen in the black "conspiracies" and public hysteria of 1712 and 1741.

Between 1715 and 1767, some 4,551 slaves were imported into New York and New Jersey, but of these only 930 were African born. The vast majority came from the Caribbean, and even some of those designated as African born may have lived for a period—or been "seasoned"—in the West Indies. Despite the periodic scarcity of slaves, their prices remained relatively constant through this period: a young and vigorous male might sell for fifty pounds, a female of the same condition for forty-five pounds. Those beyond the age of forty cost at least 10 percent less and sometimes lower amounts, depending upon physical fitness. Few persons could afford to keep more than half a dozen slaves, but it was common throughout the colony to own a few for general labor. As aged slaves lost their usefulness and became expensive to keep, white owners would often free them in order to minimize the cost of maintenance. Many of the freedmen became pathetic beggars as a result and an unwanted expense to the communities.

Because some of the slaves received training in particular crafts and skills, white artisans and mechanics resented their competition, opposed the practice, and developed strong Negro-phobe tendencies. In 1737, for example, Governor Clarke informed the legislature that "the artificers complain and with too much reason of the pernicious custom of breeding slaves to trades whereby the honest and industrious tradesmen are reduced to poverty for want of employ, and many of them forced to leave us to seek their living in other countries." In short, the growing number of blacks in eighteenth-century New York was simultaneously a sign of economic vigor and psychological distress. An American dilemma began to make its mark upon the public consciousness. Private conscience, however, took longer.

Unlike the Chesapeake colonies, New York received few English convicts, if any. Some "transports" may have been shipped and misrepresented as "freewillers." But on the whole, white labor was supplied by free immigrants, indentured servants, and apprentices. Because of the periodic shortage of unbound laborers, apprenticeship became a dying institution, except as a method of education in the professions and skilled trades. Besides, the cost of maintaining a lad could barely be justified by the fruits of his labor. In 1711 New York City lengthened the minimum term of apprenticeship from four to seven years. In 1731, however, the law ceased to include any stipulation of a required term, and after 1747 there effectively ceased to be any legislation to regulate apprenticeship. It remained an available public institution simply as a means of obtaining freedom of the town by virtue of registration. Outside New York City the practice continued in vestigial but declining form until after the Revolution.

The 203 apprenticeship indentures filed in New York City between 1718 and 1727 are, however, indicative of the various tasks and trades being filled there and also, perhaps, of the proportional distribution of the work force. The indentures were distributed among thirty-nine trades: there were thirty-eight cordwainers, thirteen joiners, twelve shipwrights, ten coopers, nine barbers and wigmakers, eight blacksmiths, eight glovers, six mariners, six bakers, six felt makers, five turners, five merchants, four carpenters, four tailors, four goldsmiths, three hatters, three weavers, three printers, two tanners and curriers, two limners, two butchers, two periwigmakers, two saddlers, two gunsmiths, two sailmakers, two silversmiths, two pulley makers, one reaper, one painter, one leather dresser, one "Inginnear," one boatman, one tobacconist, one brasier, and one currier. An additional thirty were to give general service. Many of these were young girls apprenticed as domestics, given a promise by their mistresses, perhaps, that they would be taught to sew.

Because of a frequent shortage of young people entering the trades, it would appear that apprentices and indentured servants were, on the whole, reasonably well treated in eighteenth-century New York. The Dutch courts of New Netherland had established a precedent of fining masters convicted of mistreating their servants, requiring them to pay medical bills and holding them liable for civil damages. English legislation after 1664 provided less stringent controls, but the courts seem to have compensated by being remarkably sympathetic. Between 1695 and 1789, only thirty-nine cases of unreasonable correction came before the Court of General Sessions of New York County. In twenty-eight of these the complaining servants were released from their indentures, and in one the master was fined. The court found the charges unsubstantiated in only eight cases, all of which occurred after 1774. The Court of General Sessions was equally sympathetic to complaints from servants who had received inadequate food and clothing. It discharged the servant from bondage in every case except one, which was declared to be unsubstantiated. Significantly, few cases of apprehended runaway servants came before the courts of New York during the first half of the eighteenth century (though the figures began to rise in the 1750s with the onset of the French and Indian War). Completing the term of apprenticeship in New York was one way to obtain the franchise, and that may have served as an inducement to some who were otherwise discontented with their lot.

This metamorphosis from apprenticeship to citizenship suggests a much more important set of similar relationships, one for which the nineteenth century had a nice name: political economy. During the period 1710–31, as commercial growth occurred and the economy became more complex, both became intertwined in various new ways with the role of government and the political process. Patronage and partisan politics, for example, were affected by the emergence of self-conscious interest groups. In the decades after 1709, Lewis Morris, Sr., built a coalition of Hudson Valley farmers and New York City artisans along with small traders there and in Albany. To hold their support he offered the farmers better roads, cheaper money, and favorable land laws; he offered the petit bourgeois protection against imports, subsidies for local production, and restrictions against peddlers; and for the middle class generally, the burden of direct taxation would be shifted to imposts paid by the larger merchants. To counteract Morris's coalition and program, Adolph Philipse organized the wealthier merchants of New York City and Albany; gained the support of large landowners, too; and even tried to appeal to poorer freemen by promising to repeal the duties on rum, salt, and molasses.

Competing interest groups became locked in bitter conflicts over the relative merits of free trade as against protective duties, each side arguing that the position it advocated would best ensure the continuation of maximum economic growth. In 1715 New York's shipbuilders received an exemption from the tonnage tax for all vessels constructed in the colony. Thereafter special tariffs and monopolies began to appear with regularity: in 1719, for example, to help the coopers and cask makers; in 1720 to encourage sugar refining; in 1724 to promote the manufacture of lampblack. Some of these were soon revoked, either because of counterpressures from competitors or because the infant industry failed to develop with vigor and visible benefits.

By 1726 a pamphlet war was raging hotly, reaching a climax with the appearance of *The Interest of the Country in laying Duties: or, a Discourse, shewing how Duties on some Sorts of Mechandize may make the Province of New-York richer than it would be without them* and a rebuttal entitled *The Interest of City and Country to Lay No Duties: or A Short Discourse shewing that Duties on Trade, tend to the Impoverishing City and Country.* "On the Contrary," this author insisted, "the taking them off, and having trade free, would be greatly to the advantage and for the interest of both." Yet another screed followed in this contrapuntal debate, *The Two Interests Reconciled: occasioned by two late Pamphlets, called The Interest of the Country and The Interest of City and Country,* which in fact was as partisan as those it purported to reconcile. Written by Cadwallader Colden as an election appeal to the laboring class, it urged a direct tax upon land engrossers and usurers, argued the advantages of a locally built and home-owned merchant marine, and pleaded for the continuation of protective duties.

An examination of all the publications produced in New York during these two decades reveals that regulation of the economy was clearly a matter of paramount concern; for the pamphlets, books, and broadsides dealt heavily with agricultural production, whaling, the Indian trade, controlling pirates, regulating fees, the excise on liquors, complaints about New York City merchants and lawyers, as well as problems involving public currency and bills of credit. Beginning with his arrival in 1710, moreover, Governor Robert Hunter's annual messages to the Assembly stressed repeatedly the need "to provide a suitable support for her Majesty's government . . . and to restore the public credit in a great measure lost." *

Hunter really referred to two separate (albeit related) problems: first, the financial support of his government and ultimate control over public monies; and second, the need for a circulating medium of exchange sufficient to the needs of a growing economy. As to the first of these, the Assembly wanted stricter controls over the governor's salary, fees for provincial officials, long-term appropriations for government support, and the amendment of money bills by the governor or his Council.

---

* See Lincoln, ed., *Messages from the Governors,* I, 141–42, 148, 155, 163, 172.

Between 1715 and 1717 a series of compromises was worked out between Hunter and the Assembly whereby he received a five-year assurance of tax revenues in exchange for agreeing to spend funds according to a program designed by legislative leaders and also signing a naturalization bill being promoted by citizens of Dutch descent.

Thus, while the Assembly did not yet win full control over the colony's budget—that did not come until 1737-39—it did establish a very real basis for responsible parliamentary government by 1717. At about the same time, it expanded in size from twenty-two to twenty-six, gained some tactical advantages in future contests with the royal prerogative, and secured a real voice in the allocation of provincial expenditures. There were setbacks in the next decade (a decision in 1722 that all revenue must pass through the hands of crown officials; and a royal veto in 1730 of all Assembly acts passed in 1720-29 that prohibited "the selling of Indian goods to the French, or laying duties on them"); but groundwork had been laid for the final breakthroughs of the 1730s.

The second (and related) problem confronting Hunter concerned payment of public debts and the need for an adequate sum of circulating money. The provincial government had for too long been dependent upon the credit of a few private individuals, such as Robert Livingston and Peter Schuyler, for loans in time of need. Some of the largest debts outstanding were repaid by 1717, but thereafter the more pressing problem still involved issuance of paper money. New York first did so in 1709 in order to contribute toward an intercolonial military expedition "for the reduceing of Canada" and again in 1711 for a second unsuccessful attempt against the French. The ensuing provincial debt remained so vexing, however, that subsequent issues became necessary in 1714/15 and 1717 in order "to restore the public Credit, and add new Vigour to a then languishing Trade." By autumn of 1718, the Assembly asserted that its measures had been successful, since "the great Increase of the Trade and Oppulency of this Province, has been an Effect so visable of this Proceeding." Governor Hunter concurred, inform-

11 Ounces of Plate, or } (No. 679
16 Lyon Dollars,
At Two and a half *per Cent. per an.*

THis Indented Bill of *Eleven Ounces of Plate,* or *Sixteen Lyon Dollars* due from the Colony of New-York, to the Poſſeſſor thereof, ſhall be in value equal to Money, and ſhall be accordingly accepted by the Treaſurer of this Colony, for the time being, in all publick Payments, and for any Fund at any time in the Treaſury. Dated, *New-York,* the 1ſt of *November,* 1709. by Order of the Lieut. Governor, Council and General Aſſembly of the ſaid Colony.

A bill for 16 Lyon dollars from New York's first issue of paper money in 1709, printed by William Bradford. *Courtesy of The New-York Historical Society, New York City.*

ing the Board of Trade in August that "this is at present the most flourishing Province in Trade & Creditt. Our Money Bills are now at least Thirty Per Cent better than those of New England on their own Exchange, and equall to Silver all round about us."

It is especially significant, therefore, that during the period 1720–23 New York did not suffer so badly from the severe economic depression that especially afflicted Great Britain, Pennsylvania, Delaware, Maryland (which had not yet issued paper money), and New Jersey (where all previous paper currency had been retired). In 1723 Governor Burnet praised the paper money system in New York, and a year later he wrote the Lords of Trade that "this manner of compulsive credit does in fact keep up its value here and it occasions much more Trade and business than would be without it. . . . All the merchants here seem now well satisfied with it." Between 1724 and 1734 the colony issued no new paper and managed to retire some of the older issues with proceeds from taxes reserved for that purpose. In sum, New York's money was better managed, more stable, and less inflated than the currency of any other English colony for which adequate statistics are available. Here, for example, are the exchange values on one hundred pounds sterling for New York currency in this period:*

Years	Value (in pounds)
1709–11	150
1714–17	160
1723–34	165
1737–39	170
1740	160

Between 1709 and 1740 a total sum of £142,407 was issued, of which £62,653 had already been retired from circulation and canceled. The level of prices in New York in the early 1740s was slightly lower than it had been twenty years before. In addition to preventing inflation, the currency issues of 1715, 1717, and

---

* Derived from Lester, "Currency Issues," *Journal of Political Economy*, XLVII (1939), 201.

1737 had contributed mightily to economic recovery and growth. Local governments, moreover, derived extra income from the interest payments.

The years between 1710 and 1728, then, were particularly important ones for the economic development of New York. The paramount issues raised in Assembly elections of this period—1713, 1716, 1720, 1726, 1728—stemmed from relative prosperity and a growing proliferation of commercial interest groups. Even the prolonged recession that began in 1729 could not fully check a steady increase of economic activity. Peddlers and chapmen became so busy that a law passed in 1729 compelled them thereafter to have licenses and pay duties. In response to the growing volume of retail business in New York City, which required regularity and greater consideration for the needs of sellers as well as consumers, four public markets were established in 1731. Market "day," thenceforth, would occur six days in the week.

The symptoms and by-products of economic growth were manifold. Increased commercial activity required more lawyers to handle the consequent increase in litigation. The embryonic bar association formed in 1709 to regulate legal fees had become more complex and formalized by 1729. Similarly, the "law merchant" affecting commercial transactions underwent a process of secular adaptation as a barter economy gave way to one based upon credit (and therefore requiring instruments for the extension of credit). By 1730 promissory notes were in common use and legally established in New York, though they had not yet fully supplanted the traditional and more formal "writing obligatory."

The ultimate meaning and measure of commercial growth in these decades may be found in the augmentation of basic tendencies present since the founding of New Netherland: privatism and materialism. Most of the primary issues that arose—including Hunter vs. the Assembly over public credit, Hunter vs. the Palatines over their economic autonomy, Hunter vs. some Anglicans over ministerial livings and the control of valuable land, competition among factions and families for commercial benefits—were related to some sort of struggle for financial power and tangible gain. Hunter learned that he could not prevent the colony's merchants from trading illegally in the French West Indies—such was their opportunism; and such was their greed that they consistently sought a profit margin of 100 percent, whereas Boston's merchants accepted 50 percent. Moreover, much has been made of the fact that Europeans in New York frequently defrauded the Indians of their lands. That is quite true; but it should be recognized in its proper context: that whites defrauded whites, as well, with equal regularity and ruthlessness.

So long as exploitative opportunism and a bourgeois ethos ran roughshod over concern for human rights and civic consciousness, New York would remain one of the least attractive colonies to middling and lower-class immigrants. Land for farming was more readily obtainable elsewhere, especially because large tracts in the Hudson and Mohawk valleys continued to be held for speculation. New Yorkers commonly paid higher taxes than their neighbors in nearby colonies and lived in a complex economic environment of special monopolies given to selected persons, groups, and cities. In consequence an exodus of outwardly mobile *menu peuple* continued to flee the province, and it remained underpopulated by comparison with competing colonies. The frustrations attendant upon all of these circumstances became visible in the politics of the 1720s and particularly explosive in the public turmoil of the 1730s.

8

POLITICAL CHANGES AND CONSTITUTIONAL CHALLENGES

Although New York's economy underwent a striking period of growth from 1713 until 1728, its polity changed even more dramatically between the early 1720s and about 1740. Why so? First, because of major changes in personnel. Some of the leading figures in provincial politics for more than a generation past gave up the ghost (Peter Schuyler in 1724, Robert Livingston and Abraham de Peyster in 1728) and were replaced by younger men who were prominent for decades to come. Moreover, Hunter and Burnet, the able pair who governed between 1710 and 1728, were succeeded by less skillful politicians: Montgomerie, Cosby, and Clarke (1728–43). In consequence, the governor's office suffered a significant decline in quality, dignity, and effectiveness. Whereas Hunter had been astute, detached, and respected, William Burnet managed to alienate some of the colony's most powerful economic interests. Nevertheless, Burnet was at least intelligent, vigorous, and a champion of imperial needs as against the particularistic schemes of New York's fur traders. By contrast, John Montgomerie had few principles or convictions and readily sacrificed those few for political expediency. Cosby was inexperienced, ill informed, and temperamentally unsuited for the office. And the nominal appointee between 1737 and 1741, Lord De La Warr, was an absentee; so the colony had to be run by a partially compromised deputy.

A second development underlying the transformation of New York's polity was the emergence of protoparties out of the older system of chaotic, impermanent factions. Political activity became somewhat more organized and professionalized than it had ever been before. In consequence it also became a means of political socialization, with more people taking an interest and participating in public affairs. By the early 1740s, a greater degree of maturity and stability was apparent: agreement on the basic nature of the political system, willingness to work within it, plus the necessary awareness and expertise to keep that system functioning.

Central to this transformation was the sequence of constitutional controversies that arose between 1732 and 1739. Their successful resolution went a long way toward clarifying the nature of New York's constitution and giving it the shape it would hold through the remainder of the colonial period. Whereas the pivotal problems between 1720 and 1731 had involved economic issues—whether and how to reorganize the Indian trade in the north and west, governmental protection for the manufacturers and artisans vs. free trade for the landed interests and import-export merchants, the expense of frontier defense, and so forth—critical problems of the next decade seemed to be matters of first principle: the prerogatives of governors as against Council presidents; the proper authorization and jurisdiction of equity courts; the propriety of political opposition and freedom of the press; the very legitimacy of Clarke's administration; and the duration of Assembly financial support for the governor.

In order to particularize the nature of this transformation, it may be useful to juxtapose several comparable episodes. After the Assembly adjourned in 1714, Samuel Mulford published a speech he had made in which he attacked economic aspects of the majority faction's program. For so doing he was expelled by the next Assembly. In addition, Governor Hunter had him indicted for libel on grounds that the speech had accused the Morrises of acting for their own profit. Mulford was thereby remanded from one session of the Supreme Court to the next;

and Hunter would not drop the prosecution until Mulford apologized. Similarly, when Lewis Morris intemperately attacked the governor and Council in 1729, he was promptly suspended. But in 1734–35, when the famous case of John Peter Zenger occurred, popular opinion effectively permitted printed criticism, refusing to deem it libelous if true. A significant shift thus occurred between 1715 and 1735, one in which muzzling and purely partisan matters gave way to open opposition and problems involving basic principles. Resolution of the latter provided a new and firmer framework for provincial affairs between 1740 and 1776.

During William Burnet's governorship, the most enduring political controversy concerned the propriety of fur trading between Albany and Montreal. The return of peaceful relations between France and Britain after 1713 provided a boon for Albany's traders, who promptly increased their commercial activity to the north and west. After 1714 a few tribesmen from the "Far Indians" (i.e., around the Great Lakes) began coming to Albany with their pelts, and after 1716 some of the Dutch and English even began to venture westward through the Mohawk River valley in search of furs. But the Albanians basically preferred their flourishing trade with Montreal, a practice that had implications offensive to Burnet, Robert Livingston, and Lewis Morris. When furs from the Far Indians came to Albany by way of Montreal, it meant that the French were selling their goods to those Indians and thereby maintaining geopolitical influence over them. If the western tribes came directly to Albany, however, or else bought goods from Albany traders out on the lakes, English influence would presumably increase. In any case, when the British reproached the Five Nations for trading with *coureurs du bois,* the Iroquois sachems stolidly pointed out that the French obtained their trading goods from Albany anyway!

Governor Hunter had tried to curtail the Montreal trade, but without success. Burnet arrived in September 1720, determined to abolish this subversive traffic. Within six weeks Lewis Morris

had introduced a bill in the Assembly making the Albany-Mon-
treal axis illegal; it passed into law sixteen days later. It was
reinforced the next year by a law providing that anyone even
suspected of trading with New France might be tendered an
oath. All who refused would be regarded, ipso facto, as guilty.
Then, starting in 1722, Burnet extended the second prong of his
new imperial policy: he sent out trading parties with access to the
Niagara frontier. In 1725 a post was established at the mouth
of the Onondaga River—a location subsequently known as
Oswego—and in 1727 the British put a fort there.* Its presence
infuriated three major groups: the French, because it reduced
their effectiveness in that area; the Iroquois, because it lessened
their role as middlemen and violated their sense of territoriality;
and many of the Albanians, because it competed with their now
illegal trade to Montreal.

Burnet's interdiction of 1720–21 had, to some degree, encouraged English trade to the west; and, at first, his new policy
seemed successful. But the contraband commerce continued
nevertheless. Between 1723 and 1725 Burnet's critics became
more vocal and powerful, and by 1726 he had to admit the
failure of his scheme. It could not curtail the Montreal fur
runners, and so in 1726 a double tax replaced the absolute ban;
but even so, evasion continued. Burnet was transferred to
Massachusetts in 1728, and soon thereafter George II vetoed all
Assembly acts passed between 1720 and 1729 that might impede
any segment of New York's fur trade. In doing so he bowed to
lobbying pressure from English merchants trading to New York.
Never again would the province pass such legislation, and
Albanians continued to trade actively with Montreal until 1744,
when war broke out once again. Nevertheless, Burnet's scheme

---

* In 1755 it was replaced by Fort Ontario, which was rebuilt in 1759 and
regarrisoned by the British in 1782 and by the United States in 1812, 1838–44,
and 1863. It was converted to a training post in 1903–5 and used as a general
hospital in the First World War and a training camp in the Second. Since 1949
it has been developed as a historical museum property by the State of New
York. Its guardhouses, barracks, powder magazine, bastions, casemates, and
parapet crests offer an interesting vista upon the living past.

William Burnet (1688–1729), governor of New York, in´ 1726. Portrait attributed to John Watson. The fort depicted in the left background is most likely Oswego, where Burnet established a trading post and garrison. *Colby College Art Museum.*

had been a sensible one, had many admirers among his contemporaries, did cause the western trade via Oswego to develop significantly, and thereby broke Albany's long-standing monopoly over the provincial fur trade.

All of this, moreover, had significant impact both upon Albany's internal politics and on the city's situation within the balance of provincial power. Before the early eighteenth century, New York's Indian trade had been conducted under a code of regulations drawn up by the Albany Common Council and enforced by the constable and sheriff of Albany County. The Assembly paid little attention to the trade except to tax it. Beginning in 1713 and 1714, however, the Assembly passed a series of laws forbidding the sale of rum to Indians in Albany, regulating the fur trade, and gradually supplanting the city's regulations in this regard. Once again the struggle between central and local authorities would temporarily tip toward the central. For fifteen years after 1728, however, Indian affairs would become less important and less controversial. Administrative details therefore devolved back upon the Albany commissioners and the Oswego commissioner, who was responsible to them. When the Anglo-French rivalry heated up once more in the 1740s, problems arose that were far too difficult for these local officials to handle. At that point a new administrative structure had to be devised.

Meanwhile, Albany's local politics became less homogeneous and more fractious. Between 1710 and 1721 the fur traders there had dominated the Common Council, en bloc; but thereafter some of the smaller traders favored Burnet's westward scheme, while the larger and more established traders preferred their traditional ties to Montreal. Albany's commercial community lost its united front as fur traders fought with merchants and skilled artisans. Ever so slowly the balance of power swung into the hands of the latter coalition.

The diplomatic consequences were equally complex and far-reaching. Although New Yorkers might trade with the French at Oswego; and although equal duties were paid (after 1729) on goods shipped to Canada or Oswego, the French came to despise Oswego as a hamstring to their hegemony on the Great Lakes. When an opportunity occurred in 1756, Montcalm gladly destroyed the British garrison.

The Iroquois also resented Oswego, for it violated the bases of their power that had been built during the second half of the seventeenth century. They owed their success to firm control over one of the few passes in the Appalachian mountain chain. That control had given them access to both the western fur supply and the eastern markets, which in turn had helped them to acquire better armaments than their Indian rivals. Superior political organization had enabled them to use their military advantage with maximum effectiveness, and the growth of Anglo-French competition after the 1680s had given them a good bargaining position as both sides sought the Indians as auxiliaries.

By 1700 the Iroquois Confederacy had become fully aware of the risks involved in being whipsawed between the French and English. In the summer of 1701, therefore, the Iroquois signed treaties at Albany and at Montreal—treaties that initiated a new era in their foreign policy. That policy, which would endure in principle until 1795, was based upon the following strategy: peaceful relations with the Far Indians, political manipulation of neighboring tribes, and an armed neutrality vis-à-vis the French and English. The ultimate objectives, of course, were commercial profit and a balance of power between the contending Europeans. Such a policy required as much duplicity toward the Europeans as they had traditionally practiced toward the Iroquois. The measure of Iroquois success may be found in two factors throughout the first half of the eighteenth century: first, the French and English could never really be certain whether the confederacy was friendly or alienated; and second, the Europeans sought Iroquois neutrality much more often than they aspired to outright alliance. Exclusive collusion with the Indians occurred only occasionally and as a secondary tactic; it rarely endured and could not be relied upon.

The Peace of Utrecht, signed in 1713, specified that the French were not to molest members of the Five Nations (addition of the Tuscaroras in 1714 made them six) "subject to the

Dominion of Great Britain"; and the English in turn were to respect the French sphere of influence. Both sides were to have liberty to come and go as they pleased for purposes of trade, and the Indians were free to favor the French or English as they wished. But article fifteen of this treaty left it extremely unclear just which Indians were part of the English sphere and which were part of the French—a matter reserved for determination by a commission to be appointed some time in the future. The ambiguity of this article became a cause of many subsequent controversies.

One result of this situation was that Albany emerged as the principal pulse-taking place for white-Indian relations in North America. As the inhabitants of Albany stated in September 1720, "The said Five Nations are the balance of the continent of America, who if the French bring [them] over to their interest will prove the ruin of many thousand families." The first intercolonial conference concerned with Indian affairs had been held at Albany in 1684, attended by representatives from Virginia, Maryland, Massachusetts, and New York. In 1691, the crown entrusted New York's governor with responsibility for maintaining the Iroquois alliance, and additional intercolonial sessions met at Albany in 1694 (New Jersey and Connecticut joined New York and Massachusetts) and 1700 (when Pennsylvania and the Chesapeake colonies came).

The grandest of all these confabulations, however, occurred in September 1722, when delegations from New York, Pennsylvania, Virginia, and the Iroquois gathered in Albany at Burnet's behest. According to the treaty they negotiated, the Iroquois agreed not to make raids to the south but insisted, nevertheless, on freedom of travel. The Iroquois forgave the murder of some Seneca Indians by Conestogas. The most sensitive issue at stake, however, was a Virginia law that any Indian of the Five Nations found south of the Potomac or east of the Blue Ridge without a passport from some governor would be killed or banished overseas, while any southern Indian going north could be put to death by white or red men. The conference decided, rather unrealistically, that passports could be issued to no more than ten Indians at a time to go beyond the boundaries.

Although Governor Spotswood of Virginia claimed absolute sovereignty over a vast area in the king's name, he carefully avoided confronting the Iroquois with that claim. The confederacy agreed to respect Spotswood's dividing line and not cross it without his permission, but they shrewdly insisted that his division was not simply a separation between themselves and the Indians under his protection. Rather the line represented the "Frontiers of Virginia," and they thanked him for renewing the peace "as well in the behalf of the Christians as the Indians of Virginia." Once again, however, the whole problem of territorial sovereignty seemed beyond solution. Belts of wampum were exchanged and a practical pattern of traffic control agreed upon. But political supremacy and territorial rights remained for another generation to redefine.

Thus the history of New York's "foreign relations" in the century since 1626 was really a dual one. The principal object of concern to the east shifted steadily—New England in the 1620s and 1630s, England in the 1650s and 1660s, the Netherlands in the 1670s, France from the 1690s forward—while Indians to the west and north remained a constant factor and would continue to be so through the revolutionary war.

During the 1730s, when Indian relations were perhaps least problematic and pressing, New York's situation in the structure of Anglo-American politics became most visible. Being a royal rather than a proprietary or chartered colony and having a heterogeneous population that could be politically manipulated more readily than that of, say, Massachusetts or Virginia, New York had been more closely integrated into imperial schemes, such as they were, than any of England's other North American possessions. In 1709, for example, the Board of Trade made the interesting assumption that impulses to develop industries that would rival those "at home" could be controlled more easily in New York than in her neighbors. New York's officialdom was more closely tied to the British patronage system than was that of

Massachusetts, Pennsylvania, Virginia, or South Carolina; so provincial politics in New York were less self-contained than elsewhere and more subject to the vagaries of pressure from overseas. A few ranking politicians such as Lewis Morris recognized that the ultimate source of authority rested in London. When he wanted to depose Governor Cosby in 1735, Morris requested a leave of absence from the Assembly in order to nurse his "sore leg" (earlier it had been called his "politic shin") in London. He and his son stayed there for eighteen months, accomplished some of their objectives, but ultimately decided that their costly mission had failed.

In another sense, however, the decades between 1728 and 1748 were rather free and easy ones for New York in imperial affairs. There was an overall relaxation of pressure from London, an augmentation of provincial autonomy, and a consequent acceleration of political maturity. New York had no colonial agent, or official lobbyist, in England between 1730 and 1748. Because of a dearth of clearly defined issues and deserving applicants, Anglo-American politics became more personal, private, and petty. The Duke of Newcastle, who was determined to secure complete control over all American patronage, cared little about policy. So in June 1731 he selected William Cosby, a relation by marriage, to be governor and thereby set the tone for a decade. There is evidence that all but the best-informed colonial politicians did not fully comprehend the mainsprings of power overseas, and some of them understandably came to believe that the ultimate locus of power lay in the localities: in county ballot boxes, in the Assembly, and in the newspapers of New York City.

By 1739 there were many in the province who claimed for its Assembly constitutional privileges equal to those held by the House of Commons: namely, that the Assembly majority should control the administration of government, that the governor should be responsive to the legislative direction of that majority, and that the Assembly should sit as a high court to judge the misdemeanors of executive officers and interpret colonial laws. These goals had not yet been realized by 1739, but to many they seemed to be the logical blueprint for good government. More-

over, just as avant-garde voices in English politics first advocated
the legitimacy of party and of acceptable opposition during the
1730s, so too there were exponents of these newfangled phenomena in New York during the same decade. Even English
writers who were strongly opposed to the presence of parties had
to admit in 1736 that "their effect could not be as virulent as
commonly supposed, or the nation would long ago have disappeared." The same concession most certainly had to be made in
New York; and there even were a farsighted few who saw
advantages in open conflict. Although the 1740s and 1750s would
have less toleration of opposition and considerably less sympathy
for faction than for party, it is reasonable to assert that
responsible opposition had a respectable genesis, in England and
New York, during the 1730s.

As an accompaniment to this development, the role of the
royal governor underwent significant alterations. In the early
eighteenth century his office stood as the very pivot of political
life. By 1740, although the governor was still a figure of
consequence, there were also enduring issues and parties to give
public life its shape and substance. The governor's person was
less dominant, his formal and informal powers diminished. Legal
advisers to the crown decided in 1735 that the governor should
no longer participate in deliberations of the legislative council,
an activity that had given him added leverage until that time. In
1738 they decided that the governorships of New York and New
Jersey should go to two separate persons, a move that also
diminished the prestige of what had been a dual office for more
than a generation.

In addition, between 1736 and 1741 the Assembly asserted its
ultimate control over the power of the purse. New York's
executive office had been the most lucrative of all the colonial
governorships: an excellent base salary plus all sorts of perquisites and fees. Until 1736 the incumbent could expect to clear
some twenty-six hundred pounds annually from his function as
garrison commander alone. Thereafter, however, he could no
longer pocket money by underpaying the soldiers. His appropriations for trips to Albany and presents for the Indians ceased to be

automatic. In 1739 the Assembly won its fight for annual rather than long-term revenue appropriations. Thereafter there would always be a disparity between the sum suggested in the governor's instructions and the amount legislators would allow. In 1741 the Assembly eliminated Clarke's stipend for supplying the garrison and repairing the fort.

Thus the governors' salaries and fees declined over the first half of the eighteenth century, for they were caught in a tangled web involving Whitehall, the Assembly, currency inflation, and a diminished military command. Cornbury's salary in 1703 had been £1,200 sterling; Hunter's in 1715 nominally rose to £1,560 in New York currency (worth only £1,100 sterling). Between 1722 and 1753 the actual value of that salary never rose above £950 sterling, and the ancillary sources of income began to be stripped away. No wonder Archibald Kennedy, an honest placeman, remarked at mid-century that "from an Assembly . . . we have everything to dread; they have the purse on their Side, which greatly preponderates in the Balance, and will be doing (I wish I could say fairly) what every other monied Person does; that is, turn it to their own particular Advantage."

What had been developing for half a century was essentially a system of fiscal responsibility. In 1692 the Assembly had requested that the executive account for the specific disbursement of funds voted in the previous session. By 1739, salaries to public officials had to be indicated by name and individual amounts, rather than in a gross lump, a provision that constricted the governor's power of appointment; for if his appointees were unacceptable to the Assembly, their salaries would not be funded.

Quite obviously, a not-so-quiet transformation had taken place in the nature and role of the Assembly. It occurred largely in the 1720s and 1730s and was characterized in 1734 by Lewis Morris's condemnation of Cosby's administration as the reign of "a God damn ye." No governor after Hunter could safely ignore the Assembly's wishes and hope to survive. During the 1720s, that body began to be more sensitive to its electorate, more concerned with wooing votes from the uncommitted, and more given to the use of pamphleteering. Creation of a disciplined minority within the Assembly made it necessary to abandon the committee of the whole as a suitable body to discuss and develop legislation. After 1722, there would be special committees for particular bills, a sign of growing complexity in the political system. By 1727, moreover, the constitutional relationship between Assembly and governor had become better defined, for Burnet realized that he could not simply be a partisan chieftain but would have to be responsive to whichever party controlled a majority of the Assembly.

Robert Hunter had cooperated with Lewis Morris in forming a cohesive party based upon patronage, discipline, economic protection for artisans, shopkeepers, and yeoman farmers, and toleration for dissenters (especially in Queens and Westchester counties) and for Dutch descendants. By 1720 an opposition party had emerged, headed by Peter Schuyler and Adolph Philipse, dependent upon wealthy merchants, major landowners, and leading Anglicans. Each side was eager to gain control of the Assembly in order to use it for economic advantage: land grants, suitable tariffs, debt and usury bills, and the like.

When Burnet arrived, he sided with the Morris party; but being less skillful than Hunter, he alienated the opposition, especially the wealthy merchants of New York and Albany. By 1725 the Morrisites had declined in power and prestige, so Burnet was clearly in serious political trouble. The Philipse party implemented some of its policies in 1726–27 and essentially controlled the Assembly thereafter until 1733. When the Morris party went formally into opposition in 1728 (for the first time in its experience) it convulsed New York politics and drew the battle lines that would endure for more than a decade.

The words of identification used by contemporaries after 1732 were *Court* (Philipses) and *Country* (Morrisites). Each group had its leadership, to be sure, and each had a fairly distinct program. The Country party was the more provincial in orientation. It hoped to develop an indigenous economy and had a more insular view. The Court party was the more cosmopolitan. Members

Lewis Morris (1671–1746), provincial politician and chief justice, by John Watson, ca. 1738. *The Brooklyn Museum, Dick S. Ramsay Fund.*

traded more with Montreal and overseas, and they were likely to be involved in the coastal and slave trades and in Indian diplomacy on the frontier. The varied composition of both coalitions reflected the heterogeneity of the colony's economy and revealed that simple family allegiances (the substructure of politics in Leislerian times) had given way to a more mature system in which marriage alliances still mattered, but less so than economic interests, constitutional issues, and the harsh clash of personalities. As William Alexander wrote at mid-century: "Interest often Connects People who are entire Strangers, and sometimes separates those who have the strongest natural Connections."

Nevertheless, it is important to recognize that these two major parties did not comprise the whole political spectrum. There were several lesser blocs as well: a Beekman coalition in Ulster and Dutchess counties, a splinter group in Albany, and a constellation around James De Lancey that grew in luster with the passage of time. Moreover there was internal fluidity within the two dominant blocs. Their composition and sources of support shifted. As Philip Livingston put it in 1737, "We Change Sides as Serves our Interest best, not ye Countries." The Philipse group gradually became less a party of the well-to-do, and the Morrisites took on a more conservative hue by the later 1730s. Lewis Morris and James De Lancey, in fact, were ideological chameleons. Both elements were dominated by elites, both sought to manipulate the lower segments of society for partisan advantage, and both were capable of appearing either liberal or conservative as it suited their purposes.

The reasons underlying this fluidity are revealing. First, so many important issues surfaced simultaneously that a man, or group of men, might vote on one side of a constitutional question but the opposite side of an economic issue. Second, the pluralistic matrix of politics—with its class and ethnic diversity, techniques of popular appeal, and crosscutting issues—was almost too advanced for the colonists' ability to conceptualize and rationalize the changing political process. Petitions and contradictory demands on the Assembly may have placed greater strain upon legislative procedures in New York than in most of its more homogeneous neighbors. In any case, it is clear that the fact and legitimacy of opposition developed early in New York. Ever since 1664 there had been de facto opposition, that is, a majority of the population who agreed to remain and accept a government whose particular policies were not always agreeable.

Between 1733 and 1735 an episode occurred that would achieve a certain immortality as a shibboleth for freedom of the press in American history: the Zenger case. Its significance in our context, however, is that it gathered all of the aforementioned strands that had been unraveling from an earlier patchwork of politics and embroidered them into the sampler for a new one. Assembly elections in 1728 had been particularly virulent, typified by a series of newspaper "Letters to Ape" written by the Morrisites about Adolph Philipse and his followers. During the next five years, as public opinion was perceived to be an important factor in politics, campaign techniques came into their own. The likes of Lewis Morris would play to public opinion, trying to agitate and shape it. Party rallies, printed publicity in broadsides and pamphlets, pressure exerted in personal interviews, all became voguish—though with just what effect it is hard to say. Henry Beekman reported early in 1734 that "our paper war still goes on by the parties, but the people here [New York City] look only on them . . . as party affairs, and a nuisance."

In 1732 the Morrisites sided with Rip Van Dam, chairman of the Council and acting governor between Montgomerie's death and Cosby's arrival, in a dispute with Cosby over salary perquisites. When Cosby created a chancery court that would rule in his favor, Chief Justice Morris attacked the constitutionality of such a court, whereupon Cosby fired the chief justice. When a by-election occurred in Westchester County in 1733, both Morris and his son ran and won. Shortly thereafter, in November, they established an opposition newspaper, the *New-York Weekly Journal*, put out by a young printer named John Peter Zenger. The *Journal*, edited by James Alexander, heaped hosannas on the Morrisites and poured abuse upon Cosby. After the governor ordered that this scandalous sheet be burned and

Zenger arrested for libel, Cosby's new chief justice, James De Lancey, disbarred precisely those lawyers who might have given Zenger legal aid. At that point the Morrisites, masterminded by James Alexander, imported a brilliant barrister from Philadelphia, Andrew Hamilton. His strategy, worked out with Alexander, was to argue that the jury, rather than the chief justice, should decide whether the published statements were false and therefore seditious. If they were indeed true, Hamilton insisted that they could not be libelous. He then persuaded the jury that what Zenger had published was true, at which point the jury acquitted his client. The case later became a landmark in the saga of a free press for the future United States.

In fact it was less than that, for in the next two generations some comparable cases were handled and decided in the traditional manner. Nevertheless, an important precedent had been set, and Alexander's *Brief Narrative of the Case and Tryal of John Peter Zenger*, published by Zenger in 1736, became (with the possible exception of *Cato's Letters*) the most widely known source of libertarian thought in America during the eighteenth century. Thus the press had been utilized as an effective weapon in opposition to the royal prerogative, New York would never again be a one-newspaper town, and public opinion had been mobilized in politics as never before.

In 1737, a little more than two years later, the Assembly agreed to publish its division lists and reveal how its members had voted. In 1734 the Assembly had expanded in size to twenty-seven—the result of population growth—and thereby reached its mature size.* In 1736 the Council chose a Speaker for the first time and began to regain some of its former importance as an upper house. In sum, the growth of legislative power during the 1730s seemed to be directly proportional to the decline of executive authority.

The rise of legislative power at this time also coincided with an awakening and possibly an expansion of the electorate. In 1701 New York had passed an act permitting any white adult male

---

* Four more seats were added in 1773.

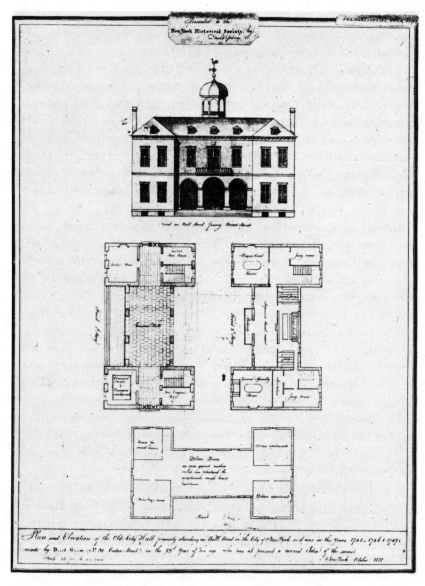

A plan and front elevation of New York's old City Hall, depicted in 1745–47. The first City Hall was constructed on the same site in 1703, and the provincial Supreme Court met here throughout the eighteenth century. Drawing by David Grim, 1818. *Courtesy of The New-York Historical Society, New York City.*

with an "estate freehold [worth forty pounds] during his life" to vote in Assembly elections. Local suffrage, unless otherwise provided for by city or borough charter, was also confined to freeholders. The size of the electorate in rural New York was roughly comparable to that in its neighboring colonies: slightly more than half of the white adult males. To compensate for the relatively inequitable distribution of land in New York, there were more leaseholds (land tenure held by virtue of a lease) that qualified as freeholds than existed anywhere else with the possible exception of Virginia.

In New York City and in Albany the freemen were those merchants, artisans, and laborers who had been admitted to freedom of the town by the municipal corporation—a status rather generously bestowed. Freemen could vote in municipal and provincial elections, like freeholders, and could hold municipal office as well. Although one could purchase citizenship by literally buying freemanship, a decree of the New York Common Council in 1703 had admitted gratis those "that are poor and not able to purchase their Freedoms." There were, in addition, persons admitted as "Registrants": those who, by virtue of birth or citizenship, merely had to have their names recorded on the rolls and pay nominal clerical fees. Significantly, between 1735 and 1740 three times as many persons registered for freemanship as purchased it.

Just as important as the question "Who could vote?" were two related queries: "Who did vote?" and "How frequently?" In 1733 it appears that 33 percent of those eligible did actually vote. In 1735 the proportion rose to 55.4 percent and in 1761 to 56.1 percent. In 1737, a hotly contested election year, votes by Jewish inhabitants were disallowed as the result of an anti-Semitic appeal, and for about a decade thereafter Jews were officially disfranchised.

That election of 1737 had a very positive attribute, however. It marked the beginning of regularity in Assembly elections. Previously they had occurred at irregular intervals—1716, 1726, 1727, 1728, and 1737—on the death or accession of a king or some other special occasion. In 1734 the Assembly sought a measure establishing elections every three years on a regular basis. The Council blocked the bill, and the lower house revived it in 1737. But in 1743 a Septennial Act was approved which regularized colonial elections thereafter at intervals no greater than seven years. In fact they would occur in 1743, 1745, 1747, 1750, 1752, 1759, 1761, 1768, 1769, and 1775.

Between 1720 and 1731, the major issues in public life had involved economic affairs, Indian relations, and factional organization. Between 1732 and 1741, however, the great questions were constitutional in nature: (1) the salary payments to an absentee governor; (2) the propriety and proper jurisdiction of chancery courts; (3) the right of opposition, the limits of censorship, and freedom of the press; (4) the proper grounds for removing a governor; (5) the legality of Clarke's administration; (6) the proper duration of financial support voted by the Assembly; and (7) the right of artisans to take concerted action to improve their lot. Gradual resolution of these matters over a decade left New York's constitution much more clearly defined than it had ever been before. The provincial judicial system would also undergo alteration and rationalization at this time with far-reaching consequences for the society and its sense of stability.

A few of these constitutional and administrative changes had begun in the 1720s. In 1721, for example, with the appointment of Francis Harison as an admiralty judge, that position ceased to be held concurrently by the colony's chief justice, thereby diminishing the practice of plural officeholding. In addition, the vast admiralty district that had included New York, New Jersey, and all of New England (save New Hampshire) ever since 1697 was divided so that New York, New Jersey, and Connecticut comprised a discrete unit after 1721.

Then, in 1727–28, a court case known as Philipse vs. Codrington caused particular resentment against unethical conduct by some lawyers and greedy practices by officers of the Court of Chancery. In consequence a special review committee of the Council established the first Committee on Grievances in the

Practice of Law in New York. Its area of concern included abuses in the drawing of legislative bills, excessive delays in adjudication, and unnecessary expense and irregularities in proceedings. Unfortunately the committee was never as effective as its proponents anticipated or hoped. Many complaints were lodged with it; but its composition changed too often and it lacked sufficient leverage to be truly effective.

Early in 1731, there were indications that lawyers might gain a still more advantageous position. New York City's new charter that year left the traditional Mayor's Court intact but established a lucrative monopoly for a small coterie of seven lawyers. There were at this time about fifty-five attorneys practicing in the colony, and more made their appearance during the 1730s. After a buildup of resentment and a political struggle in the early 1740s, the monopoly was finally broken in 1746 by a special act of the Assembly.

Meanwhile, the single most recurrent theme in the extensive papers of James Alexander—and certainly one of the major developments of the 1730s and early 1740s—was the need for a "constitutionally established" judicial system. The emergence after the 1720s of a substantial group of trained barristers helped to bring about a considerable modernization in New York's system of legal administration. Major authorities on international law, such as Grotius's *De jure belli ac pacis* and Pufendorf's *De jure naturae,* began to be cited in arguments as early as 1729. Acts passed in 1732 provided special machinery for the trial of slaves and for the summary trial of offenses below the degree of grand larceny whenever the accused could not post bail. There is evidence by 1733 that the practice of law in New York did not lag much behind that of England in adeptness at dealing with common-law precedent. The adroit handling of the Zenger case in 1735 as compared with the cruder Bayard trial in 1702 demonstrates the rapid professionalization of the colonial bar within a generation.

Although the Morrisite party has received adequate recognition from historians for its role in supporting John Peter Zenger, what has not been sufficiently noticed is that the Morrisites mounted a broad-gauge campaign for constitutional and judicial reform during the mid-1730s. In 1734 they sponsored bills to regulate the appointment of sheriffs, to control prosecution costs, and to permit the lower house to appoint an agent in London. During the next year they championed not only freedom of the press and the right of juries to consider points of law (as well as fact) but also the principle that judges must accept the jury's verdict, that judges should have tenure during good behavior (rather than at the pleasure of the crown), and that the taking of court fees be regulated. Until 1737 the Morrisites continued to sponsor reform bills: for frequent Assembly elections, for the regulation of election procedures, and to clarify the jurisdiction of courts by statute. All of these attempts were offered in order "to preserve men from oppression." Although they were not all implemented at that time, they did establish a new consciousness of constitutionalism and an awareness of administrative reform.

No problem seems to have been more volatile at this time than the existence and jurisdiction of chancery courts. The issue was essentially this: did the governor have a constitutional right, by virtue of his royal commission (which contained the power to erect and create courts for hearing all causes according to law and equity), to erect by ordinance a court of chancery consisting of the governor and his Council, or even the governor alone? Hunter had established one in 1711 (also called a court of equity), and Burnet had strengthened it between 1720 and 1726. The Assembly mounted a serious challenge in 1727, however, thereby precipitating a major political crisis; and consequently Governor Montgomerie did not serve as chancellor during his regime (1728–31).

When Cosby filed suit against Rip Van Dam in 1732–33, he established a special court of exchequer and thereby aroused immense popular hostility. The fundamental tension involved prerogatives of the crown as against the felt need for institutions responsible to society. A complicated controversy involving disputed land along the Connecticut border, the Oblong case, kept the chancery issue alive until Cosby's death in 1736 and on into 1737, when the Assembly made its final protest. For a while the issue became dormant although unresolved. After 1750, the chancery court emerged relatively unchanged, handled a good deal of litigation, and continued to function until 1775.

No one had really objected to the use of equity law per se (as opposed to reliance upon legislative statutes and the common law). The dispute that raged on and off between 1727 and 1737 concerned the manner in which courts dispensing equity would be constituted. The crown insisted upon a narrow, prerogative basis for authorization, whereas the colonists called for legislative consent. In practice, chancery courts had too often been used as devices for the collection of royal quitrents, though admittedly they also became a convenient rallying point and rhetorical scapegoat for the Country party. While partisan politics raged during the 1730s, chancery courts would be an issue, and in the autumn of 1736 some contemporaries genuinely believed that the province was on the "verge of civil war." Lieutenant Governor Clarke was an appeaser, however; the strife began to die down after the election of 1739, and chancery courts became an accepted instrument of justice.

The significance of the 1730s for the history of judicial administration in New York, then, is not that so many fundamental issues were finally resolved, but rather that they could be raised with impunity and become for a decade the very stuff of politics. The tumultuous year 1741 gives ample evidence that equal justice for the *menu peuple* had not yet arrived. Two so-called conspiracies were prosecuted in that year, and neither does much credit to the Anglo-Saxon tradition of impartial proceedings.

The pertinence here of New York's slave "revolt" of 1741, which will be more fully examined in a later chapter, has to do with its attendant mass arrests and accusations, entailing an extended period of trials and punishments, lasting more than a year, in which 150 slaves and 25 whites were jailed, 18 slaves and 4 whites hanged, 13 slaves burned to death, and more than 70 transported to the West Indies. Testimony taken before the Supreme Court suggests a pattern of terror and intimidation in which blacks were offered pardons only for "telling the truth,"

which really meant confessing and implicating others. Denials
and professions of innocence went unheeded. The magistrates
succumbed to popular hysteria, Negrophobia, and anti-Catholicism. Conflicting and contradictory testimony was ignored,
attempts were made to discredit witnesses when necessary,
crucial questions of fact remained unanswered (Where had the
plotting been done? Who were the leaders? How had marginal
"conspirators" been brought in? By what means were confessions
extracted?). Two slaves, for example, were bound at the stake
with faggots lit while their "confessions" were being recorded. In
this manner the state "proved" the existence of a seditious
conspiracy.

On April 20, 1741, the *New-York Weekly Journal* reported that
"last Week there was a general Combination of the Bakers not to
Bake, because Wheat is at a high price, which occasioned some
Disturbance, and reduced some, notwithstanding their Riches, to
a sudden want of Bread." News of this strike apparently
unnerved a city already tense over numerous fires, robberies,
rumors of racial homicide, and rapidly rising food prices.
Consequently an agreement among bakers not to work until city
authorities raised the price of bread was prosecuted as a criminal
conspiracy. That no convictions were obtained, even though
there existed precedents in Anglo-American law for such a
prosecution, may counterbalance in small measure the brutal
punishments meted out in the "Negro Plot"; but it also suggests
that white "lawbreakers" were treated less harshly than black
"lawbreakers" and stands, like the Zenger case, as an ambiguous
benchmark. Labor strikes did not suddenly become legal after
1741; but a precedent had been established, and future "combinations" would be more common as a result.

It is not easy to summarize the political changes and
constitutional challenges of the 1720s and 1730s. Despite considerable instability and upheaval, despite contradictory allegiances
to family groups and economic interests, despite the intersection
of ethnic and class conflict, there were nevertheless marked
continuities in the political alignments of that era. Moreover,

those alignments cut across class and ethnic lines and gave rise to significant constitutional issues whose discussion signaled a new maturity in the public consciousness of New Yorkers.

By the early 1740s, certain trends were beginning to surface with some clarity: the law, the courts, and the administration of justice would require further attempts at rationalization and adaptation to provincial needs; social diversity required institutional heterogeneity, such as church establishments in some counties but not others; self-interest would be more determinative in politics than family, class, or even ethnic identity; localism and parochialism would give provincial affairs a peculiar cast, for few persons had any sense of the province as a whole. New York was more of an artificial designation than a conscious, cohesive entity; for residents of Suffolk County, Manhattan Island, Marbletown, and the Mohawk Valley had little in common.

The third and fourth decades of the eighteenth century were years of political awakening and modernization in New York. The meaningful changes largely affected elite groups and took the form of altering power relationships among executive, legislature, and courts. There still remained a great deal of social deference and political indifference, however, as William Smith, Jr., observed as late as 1756 when he remarked upon "that torpor which generally prevails when [the multitude] are uninfluenced by the arts and intrigues of the restless and designing sons of ambition."

The two decades after 1756 would bring to fruition seeds planted during the 1720s and 1730s. Political techniques and organizations would flourish, the lesser segments of society would be brought into still fuller participation, and the interaction of social groups would become as problematic as institutional relationships had been in the days of Lewis Morris, Adolph Philipse, and William Cosby. Once the role of governors, assemblies, and courts had been clarified, however, men might turn their attention elsewhere; and they soon did.

9

SECTS AND THE STATE IN
A SECULAR SOCIETY

The spiritual life of eighteenth-century New York underwent permutations that reveal a great deal about social change in an ever more secularized society. The causes and consequences of those changes are to be found in the interaction among sectarianism, the state, and the inevitability of accommodation in an unusually heterogeneous province. Regardless of which denomination is examined, the story is roughly the same: slow growth, insufficient clergy, inadequate funds, conflicts with the governor and Assembly, theological conservatism, internal schism over pietism, fluidity across congregational lines, and, ultimately, the emergence of toleration and a kind of ecumenical "civil religion." These themes recur among problems of church and state, attempts to spread the gospel through missionary work, controversies pitting formalists against evangelicals, and tendencies toward "americanization" among the Dutch Reformed, French Protestant, Jewish, and Lutheran denominations.

Residents and visitors alike agreed that piety had not been a prominent aspect of provincial life. "A great complaint was made to me," George Whitefield wrote in 1740, "by some of the most serious inhabitants . . . that a work of God had never been carried on in [New York], since its first settlement." When Henry Melchior Muhlenberg preached in New York City in 1751, he raised a series of fundamental issues "but addressed the questions to myself in catechetical form, for I have observed among the listeners a great ignorance of and blindness to the most essential, basic truths, because for so many years they have been sustained with non-essentials, speculations, and polemical disputations and thus have been more driven away than gathered together."

Although Muhlenberg was invited to fill the Lutheran pulpit in New York City in 1751 and again in 1752, he decided against taking it permanently, thereby repeating a symptomatic pattern cut by Jonathan Edwards in 1723 and continued by the Presbyterian Joseph Bellamy in 1754. On the whole, New York's churches could not lure or keep clerics of high theological ability and aspiration. New England, New Jersey, and Pennsylvania remained far more attractive to men of the cloth; and therein lies a significant ingredient of New York's secularized nature. The quality and quantity of its clergy was, for the most part, undistinguished and inadequate. Most of them were educated and ordained elsewhere—at Harvard or Yale, in England or on the continent—and therefore lacked roots in the indigenous communities. Few of them ever gave sermons sufficiently significant to be publishable; and the best of them, such as Gualterus du Bois (Dutch Reformed minister in New York City, 1699–1751) or Ebenezer Pemberton (Presbyterian minister there from 1726 until 1753), have scarcely become memorable figures in American church history.

There were at any given moment a great many churches without regular pastors. Some congregations saw an ordained minister only three or four times each year; and so the paucity of numbers, along with the lack of intellectual distinction, contributed to the secularization of New York society.* The process was circular, to be sure: because the communities were socially diverse and grossly materialistic, quality clergymen could not be

---

* Church buildings were commonly in disrepair, and funds were not available to improve them; rural parishes covered vast expanses of wilderness; countless arguments occurred over legal title to church lands and their proper boundaries.

The Reverend Gualterus du Bois (1671–1751), Dutch Reformed pastor in New York City, 1699–1751. Portrait by John Wollaston, ca. 1751. *The Minister, Elders, and Deacons of the Reformed Protestant Dutch Church of the City of New York. Photo by Elmer Ansley.*

readily attracted; because the clergy remained undistinguished and pulpits vacant, the society became even more secularized.

Still another result was the development of a dualistic pattern among New York's churches. Their regular clergy tended to be conservative and therefore opposed to such evangelical visitors as Theodorus Frelinghuysen and George Whitefield. Nevertheless, these vigorous preachers attracted a modest following of their own in the colony, so that religion in New York tended to be either orthodox and formulaic or else heterodox and pietistic. There was relatively little of what one might call liberal or rationalistic religion in between.

Yet another dualism emerged during the middle third of the eighteenth century: a sharp contrast between urban and rural environments, with differential impact upon religious life-styles. Countryfolk saw ministers less often and seem to have had a different manner of responding to visitors. In Rhinebeck, Henry Muhlenberg found that the people "are accustomed to judge a strange preacher by his physical health and strength; they insisted upon hearing some conversation and answers to their questions." In New York City, however, refined citizens required more attention to rhetoric and to proper appearances. On Pentecost in 1751, for example, Muhlenberg observed that "here in the city I must bestow greater pains upon the English language than I did in the country because here the ears are more *delicate* and also because the English congregations have more *delicate* orators." A few days later he remarked that "when I am at home in my country congregations I have to get along, just like other peasants, with clothing which my wife spins and sews for me, as necessity teaches us to do. I would not dare to appear in such apparel here, however, unless I wanted the children on the streets to laugh at me behind my back." When he saw du Bois's personal library, manuscripts, and extensive notes on Scripture, Muhlenberg felt that "those preachers are fortunate who have time during the week properly to meditate upon their sermons and write them out," unlike the rural itinerants who "too often have to study and meditate in the saddle on horseback."*

The provincial clergy, urban and rural alike, was not very well paid; as William Smith, Jr., the colony's foremost historian, put it in 1756: "It is true they live easily, but few of them leave any thing to their children. The Episcopal missionaries, for enlarging the sphere of their secular business, not many years ago attempted . . . to engross the privilege of solemnizing all marriages. A great clamour ensued and the attempt was abortive." As early as 1704, the Society for the Propagation of the Gospel, overseas arm of the Church of England, had appealed to the Lords of Trade and Plantations for financial support, particularly for its two new missionaries in New York: "The said Gentlemen [are allowed] 100£ per annum each, over and above which they will have 20£ a piece to buy them utensils for the little Caban they are supposed to have among the Indians, and 10 or 15£ for books etc. . . . the Society having done so much . . . they would gladly know what assistance they may expect in an affaire, that does at least as much concerne the State as the Church." Their lordships' reply was less than encouraging, for it offered little more than moral support plus the small sum already established for transporting Anglican ministers to America. They ordered Secretary William Popple "to acquaint you that her Majesty does allow £20 a piece to all Ministers going to the Plantations for their passage; that they are of opinion it will be a great incouragement to such Ministers if they can be assured of a Benefice in England after so many years service (as may be thought reasonable) among the Indians."

The financial relationship between church and state *within* New York was even more delicate. As we have seen, the Ministry Act of 1693 had effectively established the Church of England in four downriver counties: New York, Richmond, Queens, and Westchester. Although it referred only to "good sufficient Protestant" ministers, its interpretation and enforcement by the governors meant that tax assessments against all ratepayers

---

* These quotations are drawn from a priceless source for the spiritual life of New York in the middle of the 18th century, *The Journals of Henry Melchior Muhlenberg*, 3 vols. (Philadelphia, 1942–58), I, 248, 279, 280, 283.

would be used for salaries given to Anglican incumbents. Disputes over the nature and meaning of this law endured with intensity, especially between the governor and the Assembly, throughout the 1690s. By the turn of the century, however, executive authority and Dutch Reformed accommodation resulted in a compromise of sorts that was highly favorable to the Anglican minority in these counties. In 1697 Governor Fletcher granted a corporate charter to Trinity Church, thereby legally establishing it in New York City. The Reformed congregation continued to enjoy an exemption from supporting Trinity as well as the privilege of raising funds to pay its own pastor. The Dutch church thus enjoyed a special status above all other dissenters and therefore continued to give anomalous assent to an Anglican establishment. Being number two in a British royal colony was clearly preferable to being merely one among many subordinate nonconformist sects.

When the Assembly adopted a bill in 1699 for the support of *all* Protestant ministers in New York, Bellomont had it defeated in Council. His instructions did not allow him to accept any measure that might jeopardize the special status of the Church of England. Dissenters did, however, obtain one concession in 1699. A bill went through that allowed towns to raise funds from general taxation for building and repairing meetinghouses. That act could be construed to permit construction of dissenting churches at public expense. So, by 1700, nonconformists in New York at least enjoyed the privilege of public worship in churches, and with ministers of their own choosing. In effect, the colony's ecclesiastical solution for its pluralistic society was state support according to local option, plus a special requirement in the four lower counties that dissenters there also pay taxes to aid an embryonic Anglican establishment.

It was not the best of all possible arrangements for anyone, actually, and would cause periodic flare-ups. Between 1702 and 1708, Cornbury consolidated a number of triumphs for Church of England zealots. In 1704 he forced the Assembly to accept Trinity's corporate charter. He filled vacant parishes with Anglican clerics, even jailing the competition in order to do so.

He encouraged activity by the Society for the Propagation of the Gospel and tried to suppress public preaching by unlicensed itinerants. He also, however, left a bitter legacy of unrest as well as unresolved disputes in particular parishes.

Jamaica parish in Queens County, for example, consisted largely of Presbyterians who had been accustomed to maintaining their own minister with town taxes ever since 1665. They were determined not to allow Anglican control over their new church, and they even rioted in 1704 in order to regain possession of it by force. Cornbury's high-handed tactics temporarily won the day, and the Anglicans took over. But the bitter issue resurfaced in 1710, again between 1716 and 1719, during the 1720s, and once more in the 1760s. Inhabitants of Jamaica refused to pay the salary of an Anglican incumbent and brought suit to repossess their own building. They lost the battle in 1719, won in 1732, and lost in 1768; but they won the war, in a sense, because they steadily stirred up public opinion against the Anglicans and thereby helped to prepare the populace for total separation of church and state.

Cornbury's successors tended to be less zealous and were inclined to respect the rights of an acquiescent Dutch Reformed plurality. In consequence there was a period of comparative calm between about 1710 and 1750, a period in which Anglicans were less militant, the dissenters increased in numbers, and toleration became prevalent on an ad hoc, expedient basis. It is true that a law passed in 1712 effectively tightened up taxing provisions of the Ministry Act by setting harsher penalties for vestrymen who failed to do their duty promptly; and it is true that there were outbursts of hostility between Anglicans and nonconformists: at Brookhaven in 1719 and at Newburgh in 1743, for example. But these were relatively isolated and infrequent. The serious tensions between 1710 and 1750 occurred *within* rather than between denominations.

Much of the divisiveness among Anglicans was due to the acerbic personality and conservatism of William Vesey. Born in Braintree, Massachusetts, he graduated from Harvard in 1693, preached on Long Island from 1693 until 1695, was ordained by the Church of England in 1697, and was then inducted at Trinity Church in New York City. After Cornbury's departure, Vesey became involved in a series of fierce controversies with royal governors and other officials over the rights vested in Trinity and its rector, over the rector's salary, over use of the fort chapel for services, over the Presbyterians' cause in Jamaica, and over land grants. From 1714 until his death in 1746, Vesey served as the Bishop of London's commissary, or agent, in New York and New Jersey. As such he became a great advocate of Anglican prerogatives, tried to prevent evangelicals such as Whitefield from preaching in New York, and provoked such publications as *To the Reverend Mr. Vesey and His Two Subalterns, viz. Tom Pert the Beotian, and Clumsy Ralph the Cimmerian*, printed by John Peter Zenger in 1732.

Vesey's biggest battle, perhaps, occurred with Robert Hunter; it demonstrated for all to see that the Anglican interest in New York was anything but monolithic. Hunter called meetings of the clergy without bothering to notify the testy Vesey and drew off some of Vesey's disaffected parishioners from Trinity to the fort chapel. Vesey lacked sufficient leverage in London to have Hunter removed from office, but he did make life miserable for the governor in 1712 and 1713. Hunter complained to Jonathan Swift that he was "used like a dog" and had "spent these years of life in such torment and vexation that nothin in life can ever make amends for it."

After 1716 a disagreement developed among the Anglicans over how best to promote the Church of England in New York. Gradually the tolerationists came to prevail over the zealots. Caution and conciliation became the dominant Anglican policy for a generation and in a curious way contributed to the development of a civil religion in New York. Governors felt free to write about theological and ecclesiastical matters,* while

---

* See *By His Excellency Robert Hunter, Esq. . . . A Proclamation: Considering that True Religion and Piety are the Only Firm Foundations. . . .* (1711) in Evans, comp., *American Bibliography*, no. 1523; and William Burnet, *An Essay on Scripture-Prophecy; Wherein It Is Endeavoured to Explain the Three Periods Contain'd In the XIIth Chapter of the Prophet Daniel* (1724), in Evans, comp., *American Bibliography*, no. 2509.

ministers commonly gave sermons on political subjects and commented upon politics from the pulpit. Henry Muhlenberg, moreover, noted in 1751 that "it is customary and necessary for a preacher who comes to New York to visit the supreme authorities of the government and present his credentials," a custom that brought that cleric into a lengthy interview with Chief Justice James De Lancey.

This tendency toward secularized civil religion involved the invocation of divine help on behalf of the state, the proclamation of thanksgiving days, and even an official *Form of Prayer . . . to Be Used in the Churches Throughout the Province . . . for a General Fast and Humiliation: To Implore the . . . Divine Blessing on His Majesty's Arms, By Sea and Land, Especially Those Employed More Immediately for the Security of These Colonies.* It reached a culmination of sorts during the French and Indian War. Theodorus Frelinghuysen the younger, also a Dutch Reformed minister, preached in honor of the Albany Treaty (1754) and on the occasion of *Wars and Rumors of War, Heaven's Decree Over the World* (1755). Special prayer forms were decreed in 1757, 1758, and 1762. Abraham Keteltas preached about *The Religious Soldier* (1759), Ebenezer Prime addressed *The Importance of the Divine Presence with the Armies of God's People in their Martial Enterprises* (1759), Chauncey Graham delivered *A Sermon Against Profane Cursing and Swearing . . . to the New-York Forces in their Camp* (1761), and Joseph Treat offered *A Thanksgiving Sermon on The Glorious News of the Reduction of Havannah Preached at the Presbyterian Church in New York* (1762).*

Attempts at spreading the gospel among the heathen in New York grew by fits and starts during the first half of the eighteenth century. Both Cornbury and Vesey cooperated with the S.P.G. after 1701 in providing missionaries and teachers and in establishing a charity school under Trinity's auspices. Elias Neau, a Huguenot refugee of saintly character, abandoned a successful career in commerce in order to become the S.P.G.'s catechist in New York. From 1703 until his death in 1722 he

---

* See Evans, comp., *American Bibliography*, nos. 7199, 7421, 7888, 8120, 8383, 8473, 8865, 9111, 9287, 41157, 41159 [Bristol, *Supplement*, nos. 2166, 2168].

worked with slaves in the city, teaching them literacy and Christianity—largely at night when their masters' work was done—despite opposition from whites who feared that educated slaves would be more rebellious. Although Neau disavowed any abolitionist beliefs, the number of his pupils declined until the Assembly, at his request, decreed that the legal status of a slave would in no way be altered by his evangelization!

In April 1712, another sort of problem threatened the existence of Neau's school. During the night of April 6/7, some twenty-five slaves gathered at an orchard where they had previously concealed weapons. After setting fire to a nearby outhouse, they took cover behind some trees and awaited the response. An alarm roused the city's white citizens; and when they rushed to the scene, the conspirators killed nine of them and wounded seven. Whites who escaped warned the garrison, the slaves dispersed, and the next day New York's militia captured all of the insurrectionists except for a few who killed themselves rather than be taken. Twenty-seven slaves were tried for conspiracy as a result; twenty-one of them were convicted and executed.

A great deal of the anxiety that followed took the form of hostility toward Neau's school. Although only two of the condemned slaves were his students, and one of them was subsequently exonerated, there were demands that the catechist cease his work. The Common Council prohibited any black from being out at night without a lighted lantern obtained with his master's consent. Neau's classes declined, consequently, and in 1718 he temporarily lost his appointment. He was reinstated in 1719, however, and after his death in 1722 his successor, William Huddleston, reported that "swarms of negroes come about my door . . . asking if I would be pleased to teach them and build on Mr. Neau's foundation."

Succeeding catechists, such as James Wetmore, Thomas Colgan, Richard Charlton, and Samuel Auchmuty, continued to teach the city's blacks. Huddleston also enjoyed great success as the S.P.G.'s schoolmaster for Dutch and French children in the city. By 1715 he had taught 650 of them to read and write

English. In 1718 he had 50 students learning literacy and the catechism. One result would be a steady flow of Dutch descendants into Trinity Church and the two Anglican chapels in New York City.*

Neau had originally hoped to bring the gospel to red men as well as black; but like most of the early S.P.G. missionaries, he became disenchanted with the prospects for success among the Indians. As he wrote in 1705, "God would sooner bless the works of pious persons who employ themselves at this work [i.e., catechizing blacks] than to run up in the woods after miserable creatures who breath nothing but blood and slaughter. . . . In a word, they are people who have nothing but the figure of men."

The Iroquois were not unreceptive to Christianity, but their (perhaps intentionally) whimsical understanding of Western ways and European power made them frustrating creatures for self-righteous proselytizers to handle. Here is the report of one S.P.G. missionary, John Talbot, late in 1702: "I have baptized several persons. . . . Even the Indians themselves have promised obedience to the faith. . . . 5 of their sachems or kings told [Cornbury] . . . they did not admire at first what was come to us, that we should have a squaw sachem vizt a woman king [Queen Anne], but they hoped she would be a good mother, and send them some to teach them religion, and establish traffic amongst them that they might be able to purchase a coat and not go to church in bear skins."

Most of these early missionaries came to feel, as Neau did, that the Indians were barbaric and alcoholic, would soon disappear, and were therefore a waste of time. Moreover, white "heathens" needed help more than red ones. As the Reverend Thoroughgood Moore wrote in 1705, " 'Tis from the behavior of the Christians here that they [the Indians] have had and still have their notions of Christianity, which God knows has been and generally is such that I can't but think has made the Indian hate Christianity."

A missionary located at Mohawk Castle in 1713, William Andrews, did not favor teaching English to the Indians because

---

* See Evans, comp., *American Bibliography*, nos. 1740, 3297, and 3615.

that would enable them to converse with whites "and so to learn their vices." Andrews's duties included preaching and baptizing, as well as preparing translations of Scripture and liturgy for publication in the Mohawks' language. He encountered interference from fur traders, French competition from Canada, and the problem of teaching theology to adults in a language he did not himself know well. Andrews made relatively little progress, gave up in 1719, and left the Albany area. At that he fared better than his successor, the Reverend Thomas Barclay, who went mad in 1722: "Of late many misfortunes successively attending him have at length brought him to an outrageous distraction such as obliged his friends to confine him to a dark room."

Whether or not missionary work among the Indians was worthwhile remained a controversial question through succeeding decades. The Reverend John Miln, who succeeded Barclay at the Albany station, informed William Vesey in 1732 that it was crucial to have missionaries fluent in Mohawk. Otherwise ideas had to be conveyed "by the means of an interpreter whose immoral life contributes to lessen the impression of his dictates." In 1742 Dr. Henry Stebbing gave the S.P.G.'s annual sermon and asserted that the society's primary objective should be the salvation of white souls; "the Converting of Heathens is a *secondary, incidental* Point."

Between 1749 and his death in 1774, Sir William Johnson pressed for Christianization, and in 1752 the S.P.G. decided to concentrate its efforts upon the younger Iroquois. Even so, the same cynicism that had been evident for half a century continued to prevail. John Ogilvie, the Anglican missionary at Albany from 1750 until 1763, reported in 1752 that "the generality of the professors of Christianity who have any considerable dealings with the Indians by their conduct give the most convincing proof that they regard them only . . . to promote their secular interest." By 1760 a strong sense of failure prevailed. Ogilvie wrote to London about French Jesuit successes all through the Ohio and Mississippi valleys and wondered "how ought we to blush at our coldness, and shameful indifferences in

the propagation of our most excellent religion? The Harvest truly
is great but the labourers few."

If the "harvest" among Indians and blacks never really
achieved its potential in New York, it was not appreciably richer
among the white communities either. Pietism was introduced to
the colony early in 1720 by Theodorus Jacobus Frelinghuysen,
then a twenty-eight-year-old Dutch Reformed clergyman from
Germany who had been called to serve the Raritan Valley
communities of northern New Jersey. He stopped in New York
City on his way to the Raritan and, at the invitation of his
pastoral colleagues, preached to the congregation. Then, and on
subsequent visits during the quarter-century that followed, he
made innovations in manner and message offensive to more
traditional clerics and parishioners. He emphasized spiritual
regeneration, seemed to advocate doctrinal deviations, omitted
the Lord's Prayer, refused to perform the baptismal rite,
reportedly displeased "his audience with his howling prayers,"
and even had the audacity to criticize the senior pastor, du Bois,
for indulging in the luxury of having a mirror in his home.

Through the 1720s and 1730s, Frelinghuysen became the focal
point of conflict within the Dutch Reformed denomination. His
opponents in New York, led by the deeply conservative pastor
Henricus Boel, published a formal complaint against their
evangelical enemy in 1725. The 146-page *Klagte* threatened
excommunication but had little actual effect upon Frelinghuysen, who continued to insist that a formally righteous man
might nevertheless be an ungodly man because still unconverted.* A truce of sorts was achieved in 1737–38. But in the
decade remaining to Frelinghuysen, he advocated autonomy
from the Classis of Amsterdam for the Dutch Reformed congregations in "our American Jerusalem," supported the formation of
an indigenous Coetus (an American council of Dutch churches),
and published seven collections of his sermons. Although he

---

* See Evans, comp., *American Bibliography*, nos. 2605, 39964 [Bristol, *Supplement*, 841]; and Hastings, comp., *Ecclesiastical Records*, IV (1902), 2244–92.

became anathema to conservative congregations in New York and unwelcome among them, his reputation and activities between 1720 and 1738 helped to pave the way for George Whitefield and the Great Awakening in New York—such as it was—between 1739 and 1741.

Whitefield, the young ecumenical evangelist from England, reached New York City in his seaboard tour on November 14, 1739. He spent barely five days there and made a splashy but ultimately ephemeral impact. He had an unsatisfactory, indeed hostile, interview with William Vesey, who would not permit him to preach at the Anglican service and even posted constables "at the door of the English Church, lest [Whitefield's] adherents . . . should break it open and take it by force." Only one minister offered the itinerant a pulpit, Ebenezer Pemberton at the Presbyterian church; and so most of Whitefield's preaching was done in open fields before huge throngs. "The people seemed exceedingly attentive," he observed in his journal, "and I have not felt greater freedom in preaching, and more power in prayer, since I came to America, than I have had here in New York. I find that little of the work of God has been seen in it for many years." *

Whitefield returned to New York from April 29 until May 5, 1740, and once again in October and November. He preached (from a specially constructed scaffold this time) to crowds ranging from five thousand to seven thousand persons; met with other leading evangelists, such as William and Gilbert Tennent; collected funds for his orphanage; listened in disappointment to uninspired Anglican sermons; and visited churches in Brooklyn, Staten Island, Rye, and East Chester. He also inspired James Davenport, a twenty-six-year-old preacher from Connecticut who had served the church at Southold, Long Island, since 1738. Davenport conducted enthusiastic revivals on eastern Long

---

* For his fascinating account of visits to New York, see *George Whitefield's Journals* (London, 1960), 347–51, 359–60, 415–17, 483–86. For Whitefield's writings published in New York, see Evans, comp., *American Bibliography*, nos. 4452, 4456, 4457, 4588, 4645, 4656, 40870 [Bristol, *Supplement*, 1847].

Island during the spring of 1740, then he joined Whitefield in his travels, got into trouble in Connecticut in 1741, was judged not fully sane, and was sent back to Southold in 1742. His congregation there censured him for his absences and eccentric behavior and eventually dismissed him in 1743.

All in all, the Awakening may have had less impact in New York than in any colony north of the Carolinas. Revivalism among the Presbyterians of Long Island was really a segment of the New England Awakening. Aside from episodic activity in Manhattan and Staten Island, evangelical religion was lightly felt in the province. "As to religion," remarked a visitor from Maryland in 1744, writing in Albany, "they have little of it among them, and of enthusiasm not a grain." New York's communities were long since too secularized, materialistic, and in many cases isolated to be very seriously affected. There was no need to rebel against ministerial authority because too few of New York's clergy had ever been very authoritative. Most of all, they were quite literally too few. A congregation could not reject an "unconverted" minister without the risk of having a vacant pulpit for a protracted period of years. Conservative opponents of the Awakening in New York feared that freedom of conscience might occur in epidemic proportions if an excess of sectarianism were allowed. Perhaps, alongside secularism, that anxiety served to restrain pietism in New York. A society already plagued by pluralism in politics and social relations could scarcely afford additional schisms within its churches.

Schisms it would have, however, although the worst of them would not occur until the later 1740s and 1750s. Henry Muhlenberg visited the Lutheran church in September 1750 and commented perceptively about the situation he found. His analysis applies with equal validity to divisions among the Presbyterians, Dutch Reformed, and other groups:

It is a deplorable thing when such strifes arise in the congregations, since the members are almost without exception interwoven with one another by marriage, relationship, and the like, and the disaffected will not rest, but continue to agitate to gain a following and accomplish their purpose. And since the preachers must obtain their salary from the individual members of the congregation, it is diminished in the same ratio in which the number of the discontented increases, and the others lose courage and fear that the whole [financial] burden will fall upon them alone. In short, under such circumstances it is easier to be a cowherd or a shepherd in many places in Germany than to be a preacher here, where every peasant wants to act the part of a patron of the parish, for which he has neither the intelligence nor the skill.*

In May 1751, Muhlenberg came to New York once again in order to serve the Lutherans there on a trial basis. His comments on the circumstances he found are symptomatic of several central tendencies in provincial life: the decline of "enthusiasm," persistent religious formalism, ethnic pluralism, and the growth of a pervasive secularism in society.

I observed at the first service that the little Dutch and German group which clung to the church sang in a manner that was slovenly, poor, and wretched, bawling out in both German and Dutch as though they were stuck on a spit. . . . These poor souls have been lulled and consoled for so many years . . . that they consider a two-hour service in church on Sunday as quite sufficient for justification [preparation for salvation]. They think that their works without faith are Christian weaknesses, and whatever is said that does not sound like the old doctrine, but which urges conversion to God and living faith in the Lord Jesus, seems dangerous to them. (Muhlenberg, *Journals*, I, 278.)

Many of these folk were barely cognizant of the theological distinctions Muhlenberg had in mind, and the province remained stony ground on which to cast the seeds of spiritual discourse. Apart from a tiny handful of published sermons by Pemberton, Samuel Buell (the Presbyterian minister at East Hampton, Long Island), and Jonathan Edwards (who preached

---

* Muhlenberg, *Journals*, I, 251. For the conservatism of New York's clergy, see ibid., 237. Although Muhlenberg may have been a spiritual democrat in wishing to convert Everyman, he was not a social democrat. Departing from Kingston, N.Y., after a visit with the divided Dutch Reformed church there, he wrote that "we sailed away on our small ship, thanking God for granting us a decent ship's company, which is something that seldom occurs. Often one is compelled to sit with company that gives one a foretaste of hell." Ibid., I, 253.

before the Synod of New York in 1753), there were comparatively few indigenous writings for the populace to read.*

In the quarter-century from about 1730 until 1755, during which a full-scale Awakening failed to materialize in New York, a more important social phenomenon did occur in the churches. It might be referred to as americanization, but more accurately still as acculturation. Its causes were pluralism, once again, as well as the elusiveness of ecclesiastical boundaries, the proportions of immigration by national origin, and the fact that a sizable new generation, native born in New York, was coming of age. Its symptoms were the adoption of English language liturgy and preaching, ecumenical tendencies among some groups, and, especially, intermarriage.

As one observer noted in 1750, "in the *province* of New York *Ecclesia Calviniana* is predominant. Most of the marriages are mixed, so that one is a Lutheran and the other a Calvinist." Even the clergy crossed denominational lines casually. After Pemberton's wife died in 1751, the Presbyterian minister married a Baptist, who subsequently reported to a friend that she "had the happiness of marrying One who is a friend to God . . . & a friend to liberty of conscience. . . . I have had no difficulty from this quarter, but on the contrary have been treated with the utmost generosity, & indulgence." The Sephardic Jews intermarried with Gentiles to such an extent that by the century's end a discrete Jewish community barely survived. When Phila Franks married Oliver De Lancey in 1742, her family was shocked and disappointed. Realistically, however, the number of eligible young Jewish men was small, and mother Abigail Franks had previously expressed a low regard for most of them. In succeeding years the union of Christian with Jewish families became increasingly common.

In 1724–26 a fierce quarrel divided the French Protestant church, during which many of its members shifted their alle-

---

* See Evans, nos. 5268, 6966, 7449, 8538, 8559, 8808, 40939 [Bristol, *Supplement*, 1922].

giance to Trinity. In 1751 Muhlenberg noticed that "the Dutch
Reformed church was once the leading and predominant church,
but in a very few years the English church has had an increase of
many thousands, with the result that a very large building can no
longer contain the members and the second large church is now
in the process of construction and will be completed in the near
future. The reason for this is that the Dutch children forget their
mother tongue and learn English. Since they cannot hear
English in their own church, they go over to the other to hear
what they understand and like." Albany had been a Dutch
Reformed bastion throughout the seventeenth century; but a
small Lutheran group developed in the earlier eighteenth
century, an Anglican community between 1754 and 1763, and a
Presbyterian church in 1763. Albany had by then become
multidenominational, like the rest of the colony.

As the Lutherans in New York became multinational after
1740, the conflicting demands of Dutch and German resulted in
English as a compromise language early in the 1750s. Similarly,
between 1760 and 1766 a series of English-language Jewish
prayer books was printed in New York, including one for regular
services as well as one for the High Holy Days.* When Baruch
Judah, who had been elected a constable in the 1730s, collected
the parish levies for Trinity Church, he signed his bond for
faithful performance of duty in Hebrew as well as in English.
Joseph Jessurun Pinto, who served as cantor of Congregation
Shearith Israel ("Remnant of Israel") from 1758 until 1766, was
a competent Hebraist; knew Dutch, Spanish, as well as Portuguese; and also wrote fine English in a fair hand. In 1768 the
synagogue chose—for the first time—a native-born Jew, twenty-
three-year-old Gershom Mendes Seixas, to be precentor. All
previous teachers had been foreign born as well as educated
abroad.

---

* See Evans, comp., *American Bibliography*, nos. 7262, 8890, 41133 [Bristol,
Supplement, 2140], as well as the books, printed decisions, and certificates in the
archives of the American Jewish Historical Society in Waltham, Mass. One of
these certificates, issued by Rabbi Abraham ben Isaac of New York, asserts that
meat being shipped to Barbados by Zevi ben Mordecai, a merchant, is kosher.

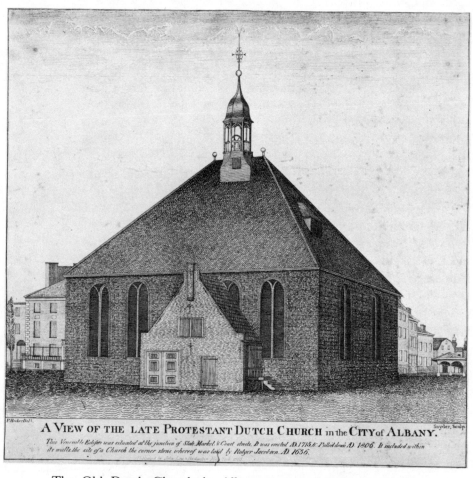

The Old Dutch Church in Albany (1715–1806); engraving by Henry W. Snyder after a drawing by Philip Hooker. *Collection Albany Institute of History and Art.*

This process of acculturation was most difficult for the Dutch Reformed congregations. Some new churches had appeared during the first third of the eighteenth century; but growth overall had been sluggish, hampered by an insufficiency of clergymen, a decline in rigorous adherence to Calvinism, and weakened ties with the Classis of Amsterdam. In 1735 the Classis inadvertently set in motion a crisis that would get steadily worse and endure until 1771. "We should be especially pleased," it wrote the ministers of New York, "if we could receive from you some Plan, which might tend to promote the union of the Dutch churches in your portion of the world, in doctrine and ecclesiastical business . . . but without impairing our Correspondence."

In March 1737, a New Jersey minister submitted to the New York Consistory a proposal for the creation of a Coetus. He contended that there had to be some authoritative body in America to settle disputes, deal with irregularities, and maintain "good order" among the churches. Consequently a convention met later that year in New York City, approved plans for a Coetus, and sent them off to Amsterdam for approval. Within a week, however, four prominent ministers decided to oppose the plan, sent their criticisms to the Classis too, and charged that supporters of the Coetus had ecclesiastical independence in mind.

By 1738 the need for some sort of autonomy was glaringly apparent. There were sixty-four Dutch Reformed churches in New York and New Jersey being served by only twenty-one ministers. By 1740 the proportions were sixty-five to twenty. Two pastorates had been vacant for nine years, despite regular appeals to Amsterdam. In March 1738, a travel-battered letter, dated in Amsterdam on October 1, 1736, finally arrived containing Classis sanction for a request made in 1734 by the Schoharie community for permission to examine and ordain John Schuyler, thereby avoiding the danger and expense of a trip to Europe. By 1738 the Frelinghuysen faction had already begun to train indigenous ministers informally, so some action was inevitable.

On April 6, 1739, the Classis gave its approval for an

ineffectual organization—so long as "no opinions be expressed in such Coetus concerning Doctrine; and that no examinations be held, preliminary or final, for licensure or ordination." The americanizers had hoped for much fuller jurisdiction, their spirits sagged, and the whole project fell dormant for eight years, but not without grumbling and friction. The conservatives led by Boel, the moderates led by du Bois, and the americanizing pietists led by Frelinghuysen relentlessly sought to undercut one another. They argued over the exclusive use of Dutch in services and over certain irregular local ordinations. Although the liturgy, psalms, and hymns had all been translated into English by about 1748, none was in common use. Dutch parochial schools had been reactivated since the 1720s, in fact, in order to combat americanization. As one lament put it, members were guilty of "a wretched carelessness of necessary things, [and] have now for some years neglected to have their children receive instruction in the Netherlandish tongue." Meanwhile, the number of intermarriages and private baptisms (in the home) continued to increase. Something had to be done.

When the Classis granted a Coetus to the German Reformed churches of Pennsylvania in 1747, it could hardly deny the same privilege to its Dutch Reformed members. So in September of that year a convention met to organize a Coetus that would comprise all the Dutch churches in America. It acknowledged subordination to Amsterdam, agreed only to consider ecclesiastical (and not doctrinal) matters, and allowed for a right of appeal to Amsterdam. Although American ordinations began to occur in 1748, the Albany Consistory and half a dozen prominent ministers refused to accept the Coetus. When criticisms began to be sent by the Classis of Amsterdam, the americanizers became so incensed that in 1753 they proposed the creation of an autonomous American Classis. That led in 1754 to a full-fledged schism within the church, accompanied by all sorts of anomalies. The conservatives got involved in collusion with the Anglicans and supported their appeal for a college in New York with Church of England hegemony.

Led by older men who were Dutch-born and trained, the

Conferentie party, as it was called, insisted upon subordination to Amsterdam, purity of doctrine, and continued use of the Dutch language. The Coetus party, more pietistic and led by younger men, many of them educated in America, wanted to be able to ordain and discipline clergymen without recourse to Amsterdam. The result was pamphlet warfare, lockouts, ministers assaulted in their pulpits, closed churches, and numerous communicants who stayed at home in disgust. The Coetus party had the support of a majority, however, established an American Classis in 1755, and backed the movement for English-language preaching and services.

In 1762 the New York Consistory decided to call an English-speaking pastor to fill its vacancy. Archibald Laidlie, a Scot who had settled in Holland, arrived in 1764 and on April 15 preached the first English sermon ever heard in a Dutch Reformed church in America. He refused to side with either faction fully, began a slow process of conciliation, and enjoyed considerable success. Finally, under the leadership of young John Henry Livingston, who had been thoroughly trained in Holland and had returned to New York in 1770, a plan of union was approved by the Classis of Amsterdam and became the basis for a settlement in 1771. American ordination was approved, but doctrinal appeals could still be carried to Holland. The churches ratified the plan in 1772.

One important consequence of all this turmoil from the later 1730s onward was that the Dutch Reformed church lost its position as the dominant group among dissenting denominations. Some Reformed leaders had been much too cozy with the Anglicans for several generations past, while the Presbyterians had become stronger and more aggressive about the rights of nonconformists. The first Presbyterian minister appeared in New York City in 1716, and steady growth took place during the next two decades. The Presbytery of Long Island, organized in 1717, merged with the Presbytery of East Jersey in 1738 to form the Presbytery of New York, which then continued throughout the colonial period. A Presbytery of Suffolk County (Long Island) was formed in 1749 and one in Dutchess County in 1766.

Schisms occurred as a result of the Awakening, to be sure. Between 1745 and 1758 the Synod of New York broke away from Philadelphia's "New Side" influence, but they were formally reunited in 1758 and began to achieve genuine harmony after 1762.

What is significant about all of these organizational convolutions is that the years between 1745 and 1760 were years of rapid growth for the Presbyterians—growth based upon the influx of groups quite diverse in social origin. There were Puritans from New England and Long Island, Scots-Irish immigrants from abroad, converts drifting in from the divided Dutch Reformed communities, and members such as the Livingstons from intermarriages between Scottish and Dutch families settled in the colony since the seventeenth century. Such amalgamation could not occur without strife. Pemberton's congregation in New York City, for example, had received by mid-century an influx of what Mrs. Pemberton described as "bigotted Scotch Irish Presbyterians." When the elders and deacons suggested introducing Isaac Watts's version of the Psalms (then widely used in New England) instead of the various versions causing some confusion in New York services, they urged that anyone who objected bring the matter to Pemberton. The newcomers decided instead to organize themselves as the "Scotch Presbyterian Society" and formally charged the minister with neglecting the Westminster catechism when he administered baptism, failing to pray at burials when so requested by the family, and permitting the singing of anthems. Although Pemberton resigned in 1753 and moved to Boston for the remainder of his career, the Presbyterians of New York grew steadily in strength and numbers anyway. As we shall see, they provided the most serious challenge to Anglican hegemony during the 1750s and 1760s.

The development of religious toleration in New York made significant strides during the middle third of the eighteenth century. In part it was caused by the influence of English latitudinarianism, partially the ecumenical impact of revivalism, and in part the result of a growing pride in independence among many of the sects. Dissenters received no public assistance by the later 1730s, slowly came to regard that "deficiency" as a virtue, and prized the concomitant freedom from interference by the state. As one Dutch Reformed pastor put it in 1738: "We enjoy the free exercise of our religious services in every respect, although there is not the least provision made for our Church by the Civil Authorities. Hence, mutual affection, and unity in faith and piety . . . are the only means of preserving our Christian churches, and of making them flourishing and prosperous." This sort of attitude would lead inexorably, though not without detours, in the direction of complete disestablishment—and along the road of toleration, at that.

For two generations after 1665, Quakers received discriminatory treatment in New York. Because they would not take or administer oaths, they could not hold public office and often were disenfranchised. The Assembly approved a bill in 1691, however, to "ease People that are Scrupulous in Swearing." This act allowed Quakers to substitute a simple affirmation for an oath when giving testimony in civil cases or when asked to serve on juries. A setback occurred in 1701, however, when the Assembly passed a law providing that "no person or persons as shall refuse upon the tender and demand of the sheriff or either of the Candidates to take the Oaths appointed by Law . . . shall be Suffered to give his or their vote or votes for any Representative . . . or for any other officer whatsoever."

A reversal finally came in 1734 as a result of the Cosby–Van Dam controversy. When Lewis Morris ran in the Westchester by-election of 1733, he attracted a good deal of support from Quakers who approved of his position sympathetic to dissenters. The sheriff, a Cosby man, insisted that the Quakers swear that they were qualified freemen. When they declined, he denied them the right to vote. Morris won the election anyway, but his supporters made a great issue of the rejection in Zenger's *Weekly Journal.*

The Quakers thereupon petitioned Cosby that they had in practice been allowed to make an affirmation for years, that the law of 1691 served as a precedent, and that a parliamentary law of 1722 permitted Quakers to use a simple statement in place of an oath when voting or testifying in civil cases. Cosby referred the case to his attorney general, who ruled negatively. But in 1734 the Assembly finally settled the matter by deciding that "the legislation of New York should conform as near as possible to that of England," and it passed a bill giving New York Friends the same status as English Quakers. Cosby gave his reluctant approval, and thereafter Quakers could vote without being challenged in New York. Not until after independence, however, would they be allowed legitimately to give evidence in criminal cases or to hold significant public office.

Nor could Jews do so, though they made progress in other areas once their community gained size and substance. By 1706, when the Jews of New York City prepared a kind of "constitution" for their own regulation, they enjoyed economic as well as some civil rights. They voted (if no one challenged them to take a Christian oath) and conducted public worship. In 1718 they won the privilege of naturalization through special acts of the Assembly, a privilege that enabled them to own land. By 1727 they seemed to have won full suffrage, and by 1731, when there were some seventy-five Jewish families in New York, they had dedicated the first synagogue to be constructed as such in British North America, had erected a separate school building, and had been allowed to expand their burying ground.

At the election of 1737, however, their right to vote was successfully challenged. William Smith, Sr., played heavily upon anti-Semitic prejudices in persuading the legislature to disallow Jewish votes for assemblymen as well as Jewish testimony in court. Between 1748 and 1761 these privileges were regained, and the Constitution of 1777 finally gave Jews (as well as Roman Catholics) full political equality.

That document was to be a genuine benchmark in New York's movement toward complete secularization. It declared "that the free exercise and enjoyment of religious profession and worship, without discrimination or preference, shall forever hereafter be allowed, within this state, to all mankind." It also decreed that no minister or priest would be eligible to hold any civil or military office. Official toleration and formal separation had been achieved. Most communities had more than one church, and some even had more than one of the same denomination. After the mid-1750s there would not be another effort to attract sectarian support throughout the province on a public issue, though local religious antagonisms might affect elections within a particular county. Actual toleration would be greater in New York City than in many of the rural areas; but freedom of conscience had become characteristic of the colony as a whole and was one of the salient attributes of thought and culture in New York after mid-century.

10

A UTILITARIAN CULTURE AND
THE USES OF LEISURE

At first glance, provincial New York may seem to have been what H. L. Mencken once called the South, a "Sahara of the Bozart," that is, a cultural desert. In 1688 Charles Lodwick was requested to provide the Royal Society with "a compendious Naturall History of that Countrey." He apologized for taking four years to do the job but explained in 1692 that "where Masters of Ships are ye chiefest Mathematicians & ye Natives [the chief] Geographers, with such tools you must not expect a good Fabrick. . . ." James Petiver, a prominent Fellow of the Royal Society, tried for three years (1692–95) to establish a scientific correspondence with Dr. Alexander Innis at Boscobell House, near Hempstead, Long Island; but Innis never replied. Petiver tried again with one Robert Gamble in 1713–14; yet, once again, silence from New York. Three decades later, in 1742, Cadwallader Colden expressed his appreciation to a London correspondent for the opportunity "to communicate some thoughts in natural philosophy which have remained many years with me undigested, for we scarcely have a man in this country that takes any pleasure in such kinds of speculations."

It is true that formally learned men did not abound among the inhabitants of colonial New York and that science, philosophy, and knowledge for its own sake were low priorities for provincial aspiration. But there was, nevertheless, a culture of some consequence, particularly in the four decades after 1730. What we find in that period is, first, that culture, by and large, had to be utilitarian; second, that this was a society quite literally learning how to learn; third, that the process of urbanization had much to do with the blossoming of a cultural life in New York City at mid-century; and fourth, that while many cultural phenomena occurred for the first time during the 1730s (e.g., theatrical performances and an opposition newspaper), they did not become firmly established until the early 1750s, which seems to have been the "takeoff" point for an autonomous cultural life in New York.

There is a sense in which colonial culture before 1750 was factual and literal in its achievements. Its agents—whether they were limners doing portraits, lawyers pleading cases, or scientists describing nature—hoped to get a true likeness, to establish the truth of a libel, to be accurate in detail; whereas after 1750, the colonists sought to *improve* upon nature: to romanticize their portraiture, exaggerate their theatrical extravaganzas, and use applied science for the betterment of public health. Although Governor Burnet turned his attention to some serious astronomical observations in 1723 and 1724, a scientific community did not emerge in the province until the 1750s. Although Cadwallader Colden "retired" to his country estate, Coldengham, in 1739 to start systematic studies in botany, physics, and medicine, his inquiries did not begin to achieve fruition for some years to come.

For the most part, moreover, cultural achievements would have to be visibly useful in order to be generally desirable. When William Livingston established *The Independent Reflector* in 1752, his first number explained that science, education, politics, and religion would be discussed in terms of social betterment. "But in Subjects meerly literary, I shall rarely indulge myself." In 1768, relying upon a bit of hyperbole, he put it even more boldly: "We want hands . . . more than heads. The most intimate acquaintance with the classics, will not remove our oaks; nor a taste for the *Georgics* cultivate our lands."

The cultural life of provincial New York, then, is not to be found in the customary, formal institutions that preserve and transmit culture. Schools, for example, were neither free nor obligatory in the modern sense, did not educate very many people for very long periods of time, and consequently were less important than newspapers, artisans, lawyers, printers, and booksellers as sources of education. An awakening of civic consciousness after 1750, a desire to overcome parochialism and inform outsiders of New York's potential, a proliferation of clubs, societies, libraries, and pamphlet wars, would provide the colony with its first real taste of the arts and letters.

The single most striking cluster of phenomena in this period, 1730–70, involves the expansion of literacy and the dissemination of knowledge. Apparently, more than 80 percent of those who left wills could sign their names. All four generations of the De Foreest family in colonial New York (1636–1766)—a brewer, a glazier, a schoolmaster, and a printer—were literate, as were two generations of the Dominy cabinetmakers in East Hampton, Long Island. The first writing master appeared in New York City in 1737 and the second in 1753—a Mr. Elphinstone, who taught his pupils to write a good hand in an hour's lesson each day for five weeks. Three more appeared in 1763, 1769, and 1774. Ink pots, ink bottles, and inkstands began to be advertised after 1754, and sellers of writing ink began to emerge after 1758. Previously people had made their own, according to various crude methods.

The growth of newspapers also contributed to the growth of literacy and depended upon such growth for success as well. The first, Bradford's *New-York Gazette*, appeared in 1725 and lasted for nineteen years until his retirement. The second, Zenger's *Weekly Journal*, began in 1733, survived his death in 1746, and continued until 1752. The third, James Parker's *Weekly Post-Boy*, got started in 1743; and the fourth, Henry De Foreest's *Evening Post*, was both a continuation of Bradford's *Gazette* in 1744 as well as the first afternoon paper in colonial America. Altogether there were twenty-two separate newspapers published in New York between 1725 and 1776, all but one of them in New York City. Most of them were published weekly (a few less often); they were small

(about four pages); and they had at best a printing of perhaps
350 to 550 copies per issue. Needless to say, each copy was seen
by more than one person. So it was that a plural society spawned
many newspapers, especially after the 1750s, quite consistent
with the observation of one visitor in 1760 that being "of different
nations, different languages and different religions, it is almost
impossible to give them [New Yorkers] any precise or determi-
nate character."

There were three printers active in the city by 1742, four in
1750, six in 1762, and twelve by 1777. Their activities are useful
indexes in many ways. By 1757–58, for example, James Parker
may have been the busiest printer in all of the colonies and Hugh
Gaine almost as prolific.* Most striking is the gross increase in
every sort of publication—books, pamphlets, broadsides, etc.—
from the 1740s onward. Compare the average number of titles
printed per annum after 1730: approximately 20 per year during
the 1730s, 25 per year during the 1740s, 32 per year during the
1750s, and 55 per year during the 1760s. In 1774 alone there
were 155 titles, and the number increased steadily thereafter.

By 1750, politics had come to have a significant impact upon
literary productivity and consequently, perhaps, upon literacy as
well. The fact that provincial elections occurred in 1726, 1737,
1743, 1745, and 1747 caused no discernible rise in the number of
provincial publications in those years. The election year 1750,
however, elicited 40 titles, the greatest number until that time;
and the election years of 1759, 1761, 1768, and 1769 brought
forth 43, 59, 64, and 135 titles respectively—each a new annual
high. These figures would seem to suggest that popular appeals to
the broader electorate did not get fully under way until the 1750s
and that thereafter elections may well have been a stimulus to
the growth of literacy.

There were, of course, a variety of notable publications that

---

* The process of americanization is also worth noting. Bradford had been
born in England and came to America at the age of 22; Zenger was born in
Germany and came at the age of 13. Parker, De Foreest, and Benjamin
Mecom, however, the next three to set up in New York, were born in New
Jersey, New York City, and Boston.

appeared during these decades. Robert Hunter (probably assisted by Lewis Morris) had written the first indigenous American drama, *Androboros: A Biographical Farce in Three Acts*, a sharp satire against the Anglican clergymen of New York and New Jersey as well as opposition leadership in the Assembly. Although it was never performed, Bradford published it in 1714. In 1727 Bradford produced the first edition of Colden's *History of the Five Indian Nations Depending on the Province of New York in America*, an influential volume. In 1724 Bradford had included in Colden's *Papers Relating to an Act . . . For Encouragement of the Indian Trade &c* a map of western New York and the Great Lakes region that is considered to be the first map ever engraved in New York. Later that year he reissued the map alone as a separate publication (13¾ by 8½ inches, on a scale of eighty miles to the inch). In 1731 Bradford brought out James Lyne's "Plan of the City of New York from an Actual Survey," the earliest map or plan made of the city.*

By mid-century the significant and innovative publications were growing in number: Colden's speculative work on gravity (1745); James Parker's edition of *Pamela*, by the English novelist Samuel Richardson (1744); Parker's edition of Lewis Evans's map of all the middle colonies (1749); Isaac Watts's devotional lyrics (1750); "The Yearly Verses of the Printer's Lads," also in 1750; *The American Mock-Bird: A Collection of the Most Familiar Songs Now in Vogue* (1760, revised in 1761); and "An Evening Thought: Salvation by Christ, with Penetential Cries" (1760) by Jupiter Hammon, a slave on Long Island.†

An increasing volume of publications necessarily stimulated the business of booksellers, and their catalogs of local and imported books began to appear regularly after 1754: first those of Noel Garrat, then Hugh Gaine's, and in 1760 that of James Rivington. Equally important, it stimulated the establishment in

---

* See Evans, comp., *American Bibliography*, nos. 1681, 2512, 2513, 2849, 3438.
† See Evans, comp., nos. 5485, 5564, 6316, 6620, 8528, 8940; and Bristol, *Supplement*, 1503. Hammon's 88-line poem, which appeared as a broadside, was the first publication by a black person in America.

1754 of the colony's first enduring circulating public library: the New York Society Library. A subscription library, it accepted anyone to membership at a uniform rate and reflected a strong desire for civic culture on the part of the city's intellectual leaders. They believed that a "Publick Library would be very useful as well as ornamental to the city" and in 1758 designed a bookplate depicting New York as the American Athens.

There had, in fact, been earlier attempts at establishing libraries in New York—the Trinity Parish Library, founded in 1698; the public gift of Chaplain John Sharpe's library in 1713; the Corporation Library, bequeathed by Dr. John Millington to the S.P.G., arrived from England in 1730—but these never took hold as public institutions, were kept at City Hall in several phases of desuetude, and were largely destroyed or dispersed by British troops in 1776. The library of King's College began with a bequest from Joseph Murray in 1757, and the Union Society Library started in 1771 with a collection of close to one thousand volumes. Finally, from 1763 onward some of the more enterprising booksellers, such as Noel Garrat and Samuel Loudon, kept circulating libraries to which subscribers would pay five dollars a year for the privilege of taking home one book at a time. In 1765 Garrat ran advertisements in the *Gazette* to inform his patrons "that there is an Addition made of several new Books, and more expected for their entertainment, and of those who shall think proper to become encouragers of this useful undertaking"—once again, the emphasis was upon the *utility* of culture.

In 1762 a new form of literature made its first appearance in New York—books for small children—and they, too, would be made useful by design. Hence the publication of *Food for the Mind; or A New Riddle Book*, by Jack the Giant Killer; and *A Little Pretty Pocketbook, Intended for the Instruction and Amusement of Little Master Tommy and Pretty Miss Polly*; and *The Private Tutor for Little Masters and Misses*; and Tommy Trapwit's *Be Merry and Wise*. Such items extended to a lower age group the sort of self-help manual that had been appearing in New York since the later 1740s. These guides quite clearly played a significant role in the informal education of adolescents: *The Friendly Instructor: or A Companion for*

Young Ladies and Young Gentlemen (1746); *The Countryman's Help and Trader's Friend; or A Pocket Companion for Debtor and Creditor, Buyer and Seller* (1747); *The Lady's Preceptor* (1759); *The Servants' Directory or House-Keeper's Companion* (1760); *The American Instructor: or, Young Man's Best Companion. Containing Spelling, Reading, Writing, and Arithmetick, in an Easier Way than Any Yet Published; and How to Qualify any Person for Business, without the Help of a Master* (1760); *The Complete Letter Writer; or Polite English Secretary* (1763), and numerous others.*

During the middle third of the eighteenth century, there also began to be available a variety of books designed to assist in the process of formal education. Some of these were language books, such as *The English and Low-Dutch School-Master*, printed by Bradford in 1730, and *A New Complete Guide to the English Tongue* (1745), as well as several for instruction in Spanish and Latin (1751, 1752). Others were primers for instructing youngsters in reading, writing, and religion, such as *The New-York Primer*, which Henry De Foreest made available regularly from 1746 onward.† These contained a catechism approved by the Westminster Assembly and were used in the so-called Dutch School—which was regularized as a charity school by the Dutch Reformed church after 1725—as well as by private schoolmasters throughout the province.

There may have been as many as fifty such schoolmasters in New York City between 1695 and 1775, and their role in the process of elementary education is only slightly less obscure than the institutional history of primary schools in colonial New York. During the eighteenth century, a very slow but steady shift occurred in which education came to be identified less with a particular person or schoolmaster and more with an institution— what finally emerged, in 1805, as the free public grammar school. Despite periodic attempts to move in this direction—an Assem-

---

* See Evans, comp., *American Bibliography*, nos. 5774, 5960, 5961, 8296, 8607, 8736, 9148, 9159, 9248, 9281, 9286, 9354, 9377.

† See Evans, comp., *American Bibliography*, nos. 5648, 5838, 6033, 6572, 6741, 6775, 6928; and Bristol, *Supplement*, 821.

bly act in 1702, an English school in New York City in 1705, another act passed in 1732 that provided for a public school to teach twenty pupils (the school expired in 1738)—most children learned to read and write at home, at small, private neighborhood reading schools, or at the denominational charity schools run by the Dutch Reformed, the Anglicans, and the Jews. An intellectual, such as Colden, had all of his children educated at home, and his son David would later remark that he "never so much as saw any publick School or University." In 1752 William Smith, Jr., "wondered that this Province should have been near a whole Century, in the Hands of a civilized and enlightened People; and yet, not one publick Seminary of Learning planted in it."

The school was not yet the focal point of education that it would become later in the nineteenth century. The scope and responsibility of lower schools were not clearly defined because other agencies could and did teach the same skills. The family and the church had primary responsibility for moral education. Accounting could be learned in the countinghouse and crafts in apprenticeship. It has been estimated that in 1770 only about three-sixteenths of the white children younger than age sixteen were in school in any given year. A "school," moreover, was an ephemeral thing, for arrangements were often temporary, schoolmasters moved about, and students sought out different masters for different subjects. There were also evening schools especially arranged for apprentices. In 1767, for example, one teacher announced lessons to be given both morning and evening in order to "suit some of both Sexes, who attend other Places of Education at different Periods, for other purposes." Teaching was more of a trade than a profession; there were no standards for preparation or qualification, nor was there a system of promotion or provision for job security. The pay was so poor that most schoolmasters taught only part-time and had to have some other means of livelihood.

Strange as it might seem, there existed a genuine prejudice against free public schools, but the reasons are not hard to discern. Those eighteenth-century schools that were subsidized by the Dutch Reformed congregations, by the Jewish community, and especially by S.P.G. missionaries were considered charity schools for poor parishioners and others who could not provide any education for their children. Middle-class parents who were wary of being identified with pauperism therefore kept their youngsters away from these "charity" schools. Prejudice against the Church of England, moreover, kept many children away from S.P.G. schools where tracts, sermons, and Anglican books were distributed in abundance. Such prejudice against S.P.G. schools was ironic, for the society steadily concentrated many of its best efforts on New York. It sent a disproportionate number of missionaries there because New York seemed to offer larger opportunities than other colonies, what with Indians, blacks, a secularized society, and no single group strong enough —such as the Congregationalists in Massachusetts or Quakers in Pennsylvania—to provide concerted opposition. When the S.P.G. was given an extensive personal library in 1728 with the stipulation that it be sent to America, officials chose New York as the likeliest location.

No wonder, then, that when William Livingston considered the problem of educational institutions in 1753, he recognized that nonsectarian schools were the only solution for a heterogeneous society. "For as we are split into so great a Variety of Opinions and Professions," he noted, with respect to creating a nondenominational college, "had each Individual his Share in the Government of the Academy, the Jealousy of all Parties combating each other, would inevitably produce a perfect Freedom for each particular Party." In keeping with this view, Livingston also proposed a scheme that, for 1753, was wildly avant-garde: a system of county grammar schools, managed by elected local boards, with the teachers paid from local taxes. Despite a most reasonable presentation on behalf of his plan, it never even reached the stage of legislative consideration by the Assembly.

Livingston's college proposal—which was stillborn in the Assembly as well—has attracted considerable attention from historians because its discussion, in the polemics of 1753–55, provides an ideal laboratory for examining diverse positions then held concerning the proper relationships among church, state, and education. For our purposes here, however, Livingston's most significant contention was that the primary purpose of higher education is to produce public-spirited citizens who would be useful to the community. Once again, culture was to be utilitarian. "The true Use of Education, is to qualify Men for the different Employments of Life . . . in a word, to make them more extensively serviceable to the Commonwealth . . . [and] better Members of Society." Livingston's nonsectarian college would have offered freedom of religion to all Protestants—he even proposed a set of ecumenical prayers for chapel—but, significantly, not to Roman Catholics. Even for this most advanced radical thinker, the palisade of Protestantism provided the outer boundary of respectable heterodoxy. The very presence of a few persons beyond the consensus, however, may have eased the way for more deviant nonconformist groups at that moment in time. Quakers and Moravians looked somehow less odious when placed alongside the specter of papistry.

In any case, the Anglicans had been hoping for some time to have a northern colonial college under their control as a foil against Harvard, Yale, and Princeton, which were Congregationalist and Presbyterian. Consequently, the college they sought for New York in 1752–54 would be founded on a royal charter, have an Anglican president, and use the Church of England's liturgy in its chapel services. By making an alliance with conservative leaders of the Dutch Reformed church and by gaining the approval of Lieutenant Governor James De Lancey, they beat Livingston's Presbyterian party, secured their charter, and created a distinct Anglican hue for the embryonic institution. Livingston's forces had strength enough, however, to prevent the college from receiving full financial aid through the Assembly.

Reverend Samuel Johnson, Anglican minister at Stratford, Connecticut, and a prominent American churchman, gladly received the call to serve as first president of King's. Johnson did not doubt that he was going to preside over an "Episcopal

College" and "a Seminary of the Church." He nursed it along as best he could for nine years, but after his retirement he had to concede that it was not flourishing. The reason, in part, was that the absence of good lower schools caused many prominent families to send their sons elsewhere—to New or old England—for education; and those native sons who did matriculate came inadequately prepared. Johnson congratulated a group of citizens in 1764 on finally establishing "so good a grammar school, without which as I often inculcated, the college could never flourish, and for want of which only . . . its reputation much suffered and mine with it." Between 1758, when the first class graduated, and 1775, the last class before the Revolution, 155 students entered King's College and 99 of them graduated, an average of 5.5. each year. By the end of the colonial period, it was becoming customary for most New York boys who went to college at all to attend King's, or else Princeton (then called the College of New Jersey).

There were at that time no law schools as such. Those who aspired to legal training underwent apprenticeship with an experienced practicing lawyer, such as James Alexander or William Smith, Sr. In 1745, while William Livingston worked in Smith's office, he noted that lawyers were not highly regarded as a professional group in New York. "There is perhaps no Set of Men that bear so ill a Character in the Estimation of the Vulgar, as the Gentlemen of the Long Robe." During the next two decades, however, the New York bar underwent a striking expansion and transformation. "Heightened commercial activity," as Milton M. Klein has observed, "produced an astonishing increase in litigation, and this, in turn, created an enlarged demand for legal services. . . . As the bar became financially more attractive, men of greater ability and education entered its ranks; and by their achievements and their learning they helped to overcome much of the public hostility formerly directed against the profession."

Even so, apprenticeship remained the route to legal education, just as it did for all manual vocations in the colony. The surest path to occupational success did not lead through a schoolhouse door, but rather through the workshop of a skilled craftsman. Although many apprentices' indentures guaranteed them some sort of formal schooling to supplement their trade—usually in the guise of reading, writing, and ciphering at night school—that was looked upon as being much less important than the skill actually acquired through on-the-job training. Thus a lad of humble origins, if all went well, might attend a charity school for two or three years (usually between the ages of seven and ten) and then be apprenticed to an artisan. Here, in abridged form, is a typical eighteenth-century indenture:

This Indenture Witnesseth that Thomas Hill about twelve years of Age with the Consent of William Hollins his father in Law [i.e., guardian] . . . voluntarily and of his own free will and accord put himselfe Apprentice unto Christopher Giliard, Cordwainer in the City of New York in America for the space and Term of seaven years . . . during all which Term the said Apprentice . . . faithfully shall serve his secrets keep his lawful Commands gladly Every where Obey [.] He shall doe no damage to his said Master nor see to be done by Others without letting or giving Notice thereof to his said Master. . . . He shall not Committ Fornication nor Contract Matrimony within the said Term [.] Att Cards, Dice or any other unlawfull Game he shall not play. . . . He shall not absent himselfe day nor night from his Master's service without his leave nor haunt Ale houses, Taverns or Playhouses but in all things as a faithful Apprentice he shall behave himselfe toward his said Master and all his During the said Term and the said Master during the said Term shall find and provide unto the said Apprentice sufficient meat drinke Apparell Lodging and washing fitting for an Apprentice and after the Expiration of the Said Term of seaven years to give unto his said Apprentice two new suits of Apparell the one for working days the other for Sundays and holy days and to Instruct and teach his said Apprentice in seaven years to read and write English and in the Cordwainer's Trade according to his Ability.*

Significantly, the state had very little supervisory authority in the education of children generally or of apprentices in particular. The Duke's Laws of 1665 had contained a brief directive:

---

* From Robert F. Seybolt, *Apprenticeship & Apprenticeship Education in Colonial New England & New York* (New York, 1917), 88–89.

"The Constables and Overseers are strictly required frequently to Admonish the Inhabitants of Instructing their Children and Servants in Matters of Religion and the Lawes of the Country, And that Parents and Masters do bring up their Children and Apprentices in some honest and Lawful Calling Labour or Employment." Enforcement of so broad a requirement was haphazard, however; and there were no other statements after 1665 except for one in 1736, when the Common Council of New York City requested that "such parish children as may be hereafter sent to the poorhouse for Maintainance . . . be religiously educated and taught to read, write, and cast accounts."

Not much is known about life on the premises of an artisan's workshop; but from newspaper advertisements, surviving artifacts, furnished rooms that have been reconstructed (in the Museum of the City of New York, for example), and the rare case of the Dominy craftsmen of East Hampton, whose actual shop, tools, letters, accounts, weather books, and products have all endured, it is clear that shop life was crowded, dark, and dirty by modern standards. Ceilings were low, windows small, smells pungent, and the hours of work long. Cash income, moreover, was elusive. Only by keeping their own farm lots and accepting goods in barter could the rural craftsmen remain solvent and supply their families. Here, for example, is a breakdown of the Dominy family accounts during the period 1765–75:*

Date	Production accounts debited or charged			Income cash and services credited			Debit to credit relationship		
	£	s	d	£	s	d	£	s	d
1765	10	8	5½	10	11	4	0	2	10½
1770	50	8	6½	44	10	6	−5	18	½
1775	22	5	0	13	13	0	−8	12	0

* From Charles F. Hummel, *With Hammer in Hand: The Dominy Craftsmen of East Hampton, New York* (Charlottesville, 1968), 219.

An oak dowry chest with red and green painted scenes on the front panels, made in the Hudson Valley during the eighteenth century. There are floral scenes on the end panels. *Courtesy of The New-York Historical Society, New York City, Garbisch Gift.*

Payments received in "kind" by the Dominy family—such as woven coverlets, linen, shoes, skeins of wool, spoons, hats, blanketing, "Sundries of Earthen ware," lumber, paint, varnish, and delivery of products—had a relatively low cash value as then reckoned, but considerable utility for day-to-day living.

Silversmiths, in particular, were important to people of means in New York because silverware of various sorts was a standard repository of wealth. In the absence of banks and secure safes, silverware was functional, could be melted down if necessary, and was less likely to be stolen than cash since each piece had its characteristic design and identifiable marks. So it was that Peter Van Dyck (1684–1751) and Myer Myers (1723–95), prominent silversmiths in colonial New York City, were also, in a sense, leading investment bankers. Here is part of an advertisement that appeared in the *New-York Gazette* on March 18, 1754: "The Dwelling House of Isaac Seixas, nigh the New Dutch Church, was last Night broke open, and sundry Things stolen therefrom; among which were two large Silver Table Spoons, mark'd with the Cypher I R S. Maker's Name M M; six Tea Spoons, mark'd R. L. and Sugar Tongs; a Silver Pepper Box, and a Salt-Celler with the same mark."

Needless to say, somewhat more is known about the domestic culture of prosperous provincials than about the poor and middling folk. During the 1740s, for example, the sitting room of a merchant's home in New York City might have contained a beechwood armchair, a slat-back armchair of maple and hickory, together with several sturdy side chairs that could also be used at the dinner table; a wall cupboard full of salt-glazed stoneware, pewter, and possibly silver tankards; a game table for cards, checkers, and backgammon; a few porcelain dishes made in Japan for the export trade; a Feraghan rug; perhaps some damask window curtains; and even a mahogany looking glass with gilt ornamentation.*

---

* The American wing of the Metropolitan Museum of Art in New York City contains the original great hall from the Van Rensselaer manor house in Albany, built between 1765 and 1769. The woodwork and paneled doors were

Although little residential architecture of this era has survived in New York City, a fair amount remains in the upper Hudson Valley and on Long Island. The Glen Sanders house, built in 1713 in Scotia, reflects the life-style of the early Scots immigrants to Schenectady County. The Bronck house in Coxsackie (Greene County), built of stone in 1663, enlarged in 1685, and expanded with a considerable brick addition in 1738, provides a superb example of rural Dutch construction. And the Abraham Yates house, built about 1730 in Schnectady, offers a vivid sense of Dutch-style architecture for village life. It began as two rooms plus a hall and was then added to on several occasions. The brick gable end, flush with the street, remains unaltered, and the side walls are covered with clapboards, or what contemporaries referred to as "weatherboards." We know that the Yates house is characteristic of the period because we have this excerpt from Peter Kalm's visit to Albany in 1750:

The houses in this town are very neat, and partly built of stones covered with shingles of white pine. Some are slated with tile from Holland, because the clay of this neighborhood is not considered fit for tiles. Most of the houses are built . . . with the gable-end towards the street, except a few, which were recently built in the modern style. A great number of houses are built like those of New Brunswick . . . the gable-end towards the street being of bricks and all the other walls of boards. The outside of the houses is never covered with lime or mortar . . . and the walls do not seem to be damaged by the weather. The eaves on the roofs reach almost to the middle of the street. This preserves the walls from being damaged by the rain, but it is extremely disagreeable in rainy weather for the people in the streets, there being hardly any means of avoiding the water from the eaves. The front doors are generally in the middle of the houses, and on both sides are porches

---

made by native craftsmen. The scenic wallpaper was custom made in England, ca. 1768, according to specifications sent over by the family. The scenes were copied from French prints of the period and painted in tempera on sheets of watercolor paper. The pieces of furniture shown in this section are all variations on Chippendale patterns and were made in New York between 1750 and 1770; they will be found in this great hall. They are not, however, original to the manor house, which was built by Stephen van Rensselaer, who died in 1769, and was then passed on to young Stephen, called "the last of the patroons."

A mahogany side chair with ball-and-claw feet, made in New York ca. 1750. The cipher of Robert and Margaret Beekman Livingston is worked into the splat. *Courtesy of Richard Aldrich and others, Barrytown, N.Y.*

A sofa with ball-and-claw feet of mahogany, made in the New York workshop of Joseph Cox (1757–60). The secondary woods are oak, cherry, and pine; the upholstery is crimson damask. *The Metropolitan Museum of Art, Gift of Mrs. John J. Riker, 1932.*

A marble-top mahogany pier table made in New York ca. 1760–70.
The Metropolitan Museum of Art, purchase 1946, Joseph Pultizer Bequest.

A triple-top gaming table (checkers, chess, backgammon, and cards) made of mahogany veneer on beech, with rosewood and satinwood inlays. New York, ca. 1765–70. *The Metropolitan Museum of Art, Rogers Fund, 1937.*

A mahogany wing chair with ball-and-claw feet, upholstered in brown leather, made in New York before the Revolution. The secondary wood is beech. *The Metropolitan Museum of Art, Rogers Fund, 1933.*

A mahogany chest-on-chest with secondary woods of white pine and poplar, made in New York ca. 1770. *The Metropolitan Museum of Art, Gift of E. M. Newlin, 1964.*

with seats, on which during fair weather the people spend almost the whole day. . . . In the evening the verandas are full of people of both sexes; but this is rather troublesome because a gentleman has to keep his hat in constant motion, for the people here are not Quakers whose hats are as though nailed to the head.*

From restorations being made in the old community of Kinderhook (Columbia County), we achieve a subtle sense of the anglicization of Dutch architecture over the course of the eighteenth century. A farmhouse built in stages after 1713 is purely Dutch, with its high gable roof, as is the Adam Van Alen farmhouse, with its parapet-gables, built in 1737. Its exterior gable ends show "mouse-teeth" brickwork designs. The interior ceilings all have large, exposed beams, held at each end by "knee braces" to provide extra support for the roomy attic, which was often used as a grain storage area. There are the traditional half-doors (designed to let in fresh air but not smelly animals), transom windows over the doors, small garret windows, and wide floorboards of durable pine.

The Johannis Van Alen farmhouse, however, built about 1760, has a gambrel roof and shows a mixture of Dutch with English Georgian characteristics. It is taller than its predecessors and consequently has spacious bedrooms on the second floor. In the main hall the ceiling is plastered, in the Georgian style; but in the adjacent dining room the beams and ceiling boards are left exposed, according to Dutch custom. This same pattern of hybridization occurs in the John Pruyn house, built in 1766. But the Van Schaack house, constructed in 1774, has the pure elegance of late Georgian design: hipped roof, Palladian window in the center, and an elaborately architectural doorway. Kinderhook, then, provides a magnificent display of country architecture, adapted generation by generation to the cultural tastes of upstate New Yorkers.

Architectural changes are less visible on Long Island. The Sherwood-Jayne house in East Setauket, which has been beauti-

---

* See Adolph B. Benson, ed., *Peter Kalm's Travels in North America: The English Version of 1770* (New York, 1937), I, 341.

The "Hardenberg bedroom," Hudson Valley interior from the 1760s. *Courtesy, The Henry Francis du Pont Winterthur Museum*

fully restored by the Society for the Preservation of Long Island Antiquities, was built around 1730 by the son of William Jayne, a chaplain in Cromwell's army who had immigrated in 1678. The saltbox type, with its shingles (then called "wood shakes"), is not discernibly different from those built in 1700—only a bit roomier—or those in 1760. Even the Custom House in Sag Harbor, built between 1765 and 1770 and preserved today with many original furnishings intact, does not deviate significantly from the Thompson house of 1700 or the Sherwood-Jayne residence of the 1730s.

By the middle third of the eighteenth century, a good many of these homes contained depictions of their owners and families. The history of painting in colonial New York, in fact, is one of the most useful yardsticks available for the process of secularization and the phenomenon of materialism, not to mention attitudes toward art, culture, and leisure. There are really three phases to the story: the period until about 1715, which shows strong Dutch influence, and about which we know little; the period 1715–50, a fascinating era of native folk art, concentrated especially in the Albany-Kingston areas; and the English-influenced phase of fine portraiture, focused on New York City between 1750 and 1775.

Each period has rather distinct characteristics that are symptomatic of different social tendencies and traditions. The untrained patroon limners of the upper Hudson Valley, with their bright colors, full-length portraits, and linear designs, were quite distinct from the British emigrant artists trained in the late baroque or rococo Georgian styles, doing busts, by and large, with their self-conscious techniques. Most of the paintings done before 1750, moreover, are either scriptural or domestic in subject matter, memorializing entire families. After 1750, however, when civic bodies as well as private persons began to patronize artists, there were fewer portraits of women and children and more of politicians, soldiers, and ministers depicted in heroic guise.

The earliest substantial "school" of art flourished around Albany during the first quarter of the eighteenth century and

Elsje Rutgers Schuyler, the wife of Dominie Petrus Vas of Kingston.
Portrait attributed to Pieter Vanderlyn, 1723. *Collection Albany
Institute of History and Art.*

concentrated upon religious subjects, such as the finding of Moses, and Christ on the road to Emmaus. In 1744, when Dr. Alexander Hamilton of Maryland visited Albany, he noticed that "they affect pictures much, particularly scripture history, with which they adorn their rooms." Between 1715 and 1745, however, merchants and planters of the Hudson Valley patronized an anonymous cluster of about twenty remarkable limners, and some 185 of their canvases are now known. They constituted the first major group of American artists in any locale, and their productivity was unmatched in the colonies before 1750.

Although it may seem unlikely that the first flowering of American art should occur there, in a parochial setting, the reasons are not really obscure. Because they were Dutch, they inherited a strong seventeenth-century tradition of domestic art. Precisely because they were insular, they wanted pictures of themselves rather than the English art coveted by their contemporaries in the Chesapeake area. Because they were secularized, they had no hesitation about making graven images. And because they were prosperous, they had the money and time to have their likenesses done. There were close to 350 freeholders living in the Albany area between 1715 and 1725, and 66 portraits have survived from that time and place. A society thereby sat for posterity—and its own gratification: many patrons, many limners.

Most of the paintings followed the stylistic conventions found in European mezzotints of the later seventeenth and early eighteenth centuries, including certain stock architectural backgrounds. Most of them are two-dimensional, very colorful, and rather static in their lines except for the actual faces. In most of them the eyes are narrowed because of a characteristic faint smile. Yet there also appears to have been a strong sense of territoriality among the limners, and each one had a distinct style in matters of detail. Whereas the "Aetatis Sue" (from his characteristic identification of the sitter's age) limner's subjects (1715–25) were largely patricians, the Gansevoort limner's patrons (1730–45) were mostly middle-class people. His men and boys wear no wigs, their clothes are bourgeois, few props clutter the portraits, and there are occasional farms and mills to be found in the backgrounds.

There was no comparable flourishing of painting in New York City during the first half of the eighteenth century. The Duyckinck family did most of the portraits that were commissioned: Evert (1621–1702), who had arrived in New Amsterdam by 1657; Gerret (1660–1710) and Evert III (1677–1727), both of whom became freemen in 1698; and two named Gerrardus who lived until 1742 and 1756. Their principal livelihood, however, came from the sale of paint and mirrors as well as from varnishing, gilding, and glazing. Robert Feke (1705–ca.1750), who became a major figure in early American art, left his home in Oyster Bay for Newport, Rhode Island, because a portraitist's prospects were not good on Long Island or in New York City during the 1720s and 1730s.

Beginning in 1749, however, a series of talented visitors came to New York and stayed for as long as patronage sustained them. They made New York City a major art center, and they are impressive both for the quantity as well as the quality of their work. They did no religious art at all and few landscapes. They did neither exteriors nor interiors of homes and no casual depictions of working people at their trades. They painted almost exclusively portraits of public and military officials, professional men, the mercantile elite, and their families. John Wollaston began this extraordinary era, arriving late in 1749, staying for more than two years, and painting about one hundred prominent subjects. Lawrence Kilburn came in 1754 and stayed until 1775. Benjamin West visited in 1759. A series of artists took up permanent residence during the 1760s, including William Williams. And then, during the second half of 1771, John Singleton Copley took the town by storm and enjoyed incredible success. The "best people" had Copley "do" them; and he, in response, did some of his finest American portraits.

Between being lionized socially and having more prospective clients than he could handle, Copley's visit was a breathless one. He felt that his patrons were discriminating: "The Gentry of this place distinguish very well, so I must slight nothing." He charged higher prices than he did in Boston and got what he asked: forty guineas for a full-length canvas, twenty guineas for one fifty by forty inches, and ten guineas for one thirty by twenty-five inches; rates for children were higher. He also came into his own during this challenging visit, and he knew it. "I have done some of my best portraits here," he wrote a relative, "perticularly Mrs. Gage's. . . . It is I think beyond Compare the best Lady's portrait I ever Drew." He was correct; it would be exhibited in London at the Society of Artists in 1772.

Copley was hardly the first outsider to take note (and advantage) of New York's commercialism. A characteristic formal portrait by John Wollaston in 1750 depicted Nathaniel Marston at his desk reviewing his account books. This was a bourgeois society that was rather proud of the fact. John Galt, the friend and biographer of Benjamin West, observed that "in New York [1759] Mr. West found the society wholly devoted to mercantile pursuits. A disposition to estimate things, not by their . . . beauty, but by the price which they would bring in the market, almost universally prevailed." Dr. Hamilton had found the same ethos at Albany in 1744: "The chief merit among them seems to be riches, which they spare no pains or trouble to acquire . . . their whole thoughts being turned upon profit and gain."

During the second quarter of the eighteenth century, visitors and natives alike began to notice the relative boorishness of New York's society and the vapidity of its cultural life. When Benjamin Franklin passed through in 1723, he was struck by the absence of books. "Those who lov'd Reading were oblig'd to send for their Books from England." Abigail Franks was apologetic about the province when it was criticized by outsiders. There were just as many fools in England, she insisted, and more pretentious ones at that. But to insiders she complained about the gaming and drinking that lasted from "Sunday night to Saturday morning." She lamented the lack of learned citizens and criticized the "ignorant Dutch," but also the ladies at her synagogue—"a stupid set of people."

Hamilton was appalled by the crude quality of manners and

conversation he encountered in New York. He saw a good deal of heavy drinking by "toapers" and "bumper men" and found that "to talk bawdy and to have a knack att punning passes among some there for good sterling wit." He remarked particularly upon one lout who "exceeded everything I had seen for nastiness, impudence, and rusticity. He told us he was troubled with the open piles [i.e., hemorrhoids] and with that, from his breeches, pulled out a linnen hankercheff all stained with blood and showed it to the company just after we had eat dinner."

By mid-century, a nucleus of citizens who were sensitive to both the boorishness and its critics, decided to do something about it. Social organizations, such as the Scots Society or the "Hungarian Club," had existed for some while; and there would be a bevy of others: a St. Andrew's Society, a St. Patrick Society, and so on. But these were primarily for eating, drinking, and conviviality. In 1748, however, a small group of ambitious, mostly young literati formed a discussion club which they called the Society for the Promotion of Useful Knowledge. They hoped that it would become an American counterpart to the Royal Society. Although they were destined for disillusionment, they did set a precedent by stimulating others to start comparable organizations in New York: a medical society in 1749, a society for the arts in 1764, and a debating club in 1768 (largely a forum for the exchange of views among lawyers).

These intellectuals also decided to create a periodical in which issues of public importance might be openly aired. Their intention, stated in 1749, was simply "improving the Minds of our Fellow Citizens." It came to fruition in 1752–53 with weekly publication of *The Independent Reflector*. The authors—William Livingston, John Morin Scott, and William Smith, Jr.—kept it going for exactly a year. It enjoyed considerable popular success: subscriptions exceeded four hundred copies. And it paved the way for a series of short-lived journals of opinion which stimulated the public mind in years to come: *The Occasional Reverberator* (1753), *The Plebean* (1754), *The Instructor* (1755), *John Englishman* (1755), and *The Pacquet* (1763).

At this same moment in time, when literary clubs, libraries,

and magazines began to appear, New York also got its first
sustained taste of theater and dramatic publications.* Back in
1709 the Provincial Council had forbidden any "play-acting and
prize-fighting." Not until 1730 did the first theatrical performance occur in New York, an amateur group's rendition of
Romeo and Juliet (also the first known production of any Shake-
spearean play on an American stage). In 1732 New Yorkers
could see *The Recruiting Officer* and four other plays in an extended
season; but from 1734 until 1750, although there were public
entertainments of various sorts, there were no more plays. In
February 1750, the Murray-Kean company of players arrived
from Philadelphia, set up a theater seating some 280 persons in a
warehouse and opened a sixteen-month run (with *Richard III*)
that effectively established the drama in colonial New York.

During the next decade there would be a good deal of public
discussion about "the taste of this place" plus intermittent
hostility to various aspects of dramatic productions. Even William Livingston suggested in 1753 that a troupe of comedians
would be injurious to public morals, and in 1761 there was a
shrill controversy over the propriety of ladies attending the
theater. When "Philodemus" insisted that ladies who went to
plays lacked modesty, "Armanda" replied by calling "Philodemus" a "superannuated animal that has past his grand
climacteric, and whose early times of life had been employed in
luxury and debauchery, and now being satiated, concludes that
all is vanity and every pleasure criminal." Nevertheless, the
1750s had brought a steady procession of comedies, ballad
operas, concerts, acrobats (including the "Female Sampson"),
benefit performances, and the Douglass Company in 1758 and
again in 1761. Thereafter, although people occasionally did
"throw Eggs from the Gallery upon the Stage," complaints about
the social behavior of actors began to diminish and public
acceptance was won.

---

* For New York imprints of such plays as *The Beggar's Opera* and broadside
advertisements for theatrical productions (all 1748–53), see Evans, comp.,
American Bibliography, nos. 6164, 6673, 7077, 40557, 40631, 40660 [Bristol,
Supplement, 1498, 1580, and 1618].

What made theater particularly vulnerable to criticism, of course, was that it was frivolous rather than useful. By the same token, intellectual endeavor for its own sake was suspect, and there was not a great deal of it in New York. Governor Burnet was a cultivated man, the son of a distinguished bishop and historian, educated at Cambridge, England, and called to the bar. He found himself so starved for stimulating conversation in 1724 that he summoned Benjamin Franklin, then an eighteen-year-old who happened to be passing through, for a tête-à-tête. Burnet, according to Franklin, "hearing from the Captain that a young Man, one of his Passengers, had a great many Books, desired he would bring me to see him. . . . The Governor treated me with great Civility, show'd me his Library, which was a very large one, and we had a good deal of Conversation about Books and Authors."

The most systematic inquiries into science and philosophy were undertaken by Cadwallader Colden, who had studied at Edinburgh and London, practiced medicine in Pennsylvania, and published his first scientific work, *Animal Secretions*, in 1715 at the age of twenty-seven. He came to New York in 1718, immersed himself in administrative affairs and politics, but also found time later on to write treatises on botanical topics, disease, gravitation, calculus, and philosophy. He corresponded with eminent European scientists and introduced the Linnaean system of classification to America (1742–44) soon after its original publication in 1737. Colden has perhaps been overrated as a scientist. He did little experimental work, often ignored empirical evidence that did not jibe with his speculative theories, and received considerable criticism as a result. He did, however, have real ability in the realm of natural history, especially at identification and classification. His ultimate significance as a scientist, however, lies less in any particular discovery or theory than in his role as an organizer and correspondent. He helped to bring Newtonian and Linnaean science to the New World, and he brought naturalists in the various colonies into contact with one another.

Although Colden had been trained as a physician, he ceased to

Cadwallader Colden (1688–1776), scientist and politician. Portrait by John Wollaston, ca. 1751. *The Metropolitan Museum of Art, Bequest of Grace Wilkes, 1922.*

practice after settling in New York—a decision of symbolic importance because it calls attention to the poor quality of medical knowledge and treatment there in the eighteenth-century. Moreover, although he ceased to practice, Colden continued to write about medical matters—behavior very much in character for him. He published a treatise on intestinal disorders (1741), an expansion of Bishop Berkeley's claims for the curative qualities of tar water (1745), and *An Essay on Yellow Fever* (1745)—even though he had never seen a case! In 1751 he printed an article on the value of pokeweed as a cure for cancer; two years later he wrote a letter "Concerning the Throat-Distemper" which was published in the London *Medical Observations and Inquiries*, and in 1765 a more ambitious work entitled *Treatise on Wounds and Fevers*.

Under the circumstances, it will come as no surprise that public health was precarious in provincial New York. The smallpox epidemic that struck during the summer and autumn of 1731 proved devastating, helped not at all by the appearance of a four-page *Treatise on the Virtues of Dr. Bateman's Pectoral Drops* (printed by Zenger). Dr. Hamilton of Annapolis observed that Albany's doctors had "no knowledge of learning. . . . They study chiefly the virtues of herbs. . . . The doctors here are all barbers." At Huntington, Long Island, he met "a fellow with a worsted cap and great black fists. They stiled him doctor. Flat told me he had been a shoemaker in town and was a notable fellow att his trade, but happening two years agoe to cure an old woman of a pestilent mortal disease, he thereby acquired the character of a physitian, was applied to from all quarters, and finding the practice of physick a more profitable business than cobling, he laid aside his awls and leather, got himself some gallipots, and instead of cobling of soals, fell to cobling of human bodies." Little wonder that people preferred self-diagnosis to such primitive medicine. When Henry Muhlenberg got laryngitis in 1750, he "took a strong vomitory in order to break up by force the viscidity of the blood and humors, facilitate the circulation of the blood, and restore my speech."

❖   ❖   ❖

In sum, there was unquestionably an increase in cultural awareness and curiosity at mid-century—medical backwardness notwithstanding. Advertisements in New York newspapers after 1750 indicate a rise in provincial consciousness and native chauvinism: "They are equal if not superior in quality to any imported from Europe" and "preference to what is American made" were typical claims. There was, however, a certain ambivalence behind their bravado. Such literati as the authors of *The Independent Reflector* imitated the political rhetoric and phraseology of Augustan England, even where it did not fit truly with the realities of provincial life. More inconsistent still, they borrowed rather indiscriminately from two different views of society and public behavior: the libertarian view of the whiggish commonwealthmen and the "country party" ideology of Swift and Bolingbroke. Hence the political philosophy that characterized New York essays of the 1750s was a hybrid, at once radical and reactionary, forward looking in some respects but unrealistic and derivative in others. Hence the lack of an appropriate congruence between ideas and reality, which would require adjustment in the decade after 1765.

Meanwhile, as New Yorkers tried to sort out those aspects of British culture worthy and suitable to the American strand, some in Great Britain even began to discover American materials as the stuff of cultural creativity. In 1755, for example, Dr. John Shebbeare published a novel in London entitled *Lydia, or Filial Piety*, in which Cannassatego, an Onondaga sachem, sails to England, meets Lydia Fairchild (a native of New York) on board his ship, sees the royal court, and returns to New York where, along with the Cayugas, he and his tribal brothers declare their intense dislike of England.

There were even some who predicted that *American* authors would eventually use their native resources for literary and political expression. "The next Augustan age will dawn on the other side of the Atlantic," Horace Walpole declared in 1774. "There will perhaps be a Thucydides at Boston, a Xenophon at

New York." Washington Irving and Fenimore Cooper were still a generation away; but the material for a military historian of high caliber was almost at hand.

11

EXPANSION, URBANIZATION, AND THE PROBLEM OF COMMUNITY

Having treated the constitutional, ecclesiastical, and cultural developments that were most salient in eighteenth-century New York, we must turn next to social life within particular localities. This is necessary because of the colony's diversity; because such varied matters as poor relief, land speculation, and landlord-tenant relationships affected a great proportion of the provincial population; because the middle third of the eighteenth century was an important period for the development of social institutions; and, most of all, because only by examining the localities can we fully perceive the most critical social problem of that generation: the problem of achieving community in a heterogeneous and burgeoning society.

We might well begin by looking at a few comparative figures in order to get a clearer sense of demographic change, both within the colony and by contrast with its neighbors. Rough population statistics for the six largest colonies (stated in thousands) are revealing:

Colony	1750	1760	1770
Virginia	275.0	346.0	450.0
Massachusetts	180.0	235.0	265.0
Pennsylvania	150.0	220.0	250.0
Maryland	137.0	162.0	200.0

| Connecticut | 100.0 | 142.0 | 175.0 |
| New York | 80.0 | 113.0 | 160.0 |

Notice that New York was only the sixth most populous colony in 1750 and still was in 1770. On the other hand, it was the only colony among the six to double its population during those two decades. Much of that rapid increase occurred in Albany and New York City. Although in 1743 New York was the third-largest American city, by 1760 it was second only to Philadelphia. (Between 1783 and 1786 the population of New York City more than doubled, and by 1820 it had the largest urban population in the United States.)

City	1743	1760
Boston	16,382	15,631
Philadelphia	13,000	23,750
New York	11,000	18,000
Charles Town	6,800	8,000
Newport	6,200	7,500

More important than these gross figures, however, was their distribution in the social structure and the sense contemporaries had of that distribution and its significance. By mid-century, for example, both an urban as well as a rural proletariat had begun to emerge. Between about 1735 and 1755 there was a distinct development of uneasy class consciousness and in the following fifteen years a good deal of social conflict: rural flare-ups during 1751–57 and 1763–66, as well as urban unrest in the decade after 1758. Election campaigns exploited these frictions and thereby exacerbated them.

Contemporary discussions of social structure and politics indicate, however, that people thought about the organization of society not so much in terms of region or class as in terms of economic interest blocs. In 1765, for example, Cadwallader Colden informed the Board of Trade that "the People of New York are properly Distinguished into different Ranks:" (1) landowners with more than one hundred thousand acres, (2) lawyers and judges, (3) merchants, (4) farmers and artisans. "This last Rank comprehends the bulk of the People," he added. When Robert R. Livingston wrote an essay in opposition to a land tax (1752), he too discussed political society in terms of these vocational distinctions.

Emphasis upon such socioeconomic lines of affiliation unquestionably created obstacles to achieving a sense of community among different occupational groups in any given locality. But to complicate matters, there was not even a strong sense of cohesion *within* these groups. Members of the elite fought each other bitterly: De Lanceys against Livingstons, Beekmans against Philipses. Agrarian tenants on the eastern frontier of the Hudson Valley did, too: farmers of Dutch descent against New England squatters. And even radicals failed to make common cause: Westchester "Levellers" and Sons of Liberty refused to cooperate in 1766.

Among the various obstacles to social cohesion in provincial New York, three stand out as being of determinative importance: ethnic diversity, the uneven distribution and system of landownership, and the process of urbanization. Where a relatively small number of men held large tracts and would neither sell nor develop them, where men greedily sought large parcels of good land to hold for speculative purposes, there could be no sense of community. After 1750 the great landowners found their privileges and practices being challenged, whereupon they became uneasily defensive and insecure.

The functional roles of New York City and Albany, moreover, as well as the nature of urban change, made any sort of community within them increasingly elusive by the end of the 1750s. Authorities on urbanization the world over have usefully differentiated between types of towns on the basis of their social functions. They distinguish between market towns and court towns, for example, and point out that changes in class structure, in family organization, and in religious orientation may proceed differently within each. In the English colonial cities, however, one consistently finds "commercial-extractive" economies, dependent upon wide-ranging patterns of trade and an open labor market. Life in these towns revolved around the pursuit of individual gain through foreign and domestic commerce as well as through related activities. New York had no royal towns like Windsor, no episcopal cities like York, no university towns like Oxford, and no pilgrimage towns like Canterbury. Its urban centers were essentially economic entities—trading marts—and their differences would result from product specialization and ethnic emphasis within the population. They were cities of Mammon: nurseries for a nation of shopkeepers.

After about 1740, when the colony began to recover from the severe economic depression of the 1730s, New York City underwent a profound physical and social transformation: from a rude outpost with a primitive economy to an expanding provincial metropolis with such commercial institutions as insurance companies. Arriving in 1744, Dr. Hamilton was impressed by all the shipping he saw in port and remarked that "in generall this city has more of an urban appearance than Philadelphia. . . . The women of fashion here appear more in publick than in Philadelphia and dress much gayer."

Thus New York now needed such urban protection as fire-fighting equipment. Its first fire engine was brought from England in 1731: a side-stroke, gooseneck, tub engine equipped with pumping handles and foot treadles. A volunteer fire company was organized late in 1737; and by 1740 the leather helmet—to protect the head from injury, to shed water from the back of the neck, and, when reversed, to shield the face from intense heat—had been developed.

Public health also began to be more problematic by the 1740s; in 1744 a cluster of laws was passed to provide for sanitation, better drainage, and the control of livestock in general and hogs in particular. After mid-century there were serious complaints about the presence and sale of putrid meat, so that in 1751 the magistrates publicly seized and burned two veal carcasses as "Carrion." In 1757 a law was passed controlling the sale of oysters during the four hot months; and in 1758 the sale of bass in wintertime was prohibited on the grounds that the catch would be "commonly unsound and unwholesome." Enforcement, however, tended ordinarily to be lax; and in 1750 Henry Muhlenberg and others complained bitterly about "the oppressive, impure, and unaccustomed air of the city."

Epidemics remained a persistent problem. Yellow fever killed about one-ninth of the city's population in 1702. Smallpox struck in 1718, measles in 1729; and the smallpox virulence in 1731 carried off some six hundred victims and led to the first experiments with inoculation in New York. Yellow fever returned in 1732 and 1743 and struck Albany in 1746. Smallpox occurred again in 1738, 1745–47, intermittently between 1752 and 1766, as well as in Albany in 1756. As the city became more crowded, smallpox became more frequent and dangerous. There were, in addition, unspecified "throat distempers" on a widespread basis in 1745, 1755, and again in the late 1760s, all of which diminished the community in demographic terms, caused psychic crises of fear and suspicion, and created an incredible drain upon the community's limited funds for poverty relief.

New York made its first significant provisions for quarantine in 1738 because of the danger of disease being brought from the lower Atlantic seaboard area. A special anchorage was established off Bedloe's Island for all vessels coming from ports known to be infected. In 1744 Governor Clinton issued a proclamation forbidding ships to dock in New York without first being visited by a physician and obtaining a health certificate. In 1739 the city for the first time had a separate structure built for destitute victims of contagious diseases; and in 1759–60 a pesthouse was constructed on Bedloe's Island, which then was designated as a quarantined area.

During the entire colonial period, New York depended upon wells, pumps, and natural streams for drinking water. (Running water from a pipeline system would not be installed until 1799.) Consequently taverns kept busy, busier than ever after midcentury when urban crowding tended to foul the water supply. New York City had 282 taverns in 1766 and 396 by 1773. A statute of 1737 forbidding tavern keepers from serving apprentices was reenacted in 1745 and 1773, but alcoholism continued to be a municipal problem.

So did prostitution. By the early 1740s, it was common knowledge that the main battery at the fort was the place to go to find "a courtezan, for that place was the generall rendezvous of the fair sex of that profession after sun set. . . . There was a good choice of pritty lasses among them, both Dutch and English." By the 1770s New York reportedly had at least five hundred "ladies of pleasure," and some of the most notorious lived along the same street occupied by King's College.

Crime was still another aspect of urbanization. During the periods 1731–37 and 1756–71, crime rates rose even faster than population growth. The year 1750 seems to have been a significant turning point in the history of urban crime in New York. Serious and especially violent crimes became more prominent immediately after 1750. There was a discernible increase in violations of public order, in acts of personal violence, in the number of disorderly houses, and in acts of theft. Moreover, the percentage of unresolved cases rose, as well as the average duration of prosecutions and the amount of recidivism. A genuine crisis of law enforcement occurred between 1750 and 1754. It continued with somewhat less intensity for the rest of the colonial period, despite the fact that penalties became harsher after 1750, all of which was worsened by the facts that qualified constables and sheriffs were hard to find, that jailor and hangman were unpopular positions, that even jurors and justices of the peace were in short supply. In sum, the incidence of crime kept well ahead of law enforcement through the final generation of the colonial period.

New York encountered its most serious threat to public safety in 1741, when the "Negroe conspiracy" occurred. To understand that frightening episode, however, it is necessary to look back another decade and briefly examine the ways in which white society attempted to control the black community, as well as the anxieties underlying those attempts. Fear of a slave plot in 1730 had proved to be unfounded. That fear nevertheless prompted the legislature to complete, by the mid-1730s, a harsh slave code that remained in effect for the rest of the eighteenth century. New York's slave population was the most sizable north of the

Chesapeake, and virtually every white person assumed that these blacks were a separate and inferior species of humankind requiring special controls. Any slave traveling alone more than a mile from his home had to have a pass. Slaves could neither sell goods without the consent of their owners nor possess weapons of any sort, and they could not even use guns unless under their masters' supervision.

Although prescribed punishments were harsh—whipping, branding, jail terms, even breaking on the wheel—the slave's value as part of a vital labor force often served to minimize the actual application of penalties. Although regarded as property, the slave's legal humanity was also recognized, which meant that he was theoretically protected from cruel abuse or tyrannical treatment. The law required that slaves receive an "adequate" amount of food and clothing, and masters were held legally responsible for the care of aged and infirm slaves. As chattels, however, slaves could also be bequeathed, inherited, and taxed as property. Judicial procedures established for slaves early in the 1730s omitted many of the safeguards accorded to white persons living under a system of Anglo-Saxon justice. Certain crimes were to be punished with death when committed by a black but not when committed by a white. The rape of a free woman was a capital offense, but not the rape of a female slave.

Because New York City had a substantial number of slaves (one-sixth of the population) and because their commercial uses made them relatively mobile, municipal authorities had more trouble enforcing their ordinances than at any other locality in the colony. Where many of the slaves worked as skilled artisans and were not under constant supervision, illicit social visiting took place. Slaves from Long Island and northern New Jersey set up vegetable markets to sell produce which often had been obtained illegally. Some taverns even catered to blacks, a circumstance that contributed to the wild hysteria and accusations made in 1741.

During a series of thefts and fires, one tavern owner who illegally served liquor to slaves was charged, along with his family and a prostitute, with robbery and receipt of stolen goods.

When additional fires and black insolence totally unnerved the town in April, a reward of one hundred pounds for information leading to the arsonists prompted sixteen-year-old Mary Burton, an indentured servant, to divulge a "Negroe plot" to burn the city, murder every white male, divide the surviving white females among the blacks, and make John Hughson (her master and the tavern owner previously accused) "King of New York."

Despite flagrant contradictions and absurdities in her charges, and despite sworn testimony from masters that their accused slaves had been at home when the fires occurred, two slaves were hanged. Trials continued for more than a year; 18 slaves and 4 whites were eventually hanged, 13 slaves were burned at the stake, over 150 slaves and 25 whites were imprisoned. Only confession of guilt could save a hapless accused person; and more than 70 who "confessed" were exiled to the West Indies. The hysteria and trials finally ended when Mary Burton began to name prominent, respectable citizens and thereby lost all her credibility. She received her hundred-pound reward nonetheless and promptly disappeared from the province.

The actual nature and extent of the "conspiracy" of 1741 may never be known. Since a cache of stolen goods was, in fact, found in the cellar of Hughson's tavern, the episode very likely did involve a theft ring and possession of stolen goods—but not political rebellion. Race relations became calmer thereafter, at least on the surface—perhaps the terrifying punishments had the desired effect—and only two other comparable episodes subsequently came to light during the colonial period. In 1761 authorities in Schenectady apprehended thirteen slaves who had been overheard in a tavern planning to burn and loot the town. In 1775 about twenty slaves were arrested for plotting rebellion in Ulster County; they were most likely devising a scheme for escape to Canada. There had been numerous runaways throughout the course of the eighteenth century. Some of them received asylum from the French; others joined Indian tribes and even intermarried. Despite offers of rewards and diplomatic pressures, the Iroquois almost never returned fugitive slaves who had come to them for help.

In the last analysis, the terror of 1741 was symptomatic of the city's lack of community. In an atmosphere of suspicion and tension (there had been rumors in 1740 that blacks would poison the water supply), "telling the truth" meant implicating one's neighbors. So slaves betrayed other slaves, just as whites betrayed whites. In addition to overt racism, anti-Catholic phobias and class resentments were visible. When John Ury, a Catholic priest, became a defendant in the case, prosecution lawyers begged "leave to say a few words concerning the heinessness of the prisoner's offenses, and of the popish religion in general." Mary Burton testified that Cuffee, one of the slaves, "used to say that a great many people had too much, and others too little." Race, religion, and class were all sources of resentment and trouble.

The winter of 1740–41 had been unusually long, cold, and harsh. Grain became exorbitantly expensive, supplies of food and wood ran low, and by February a special fund for poor relief was exhausted. That, too, was symptomatic, because New York's difficulty in handling the problem of poor relief reveals still other dimensions to the problems of urbanization, secularization, and failure to achieve community. The evolution of relief for the poor during the first half of the eighteenth century had been unsystematic and led in 1744 to the beginnings of private philanthropy whereby individual social groups looked after "their own kind." Crises of relief would recur in 1753 when merchants devalued lesser English coins in circulation, and in 1759–65 when severe inflation affected the colony. Urban poverty became a significant problem in the 1760s, caused by depression, unemployment, and boycotts, evident in the growing number of beggars and the need for poorhouse annexes by 1767.

Some explanation of this haphazard system is required, for there was no uniformity in the provincial administration of poor relief, and local responsibility was neither fully under secular auspices as in New England nor fully under the Anglican vestry as in Virginia. A pluralistic colony had a hybrid system, the result of grafting English forms onto Dutch customs. One authority, David M. Schneider, has summarized it this way: "In some parts of the province public poor relief was administered on the congregational plan with the Dutch Reformed, the Anglican, the Lutheran, or some other church exercising official or quasi-official authority; in others, the relief system was wholly secular in form. In some areas there was complete local responsibility; in others the county exerted varying degrees of control." The practice of boarding out paupers—a private solution—was also commonplace. The prevailing attitude toward dependency was one of disapproval, and authorities stigmatized it with badges of shame.

According to the Ministry Act of 1693, the freeholders were to elect (each January) ten vestrymen and two churchwardens. The latter would be chosen irrespective of religion and were charged with caring for the poor. Their favored policy, whenever possible, was to remove the indigent rather than support them. Non-residents of New York who required relief were normally removed from the city, escorted by a constable to their last previous legal residence. If residents on relief were willing to leave the city and join relatives or friends able to support them, the wardens would provide sufficient funds for the trip, even though it might be to England or Antigua.

Nevertheless, the cost of poor relief was consistently the largest single item in New York City's annual budget. Between 1723 and 1735, for example, it averaged £523. By 1734, when the sum reached £649, citizens complained about rising poor taxes and wandering beggars. In 1735, consequently, New York built its first poorhouse under civil auspices, yet another indication of both secularization and the emergence of a substantial lower class. Called the House of Correction, Workhouse and Poor House, it was completed in March 1736: a two-story stone structure, sixty-five by twenty-four feet. It was furnished "with the following Tools and Utensils (to witt) four spinning wheels, one or two large wheels for making of shoes, two pairs of wollen cards, some knitting Needles, twelve pounds of Flax, 500 pounds of old Junck, twelve pounds of wool, twelve pounds of Cotton, [and] two or three Hatchells [instruments for combing flax or hemp]."

Twelve adults and at least seven children moved in immediately. Despite the fact that people could only be admitted by order of the vestry and justices of the Mayor's Court, and despite the fact that every person receiving charity had to wear the letters *N:Y* in red on his or her right shoulder, there were 425 paupers living in the poorhouse and its annexes by 1772. The problem of poverty became steadily more serious in New York between 1736 and 1776. After the mid-1740s, poorhouses established by towns and precincts also began to appear in the rural areas.

If poor relief put a strain upon municipal resources, especially during the severe depression of the 1730s, it also dramatized how limited were the city's available funds. When the French wars resumed again in 1744, the city desperately needed to repair its pathetic defenses. A property tax was the logical solution; but to keep the tax bearable, a public lottery was conceived as a means of raising funds and reducing the tax burden. The lottery bill finally passed in 1746 and created a precedent that would be repeated for almost two decades. Lotteries to benefit the proposed college began late in 1746 and occurred regularly right through 1764. In 1757 there would be a lottery to raise money for a new jail, in 1762 to repair City Hall, and in 1763 to provide a bounty for producers of hemp. By 1747, however, a problem arose over the legitimacy of private lotteries (such as church raffles) that were not for the entire community's benefit. Critics condemned them because they "occasioned Idleness and Inattention to Business," had brought "Distress, Impoverishment, and Ruin to many Families," and had "given Birth to a dangerous spirit of Gaming." All of these reasons were given in an act, passed in 1772, to prevent private lotteries. Once again the state stepped in to stop further erosion of New York as a virtuous community.

That same erosion may also be seen in urban politics during the period 1734–75, a period when city government was more dominated by the social elite than it had been from 1689 until 1733. Almost the entire Common Council was replaced in the municipal election of 1734, and thereafter we find greater longevity of individual incumbents, fewer persons serving only single terms, and less rotation in office than had been the case during the preceding generation. Aldermen also were more consistently chosen from the socioeconomic elite after 1733; that is, more of them were merchants, lawyers, and large landowners, while fewer were artisans, shopkeepers, and farmers. Whereas city officials in the 1730s tended to resist gubernatorial encroachments upon charter rights, their successors took a more subservient attitude, as well as a more rigid posture toward popular causes.

Contributing to the weakness of the popular party in urban politics was the incredible disunity among dissenting groups. Because the Dutch Reformed received special consideration, they tended to support the more conservative Anglicans, as did many Huguenot families. The Presbyterians took over leadership of the opposition and developed a bitter hatred of Anglican influence in particular. After all, attempts by the Presbyterian church of New York City to obtain a charter of incorporation had been quashed in 1721, 1734, 1759, and 1767 because of Anglican hostility. Hence the Presbyterians' vigorous efforts to avert the appointment of an American bishop during the 1760s. Hence, too, their coalition with the Baptists in 1769 to organize the Society of Dissenters. Its purpose was to attack the Anglicans, to campaign for the election of nonconformists to the Assembly, and to end the partial Church of England establishment in the lower counties. The Council defeated these maneuvers in 1769 and 1770, but their significance in this context is that there was neither Christian fellowship nor community of any sort among the churches of New York City.

Similar tensions, equally indicative of anxieties caused by institutional growth and urbanization, surfaced between 1747 and 1753 in a public debate over the best location for King's College. Advocates of a rural site insisted that the quality of air would be better in the countryside, the cost of living (e.g., firewood) would be less, agricultural subjects might be taught more easily, and philosophical reflection would be more likely to occur. Even more revealing, however, were the risks inherent in a "downtown" location: proximity to taverns and persons of ill repute, temptations to idleness and corruption. As one worrier put it, New York City was a "Sea Port Town" where "great Numbers of all Sorts of People are collected, good and bad . . . ; and I doubt [not that] the latter will ever be, by far, the Majority."

Soon after 1750, significantly enough, newspaper advertising began to become commonplace in New York City. Most ads before that date had to do with runaway slaves, counterfeiting, real estate, and the departure of vessels. When craftsmen began to place ads for their products, it indicated the emergence of urban anonymity. In a village everyone knows everyone else, his products, and his business. Only in a complex, larger society, a society without community, is there any need to advertise one's wares and location.

Peter Kalm has left us an invaluable description of New York City in 1750:

In size it comes next to Boston and Philadelphia, but with regard to fine buildings, opulence, and extensive commerce, it vies with them for supremacy. . . .

The streets do not run so straight as those of Philadelphia, and sometimes are quite crooked; however, they are very spacious and well built, and most of them are paved, except in high places, where it has been found useless. In the chief streets there are trees planted, which in summer give them a fine appearance, and during the excessive heat at that time afford a cooling shade. I found it extremely pleasant to walk in the town, for it seemed like a garden. . . .

Most of the houses are built of brick, and are generally strong and neat, and several stories high. Some had, in the old style, turned the gable end toward the street; but the new houses were altered in this respect. Many of the houses had a balcony on the roof, on which the people used to sit evenings in the summer season; and from thence they had a pleasant view of a great part of the town, and likewise of a part of the adjacent water and the opposite shore. The roofs are commonly covered with tiles or shingles. . . .

Other visitors during the next decade were equally impressed. As Thomas Pownall approached on the *Arundel* in 1753, he noted that the buildings, the harbor, "and the multitude of Shipping

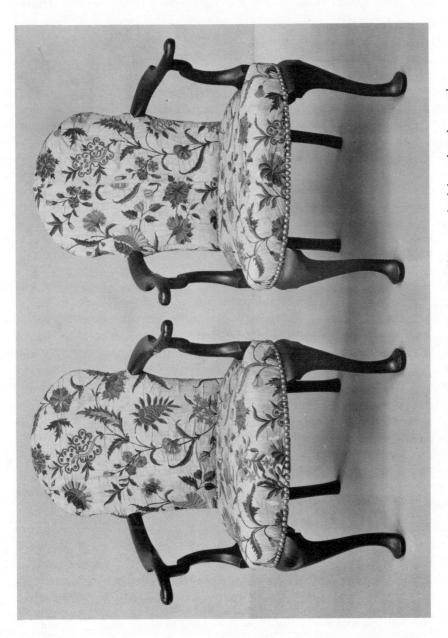

A pair of small walnut armchairs, upholstered in linen worked in colored crewels, made in New York around the mid-eighteenth century. *The Metropolitan Museum of Art, Bequest of Maria P. James, 1911.*

with which it is thronged perpetually, [make] a very striking appearance and altogether as fine and as pleasing a View as I ever saw." * According to an English naval officer in 1756, "the nobleness of the town surprised me more than the fertile appearance of the country. I had no idea of finding a place in America, consisting of near 2,000 houses, elegantly built of brick, raised on an eminence and the streets paved and spacious, furnished with commodious keys [quays] and warehouses, and employing some hundreds of vessels in its foreign trade and fisheries—but such is this city that very few in England can rival it in its show."

Population spread steadily up Manhattan Island. The municipal corporation owned the land and put it up for leases whenever it needed funds. By 1760 the King's Farm, located between Broadway and the Hudson River, had been surveyed into lots and began to be peopled. In 1762 the corporation laid out lots in portions of the Out Ward (lying between the Boston Road and the East River) and offered them on twenty-one-year leases at four pounds per annum. In 1763 it added thirty-one lots of five acres each on Murray Hill for farms or suburban homes. By 1766 New York had 8 public buildings, 5 markets, 15 churches, and 3,223 houses. "The City has more Grand Buildings than Boston," Copley wrote in 1771, "the streets much Cleaner and some broader, but it is not Boston in my opinion yet."

Residents of New York City accordingly found the expense of municipal services steadily rising during the 1760s and resented the fact that, having no more than one-fifth of the colony's population, they paid one-third of all the provincial taxes (as of 1773). Bridges, roads, and street paving and cleaning cost money, and the pinch was felt with special discomfort during the depression of 1760–65. It also provided yet another source of tension between city dwellers and countryfolk.

New York City was certainly unique in the colony, and we shall soon explore the contrasts between it and the provincial

---

* William Bradford published the first engraved map of New York's harbor in 1735. See Evans, comp., *American Bibliography*, no. 3922.

countryside. Note should first be taken, however, of certain similarities between New York City and Albany. Both began as forts and both had distinct boundaries or outer limits. Neither one had been a covenanted community, a "city upon a hill" like Boston or Philadelphia, and neither felt strong psychological pressures for communal self-purification. The nature of society in both tended to be atomistic, though Albany remained a clannish, tribal town somewhat longer. Albany's Common Council also was dominated by a patrician elite: ten families in general and five in particular, the Schuylers, Cuylers, Ten Broecks, Rose-booms, and Wendels. Albany politics also underwent a period of particular divisiveness during the 1730s, and by the late 1740s a conservative group of newer patricians began to appear in the Common Council. Finally, the cost of living by mid-century was higher at Albany than at Philadelphia. Activity in the area during King George's War (1744–48) had driven up the cost of food and lodgings, and complaints from visitors were common-place.

One of them, Peter Kalm, lived for a week with a large Albany family in November 1750. His account is as quaint as it is revealing:

There was the same perpetual evening meal of porridge made of corn meal. (The Dutch in Albany as well as those in New York called this porridge *Sappaan*.) It was put into a good-sized dish and a large hole [was] made in its center into which the milk was poured, and then one proceeded to help oneself. When the milk was gone, more was added until all the porridge had been consumed. Care was usually taken that there should be no waste, so that when all had eaten, not a bit of porridge should remain. After the porridge one ate bread and butter to hold it down. . . . For dinner they rarely had more than one dish, meat with turnips or cabbage; occasionally there were two [dishes]. They never served more than was consumed before they left the table. Nearly all women who had passed their fortieth year smoked tobacco; even those who were considered as belonging to the foremost families. I frequently saw about a dozen old ladies sitting about the fire smoking. Once in a while I discovered newly-married wives of twenty and some years sitting there with pipes in their mouths. But nothing amused me more than to observe how occupied they were with the placing of the warming pans beneath their skirts. In a house where there were four women present it was well nigh impossible to glance in the direction of the fire without seeing at least one of them busily engaged in replacing the coals in her warming pan. Even their negro women had acquired this habit, and if time allowed, they also kept warming pans under their skirts.

Although distinctive aspects of Dutch domestic life did endure in Albany, intermittent warfare between 1744 and 1763 wrought significant social changes. The town's population quadrupled between 1750 and 1770. Intercolonial expeditions brought large numbers of redcoats, regulars, and militia from other colonies. In 1756 it became necessary to quarter fourteen hundred troops in the homes of three thousand people, and several thousand more soldiers were encamped nearby. They remained there in large numbers until 1760 and proved disruptive to the community. Until mid-century, at least 80 percent of all baptisms, marriages, and burials in the Albany church records bore Dutch surnames; but that proportion declined sharply after 1760, suggesting sudden social diversification and the attendant problems of community cohesion. British military personnel married the daughters of Dutch families, and a good many brides of English descent were brought to the area. In addition, a sizable wave of German families flowed into the Mohawk River valley after 1750. One measurable result was that the proportion of voters with Dutch surnames in Albany County declined from 82 percent in 1720 to 57 percent in 1763.

Nor could there be any sense of community between the whites and Indians around Albany, so long as the former coveted the latter's lands and constantly encroached upon them. A bitter controversy occurred in 1733–36 over thirty-two hundred choice acres called Mohawk Flatts, a tract along the Schoharie River about twenty miles west of Schenectady. An accommodation was reached; but after 1744 the Iroquois' suspicion of Albany's Indian commissioners, who were hostile to William Johnson, the Mohawks' trusted friend, only made matters worse. As Edith M. Fox has written, "To evade crown regulations which restricted large-scale speculation in New York's frontier lands, prospective owners of vast tracts in the eighteenth century resorted to various devices, one of which was to acquire land in the names of other men." Where greedy men got land deceitfully, there could be no community.

Nor could there be social cohesion where restless men were on the move. During the second quarter of the eighteenth century, a little-noticed drama of internal migration occurred in New York. The population of King's County (today's Brooklyn), for example, remained stable until 1750 because its natural increase moved north to unsettled areas. By 1732 all the desirable land in Queen's County had been taken up and further agricultural expansion was impossible, so younger colonists of Dutch descent wandered to Westchester County in search of land. Many of them went to work on the manors there—Fordham, Pelham, Cortlandt, Morrisania, Philipsburgh, and Scarsdale—and by 1750 Westchester had more of a Dutch character than it had had in 1700.

Dutchess County also underwent a period of rapid growth between the 1730s and 1750s, receiving a substantial migration from Long Island and from Westchester, as well as from New England after 1740. Its population more than doubled in each decade, and one result was a desperate struggle between the Beekmans and the Philipses for control over land and for political leverage. That battle became most evident between 1745 and 1748 and demonstrated the difficulty of achieving stability in these rapidly swelling river counties. "I would act the Causious peacefull part," wrote Henry Beekman in 1747, "for it Seems that the Sead of Discord is very prevellant, & [I] would reather Suffer a Smal Indignity than Inflame the Community."

Colonists of Dutch descent also migrated across the lower Hudson into Ulster, Orange, and what is now Rockland County. They were joined there by Scottish immigrants, particularly after 1734 and into the 1740s, when Governors Cosby and then Clarke mounted promotional campaigns to attract more settlers from Scotland and Ireland.* By mid-century, therefore, most of the

---

* Many Highlanders who served in North America during the French and Indian War chose to remain in New York as residents. The royal proclamation

Hudson Valley area had been formally divided, apportioned, and subdivided. From the perspective of productive farming and inheritance patterns, a sense of crowding began to be felt. Land shares in New Paltz were minutely subdivided by 1745. On the eve of the Revolution, there were men typically holding 1/234, 1/468, or 67/720 parts. When land gets to be in such short supply, agricultural villages become uneasy communities. Not surprisingly, therefore, the lure of the Mohawk River valley became very strong at that point.

New Yorkers were able to migrate and cultivate new areas of the colony, in part, because of the development of rural roads during and after the 1730s. In the 1720s, the Assembly had begun to pay some attention to the problem of provincial travel. Although a highway act appeared on every agenda for additions and reconsideration, little of a substantive nature was accomplished at first. The Assembly did decide to increase the number of highway commissioners per county, to regulate the width of wagons (in order to reduce traffic problems on narrow roads), and to supervise the town surveyors who had responsibility for summoning inhabitants for road work (fines assessed would be put toward highway repairs). Private roads first began to be developed at personal expense during the 1720s. By the end of that decade the Assembly had come to realize that circumstances peculiar to individual counties required road legislation custom tailored for each, rather than an omnibus bill.

Considerable road building occurred during the 1730s and 1740s, therefore, including the so-called King's Highway on both sides of the Hudson. Stone markers about thirty inches high told the traveler his distance from a central point, such as City Hall in New York City, and road maps even began to appear. In 1735, for example, Bradford published "A Map of the Five Nations of Indians, with the Road from Albany to Oswego, and the Situation of the Lakes." By 1750 the pattern of highway

---

of Oct. 1763 offered generous terms. In addition, between 1765 and 1774 there were a number of large group migrations from Scotland, organized by Hugh Fraser, James Macdonald, Donald Campbell, and others. Their influx was so rapid that Charlotte County had to be carved out of Albany County in 1772.

legislation and maintenance was thoroughly established. Repair of existing roads and proposals for new ones were local responsibilities. Those who used the roads were expected to build and rebuild them, as well as pay for their upkeep through taxes, fines, and forfeitures. Local laborers coped with washouts, ruts, and stubborn tree stumps.*

Migration and immigration brought another problem, perhaps more serious even than transportation needs. Between 1721 and 1773 the colony concerned itself with vagrancy. In 1721 the Assembly passed an act "to prevent Vagrants and Idle Persons from being a Charge and Expense to any [of] the Counties, Towns, Mannors or Precincts within this Province." The act required any householder entertaining a stranger for a period of three days or longer to notify the mayor or a justice of the peace and supply vital information about the stranger. If the latter's character or economic status were questionable, he or she might be examined and a constable ordered to "Send the Said Stranger to The place from Whence he or She last Came."

This "passing-on" system remained the standard method for getting rid of the nonresident poor throughout the eighteenth century, and it became a common practice after the 1730s as a rootless rural proletariat began to emerge. In 1753 William Livingston devoted an issue of *The Independent Reflector* to a serious discussion of "the Importation of *Mendicant* Foreigners," and he took note of the critical tension between Christian charity and

---

* Expansion of settlement involved planting as well as uprooting trees. Yorkers who relocated were particularly fond of their familiar locust trees and seeded them all around new home sites—hence such place names as Locust Valley, Locust Grove, and Locust Lawn. Peter Kalm remarked in 1750 upon the locust's "fine leaves and fragrant scent which exhales from its flowers, [and] make it very suitable for planting in the streets near the houses and in gardens." Locust trees surround the charming old Dutch Church of Sleepy Hollow, as well as Bethlehem House, built in Albany County about 1730 (the trees were reputedly planted when the house was built). Many of the locusts in Dutchess County are descended from ones brought from Long Island between 1735 and 1750. The "champion" in the state today is a black locust in Slingerlands owned by William Waise. It is 74 feet high, more than 20 feet in circumference, and has a 44-foot crown.

community stability: "Thus we must often shut the Bowels of our Mercy, or injure the Community, of which we are Members.— Thus that which is virtuous in Theory, becomes vicious in Practice."

The problem of "strangers" arose in yet another form at mid-century: squatters from New England whose presence all along the eastern frontier made it virtually impossible to achieve any semblance of community there. During the six years after the peace settlement of 1748, Yankees began to occupy that ill-defined territory between the Connecticut and Housatonic rivers. Their presence conflicted with Robert R. Livingston's land claims; and even when he leased land to some of them, conflicts arose over the nature of their tenure and rent. This confrontation between the irregular land system of New York and the expansive inclinations of New England farmers (suffering from poor soil and wheat rust) was symptomatic of a series of such crises that occurred between New York and its neighbors—Massachusetts, Connecticut, New Hampshire, and New Jersey—in the generation after 1735. It led to intermittent nastiness in 1751–53, 1755, and 1757 in which there were few pitched battles and little bloodshed but considerable destruction to homes and fields, as well as arrests and kidnappings.

It also opened up for discussion the whole question of provincial taxation. The subject had been controversial during King George's War when defense needs made direct taxation mandatory. New York and Albany counties, with some 32 percent of the colony's population, were called upon (by a 1746 bill) to pay about 65 percent of the total levy. Assembly division lists indicate that all the other counties ganged up to impose this unjust apportionment. Although the Council vetoed the maneuver and adjusted distribution, residual bitterness lingered between rural and urban areas.

One source of resentment arose from the fact that before 1753 no county in New York seems to have assessed unimproved land. After that date, some of the southern and more populous counties required taxation of all land, but none of the northern counties permitted assessment of undeveloped land before the Revolution.

The threat of such a tax in 1752–53 prompted Robert R. Livingston to write an elaborate defense of the manorial system of landholding as a social and political bulwark for the people of New York as well as an economic boon for Great Britain. In seeking to preserve a privilege of great value to his family and class, he advocated instead an income tax scaled according to the individual's ability to pay. Realistically, the absence of survey plats often made it impossible to ascertain the precise ownership of particular tracts and therefore made collection of any tax on such lands all but impossible. Since almost every rural property holder possessed some undeveloped acreage, a widespread prejudice existed against the taxation of unimproved land.

The true nature of the economic, social, and political relationships between landlords and tenants in colonial New York has been a complex and controversial subject among historians. It appears certain, however, that the crux of their delicate relationship was not the existence of feudal privileges for the landlord, nor even political domination at polling time, but rather the fact that landowners withheld from the market several million acres of prime land, an action that exasperated lesser farmers who felt excluded from ownership in a fertile region. On the one hand, as Philip Livingston put it in 1739, "selling I am not fond off att all." But on the other hand, as Cadwallader Colden wrote in an undated (and timeless) letter, "the hopes of having land of their own & becoming independent of Landlords is what chiefly induces people into America & they think they have never answer'd the design of their coming till they have purchased land which as soon as possible they do."

What, then, was the actual situation? Land grants had to be obtained officially from the governor in Council, and all land in New York was subject to the payment of quitrents. A prospective patentee had to secure, successively, a warrant to purchase land from the Indians, a warrant to survey it, a warrant for the patent itself, and what were then called letters of exemplification. Because imperial instructions prohibited any individual from obtaining more than two thousand acres (reduced by half in 1753), clandestine procedures came to be used, such as multiple

acquisitions through fictitious names or "trustees." Consequently
the actual pattern of landownership in eighteenth-century New
York is to be found in the private leases and releases made *after*
approval of the patents, not in the initially recorded letters
patent.

Because of a reasonable enforcement by Hunter, Burnet, and
Montgomerie of imperial restraints upon land distribution,
speculators by 1731 were suffering from what seemed to be a land
famine as well as a lack of available settlers. After 1732, however,
and continuing to 1775, an era of extravagant, concealed-owner-
ship grants began, especially beyond the west side of the Hudson.
George Clarke, as provincial secretary and then lieutenant
governor, used his position to engross incredible amounts of real
estate between 1732 and 1743. When he departed for England in
1745, he left behind a thriving settlement on his lands in Cherry
Valley, a straggling cluster on what was called the Corry tract,
plus many thousands of acres of unimproved land that would
paradoxically impede the settlement and development of the
Mohawk Valley, a design he especially had consistently advocated.

By the middle of the eighteenth century the position of
landlords with large holdings was ambiguous but more vulnerable than we have realized. Only a handful of the old manors
survived—Rensselaerswyck, Philipsburgh, Morrisania, Livingston Manor, Cortlandt, and Gardiner's Island in Long Island
Sound—and so the manorial system was in decline.* It is difficult
to generalize about the nonmanorial patents because some had
been canceled by the crown, others had been divided or sold off
in individual lots, while still others remained intact. By the early
1750s, however, most of these landowners were feeling considerable unease: because of unextinguished Indian claims and, hence,
cloudy titles; because of conflicting border claims with neighboring colonies; and especially because of pressure from royal

---

* There were few operative differences between manorial and nonmanorial
estates in New York, only the form of the deed and the fact that manors were
entitled to send a representative to the Assembly.

officials. When Sir Danvers Osborne came to be governor in 1753, his instructions included six articles dealing with land matters. The ceiling on individual grants was cut to one thousand acres; the quitrent of two shillings sixpence per hundred acres was to be strictly collected; and undeveloped land grants were to be investigated and reclaimed by the state. By 1772 the crown had indicated explicitly its partiality for small farmers who would improve the land and thereby develop the colony.

Nevertheless, Osborne's successors—he committed suicide soon after his arrival—were loath to enforce these new directives, and the great land barons did have certain securities. So long as they were influential in the Assembly and on the Council, so long as their relationships with governors were good, and so long as they enjoyed judgeships on the courts that heard land cases, their titles were reasonably safe.

The political power they exercised over their tenants has most likely been exaggerated. Influence they had, but not "control." There were many aspects of their leases, moreover, that were fair by the standards of the time. There were leases in "fee simple" requiring a modest rent in perpetuity and term leases for the life of a tenant or some specified period of years. The actual rental fees were normally reasonable, and the services required, such as labor on the manor roads and fences, were no more onerous than those rendered by any resident of a town. There is evidence that some tenants eventually accumulated sufficient income to purchase farms outright and that others sold their leases at a profit after making substantial improvements. There was, apparently, a certain amount of mobility among the tenants.

There were also, however, various economic restrictions and controls that were vexatious. Tenants had to bring their grain to the landlord's mill for grinding, which allowed him to fix prices at will. They had to offer the proprietor "first refusal" on their crops. Only if he declined to buy could they sell on the open market. And there was bitter resentment of the alienation fees that were charged when leases were transferred or resold, often compelling a tenant to give his landlord as much as one-third of the price of his farm. In sum, the tenant could not keep all of the fruits of his improvements on the property, and he often had to pay interest on rent arrears.

Certainly, then, there could be scant sense of community between most tenants and their landlords; and New York's system of tenancy proved to be unattractive to yeoman farmers, antiauthoritarian types, and persons who had already had a bad experience with such systems in the Old World. The land riots of the 1750s and 1760s did not simply constitute desperate actions on the part of an exploited peasant class. They involved an influx of New Englanders, as we have seen, who had been accustomed to greater autonomy in landownership, as well as a complex system of manors, patents, and real estate speculation that was under attack from above as well as below by 1753. Most of the tenants and squatters who rebelled were not "levelers" eager to alter an unjust system of social class and vicious economic exploitation. They were themselves landowners *manqués,* men who wanted a piece of the system more than they wanted to revise it.

The bitterness and brawling that occurred sporadically along the Hudson between 1751 and 1757 broke out with even more dramatic impact in 1766. Its first impulse came from the proprietors of the Philipse Highland Patent (a large tract in Dutchess County), who began to assert their claims to eastern portions of the patent that touched the Connecticut border. New Englanders had been moving into this area since 1740, and some had even received permission to live there. To complicate matters, the Wappinger Indians also had claims to sections of the Highland patent. When the Philipse proprietors initiated a series of successful lawsuits in 1763 to eject farmers holding titles from the Indians, New Englanders resisted and Indians petitioned the government of New York for assistance and redress. In 1765 the Council and Colden rejected the Wappinger claims and effectively confirmed title to the Philipse heirs.

Late in 1765 the evicted farmers began to organize, and by the spring of 1766 the whole border area was in an uproar. Mobs ranging from one hundred to five hundred men, armed with guns, swords, and clubs, roamed about the countryside menacing tenants loyal to the proprietors, burning barns, destroying crops, stirring up trouble, and confronting posses. They were extremely well organized, and their agitation spread to adjacent counties, particularly the Manor of Cortlandt in Westchester. After an unsuccessful attempt in May to march on New York City and free some prisoners jailed there—Governor Moore stopped that move by calling out the militia—the uprising spread to Albany County. In late June there were armed clashes on Van Rensselaer lands and at Livingston Manor. When hundreds of rioters gathered at the Poughkeepsie jail, Moore decided to take concerted action. He dispatched the 28th Royal Regiment to Dutchess County and issued proclamations for the arrest of the ringleaders.

After several skirmishes, the rebellious tenants were terrorized into submission. A contemporary account written by someone sympathetic to them describes the event:

It was beyond the powers of language to paint in lively images the Horror! the surprize and astonishment of this poor distressed people on that occasion. To see their habitations, some demolished, some robbed and pillag'd, and others of them invellop'd in flames of fire . . . to see them at once, as it had been, deprived of all their sustenance for which they had labored, sweat and fatigued themselves all the days of their lives; and thus driven therefrom in such hostile manner; and to see others coming in to reap the fruits of their labors, to reap whereon they had not sowed.

The fighting ceased in Albany County later that fall only when detachments from two regiments plus the 19th Infantry were sent into the area. Most of the men indicted for riot pleaded guilty and were punished with "fines, imprisonment and pillories." William Prendergast, a major leader of the Dutchess insurgents, had an elaborate trial and was indicted for high treason, convicted, and sentenced to death. After a plea for clemency, however, George III pardoned him in December 1766. Thereafter calm returned to the countryside.

Obviously, these intermittent conflicts over land had complex origins and consequences. They involved class, regional, and ethnic resentments. They pitted New England yeomen against New York landlords, whites against Indians, and loyal tenants against interlopers. They also reveal that implementation of imperial policy tended to exacerbate local tensions and instability. After the 1740s, for example, New York's governors often appointed Englishmen or New Englanders to offices, especially on the upper Hudson where the Dutch and their descendants had been entrenched. By so using their patronage powers, the governors thereby helped to undermine community cohesion in yet another way.

British officials who resented the whiggish principles of members of the provincial elite also hoped that such instability would give them their come-uppance. As General Thomas Gage wrote in June 1766: "They [the landlords] certainly deserve any Losses they may sustain, for it is the work of their own Hands. They first Sowed the Seeds of Sedition amongst the People and taught them to rise in Opposition to the Laws."

A government of laws, and not men, is always an elusive thing; but it was particularly fragile in New York during the middle decades of the eighteenth century. One writer, "Philanthropos," argued in February 1768 that the tenants had been pushed to violence because the law "was absolutely barred against them . . . the lawyers generally refusing to take their cause in hand." That was true and had been for quite some time. No provincial lawyer would defend the accused conspirators in the "Negroe Plot" of 1741. No lawyer would take the case of those tenants evicted from Philipse Manor in 1765. And no lawyer could be found to handle the Wappinger Indian claims in 1767. There was some validity to the farmers' complaint that there was "no Law for poor Men" in New York. Urbanization and expansion had made it difficult, indeed, to achieve any semblance of community.

12

WAR, TRADE, AND EMPIRE

New York's position in the British Empire was both important and uncertain at mid-century. The province played a relatively minor role in King George's War (1744-48) but thereafter became literally a linchpin among the continental colonies. New York generally, and the area from Albany to Ticonderoga in particular, became the most critical sector during the French and Indian War, and between 1755 and 1760 Albany was the nerve center of British operations in North America. The formal onset of war in 1756, moreover, marked a significant turning point in New York's history because it diverted attention from civic problems, such as the King's College controversy, to military, diplomatic, and economic matters of greater moment.

During the governorship of George Clinton, 1743-53—the longest term for any English governor in the colony's history—the structure of political alignments in New York underwent several major convolutions. Admiral Clinton came to New York with strong connections to the Newcastle-Pelham party in England and with twenty-five years of experience in the Royal Navy. He needed the governorship for its perquisites because his personal finances were very frail; but he found the office (and the province) a devilish political pressure cooker, and he exacerbated it decidedly by virtue of the constitutional concessions he ultimately had to make.

As an imperial official, Clinton was obliged to pursue a vigorous war effort against the French after 1744. He found, however, that New York merchants enjoyed an extensive trade with the French West Indies and that the Albany merchants and their political allies hoped for a policy of neutrality so as not to disrupt Indian relations and the fur trade to Montreal. He found, too, that when military activity became unavoidable in 1746 the Assembly's determination to control expenditures for provisions, transportation, construction, and management of military stores all encroached upon his prerogatives as captain general. James De Lancey led the opposition to Clinton and put together a coalition of Albany traders, New York City merchants with ties to the fur trade, farmers who worried about disruption of their harvests, and residents generally who feared that a significant war effort would require a rise in taxes.

As a result of De Lancey's enmity and provincial ambitions, Clinton broke with him in 1746 and turned for support to those few who shared his imperial outlook, especially Cadwallader Colden, Archibald Kennedy (receiver general and collector of customs for New York since 1722), William Johnson, and, subsequently, Thomas Pownall, Peter Wraxall, and some others who wanted Clinton's patronage. After 1749 he also made an alliance with the old Morrisite group, including James Alexander, William Smith, Sr., and Lewis Morris, Jr. By that time the damage—political and military—had been done, and public affairs within New York were comparatively calm between 1750 and 1753.

Another consequence of De Lancey's concerted opposition was the weak war effort made by New York during the 1740s. King George's War was more noteworthy in New York for what did not happen militarily and for the economic advantages of privateering at sea than for exciting conflicts or major conquests. The fray began on November 28, 1745, when a party of French and Indians destroyed the village of Saratoga, killing and capturing more than one hundred persons. In July 1746, an intercolonial force assembled in northern New York for an expedition into Canada with Clinton in charge; but the British regulars never arrived and the colonial militia had to be dispersed. Subsequent plans to seize Crown Point on Lake

Champlain also had to be abandoned in September on account of forces being diverted to Louisbourg and Boston. New York's unpaid levies became mutinous at that point, and the Iroquois— deprived of their customary presents by a costive Assembly— were barely kept from deserting the English cause. Abandonment of the fort at Saratoga in the autumn of 1747 revealed the colony's very real paralysis. Albany was almost blockaded by the French, and the settlements north of Albany were deserted, providing some justice to William Livingston's caustic criticism of the Assembly for "proclaiming war against Cows and rattlesnakes" instead of prosecuting the war effort vigorously. The only other skirmish occurred near Schenectady in 1748 when Indians burned some cabins and seventy Yorkers marched in pursuit to drive them away.

Paradoxically, New York alone among all the continental colonies had had an assignment of regular British troops throughout the period of royal rule. Four independent companies of foot soldiers had been stationed there because of the colony's strategic importance and because of the strongly felt presence of Iroquois Indians. These companies were consistently neglected and unsupervised, however, and consequently had little military value. They could not forestall French aggression on the frontier, could not provide effective cover for advancing settlements, and could not help to control the Indian trade. They saw no real engagements until 1755, when two of them participated in General Braddock's catastrophic defeat at the Monongahela River, and again in 1757, when they were involved in the capitulation of Fort William Henry on Lake George. For the rest of the war they were more of a hindrance than a help to the British commanders, and in 1763 they were disbanded.

British neglect of these companies throughout the first half of the eighteenth century was fairly characteristic of imperial indifference to colonial concerns during much of that period. In 1750, however, a change began to occur. The shift was precipitated particularly by French aggressiveness on the Ohio frontier and is clearly discerned in the language of several major documents of the period. In October 1750, the Privy Council

ordered the Board of Trade to prepare a summary or "State" of
New York since the beginning of Governor Clinton's administration. It was, in Clinton's words, a "confounded long" compilation
of documents;* but it revealed to imperial authorities that the
"most essencial powers of Government" had been pulled from
the governor's hands, that provincial defenses had been neglected, that the Iroquois alliance had lapsed, and that "every
thing which the Crown has a right to demand, or the Province
for their own sakes, in interest oblige to provide, has been denied
merely in resentment from personal quarrels, and on account of
differences between the Governor and some members of the
council and assembly."

Other documents indicative of this awakening at Whitehall
came from the pen of Archibald Kennedy, a faithful servant of
the crown who, between 1750 and 1755, wrote six tracts
concerning imperial defense, Indian policy, and the northern
colonies. He warned of the dangers from French designs,
advocated intercolonial cooperation, fair dealings and greater
attention to Indian relations, an end to the commerce between
Albany and Montreal, and a serious effort to gather the royal
quitrents in New York. Not until 1755 did the Assembly pass a
bill for the collection of quitrents that Whitehall could approve
(it would be renewed in 1762 and 1768); but even then the
quitrent system in New York remained a failure. Kennedy could
only collect about eight hundred pounds each year, rather than
the forty thousand pounds due upon enforcement of the two
shillings sixpence per hundred-acre legal rate. Nor was he much
more successful in the collection of customs duties.

Another loyal advocate of imperial interests at this time,
William Johnson, had an equally difficult time persuading
provincial New Yorkers to take a broader view of North
American diplomacy and colonial interests. Johnson certainly
had a better understanding of the Iroquois than anyone else in
North America: he had danced their war dances and loved their

---

* Published in O'Callaghan, ed., *Documents Relative to the Colonial History of
New-York*, VI, 614–703.

Sir William Johnson (1715–74), entrepreneur, politician, and Indian agent. Portrait by John Wollaston, 1751. *Collection Albany Institute of History and Art.*

women. But his sympathies and priorities must be clearly understood. He was always eager to engross land for himself and often identified his own interests with those of the empire. In 1765 he wrote a revealing letter in which he stated:

I have laid it down as an invariable rule, from which I never did, nor ever shall deviate, that wherever a Title is set up by any Tribe of Indians of little consequence or importance to his Majestys interest, & who may be considered as long domesticated, that such Claim unless apparently clear, had better remain unsupported than that Several old Titles of his Majestys Subjects should thereby become disturbed:—and on the contrary, Wherever I found a Just complaint made by a People either by themselves or Connections capable of resenting & who I knew would resent a neglect, I Judged it my Duty to support the same, altho it should disturb ye property of any Man whatsoever.

Johnson came to New York in 1738 at the age of twenty-three, the son of a Protestant Irish farmer. More important, however, he was the nephew of Vice-Admiral Sir Peter Warren, who had arrived in New York in 1730 as the commander of a twenty-gun frigate, married Susannah De Lancey (James's sister), purchased tracts on Manhattan as well as fourteen thousand acres in the Mohawk Valley, became a member of the Council, and stayed for seventeen years. He invited his nephew to manage his estate at the confluence of the Mohawk and Schoharie rivers, and young Johnson parlayed the opportunity into an extraordinary career. He brought over Irish tenant farmers, sold tracts of Warren's real estate, operated a storehouse, constructed wilderness trading posts, and developed a relationship of trust with the Iroquois, who named him Warraghiyagey—"one who does much business."

In 1744 Johnson sold about two-thirds of his uncle's land around Warrensburg and moved to several thousand acres newly purchased near the present site of Amsterdam on the northern bank of the Mohawk. There his business operations expanded. He settled Irish, Scots-Irish, and Palatine families on his land; gave them long-term leases at nominal rents; and helped to relocate pioneer families. He also established schools and S.P.G.

mission churches among the Indians and often defended their land claims. They, in turn, trusted him to handle their transactions and even asked him to recommend purchase prices. In 1749 he could fairly inform his uncle that his "Scituation among the Indians, & integrity to them, made those poor Savages Seek to me, so that I have a Superior Interest with them, which Sort of Interest is the most advantageous to this Province."

In 1746, when Clinton sought to defend the northern frontier, he sensibly turned to Johnson for help. The governor made him provincial Indian agent and ordered Johnson to provide arms and supplies for those Iroquois willing to serve under his command. Johnson succeeded in obtaining the loyalty of many Iroquois during King George's War, but two of his attendant experiences embittered him and shaped his role and behavior during the important quarter-century to come. First, he bypassed the Albany merchants (whom he cordially disliked) and purchased goods directly from New York City traders; and second, he found that the miserly pro-Albany Assembly would not reimburse the heavy out-of-pocket expenses that he had incurred in wartime. By 1750 the province owed him five thousand pounds; the next year, in a fury, he resigned his post as Indian agent. He maintained ever after that the Iroquois were a "Foreign People" and as such should be dealt with directly by the crown rather than by provincial legislatures. In 1753, the New York Assembly paid Johnson about a tenth of the seven thousand pounds due him by then. After this token gesture of contempt and the Council's failure to support him vigorously, he left a Council meeting on July 2, 1753, and never again returned to participate in its deliberations.

Thereafter Johnson remained relatively aloof from the power struggle between governors and assemblies. He made little effort to build political alliances with influential New Yorkers outside of his valley and did little to shape the Assembly's understanding of Indian affairs on the frontier. His preference for friendship and diplomatic or marital alliances with the Indians would bring him enormous power on the frontier; but his understandable disdain for the Assembly and provincial politicians contributed to that body's failure to pass laws that would control traders and settlers more effectively, especially after 1760 when the French demise ceased to restrain expansive tendencies. Almost inevitably, then, most of the Iroquois would be antipatriot and pro-British when the Revolution began in 1776.

Indian gifts, such as fabrics, hardware, munitions, food, jewelry, clothing, and liquor, had long been established as effective (and expected) factors in frontier diplomacy. Their presentation developed from an old Indian custom; therefore, when Johnson resigned in 1751 and ceased to distribute largesse from George II to the Iroquois, New York's prestige among the Six Nations declined.* During the early 1750s, moreover, the Mohawks became especially resentful of illicit encroachment on their lands. They complained bitterly in 1754 about white claims to the Kayaderosseras and Canajohary patents (north and south of the Mohawk River), claims that dated back to the first years of the eighteenth century, and produced a territorial impasse between 1754 and 1768. It should surprise no one, then, that few Iroquois were eager to attend the Albany Conference in 1754, the prime purpose of which was preservation of the Anglo-Indian alliance. The Six Nations sensibly feared being dispossessed of their lands. When Johnson, whom they trusted, presided over another conference in 1755, they attended more willingly and in much greater numbers.

Johnson first achieved diplomatic prominence in 1746 when he impressively persuaded the aggrieved Mohawks to attend a conference at Albany in order to discuss the French menace with New York and Massachusetts leaders. Because the Mohawks had been deceived on numerous occasions by the Indian commissioners at Albany, they welcomed Johnson's friendship just as much as the commissioners there resented it. Even so, because of location and accessibility by water, Albany remained the logical meeting place for Anglo-Indian negotiations, and intercolonial

---

* After Johnson became superintendent of Indian affairs in 1755, he had available £2,000 per annum for gifts and £800 cash on hand. It then became much easier for him to woo the Iroquois away from the French interest.

conferences occurred there in June 1744, October 1745, July 1746, July 1748, and July 1751—variously attended by delegates from New York, New England, Pennsylvania, New Jersey, Virginia, South Carolina, and the Six Nations. The problems discussed at these conferences were chiefly maintenance of the "Covenant Chain" with the Iroquois, defensive measures against the French, and means of legitimizing English claims to the western country. New York had a vital stake in the solution of all these problems: the Hudson-Champlain route had strategic importance for north-south communication and control, and the Hudson-Mohawk river system provided the best access then available to the Ohio Valley.

Understandably, then, when Whitehall became concerned in 1753 that impending war with France might coincide with complete Iroquois alienation, imperial officials proposed that an intercolonial meeting be held with representatives of various tribes to permit them to state their complaints and achieve some reassertion of Iroquois loyalty "in one general treaty to be made in his majesty's name." Besides, the Indians were at least nominal owners of the interior lands then in dispute between Britain and France. So a major conference was called for June and July of 1754, to be convened in Albany.

Ironically, New York played a weak and peculiar role at this gathering. Its delegates alone attended without official commissions. Lieutenant Governor James De Lancey was the official host and presided, but when his proposal for intercolonial financial contributions for a chain of forts on the New York frontier was ignored by the other delegates, he subsequently refused to support their plan of union. When Chief Hendrick of the Mohawks, a good friend of William Johnson, presented an accurate list of legitimate grievances,* De Lancey denied their validity. Even so, the Indians were brought around to tentative

---

* Namely, that whites had defrauded Mohawks of their land, had supplied too much rum but too little in the way of more useful gifts, that Pennsylvania and Virginia were encroaching on Iroquois-claimed land in the west, and that Albany traders were selling arms to the French while urging the Iroquois to attack them!

conciliation by Johnson's cajoling; and they departed in July with thirty wagonloads of gifts, though a treaty of alliance was not achieved. The twenty-three delegates representing seven colonies recommended strong defensive measures against the French, war vessels to be constructed on the lakes, a single superintendent for Indian affairs, a fort to be placed among each Indian nation, and a western boundary along the Appalachians for those colonies south of New York so that new colonies could be created inland. It was also recommended that future land purchases be made by the government with Indian approval expressed in a body at a public council and that Indian complaints be investigated and injuries redressed.

Although all of the seven colonial assemblies failed to ratify the Albany plan, Whitehall adopted much of it as policy during the next decade, thereby adding to the tensions between imperial officials and land-hungry settlers and speculators. As Johnson informed the Board of Trade in 1756, responsiveness to Indian complaints "strikes at the Interest of some of the wealthiest and most leading men in this Province, & I fear that Influence which may be necessary to succeed, will be employed to obstruct." Although additional restrictions were included in instructions to royal governors in 1761 and 1762, New York's Council continued to hand out new and lavish land grants.

The Treaty of Aix-la-Chapelle which concluded King George's War in 1748 had been surprisingly favorable to the French position in North America, and New France worked especially energetically thereafter to win over the Iroquois as allies. In 1749 Abbé François Picquet established a strategic mission, called La Présentation, at the mouth of the Oswegatchie River, which flows into the St. Lawrence where Ogdensburg stands today. During the summer of 1751, Picquet made a circuitous "journey" around Lake Ontario in order to court the Six Nations, attract some of them to his mission, and make a report to the governor general of New France concerning affairs all along New York's northern frontier. By 1752 his mission had become a fortified garrison, and he recommended to his superiors that a war party of four thousand Indians be recruited to expel the English from the upper Ohio Valley.

By the early 1750s, there were settlers from Pennsylvania and Virginia, particularly, spilling over the Appalachian Mountains to farm and trade with the Indians there. Since the French had their *habitants* and trading posts in the Michigan and Illinois country, three imponderables soon arose: whether the upper Ohio was properly part of the British Empire or the French; whether that area would be open to British influence at all; and, ultimately, which civilization would dominate the heart of the North American continent. In 1749 the governor general of New France began to force the issue. He ordered Captain Pierre Joseph de Blainville into the Ohio Valley in order to remove British "trespassers" and push them back to the eastern slopes of the Appalachians. In 1752 he destroyed the British trading center at Pickawillany and plundered all the British subjects he could find in the valley. The French remained aggressive between 1752 and 1754, seizing Fort Duquesne and capturing George Washington's small expedition at Fort Necessity in May 1754.

At that point Britain—the crown as well as many colonists—became concerned and began to act. Major General Edward Braddock was appointed commander in chief of British forces in North America. At a council of war held at Alexandria, Virginia, in April 1755, he met with the governors of five colonies to design a strategy for removing the French from the Ohio Valley and the borders of New York. It was decided that the vital French forts would be attacked simultaneously in the summer of 1755: Duquesne by Braddock himself, Niagara by Governor William Shirley of Massachusetts, and Crown Point by William Johnson. Braddock also authorized Johnson to coordinate the operations of the Six Nations and their allies. By this time Whitehall had become heavily dependent upon Johnson's advice and leadership in making decisions affecting Indian relations.

Braddock's campaign ended in catastrophe on July 9 when nine hundred French and Indians massacred his force of nineteen hundred along the banks of the Monongahela. Because

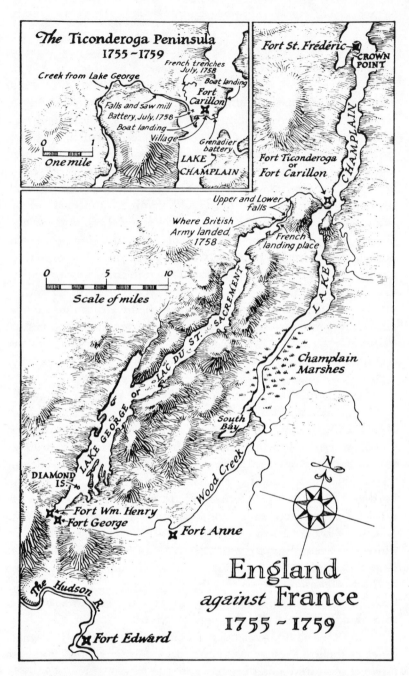

The Ticonderoga Peninsula
1755-1759

French trenches
July, 1758

Creek from Lake George

Boat landing

Fort Carillon

Falls and saw mill
Battery, July, 1758
Boat landing

Village

Grenadier battery

0   1
One mile

LAKE CHAMPLAIN

Fort St. Frédéric

CROWN POINT

Fort Ticonderoga
or
Fort Carillon

LAKE CHAMPLAIN

Upper and Lower falls

Where British Army landed 1758

French landing place

0   5   10
Scale of miles

LAC DU ST. SACREMENT

Champlain Marshes

South Bay

LAKE GEORGE or

Wood Creek

DIAMOND IS.

Fort Wm. Henry

Fort George

Fort Anne

N

The Hudson R.

Fort Edward

England
against France
1755 - 1759

The Lake George–Lake Champlain area, 1755–59. *From* Navies in the Mountains: The Battles on the Waters of Lake Champlain and Lake George, 1609–1814 *by Harrison Bird. Copyright © 1962 by Oxford University Press, Inc. Reprinted by permission.*

Braddock's captured papers revealed Shirley's plans to seize Niagara and Frontenac on Lake Ontario, the French were able to reinforce those forts and Shirley's campaign had to be abandoned. Meanwhile, in July and August Johnson brought some four hundred Indians and thirty-five hundred colonials, mostly raw New Yorkers and New Englanders, to the southern tip of Lake George where they began construction of Fort George as well as Fort Edward (on the upper Hudson) in anticipation of a French attack. In early September, when Johnson's men were divided between those two sites, Baron Dieskau, a German in the French service, diverted thirty-two hundred French and Indians out of Crown Point in order to strike at Fort Edward. Along the way he learned that Johnson's unit was largely unfortified at Lake George and prepared to attack there. Early on September 8, Johnson dispatched one thousand men to meet Dieskau's army, prompting shrewd Chief Hendrick, Johnson's ally, to remark, "If they are to be killed, too many; if they are to fight, too few."

Dieskau's first volley killed Hendrick as well as Colonel Ephraim Williams and precipitated a panicked retreat by their men. When the Frenchmen recklessly pursued their quarry, they were mowed down by Johnson and seventeen hundred effectives behind breastworks and cannon. Many French officers were wounded, their men and Indian allies became disorganized, and Dieskau was captured while sitting alone on a tree stump. Toward dusk, a militia unit coming from Fort Edward to Johnson's assistance met the retreating French force, killing many and capturing their baggage. Thus of three engagements in one very long day, the French had won the first, withdrawn from the second, and been routed at the third. Even so, the British victors had suffered more casualties—262 as against 230.

It had been a fortunate affair for Johnson in many ways. He was knighted, made a baronet, confirmed by the crown as superintendent of Indian affairs in the north, and given five thousand pounds. Although he remained at Lake George in order to complete Fort William Henry (near the site of Fort George), he could not fully control the troops there. Many of

Chief Hendrick (Thoyanoguen) of the Mohawks; ca. 1676–1755,
chief sachem of the Iroquois. *Library of Congress.*

them were insubordinate and refused to work without extra pay. The original aim of a northern advance to Crown Point had to be abandoned. By autumn Johnson realized that Shirley was trying to undercut him politically and militarily, so in November Sir William resigned the commission he had received from Braddock and decided to devote himself to his administrative duties and personal affairs. The French remained at Crown Point and planned another fort ten miles to the south where Lakes George and Champlain connect—a strategic spot the Indians called Ticonderoga. Thus the adversaries were set in position by the beginning of 1756.

Soon the length of Lake George and its surrounding wilderness became the very heart of this French and Indian War, which was officially declared by Britain on May 15, 1756. For more than a year thereafter the two sides glared at and menaced each other from opposite ends of the lake. In February 1756, the crown commissioned Johnson as colonel of the Six Nations and announced that the Iroquois were British subjects. By June he had persuaded the Iroquois to abandon their policy of neutrality and neighboring Indians to stop murdering settlers on the frontier. A conference and grand ceremony at Onondaga sealed the alliance.* During the next five years, Johnson's contributions were significant. He persuaded the Iroquois to fight for Great Britain, something the Albany commissioners had not been able to do during King George's War. He enlisted the loyalty of other tribes, as well, and he insisted upon fair prices and an honest exchange of goods.

Before turning to the military narrative of the war itself, we ought to obtain an overview of the problems it presented, particularly in New York. To begin, the colony's native defenses were weak, a condition readily recognized by Governor Charles Hardy early in 1756:

Small arms we have none in the publick Magazine but six chests that belong to the four independent companys; this city has a stand of 400

---

* In 1763, Johnson gave these figures for the Six Nations' fighting strength: 160 Mohawk warriors, 250 Oneidas, 140 Tuscaroras, 150 Onondagas, 200 Cayugas, and 1,050 Senecas.

muskets, they provided last year; and what is in the possession of private People are chiefly for Indian Trade. The Militia are by law to furnish themselves each man one good muskett, with a due proportion of Ammunition, some of them are so indigent that they cannot purchase their own arms. The Militia Law in Force in this Province, which I believe is not only the best, but the only one on the Continent that can effectually answer the good purposes of such a Law, will fully inform your Lordships of their musterings and trainings.

Second, the British regulars had scant respect for provincial troops—with whom they had to cooperate in battle. To complicate these resentments over status, skill, and style, regulations in 1756 required that all provincial officers serving with regular officers would have to accept rank as junior captains. This awkward problem was eventually adjusted, but it left rancorous feelings.

British condescension toward colonials had ironic aspects because the Royal Army proved to be exceedingly ineffective during the early years of the war. The regulars had been trained for limited warfare in the European style: systematic siege techniques to reduce the element of uncertainty, dependence upon local sources of supply and transport with consequent emphasis upon preserving the rural economy in hostile as well as friendly territory. Unfortunately, conventional linear tactics and siege techniques could only be used effectively in North America when British forces came within close range of major French strongholds. The serious logistical problem was how to get Anglo-American men there and supply them when there were few transportation routes or local sources of supply comparable to those in Europe. At a tactical level, then, the problems centered upon training regulars for backwoods warfare and bringing the full force of British firepower against opponents using Indian methods.

As it happened, however, British leaders were both cautious and inexperienced with this sort of warfare. There was a great deal of inefficiency and serious delays in the campaigns of 1755, 1756, and 1757. Governor Shirley's army should have moved west along Lake Ontario in April 1756 but was not ready until

August. There was difficulty obtaining adequate provisions, such as bread, rum, and bullocks, and desertion occurred too commonly. Campsites, such as Forts Edward and William Henry, tended to be dirty and disorganized; and, most important, difficult alternatives had to be weighed. Moving forces to attack the French at one location meant weakening the British hold at another. Shirley could not attack Niagara from Oswego in 1755 without leaving the latter vulnerable to attack from Fort Frontenac across the lake, and so he did not. Lord Loudoun's assault on Louisbourg in 1757 took vital British troops away from Fort William Henry, and so it fell to the French.

Finally, there was a tremendous problem of rabid rivalry and insufficient cooperation among Shirley, Johnson, the Dutch traders and Indian commissioners at Albany, the Iroquois, Governor Hardy, and Lieutenant Governor James De Lancey— not to mention Sir William Johnson's working at cross-purposes with Governors Morris of Pennsylvania and Belcher of New Jersey. Because of the politicking among these figures, as well as mistrust and musunderstanding in London, there were almost annual changes in the high command. When Braddock died at the Battle of the Wilderness in 1755, Shirley succeeded him as commander in chief. His lack of success and his sufficiency of enemies caused him to be superseded in March 1756, temporarily by Colonel Daniel Webb and General James Abercrombie and then in July by the Earl of Loudoun. Although he fared no better in the field and produced no significant victories, Loudoun made a long-range contribution by reorganizing the system of transport and supply in North America as well as by encouraging the likes of Robert Rogers—soon to be renowned for Rogers's Rangers—who had considerable experience in irregular warfare.* William Pitt recalled Loudoun late in 1757, and Major General James Abercrombie succeeded him early the next year.

---

* The training of regular troops with provincial ranger units eventually led the British high command to recruit special units, the light infantry, as supporting troops for the grenadier and battalion companies. Marksmanship, physical hardihood, and woods lore became the criteria for light infantry selection.

After Abercrombie suffered a disastrous repulse at Ticonderoga in July 1758, however, effective leadership passed to General Jeffrey Amherst, and he at last reaped the fruits of Loudoun's administrative efforts and Pitt's strategic commands sent from London.

The narrative of military operations in New York really divides into two phases: a steady series of British defeats between March 1756 and July 1758, followed by a flow of fortuitous victories between August 1758 and September 1760, when Montreal capitulated to Amherst and New France was finished.

On March 27, 1756, the French destroyed Fort Bull, a collection of storehouses surrounded by a palisade on the banks of Wood Creek, useful as an outpost guarding the portage to Oswego. On July 3-4, John Bradstreet met a French force in an inconclusive but advantageous skirmish nine miles from Oswego. On August 14, however, the French under Montcalm came down to Oswego from the north and destroyed the two pathetic garrisons there. The British then had to burn their own forts at the Carrying Place (near Oneida Castle) and retreat toward Albany. The loss was a terrific psychological shock to all of English America. "Oswego has changed masters," wrote a surgeon to his wife from Fort Edward, "and I think we may justly fear that the whole of our country will soon follow, unless a merciful God prevent, and awake a sinful people to repentance and reformation." The heart of the Iroquois Confederation now lay open to Louis XV.

Between March 19 and 22, 1757, a French attack over icy Lake George against Fort William Henry failed. But five months later, on August 9, a siege by French and Indians again commanded by Montcalm succeeded, and the British retreat to Fort Edward was harried by a particularly savage Indian attack. Francis Parkman describes the aftermath:

On the morning after the massacre the Indians decamped in a body and set out for Montreal, carrying with them their plunder and some two hundred prisoners, who, it is said, could not be got out of their hands. The soldiers were set to the work of demolishing the English fort;

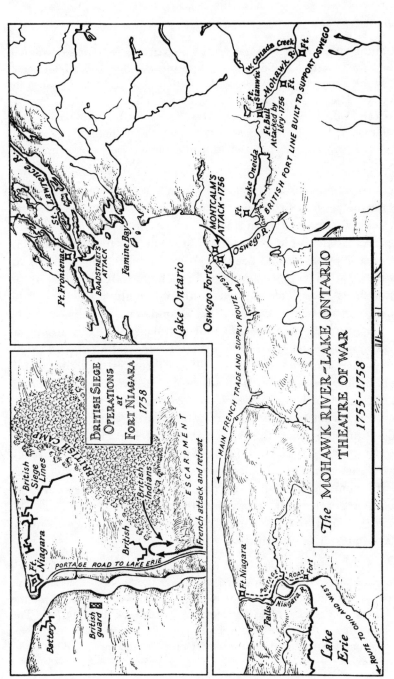

Central and northern New York, 1755–58. *From* Battle for a Continent *by Harrison Bird. Copyright © 1965 by Oxford University Press, Inc. Reprinted by permission.*

and the task occupied several days. The barracks were torn down, and the huge pine-logs of the rampart thrown into a heap. The dead bodies that filled the casemates were added to the mass, and fire was set to the whole. The mighty funeral pyre blazed all night. Then, on the sixteenth, the army re-embarked. The din of ten thousand combatants, the rage, the terror, the agony, were gone; and no living thing was left but the wolves that gathered from the mountains to feast upon the dead.*

In mid-November 1757, the French and their allies raided Palatine settlements along the Mohawk River, particularly the town of German Flats, and left the valley in a state of terror and flames. By the middle of 1758, most of the frontier settlements in central New York had been deserted. In March of that year an eerie fight took place between French and British rangers on snowshoes near Ticonderoga. Although neither side won, the stage was set for a great fiasco at Ticonderoga in July.

General Abercrombie assembled fifteen thousand troops at Lake George and marched to master Montcalm's force of only thirty-five hundred at Fort Carillon (Ticonderoga). Montcalm, meanwhile, set up a brilliant series of breastworks and entrench-ments just north and west of the fort and waited. Abercrombie did not bother to study the terrain and threw wave after wave of his regulars against the withering fire of French muskets. The carnage was horrible; the British failed even to reach the French lines, and redcoated bodies were strewn bloodily everywhere. A badly demoralized army retired in confusion. The regulars had suffered nearly 1,600 casualties, the provincials 334, while the French had 106 killed and 266 wounded. Here, once again, is Parkman's vivid description of the epilogue:

Montcalm, with a mighty load lifted from his soul, passed along the lines, and gave the tired soldiers the thanks they nobly deserved. Beer, wine, and food were served out to them, and they bivouacked for the night on the level ground between the breastwork and the fort. The enemy had met a terrible rebuff; yet the danger was not over. Abercrombie still had more than thirteen thousand men, and he might

---

* Francis Parkman, *Montcalm and Wolfe* (Boston, 1901), I, 528.

renew the attack with cannon. But, on the morning of the ninth, a band of volunteers who had gone out to watch him brought back the report that he was in full retreat. The saw-mill at the Falls was on fire, and the last English soldier was gone. . . . A panic had overtaken the defeated troops. They had left behind several hundred barrels of provisions and a large quantity of baggage; while in a marshy place that they had crossed was found a considerable number of their shoes, which had stuck in the mud, and which they had not stopped to recover. They had embarked on the morning after the battle, and retreated to the head of the lake in a disorder and dejection woefully contrasted with the pomp of their advance. A gallant army was sacrificed by the blunders of its chief.*

Seven weeks later, however, when Colonel John Bradstreet captured Fort Frontenac on the northeastern corner of Lake Ontario (the present site of Kingston, Canada), the figurative tide began to turn. The British dismantled and burned the garrison. Now New France had not only lost control of Ontario but thereby effective access to its interior posts as well. That strategic seizure provided an enormous psychological lift for the British and their colonies. It also had a salutary effect upon Indian relations, not to mention the morale of frugal provincial assemblymen.

When William Pitt came to power in the middle of 1757, he committed his government to warfare without stint in North America, even if it required higher taxes, war loans, and a promise to reimburse the colonies for their contributions. New York's Assembly certainly became more responsive thereafter than it had ever been before. On February 9, 1759, for example, James De Lancey informed the Assembly of Pitt's latest request. In less than two weeks that body agreed upon a resolution to raise, pay, and clothe New York's quota of 2,680 men. When it appeared that there might be some difficulty in securing this number by voluntary enlistments because of hardships endured in 1758, De Lancey asked whether he might secure the full number, if necessary, by making drafts from the militia. Once

---

* Ibid., II, 115–16.

The powder horn of a soldier who served in General Amherst's army during 1759. Carved on it are "New York," "Albany," and the names of various other battle sites of the French and Indian War. *McCord Museum, Montreal.* An equally superb map powder horn, inscribed "Samuel Hobbs, horn made by Samuel Davison, May 27, 1765," and depicting sites in upstate New York, is in the National Museum of History and Technology (Division of Military History), Washington, D.C.

again the Assembly agreed, and members even carried the necessary warrants issued by De Lancey into the counties so as to speed up the draft. They wanted the full complement available for service as soon as the season permitted an active campaign. As final evidence of its enthusiastic support, the legislature agreed in June to loan Amherst one hundred fifty thousand pounds; the transaction occurred in July.*

On July 25, 1759, a British force under General John Prideaux, supported by Sir William Johnson and one thousand Iroquois, attacked Fort Niagara, turned back a large French relief column sent from the west, took the strong fortress, and thereby severed France's jugular link between Lakes Ontario and Erie. A day later, as it happened, Amherst's command occupied Ticonderoga after a short siege; a week later it found that the French had also abandoned Crown Point (Fort St. Frederic) and retreated down the Richelieu River to Île-aux-Noix. Early in August the French made an unsuccessful attack upon Oswego. On October 12, the French fleet on Lake Champlain was scuttled. The British now controlled the waters south of New France. In August of 1760, the French abandoned Île-aux-Noix at the northern end of Champlain and prepared to defend Montreal, the very heart of their North American empire. Amherst took the city on September 8, and the entire province of Canada capitulated. The continental phase of the French and Indian War was over.

It had been notable for its paradoxical combination of savagery and gentility. On the one hand, almost all of the fighting was done, according to the rules of decorum, in the proper summer season. Bloody battles were interrupted by negotiations conducted under cover of flags of truce, with officers shuttling back and forth as messengers, escorted by drummers and flagmen, politely requesting surrender. All firing ceased

---

* Whereas the Assembly had raised only £72,000 for defense during King George's War, its expenditures during the French and Indian War came to about £250,000. Despite parliamentary reimbursement, New York incurred indebtedness of £291,000, of which £115,000 still remained unpaid in 1765.

during such palaver; and, following a surrender the vanquished marched out of their garrison with "all of the honors of war," granted in respect to bravery and tradition. Formality and pageantry abounded, as in Abercrombie's advance upon Ticonderoga on July 5, 1758.

Before ten o'clock they began to enter the Narrows; and the boats of the three divisions extended themselves into long files as the mountains closed on either hand upon the contracted lake. From front to rear the line was six miles long. The spectacle was superb: the brightness of the summer day; the romantic beauty of the scenery; the sheen and sparkle of those crystal waters; the countless islets, tufted with pine, birch, and fir; the bordering mountains, with their green summits and sunny crags; the flash of oars and glitter of weapons; the banners, the varied uniforms, and the notes of bugle, trumpet, bagpipe, and drum, answered and prolonged by a hundred woodland echoes. "I never beheld so delightful a prospect," wrote a wounded officer at Albany a fortnight after.

Rogers with the rangers, and Gage with the light infantry, led the way in whaleboats, followed by Bradstreet with his corps of boatmen, armed and drilled as soldiers. Then came the main body. The central column of regulars was commanded by Lord Howe, his own regiment, the fifty-fifth, in the van, followed by the Royal Americans, the twenty-seventh, forty-fourth, forty-sixth, and eightieth infantry, and the Highlanders of the forty-second, with their major, Duncan Campbell of Inverawe, silent and gloomy amid the general cheer, for his soul was dark with foreshadowings of death. With this central column came what are described as two floating castles, which were no doubt batteries to cover the landing of the troops. On the right hand and the left were the provincials, uniformed in blue, regiment after regiment, from Massachusetts, Connecticut, New York, New Jersey, and Rhode Island. Behind them all came the bateaux, loaded with stores and baggage, and the heavy flatboats that carried the artillery, while a rear-guard of provincials and regulars closed the long procession.*

And yet, wilderness warfare also brought brutality and stealth, cunning ambushes and plunder, smallpox and starvation in

---

* Parkman, *Montcalm and Wolfe*, II, 96–98. For a similar French spectacle on Lake George in Aug. 1757, see ibid., I, 505–6.

besieged forts, fever and dysentery from bad food supplies, scalping and decapitation of prisoners. Winters at the Oswego garrison, Fort Ontario, were so grim that tales of cannibalism there were carried eastward after the winters of 1752 and 1755. In September 1755, Governor Shirley inspired his troops and Indian allies at Oswego with a speech calling for a "spirit of revenge." After that he gave them a bullock for a feast, which they roasted—"pretending that they were eating the governor of Canada!" In July 1757, the Ottawa Indians at Fort Carillon boiled a disembodied Englishman in a kettle and forced ten other prisoners to watch while their comrade was devoured. When a French priest protested, a young brave replied: "You have French taste; I have Indian. This is good meat for me." On July 26, an English scouting party was captured on Lake George; a number were killed and three of the bodies were eaten on the spot. The list of such atrocities grew as the shadow of war lengthened across the forests and lakes of northern New York.

The war had many such tragic and psychic side effects. The very presence of British forces among the civilian population, for example, elicited an ambiguous response. When Lord Loudoun arrived in New York on July 23, 1756, he was greeted with cheerful cannonades, a "loyal address" from colonial dignitaries, and "at Night the City was handsomely illuminated." For the next twenty months his lavish retinue enjoyed the civilities of New York City. They drank considerable quantities of wine and wooed the local lovelies at dances held in a ballroom at the Province Arms Tavern every second Thursday evening from eight o'clock until midnight. When Amherst made his triumphal journey southward in 1760, the city was illuminated once again, fired its guns in salute, and sent Lord Jeffrey a two-thousand-word memorial of praise.

All was not sweetness and light, however, because most of the regular troops who spent their summers at wilderness bivouacs had to be quartered in colonial cities during the wintertime. Loudoun was reasonably considerate about building barracks at Albany, but a serious crisis occurred in 1756 and 1757 at New York City. Most of the British enlisted men there were placed in barracks, but the officers had to locate lodgings for themselves. When Loudoun demanded that the Common Council make provision in private homes for all of his staff as well, Mayor Cruger protested. "God damn my blood!" replied Loudoun, "if you do not billet my officers upon free quarters this day, I'll order here all the troops in North America, and billet them myself upon this city." Civilian resentment ran high over the quartering matter and because of the embargo upon their shipping as well.

Even so, the economic consequences of the war were salutary for a great many New Yorkers. Privateering had already emerged in 1744 as a profitable enterprise, the colony's privateer fleet during King George's War being second only to Rhode Island's in size and enjoying greater success. During the French and Indian War New York City became the very center of privateering in British North America. Captains and their crews became local heroes, and the lure of making a quick killing caused many men to desert the army and Royal Navy in order to sign on board a fortune-seeking cruiser. In 1757 so many warships became helpless in New York harbor because of desertions that Governor Hardy had to surround the city with troops and make a house-to-house canvass in order to find the hiding sailors and man the royal vessels. Forty New York ships were commissioned as privateers in 1756, and Loudoun estimated in the spring of 1757 that French prizes valued at two hundred thousand pounds sterling had already been brought into New York alone.

Privateering was accompanied by a good deal of successful smuggling—illicit commerce with Hispaniola, for example—a traitorous activity that enraged William Pitt, particularly after 1756. Pitt's crackdown in turn angered those New York merchants who had been shipping to the Caribbean. When profits from privateering began to fall off in 1758 and new areas for investment were sought, the merchants started carrying supplies to islands in the French West Indies that had been reduced to starvation by earlier captures of French supply ships at sea! Profiteering occurred in other sectors of the economy as well. When army contractors sought provisions for the Niagara campaign in 1755, New York City bakers took advantage of the extraordinary demand for bread to raise their prices, and Albany merchants similarly drove up the price of peas per bushel. Consequently the cost of living in New York shot up between 1755 and 1756, with great profits to some and pain to others.

These were good years for ambitious and energetic entrepreneurs. Uriah Hendricks, an eighteen-year-old Jewish youth, immigrated to the city in 1755, opened a small shop, and prospered as a merchant. He took advantage of the rising import trade, supplied army sutlers on the New York frontier, speculated in privateering shares, and sold his interest before losses began to occur in 1758. He lived next to several ironmongers; learned their business; eventually opened accounts with the major copper, brass, and iron merchants of England; and subsequently became one of the first "copper kings" in America. The records of William Beekman, extant for the period 1744–50, show him importing and reselling finished goods from England and the Continent. He also shipped provisions to coastal ports and to the West Indies and invested in conventional shipping as well as privateering. After King George's War he concentrated increasingly on the import trade, remitting no less than £11,900 sterling to his English correspondents in 1749–50. His son, James, starting with the advantages of family capital and strong connections abroad, focused almost entirely upon supplying European imports to lesser merchants in Manhattan, Albany, New Jersey, and Connecticut. His profits ran steadily between 15 and 30 percent.

New York merchants also enjoyed the perquisites of outfitting intercolonial and royal forces during the French and Indian War. Rhode Island commissioned Gerard G. Beekman to supply its troops sent against Crown Point. Robert Sanders of Albany filled the same role for Massachusetts soldiers, and along with Cornelius and Philip Cuyler he provisioned the militiamen of New Hampshire. The firm of Peter Van Brugh Livingston and William Alexander worked with Lewis Morris, Jr., and John Erving of Boston in equipping Shirley's abortive expedition to Niagara and regiments at Oswego. To reduce excessive transportation costs, these merchants selected agents at Albany and Schenectady. Similarly, English military contractors dealt with merchant factors in the colonies, to the benefit of Oliver De Lancey, John Watts, and William Bayard, all of New York City. Because the British army had its main headquarters there, its merchants reaped the greatest profits from military imperatives. And the rise in shipping risks during the war provided a strong impetus to the marine insurance business.

After 1759, when the war ceased to be a significant economic stimulus in New York, a serious depression hit and remained for half a dozen years. New York's pound continued to decline in value in relation to British sterling, and a currency shortage became acute by the middle and later 1760s. Parliament's Wool, Hat, and Molasses acts—all part of the mercantile system—remained troublesome for the colony. The first effectively required New Yorkers to buy all of their woolens in England, while the third deprived them of a necessary source of cash with which to pay for such imports. The colonists also resented the mercantile practice by which specified items they produced had to be exported exclusively to the mother country. Archibald Kennedy called this practice of enumeration a "Solecism in Trade, and the Bane of Industry."

The two wars had political and constitutional repercussions for New York as well. During King George's War, Governor Clinton was forced to approve two Assembly initiatives, both of them tactical errors from the perspective of maintaining the royal prerogative. He acquiesced in provisions that the Assembly appropriate the colony's revenue on an annual basis rather than for five years at a time and that the Assembly must approve the specific purpose of each allocation. A sharp contest took place over these terms between 1746 and 1750, with Clinton wavering in his determination to discipline the Assembly. Late in 1750 he essentially capitulated, so that the next three years were relatively calm. But in 1756 these same issues arose again, and for five years to come De Lancey and Hardy had to sacrifice the need for permanent revenue and accept temporary support bills. The Assembly spent money according to the governor's warrant and specified the amounts to be paid. Contingencies and emergencies of the French and Indian War thereby helped to strengthen the Assembly's constitutional position: precedents had been established that would be invoked just a few years later.

On the other hand, New York passed a Stamp Act in 1756 as a source of defense revenue and renewed it regularly through 1760 without causing any notable popular resentment—except among some of the colony's printers and lawyers.* The tax—which had basically been a nuisance and produced little revenue—was dropped when the fighting stopped; but it established an ambiguous precedent, one that may have been used in preparing the parliamentary Stamp Act of 1765 and may have encouraged George Grenville in his quest for additional colonial funds.

British ministries might have learned yet another lesson from the war experience: that if they wanted to keep the Indians as allies, they would have to treat them as such. They had not consistently done so during the war, and they had not responded to Sir William Johnson's recommendation for a unified and equitable system of regulating the Indian trade. When the western posts reopened in the spring of 1761, however, Amherst advised Johnson to implement personally his trade program. The superintendent visited Niagara in August and Detroit in September. His plan required that all traders have licenses and deal only at designated depots. He established fixed prices and quality controls for goods to be bartered and instructed local officials to enforce these provisions. He and Amherst simply assumed that such stipulations would put an end to Indian complaints. But Johnson himself had no authority to prosecute violators, and as the war ended in 1763 it was unclear which agency of government would provide a judicious system for Anglo-Indian relations.

---

* James Parker and William Weyman opposed the tax, but Hugh Gaine urged subscribers to his *New-York Mercury* to pay it as a patriotic duty. On the whole, the colony's printers flourished during these years. The war generated polemics and all sorts of tracts, manuals, and broadsides having to do with military affairs. See Evans, comp., *American Bibliography*, nos. 7153, 7154, 7269, 7361, 7551, 7621, 7736, 7737, 8012, 8013, 8209, 8210, 8211, 8212, 8300, 8742, 8866; and Bristol, *Supplement*, 1756, 2167, 2168.

A royal proclamation issued in December 1761 had attempted to protect the native Americans from fraudulent land claims; and provisions relating to land grants and settlement patterns that were embodied in the Proclamation of 1763 were designed to ensure some sanctuary for the Indians. Yet neither of these measures could really serve as deterrents to white expansion westward once the French threat was removed. Moreover, once a patent had been granted—even if the Indian deed had been fraudulently obtained—it was very difficult to redress native grievances because a patent provided valid title in common law. By 1763 the Indians had even lost control over areas deeded to the crown for safekeeping, a baffling loss because they felt that they had given Britain "dominion but not the property of those lands."

Hence Pontiac's Rebellion raged on the western frontier and terrified settlers for two years after 1763. An Onondaga chief explained the causes quite succinctly in 1765. "The chief cause of all the late wars," he said, "was about Lands; we saw the English coming towards us from all Parts, and they have cheated us so often, that we could not think well of it. We were afraid, that in a little time, you would be at our very Castles." The Iroquois had given permission for British construction of "a chain of small Posts on the communication through their country to Lake Ontario," but on condition that "they should be demolished at the end of the War." Because they were not then torn down, the Seneca, who felt particularly betrayed, joined Pontiac's Rebellion. In the fall of 1763, through enormous effort and the use of his influence, Johnson persuaded the other five nations to remain neutral, an achievement in which he took great pride. "As the Six Nations are the barrier of this province in particular," he wrote the Board of Trade in November, "and can easily cut off the important Communication to Lake Ontario either way, their attachment can not I conceive be too much cultivated."

In the preliminary peace terms of 1764, the Seneca were persuaded to make major concessions to the British: "That the Seneca Nation do immediately stop all hostilities, and solemnly

engage never more to make War upon the English or suffer any
of their people to commit any act of violence on the persons or
property of any of his Britanic Majesty's subjects." The Seneca
ceded land bordering the Niagara portage, with its timber and
transportation rights, to the British. In return the Seneca were
ambiguously left in full possession of their "rights," were
pardoned for past transgressions, and promised a more definite
treaty later. Pontiac's defeat would establish the Seneca in an
extremely weak bargaining position.

Thereafter Johnson continued to urge upon Whitehall that
limitations be placed upon westward expansion and suggested
that a line be drawn between the Indian lands and those open to
settlement. As he put it in June 1766, "our people in general are
very ill calculated to maintain friendship with the Indians."
Finally, in 1768, he prevailed upon the ministry to convene a
general congress to establish a line of demarcation, and the result
was the famous meeting at Fort Stanwix attended by intercolonial delegations and thirty-one hundred Indians representing the
Six Nations plus their allies and dependent tribes. This was the
largest conference of whites and Indians ever assembled, and it
lasted for several weeks. The treaty signed on November 5 gave
Great Britain all of the land east and south of a line drawn from
Fort Stanwix south to the Unadilla River; from there to the
Delaware River near Hancock, New York; then westward to
Owego, southwest to the west branch of the Susquehanna near
Williamsport, Pennsylvania, and along that river to its head;
from there westward to Kittaning on the Allegheny, along that
river and then the Ohio westward to the mouth of the Tennessee.
In sum, the Indians ceded an enormous amount of land—much
of central and southwestern New York.

At the time, this summit meeting seemed an incredible feat of
diplomacy by Sir William, the apogee of his brilliant career. He
cajoled the Oneidas, who had protested the manipulation of that
line in such a way that great chunks along the Mohawk would be
lost. He had balanced pressures from settlers, the province, and a
whole new group of land speculators, such as the Indiana
Company; and he had helped the crown and the colonies survive

a major crisis in Indian relations. The Indians, as usual, achieved ephemeral results for themselves: massive gifts in goods (worth £10,460, New York value), "guarantees" for their personal lands within the ceded areas, and a promise that the line would be respected. British governmental control had been extended without apparent loss of face or faith by the Indians.

In reality, Whitehall had been unable to restrain the aggressive settlers and speculators. Its policy of 1761–63 to protect Indian lands in central and western New York had failed, just as its hopes for an equitable settlement of the Wappinger land claims in Dutchess County were dashed in 1765–67. New York's Council rejected the appeals of Chief Daniel Nimham on behalf of the Wappingers. The Philipse Highland patent was awarded to its white claimants—an ironic reward for the Wappingers, whose braves had all borne arms in New York's service during the French and Indian War.

The British and their colonists had won that war; but the Indians on both sides may be said to have lost in the long run. By 1768, expansive settlers and speculators in New York had sown the wind—an ill wind for the Iroquois—and after 1776 they would reap the whirlwind. Sir William was New York's Hosea; and he would be prophetic. His death in 1774, however, saved him from seeing the destruction of all he had wrought.

13

"LIBERTY AND PROPERTY": FROM RESISTANCE TO INDEPENDENCE

The advent of the American Revolution in New York seems paradoxical in so many ways that it almost defies explanation. If New York's stentorian voice raised the loudest protests against British policies in 1764, it was also the very last colony to voice approval of independence in 1776. If the colony appeared aggressively radical during the Stamp Act crisis of 1765–66, it also seemed nervously reluctant during the Anglo-American breach of 1775–76. Although public affairs during the decade 1765–75 were severely complicated by class conflict, nevertheless it was class collaboration after 1776 that helped put an end to British colonialism in New York.

When the phrase "cock-pit of the Revolution" is invoked, we tend to think of Massachusetts Bay and Sam Adams, or Virginia and Patrick Henry, or possibly Philadelphia because the Continental Congress convened there. New York, meanwhile, has had the reputation of being a haven for Loyalists, or of having too many trimmers, at the least. It is certainly true that New York's Assembly did not lead the province into Revolution. In fact, the Assembly had to be revolutionized by "the people out-of-doors" before the colony could join the continental movement. Even so, despite a relative lack of memorable leaders, New York too was a

"cock-pit of the Revolution," for reasons that will emerge in the
pages that follow. Issues and self-interest mattered equally in
New York. Both were volatile and well publicized, and both
evoked significant responses. From the Stamp Act Congress held
at New York in 1765, to the establishment of George Washington's headquarters on Broadway in 1776, to the creation of the
nation's capital at Manhattan in 1789, New York served as a
fulcrum of the American Revolution. The causes and consequences of that fact are as fascinating as they are far-reaching.

Physical communication among the colonies, as well as
between them and England, improved markedly after the middle
of the eighteenth century. Parliament had first regularized a
postal system for the North American provinces in 1711.
England's postmaster general appointed deputies for the different
colonies; but the principal office was placed in New York, to
which all others were subordinate. After 1753 Benjamin Franklin
improved the mail service between New York and Philadelphia.
By October 1754, three riders left each city three days a week
and completed the trip in thirty-three hours. By the beginning of
1764, less than a decade later, the Philadelphia–New York post
had doubled in speed—a fairly strategic event for improved
communication. By the 1750s mail went at least once a week
between Boston and New York in summer and biweekly in
winter. As one contemporary remarked, "Answers may be
obtained in three weeks which used to require six weeks." In
1760, moreover, Massachusetts established postal service between
Boston and Albany in order to improve the liaison between
command headquarters and troops in the field.

In 1755, meanwhile, transatlantic packet service started
between Falmouth, England, and New York. The ships were
somewhat irregular in schedule and slower than merchant ships;
but they were exclusively for the transport of mail, and New
York was *the* North American terminus. Internally the Hudson
River served as a rapid means of travel, so that overall, New
York tended to enjoy relatively reliable contacts with England,
with the other colonies, and within.

A mahogany kneehole chest (or bureau table) with ball-and-claw feet, made in New York ca. 1760. *Courtesy, Museum of Fine Arts, Boston, M. and M. Karolik Collection.*

A mahogany slant-top desk in the Chippendale style, made in New York ca. 1760–70. Note the rope-carved apron and ball-and-claw feet. *Courtesy of The New-York Historical Society, New York City, T. Lawrence Bequest, 1952.*

Little wonder, then, that a striking feature of the New York newspapers after April 1765 is the extraordinary amount of attention given to discussions of what was taking place and being said in other colonies. Little wonder that the Stamp Act Congress met at New York City between October 7 and 24, 1765. Nor is it surprising that events in New York had considerable emotional and political impact upon its neighbors. John Dickinson's widely read *Letters from a Farmer in Pennsylvania*, for example, published in 1767, derived important constitutional arguments from the circumstances of New York's legislature being suspended without the colonists' prior acquiescence.

During a visit to the province, John Adams described New York politics as "the devil's own incomprehensibles." Roger Champagne, a modern historian, has called it "a tangled skein of expediency, intrigue, and maneuver." Both, of course, are quite correct. Since Assembly elections did not occur annually but at six- or seven-year intervals in this period (1761, 1768–69, 1776), and since only a relatively small number of local officials were popularly elected, it might be logical to assume that the development of political organizations and techniques would have been retarded in New York. But that was not at all the case. Since British policies became steadily more offensive, it might also be logical to presume progressive alienation on the part of concerned colonists. Yet the case of Hugh Gaine, a New York City printer, was not at all unusual. From radical opposition to the Stamp Act in 1765, he shifted to mild conservatism in 1768–69 because he disliked extralegal activities. In 1774–75 he was whiggish once again and welcomed the Declaration of Independence. But by the fall of 1776, demoralized by American defeats and financial distress, he turned to Loyalism. Call it vacillation? A pilgrim's progress? In either case, his was a common pattern in New York.

In order to comprehend the colony's varied response to the events of 1764–76, it is necessary to establish the identity of certain key groups and participants, as well as the character of certain trends well under way by the end of the French and Indian War in 1763. It should be noted, for example, that there

existed major and long-standing sources of antiauthoritarianism
—albeit of a parochial and often conservative sort. Dutch
resentment of English domination dated back to 1664, of course.
New England Puritans who had settled on Long Island disliked
Dutch rule before 1664 and often clashed with English royal
control in the century that followed. Then there were French
Huguenots and German Palatines whose experience with established authority had been consistently unfortunate; Indians and
blacks who encountered discrimination by law as well as by
social custom; tenant farmers with economic grievances against
their landlords; and Presbyterians who bridled under Anglican
control.

By the mid-1760s, these groups of malcontents found that they
could turn to two sorts of spokesmen for leadership. The socially
"respectable" looked to the lawyers, men already experienced in
public affairs; and the fact that lawyers played a major role helps
to explain why New York seems to have been so constitutionally
defiant in 1764–65, yet so cautious in 1775–76. New York's
legislative resolves of October 18, 1764, proclaiming the illegality
of Parliament's new revenue measure (the Sugar Act) as well as
the contemplated stamp duties, comprised one of the major state
papers of the entire prerevolutionary era. They categorically
defended colonial rights and had enormous impact in other
provinces, especially Massachusetts. New York's lawyers nevertheless believed, by and large, in *lawful* resistance and in
reconciliation, if possible. Consequently they delayed the decision for independence, so long, in fact, that on June 22, 1776,
John Adams asked, "What is the reason that New York must
continue to embarrass the Continent?"

Ultimately the likes of John Jay, Gouverneur Morris, and
Robert R. Livingston came to regard separation as inevitable;
and when that realization occurred, they determined to keep the
new government under men of their own social class and political
outlook. In order to do so, however, in order to form an alliance
with radical artisans and yeoman farmers, they had to adopt the
rhetoric of republican constitutionalism. The net effect was to
keep New York the geographic fulcrum of the revolutionary

movement, but also to ensure moderate and even conservative control of that revolution. These men swam with the tide in order to minimize social disorder. But the outcome would ultimately transform political society there. Here is Gouverneur Morris's well-known assessment of the situation (made on May 20, 1774), reviewing the decade of conflict:

The troubles in America during Grenville's administration put our gentry upon this finesse. They stimulated some daring coxcombs to rouse the mob into an attack upon the bounds of order and decency. These fellows became the Jack Cades of the day, the leaders in all the riots, the bell-wethers of the flock. . . . On the whole, the shepherds were not much to blame in a politic point of view. The bell-wethers jingled merrily and roared out liberty and property, and religion, and a multitude of cant terms which everyone thought he understood, and was egregiously mistaken. . . . This answered many purposes; the simple flock put themselves entirely under the protection of these most excellent shepherds. By and by, behold a great metamorphosis without the help of Ovid or his divinities, but entirely effectuated by two modern Genii, the god of Ambition and the goddess of Faction. The first of these prompted the shepherds to shear some of their flock, and then in conjunction with the other, converted the bell-wethers into shepherds. That we have been in hot water with the British Parliament ever since everybody knows. Consequently these new shepherds had their hands full of employment. The old ones kept themselves least in sight, and a want of confidence in each other was not the least evil which followed. The port of Boston has been shut up. These sheep, simple as they are, cannot be gulled as heretofore. In short, there is no ruling them, and now, to leave the metaphor, the heads of the mobility grow dangerous to the gentry, and how to keep them down is the question. While they correspond with the other colonies, call and dismiss popular assemblies, make resolves to bind the consciences of the rest of mankind, bully poor printers, and exert with full force all their other tribunitial powers, it is impossible to curb them.

But art sometimes goes farther than force, and therefore, to trick them handsomely a committee of patricians was to be nominated, and into their hands was to be committed the majesty of the people. . . . The tribunes, through the want of good legerdemain in the senatorial order, perceived the finesse; and yesterday I was present at a grand division of the city, and there I beheld my fellow-citizens very accurately counting all their chickens, not only before any of them were hatched, but before above one half of the eggs were laid. In short, they fairly contended about the future forms of our government, whether it should be founded upon aristocratic or democratic principles.

I stood in the balcony, and on my right hand were ranged all the people of property, with some few poor dependents, and on the other all the tradesmen, etc., who thought it worth their while to leave daily labour for the good of the country. The spirit of the English constitution has yet a little influence left, and but a little. The remains of it, however, will give the wealthy people a superiority this time, but would they secure it they must banish all schoolmasters and confine all knowledge to themselves. This cannot be. The mob begin to think and to reason. Poor reptiles! It is with them a vernal morning; they are struggling to cast off their winter's slough, they bask in the sunshine, and ere noon they will bite, depend upon it. The gentry begin to fear this. Their committee will be appointed, they will deceive the people and again forfeit a share of their confidence. And if these instances of what with one side is policy, with the other perfidy, shall continue to increase and become more frequent, farewell aristocracy. I see, and I see it with fear and trembling, that if the disputes with Great Britain continue, we shall be under the worst of all possible dominions; we shall be under the domination of a riotous mob.*

Morris was not entirely accurate about who had radicalized whom, for the second level of leadership in revolutionary New York—a kind of counterpoint to the respectable lawyers—came from the so-called mechanics, a general term referring to anyone who worked with his hands: artisans, shopkeepers, and sometimes even sailors. It must be stressed that the "popular element" in politics was not a monolith. It was divided by ethnic, religious, and economic interests and could not be so easily manipulated from above, as so many puppets. Some of the popular leaders were extremists in politics, while others were cautious and restrained. Some allied with the Livingston faction, while still others cooperated with the De Lanceys.

Nevertheless, their collective behavior in the decade after 1764

---

* From Merrill Jensen, ed., *English Historical Documents: American Colonial Documents to 1776* (London, 1955), 860–63.

added a new dimension to politics: the people out-of-doors. As one contemporary noted in 1770, the De Lanceys "had Agents without Doors who mixed with the Rabble for the Purpose of acquiring their Confidence." On October 31, 1765, a milling crowd of several thousand stood outside Fort George, "knocked at the gate, placed their hands on the top of the Ramparts, called out to the guards to fire, threw bricks and stones against the Fort." Jesse Lemisch has argued that New York's protest against the Stamp Act in December 1765—the vigorous "Petitions and Resolves"—shows the influence of a mass meeting held at Burns's City Arms Tavern on November 26, when twelve hundred freemen and freeholders adopted a set of instructions for the city's representatives in the Assembly.

Such large gatherings served from time to time to remind imperial officials as well as the indigenous elite that politicization of the "mechanics" would have to be reckoned with. The Sons of Liberty, a political organization led by lawyers, merchants, and shopkeepers, held committee meetings on street corners; large open-air dinners were served in the fields, and notices were freely posted about town. After New York City held its own tea party on April 22, 1774, members of the Provincial Assembly began to attend public meetings in order to select a committee to establish a nonimportation program against Britain. The crowd that assembled at Fraunces's Tavern on the evening of May 16, 1774, was so large that its members had to move to the Merchants' Exchange. On February 1, 1776, the citizens of New York held open-air elections for "the next general Assembly." The people out-of-doors had become more than a catchphrase. They were a reality.

While the *vox populi* grew in volume, royal authority was on the wane, and the figure who must bear much of the responsibility for undermining it is Cadwallader Colden. The irony, of course, is that this intelligent man, who served intermittently as acting governor and lieutenant governor between 1760 and 1775, wanted nothing so much as to uphold the royal prerogative. Despite all of his political maneuvering, he lacked *politique;* and for all of his vast learning, he remained one of the most naïve and tactless figures in the British colonies. It would not be unfair to call him an unwitting provocateur of the early revolutionary movement in New York. It was Colden who, in 1760, needlessly opened the issue of judges serving only at the pleasure of the king, rather than for an unlimited term on "good behavior," as had been the custom. It was Colden who, in 1760–61, overzealously decided to curtail illicit trade of long duration between New York merchants and the French West Indies. It was Colden who, in 1761–62, precipitously vacated large land patents that had been granted in violation of royal instructions.

Most of all, it was Colden who, in 1764, overturned the provincial legal practice of allowing appeals from common-law courts to the governor in Council only by "writ of error." He accepted the highly irregular pleas of one Waddel Cunningham, a merchant who had lost a civil action for assault and battery against Thomas Forsey, and thereby seemed to violate the time-honored acceptance of verdicts from trial by jury. Cunningham had asked New York's Supreme Court to review the facts as well as the law, but he had been properly turned down. Colden, however, in November 1764, stayed the court's judgment and ordered the chief justice to deliver up to him the proceedings in the case. The constitutional controversy that ensued dragged on through 1765. Colden argued the legal aspects of the case badly and managed to alienate not only the moderate Livingston party, but the conservative merchants of the De Lancey coalition as well. The entire populace now detested this seventy-six-year-old advocate of royal supremacy. As one sympathetic observer put it, "the old Body was always dislik'd enough, but now they would prefer Beelzebub himself to him."

Resolution of the case finally came late in 1765. New York's Assembly supported the Supreme Court with a series of strong denunciations of Colden's "mischievous Innovation." Then the Board of Trade expediently decided to uphold the Supreme Court's decision. Henceforth only appeals "in error" could be taken from common-law courts to the governor in Council. But the political damage had already been done. Colden's prestige, and that of the crown, were ruptured. New York's response to the

Stamp Act in 1765 was undoubtedly so strong because of the concurrent controversy over *Forsey* v. *Cunningham*. Because the custom of trial by jury was being threatened, the specter of taxation without representation and violations of the Stamp Act triable in courts without juries loomed that much more seriously as part of some concerted plot to strip the colonists of their rights as Englishmen.

Colden detested the legal fraternity in New York, perhaps because they had the advantage of expertise in just about the only subject that he had not mastered. Medicine and botany, philosophy and physics, were his; but the mysterious science of the law was theirs, and as it happened a knowledge of the law served very useful purposes in the Anglo-American crisis.

Even more important than law, however, was the ability to utilize the press, an ability Colden's enemies mastered during the years 1761–65. William Livingston, William Smith, Jr., and John Morin Scott had waged verbal warfare on Colden during the judicial tenure contretemps in 1761–62, but their success in activating public opinion had been limited. The Forsey case in 1764 and the Stamp Act, however, provided extraordinary stimuli and facilitated the politicization of "mechanics" and middle-class persons who had hitherto been apathetic. Hugh Gaine's *Mercury*, William Weyman's *Gazette*, and John Holt's *Weekly Journal* became instruments of resistance to imperial policies. They shaped public opinion by conveying a sense of anxiety about British rule, by emphasizing constitutional arguments as well as natural rights, by encouraging antipathy to the presence (or idea) of a standing army, and by creating an incipient American nationalism.

These, then, were some of the component groups and ingredients that are central to any proper understanding of the coming of the Revolution in New York. Clashes arose over imperial issues, yet it must be understood that royal forces and representatives were not well coordinated and often worked at cross-purposes. Class conflict played a major part, too; but it must also be understood that serious breaches occurred within the elite, among the "mechanics," and between the Sons of Liberty and their rural counterparts. The social groups were not monolithic.

There was, moreover, a considerable background and buildup of antiauthoritarianism in the colony; yet that impulse often manifested itself in conservative ways and in atomistic, localistic tendencies. Many of the Whig leaders had been trained in the law, as we have noted, an education that heightened their appreciation of constitutional grievances but also made them chary of extralegal activities. In consequence the so-called leaders frequently, in reality, were pulled along by public opinion and by the irresistible force of the people out-of-doors. Mass meetings often helped the lawyers to make up their minds, or brought them to action, as did the intemperate provocations of Cadwallader Colden, on the one hand, and patriotic newspaper polemicists on the other.

Most of the major trends and themes in New York's colonial history played important roles in determining the province's revolutionary experience. An excess of pluralism and materialism combined with a lack of coherent community (as well as the Iroquois' alienation) to make rebellion in New York a fairly distinctive phenomenon. The inhabitants' striking heterogeneity, as well as their sensitivity to the marketplace, meant that firm alliances were hard to make and harder to hold together. The social elite, the merchants, the landed gentry, the "mechanics," even the lawyers, disagreed among themselves and divided. As new issues emerged and as the economy waxed and waned after 1766, most of the coalitions of the early and mid-1760s came unstuck. New ones formed, to be sure, but the constant scramble made the colonists seem especially prone to be guided by expediency. In retrospect, these fluctuating coalitions seem especially confusing.

What heightens the confusion for historians, particularly when trying to narrate the revolutionary prologue in an orderly fashion, is the fact that episodes and their consequences were not neatly sequential. Their occurrence overlapped chronologically, and often their near simultaneity worked like the bursts of a Fourth of July aerial display. A controversial series of court cases called the *New York* affair, involving smuggling and enforcement of the customs law, dragged on between 1763 and 1767. Taken on its own, the series reveals that imperial reform, specifically a more efficient program for customs enforcement, should have been undertaken half a century earlier. But what made the *New York* affair so problematic was that it paralleled the troubles arising from *Forsey* v. *Cunningham* (1763–65), the Sugar Act (1764), and the Stamp Act (1765). Similarly, the Stamp Act crisis (1765–66) overlapped the passionate protest aroused in New York by enforcement of the Quartering Act (1765–67), a dispute that led in turn to Parliament's passage in 1767 of the Restraining Act. That, in turn, coincided with the furor over the Townshend duties, and so it went.

In a sense, public order and tranquillity in New York seem to have been constantly in double jeopardy between 1763 and 1768. Appreciation of this fact should help us to understand why New York had such a prominent leadership role in opposition to imperial policies during these years. In October 1764, upon learning of the proposed Stamp Act, New York's Assembly sent a petition to Parliament so bold that no M.P. could be found to introduce it. On October 31, 1765, New York's merchants entered into a nonimportation agreement: one week ahead of Philadelphia's merchants and five weeks ahead of Boston's commercial community. In sum, the boycott was first conceived and carried out in New York. Still at the radical forefront late in 1766, New York's refusal to obey the Quartering Act precipitated a special cabinet meeting in London and, from that meeting, a demand for strict adherence in the future. Early in 1767 London merchants singled out New York for special blame and charges of ingratitude (for imperial protection) after New York shippers, with support from Boston, petitioned the House of Commons for alterations in the Quartering Act and in the Acts of Trade.

No wonder, then, that when Charles Townshend presented the cabinet's resolutions to a Committee of the Whole House of Commons on May 13, 1767, he cited New York's leadership role in the decision of other colonies to defy the Quartering (or Mutiny) Act. Moreover, the American nonimportation agreement of 1768 was more rigorously adhered to in New York than in New England or Pennsylvania; New York's Sons of Liberty played a leading role for all the colonies in November 1769 (by supporting and publicizing South Carolina's refusal to provision royal soldiers); and, finally, New York's bloody Battle of Golden Hill, on January 19, 1770, preceded the more famous Boston Massacre by almost seven weeks. Thereafter, however, starting in 1770, divisiveness, indecision, and apprehension began to affect New York's situation with increasing impact, as we shall see. But first, we must bring the narrative of 1764–70 into sharper focus.

The opening salvo of the Revolution in New York may be said to have been fired on October 18, 1764. On that date the Assembly transmitted to its London agent three petitions for presentation respectively to the king, the Lords, and the Commons. These documents protested four major policy decisions that had recently been implemented, rumored, or were pending. In response to the Forsey case, the petitions insisted upon the validity and finality of trial by jury. In response to the Sugar Act, the restoration and extension of New York's commerce with the West Indies was insisted upon.* In response to the Currency Act of 1764, New York's need for paper money as well as continued bills of credit was insisted upon. And in response to the stamp bill, the right of consent was insisted upon. Here is the deferential, carefully worded summary paragraph of the petition to the king, one of these three famous documents:

These, may it please your Majesty, are the important points upon which your faithful representatives for your loyal Colony of New York, have in behalf of their constituents, and with the most humble submission, presumed to approach the throne; assuring your Majesty, that one of the principal blessings they have to expect, from a continuance of their exclusive right to tax themselves, the restoration and extension of their Commerce, the execution of law, in the ancient

---

* The Assembly had sent Parliament a memorial on Apr. 20, 1764, pointing out that New York's imports from England exceeded its exports by almost £470,000 sterling and that the entire balance was made up through the trade deriving from French molasses.

and ordinary method and the continuance of their bills of credit, will be their capacity to do the most faithful and ready services to their King and Country upon every occasion.

Earlier in this petition the Assembly had emphasized "our lives and property, and what we hold dearer than both, that inestimable liberty with which our ancestors have set us free"; and at the close, referring to taxation only with consent, they had insisted that "without such a right vested in themselves, exclusive of all others, there can be no liberty, no happiness, nor security; it is inseparable from the very idea of property, for who can call that his own, which may be taken away at the pleasure of another?" Throughout the decade that followed, over and over again, "Liberty and Property" would become the watchwords of the revolutionary movement in New York. They came to be the constant refrain of patriot newspapers, ubiquitous broadsides, and vocal Liberty Boys. It was in its implications as bourgeois and conservative a motto as it was radical. We value our freedom and our goods, they said; and they left it to others to point out that when a higher value had to be placed upon one or the other, many assigned the highest priority to property. In 1769, for example, Granville Sharp, an English abolitionist, cited an advertisement from the *New York Journal* offering the separate sale of a black mother and her three-year-old daughter as though they were a cow and calf. But chattel slavery, we well know, was for many patriots a blind spot.

Despite New York's petitions (and those of other colonies) of October 18, 1764, Parliament enacted the stamp bill a few months later on March 8, to become effective on November 1, 1765. Late in 1764 a society was organized in New York for the promotion of colonial manufactures. It offered bounties for the production of articles normally imported from Britain. In February 1765, New York's fiercely worded petition was sent to Parliament but went unpresented and unheeded. Between April and June the provincial press described imperial intentions in the most fearful tones. From July until the act took hold on November 1, a systematic protest was organized in an effort to make the law inoperative. From November onward the publicists worked for repeal. Early in October, for example, a news sheet called the *Constitutional Courant* appeared in New York. Filled with inflammatory articles, it reissued Franklin's famous cartoon of 1754: a segmented snake with the motto "Join or die."

By the time the Stamp Act Congress convened on October 7, James McEvers had already resigned his appointment as stamp distributor for New York. Fearing that a mob might destroy his store and goods, he salvaged his liberty as well as his property with a small sacrifice of dignity. On October 23, a vessel carrying the stamps, escorted by two frigates, arrived at New York. A crowd of about two thousand waited for the stamps to be landed, but they were fooled—the pernicious paper came into Fort George secretly that night. A company of artillery, just arrived from England, brought the garrison's strength to about 130 men. But the garrison's commander, Major Thomas James, lacked any sense of tact and publicly threatened to ram stamps down New York throats at sword's point. John Ketcham, a shoemaker, promised in turn to bury James alive if he caught him outside the fort.

On the night of October 31, the reassembled mob could no longer be contained. Its members hanged Colden in effigy, burned his coach and sleigh, sacked Major James's elegant home, and swarmed about the city menacing the fort and damaging some property. There was a sense of "General Terror." Frantic negotiations among Colden, his Council, the city government, and General Thomas Gage resulted in Gage restraining any return of fire from the fort, and Colden capitulating by handing the stamps over to city officials and allowing them to be "escorted" to City Hall by a throng. Gage had prudently followed the path of moderation and, with Colden, had averted "a Civil War, at a time when there's nothing prepared or can timely be so, to make opposition to it."

By November 5 the most serious threat of anarchy had passed, and a modicum of calm returned. The turmoil then and in succeeding months seems to have been guided, on the whole, by men of some standing in the community, and not by an urban proletariat. In Albany, too, the Sons of Liberty came from many of the most prominent families. And in both places their dilemma was to manipulate the "mechanics" and sailors in order to protest British policy without disrupting the traditional pattern of deference in political society. John Holt, printer of the *New York Gazette*, described to Mrs. Benjamin Franklin on February 15, 1766, an incident arising from an effort by some merchants to execute a customs bond with stamped paper:

The Matter was intended to be done privately, but it got wind, and by ten o Clock I suppose 2000 people attended at the Coffee House, among them most of the principal men in Town—The Culprits apologies did not satisfy the people, they were highly blamed and the Sons of Liberty found it necessary to use their Influence to moderate the Resentments of the People. Two Men were dispach'd to the Collector for the Stamp'd Bonds of which he had 30 in all, he desired Liberty to confer with the Governor, which was granted. The Governor sent Word, if the Stamps were deliver'd to him, he would give his Word and Honour they should not be used; but that if the people were not satisfied with this, they might do as they pleased with them—The message being returned to the gathering Multitude, they would not agree to the Governors Proposal, but insisted upon the Stamps being deliver'd and burnt, one or two men attended by about a thousand others were then sent for the Stamps, which were brought to the Coffee House, and the Merchant who had used them was order'd himself to kindle the Fire and consume them. . . . —The people pretty quietly dispersed soon After, but their Resentment was not allay'd, Toward the Evening . . . tho' the Sons of Liberty exerted themselves to the utmost, they could not prevent the gathering of the Multitude, who went to Mr. Williams's house,* broke open the Door and destroyed some of the Furniture, but thro' the Influence of the Sons of Liberty and on his most earnest Entreaty and promise in the most publick manner to ask pardon next day, or do whatever they should require of him, they were prevail'd on to leave the House. . . .

Meanwhile, the winter months of 1765–66 had brought a tense period of watchful waiting in New York. The export of flour before November 1 had been so heavy that a shortage of bread

---

* Williams was naval officer of the port of New York.

occurred just when a rise in the number of sailors in port increased the demand for food. On December 4, the customs officials opened the port in order to reduce the quantity of seamen in town (and hence the risk of mob action). Unfortunately Captain Archibald Kennedy began to stop outgoing vessels whose clearance papers were unstamped; yet he continued to permit ships to enter. Consequently the problem of a surfeit of sailors in port remained, and so the winter continued to be a lean one for too many empty bellies.

In December 1765, the lawyers of New York passed a resolution to do their business without the use of stamps. Their risk in doing so was reduced when the provincial courts decided to duck the problem of enforcement by adjourning until news of repeal arrived. That occurred in early April, whereupon the courts reopened. But in the intervening five months a great deal of economic confusion ensued. Hudson Valley farmers got some respite in paying their rents, since landlords had no way to evict for nonpayment. Speculators profited from the court shutdown, however, and serious problems of debt collection arose.

After May 20, 1766, when repeal of the Stamp Act became official, there was a mild resurgence of loyalty to Great Britain. The face-saving Declaratory Act, which preserved Parliament's right to tax the colonies, was largely ignored. Nevertheless, amid all the rejoicing, there would be a legacy of anxiety, well conveyed in the *Post-Boy* on July 3, 1766: "Were the Americans to express submission or Gratitude to the *British* Parliament for what they have done, or even to be entirely silent in declaring their own Rights at this Juncture, it would be giving up the grand Point for which they have made so glorious a Struggle, and deprive them of that Esteem and Gratitude with which their Posterity will look back upon their Ancestors of this Era." Such a concern would grow into strong apprehension during the 1770s: the fear in May 1774, for example, that the Boston Port Act would be applied to New York; the fear of bombardment from British ships between the summer of 1775 and that of 1776; the fear in January 1776 that General Charles Lee would precipitate a British attack; or the kind of fear that drove Lewis Morris, in

October 1776, simply to flee from New York to Philadelphia. Fear of political, economic, and military reprisals became a vital factor in New York's affairs after 1766.

Nor did repeal of the Stamp Act resolve New York's constitutional difficulties with Whitehall. There remained the vexatious matter of the Quartering Act. During the final phase of the French and Indian War, back in 1762–63, New York's Assembly had dutifully passed a new act to provide for the quartering of British regulars in private homes. That act expired on January 1, 1764. During the war years, Britain's government and army command had tacitly conceded the right of colonial assemblies to legislate on this matter and the related one of impressment, rather than having them imposed externally by Parliament or the military. When peacetime came, therefore, the New York leadership did not intend to give up this right, and tensions arose in 1764 over whether the civil population provided sufficient support for military imperatives. The issue grew hot late in 1764 (that same critical moment once again) when New York City refused to provide firewood for the barracks. Mayor John Cruger pointed out that there was no law for quartering in public houses as in England. Even more determinative, however, was the simple fact of economic recession. Leading inhabitants had hoped to make the city more self-sufficient, funds were in short supply, and no soldier lacked shelter anyway.

Provoked by such stubbornness, General Gage requested, and Parliament passed, a Quartering Act. Effective for a two-year term beginning in May 1765, it required civil authorities in the colonies to provide barracks and supplies for British troops. A second act, passed in 1766, covered billeting in inns, alehouses, and unoccupied dwellings. Fortunately, the British troops in New York at this point were reasonably well disciplined. A few unseemly incidents occurred; but soldiers were not to provoke civilians, and Gage managed to maintain fairly firm control. In 1766, moreover, when the army became repressive against the tenant uprising in the Hudson Valley, Gage even got a reprimand from London for excessive use of force.

Nevertheless, the New York Assembly once again refused to

comply with the Quartering Act, taking a stand this time on December 15, 1766. In February 1767, the ministry rejected the use of force as a solution, and in April the suggestion that an extra port duty be laid upon New York was dismissed as unworkable. The upshot was a spurious victory for Charles Townshend. On July 2, Parliament adopted his proposal to suspend New York's Assembly until it complied with the Quartering Act. This "Restraining Act" was never actually applied, however, because the Assembly was deemed to have complied before the effective date of the act. Each side had saved some face, but the measure of mistrust broadened.

Other colonies had objected to the Quartering Act also; but the Chatham administration singled out New York for punitive action in 1767, because that colony's Assembly had protested first and loudest on this issue and because Gage (the British commander in chief for North America) had his headquarters there. It had been ministerial policy for several years to isolate and punish the most obnoxious colony. With Hillsborough's accession to power in 1768 (with principal responsibility for colonial affairs), the prime target became Massachusetts instead of New York, a shift that helps to explain the more conciliatory mood of some New Yorkers thereafter. The major violence that simmered just beneath the surface never erupted in the years 1767–69, as one might have expected. A contributing factor may be found in the close personal relationships enjoyed by many of the army officers in New York with members of the provincial gentry. Soldiers and civilians at the lower level would taunt and fight on occasion, especially in January 1770, when the regulars tore down a "Liberty Pole" and provoked the Golden Hill and Nassau Street riots.* But by and large harmony prevailed in civil-military relations, at least until 1774, in New York.

The army played a critical role in yet another respect. Its

---

* The major tensions underlying these outbursts were socioeconomic as well as ideological. The redcoats were filling jobs that would ordinarily have been held by natives, and unemployment was an issue at the time. John Lamb and Isaac Sears encouraged the unemployed artisans and sailors with fluent rhetoric, but their real appeal was to the breadbasket.

presence brought money into the depressed colonial economies of the 1760s and especially to that of New York. This, too, contributed to the reluctance of some provincial Whigs in welcoming independence in the 1770s. In 1767–68, however, New York faced an insufficient supply of circulating money. The situation got worse when embezzlement by New York's treasurer was discovered after September 1767, counterfeiting became rife, and customs duties had to be collected in specie starting in the summer of 1768. By the fall of that year, New York had simply run out of legal tender and faced a severe economic crisis.

To make matters worse, agricultural prices had dropped, the West Indian trade had slackened, expensive British imported goods were not selling well, and land values were on the decline. The most popular solution hinged upon a plan to issue paper money on loan and thereby provide public credit, facilitate trade, and get money into circulation. That being prohibited by the Currency Act of 1764,* however, the only effective alternative was to reduce consumption. When Boston repudiated the Townshend duties with a program of nonimportation and home industry, New Yorkers joined in for sound economic as well as ideological reasons. Merchants could now dispose of excess stocks at fair prices, and sterling exchange rates soon improved. Hence one of the first acts of the New York Chamber of Commerce, newly formed in 1768, was to attempt to regulate the value of currencies circulating there. Hence also the reason New York merchants felt justified in resuming importation after July 1770. By then the Townshend duties had been repealed, and Parliament had promised to permit a new issue of paper money.

The political and economic effect of nonimportation is difficult to measure with precision, but it must have been considerable. We know that New York's imports dropped from a rough value of £573,562 in 1768 to about £188,974 the following year. Yet the

---

* Parliament finally revised it in 1770—permitting New York to issue £120,000 on loan (to be legal tender in payments to the loan office) for 14 years and to the Treasury for the same term plus one year—in order to support the conservative De Lancey-Colden alliance in New York politics and help to facilitate supply requirements of the army.

long-range growth of New York's economy, despite the recessions and problems of the 1760s, was steady. The volume of shipping more than doubled between 1754 and 1775. Some 25,192 tons entered and cleared the customhouse in 1754, as compared with 56,791 in 1775 (the figure for 1774 was 81,028, highly unusual). The number of ships owned by New Yorkers rose from 157 registered in 1749 to 477 registered in 1762 to 709 vessels in 1772. During this same quarter-century there was also an extraordinary rise in the extent of New York's intercolonial trade: joint investment with Rhode Island men in privateers, merchants with subsidiaries in New Jersey, joint ventures and actual partnerships with residents of other colonies.

One of the most significant developments in the provincial economy after 1764 involved mining and metals. Iron plantations had first appeared in the early 1740s: the Ancram works on Livingston Manor and the Stirling ironworks in Orange County. Smaller ones also emerged during the 1750s, but the major thrust occurred in 1765–66 when a consortium of English industrialists invested £54,000 sterling in ironworks at Cortlandt (and in New Jersey) under the direction of Peter Hasenclever. The manufacture of potash and pearl ash on rural farms also became possible at this time.* In 1771 the total production of metal from mines in New York and northern Jersey reached its colonial peak: 676 tons of pig iron and 1,492 tons of bar iron with a combined value of £15,708.

One suggestion that emerges from these economic trends is that there may well have been a striking contrast, during 1767–75, between the rural and urban economies in New York. Many freehold farmers seem to have enjoyed comparative prosperity and newfound security. The Indians had been pushed out of the way to a greater degree than hitherto, land speculation in many cases remained fruitful, rural manufacturing burgeoned, and the nonimportation movement encouraged local productiv-

---

* These are crude and purer forms of potassium carbonate, an alkaline substance obtained by lixiviating the ashes of vegetables and evaporating the solution in large iron pots.

ity. By contrast the economic situation in New York City was depressed much of the time: smuggling had been curtailed, nonimportation hurt the merchant community, currency was in short supply, idle and hungry sailors were stuck in port for protracted periods, and the presence of British soldiers exacerbated the problem of unemployment. Is it any wonder that the city became the center of radical political activity, while most rural areas were more evenly divided into pro- and anti-British groups?

In fact, radicalism developed outside the city only slowly. By early January 1766, Albany merchants had pledged to join their New York counterparts in nonimportation; and during the next three months some smaller towns established Sons of Liberty groups. The organization disappeared as a formal structure that summer, however, and did not reemerge until November 29, 1773.* During the intervening years provincial politics showed familiar lines of force and stress. The Livingston-dominated party had controlled the Assembly since 1761. At the election of 1768 it squeaked through by such a shaky margin that another election had to be held early in 1769. This time the De Lanceys succeeded in winning control of the legislature, in part by contending that the Livingston group had not been sufficiently hard-nosed in opposition to British policies. How did that happen?

New York had, after all, faced the prospect of military government after 1767—a prospect so grim as to be partially responsible for eliciting the Massachusetts circular letter of February 11, 1768. Yet the New York press became curiously quiet and seemingly indifferent at this point, resorting to reprints of arguments published in other colonies. As John Watts wrote to General Monckton, "our poor printers would starve if it was not for the dirty trade of copying, which they are forced to submit to

---

* It is certainly true, however, that some of the most visible "Sons" in 1765–66 rallied behind Alexander McDougall in 1769–70 when he accused the Assembly of bowing to Parliament's demands. When the New York merchants resumed importation in July 1770, moreover, McDougall, Lamb, and Sears voiced vigorous opposition.

for want of originals." The Assembly election in March 1768 was a partisan struggle along traditional lines, within the elite as well as among the middle class and their supporters. A bitter division subsequently over the proper response to Massachusetts' circular letter led to dissolution and another election in January 1769. This one may have been the most vicious in New York's colonial history. The Livingstons stirred up religious dissenters against the De Lanceys and gladly considered the use of force. One reported that "if there is not fair play shown there will be bloodshed, as we have by far the best part of the Bruisers on our side." De Lancey supporters called the Livingstons "a pack of hypocritical, cheating, lying, canting, ill-designing scoundrels" and even accused John Morin Scott of homosexuality: he "dances with, and *kisses (filthy beast!)* those of his own sex."

The De Lancey party won and in one sense would thereby control the Assembly until independence came in 1776. In reality the triumph was short-lived, however, because the coalition of merchants with Sons of Liberty could not long endure. Within little more than a year, by the spring of 1770, New York's gentry felt sufficiently threatened by the "lower orders" to make a conservative swing and join in supporting Colden. The alliance between merchants and radicals had never been very strong, anyway, and the rhetoric of McDougall (the son of a Scots milkman) and his friends frightened them. One of the popular Whig broadsides began: "In a day when the minions of tyranny and despotism in the mother country *and the colonies* are indefatigable in laying every snare that their malevolent and corrupt hearts can suggest, to enslave a free people, it might justly be expected that in this day of constitutional light, the representatives of this colony would not be so hardy, nor be so lost to all sense of duty to their constituents . . . as to betray the trust committed to them." Affiliations had changed from cleavage along family lines to conflict along class lines in little more than a year!

By jailing McDougall in 1770 for publishing a provocative pamphlet, the Assembly only succeeded in making him a martyr, an American counterpart to John Wilkes, the English radical

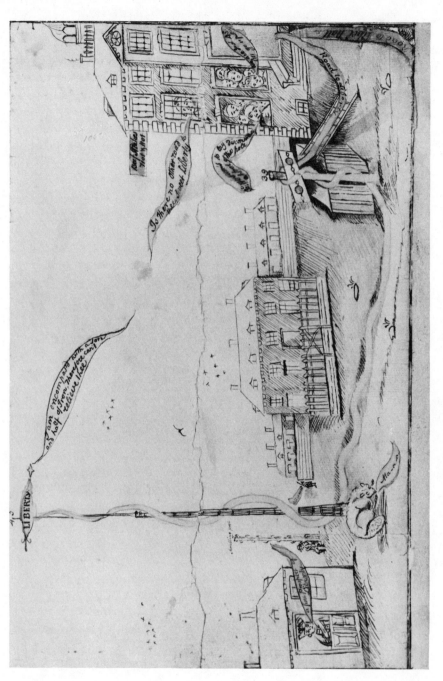

A political caricature by Pierre Eugène du Simitière (1770) showing the liberty pole, jail, and commons in New York City. *From the collections of The Library Company of Philadelphia.*

famous for no. 45 of the *North Briton*. On February 14, 1770, the
forty-fifth day of the year, forty-five of McDougall's friends
visited him in jail, dined with him on forty-five pounds of "Beef
Stakes, cut from a Bullock of Forty-five Months old." Soon after
that McDougall received forty-five "virgins" who serenaded him
with forty-five songs. One correspondent asked whether the
pleasure was diminished because the virgins were all forty-five
years of age! Heavy-handed humor, and symbolism, but effective
nonetheless in those years of intense politicization.

For more than three years thereafter, public affairs reverted to
something like the accustomed "calm" of pre-1764 times. In
1773, however, *The Tempest*, by William Shakespeare, was
performed in New York: a more significant and ominous touch of
symbolism. On December 21, 1773, Paul Revere rode into the
city with news of Boston's Tea Party. On May 17, 1774, he
returned, this time with news of Boston's patriotic resistance to
parliamentary passage of an act closing the port of Boston. New
York's own tempest soon began in earnest.

Revere's first arrival in New York forced the prerogative party
there to abandon any hope of landing and storing the tea that
was expected imminently. Fearing violence, the Governor's
Council and the tea agent reached a secret agreement with the
resuscitated Sons of Liberty to have the tea sent back to England.
As Governor Tryon informed the secretary of state for colonial
affairs, tea could have been landed "only under the protection of
the point of the bayonet, and muzzle of the cannon." As it
happened, however, the tea did not actually reach the province
until April 19. Three days later a band of "Mohawks" promptly
boarded one ship, the *London*, and performed New York's very
own "tea party." The next day a second tea ship, the *Nancy*,
hastily made a 180° turn for England. In one sense, the
proverbial Rubicon was thereby crossed.

The narrative of provincial response during the early part of
1774 ran as follows. On January 20, the Assembly had created a
committee of correspondence to protest the Tea Act. Its composition was notably moderate and conservative. On May 15 that

committee became the first public body in the colonies to suggest a continental congress. The next day a new committee of fifty-one members was appointed in a gathering at the Exchange. Isaac Low served as its chairman, and the populace ratified its existence three days later. On May 30 the City Committee asked all counties to appoint their own committees of correspondence. Two weeks later a mob carried effigies of Lord North and others through the streets of New York and burned them in public. On July 4, 1774, a public gathering denounced the Boston Port Bill, urged nonimportation until it was repealed, and ordered a subscription for the people of Boston as well. On July 28 the city elected five delegates to a congress that would meet in Philadelphia. On September 1 they set forth; and on October 20, eight provincial delegates signed the association agreement that prohibited importation from Britain. One month later a committee of sixty was chosen to succeed the Committee of Fifty-one.

The significance of this narrative is manifold and elusive. First, it enabled the radicals to reappear as an effective force. The Committee of Fifty-one had been controlled by the De Lanceys. Its successor body in November had a more whiggish composition, and the Committee of One Hundred that surfaced on May 1, 1775, would be still more defiant toward Great Britain. In the spring of 1774 the working people really emerged as an independent and organized force in New York politics, represented by a general committee of "mechanics." For about a year thereafter the radicals enjoyed their greatest visibility and influence.

By the later part of 1775, however, their leadership had begun to diverge and diminish in effectiveness. A raid into New York from Connecticut in November, led by Isaac Sears in order to disarm Loyalists and seize the type of Tory printer James Rivington, only succeeded in embarrassing the Provincial Congress. By April of 1776, Sears was busy in New Haven, Connecticut; McDougall had withdrawn from politics in pursuit of a military career; and Lamb was held captive in a Canadian prison. The Sons of Liberty had lost their leaders, and the patriotic "mechanics" thereby had less access to decision making just when separation from Great Britain and organization of a new government were the urgent issues.

Therefore the real struggle in 1775–76 would once again be between moderate Whigs led by the Livingston party and proto-Loyalists led by the De Lanceys. The Whigs could not provide forceful leadership during this period, however, for reasons that are central to an understanding of how New York came to be, effectively, in a state of nature. Caught between the volatile radicals and allegiance-oriented Loyalists, the Whigs could not claim a very distinctive position or establish a strong directional role. They themselves really hoped for reconciliation without supine capitulation. They often seemed to be indecisive and lacked effective organization. During the critical months of the fall of 1775, for example, their Committee of Safety tended to be timid and hesitant, thereby losing the initiative.

The British government, moreover, was able to maximize pressure upon New York's Whigs. Ever since 1763, New York City had been the headquarters for royal forces in North America. Even when the military presence was not large in numbers, it menaced the populace nonetheless, and especially the socially accommodating upper class. A significant number of civilian officials were based in New York as well, many of whom had imperial responsibilities and allegiances. The governor's authority filtered down through the Council, Assembly, and various courts to the sheriffs, mayors, county and town officials. Here is a knowing excerpt from the South Carolina General Committee to the New York Committee of Sixty, dated March 1, 1775: "We are not ignorant of that crowd of placemen, of contractors, of officers, and needy dependents upon the Crown, who are constantly employed to frustrate your measures. We know the dangerous tendency of being made the Headquarters of America for many years."

In addition, many patriotic New Yorkers had strong commercial bonds with Britain. They relied heavily upon English credit and traded largely within the imperial framework. Others sold goods on a commission basis for British firms, or benefited as suppliers for the military establishment. On the frontier there were Indian traders whose profitable commerce was supervised by the government. And the large landholders simply had too much at stake to risk it lightly for the sake of an imperfectly defined ideology whose social implications were not altogether clear. As one contemporary put it after the war had begun, "Such extensive property is perhaps too great a stake to be risked in a struggle with a bold invader."

Not surprisingly then, these were years of turmoil and transition as people continually reassessed their expedient positions and personal allegiances. In addition to the radicals (or "popular Whigs"), the moderate Whigs (such as the Schuylers, the Van Rensselaers, James Duane, John Jay, and Gouverneur Morris), and the Loyalists (who were more numerous and powerful than in any other northern colony), there were also a great many trimming neutrals (including one-third of the New York City merchants).

It is difficult, ultimately, to explain with any consistency or precision the decisions people made concerning their allegiances. Loyalism tended to be proportionately higher in Kings, Queens, and Richmond (Staten Island) counties than elsewhere in the province; whereas whiggism seems to have been especially concentrated in Orange, Ulster, Albany, and Tryon counties. Prominent leaders of Dutch descent in the Albany area almost entirely joined the patriot cause. The evidence reveals, however, that their hostilities were not so much directed against England per se as against particular immigrants from Great Britain who had been considered as intruders in local politics for the previous fifteen years. A careful study of social and demographic data by Alice Kenney, moreover, suggests that only in isolated areas and special cases were ethnic distinctions significant in the upper Hudson Valley and in the Mohawk Valley. "In Schenectady, an exposed situation and opposition to the Johnsons produced many Dutch Patriots. In Kinderhook isolation from constitutional and mercantile provocations and conflict with Yankee settlers influenced a large number of Dutchmen to become Tories. On the Manors, ethnic considerations were overridden by antagonism toward Patriot landlords."

Amid the political disorganization which occurred in 1774-75, many people seemed to assume that the best solution to such British policies of revenge as the Intolerable Acts was to imitate the forms of economic pressure (such as nonimportation) that had been successful in 1765-66 and 1768-70. What these colonists could not know, however, or did not realize, was that the orientation of England's economy had begun to shift away from the Atlantic community as new markets opened in the East and on the Continent. Consequently economic protest would not achieve the same results in 1774-75 as earlier. Patterns of trade had changed; the British merchants would not push for repeal this time; and, moreover, Parliament and George III had their dander up. The time had come, in their adamant view, to draw the line.

Until the later part of 1774, party differences within New York had largely concerned the question of how best to resist unpopular British measures. Thereafter a shift occurred, and differences more often seemed to be expressed in terms of conflicting allegiances to alternative sources of public authority. From the spring of 1774 until the spring of 1776 there virtually were two side-by-side systems of government in the province. There was, first, the duly constituted royal government, within which the regular Assembly grew steadily more conservative. It adjourned in January 1775 and never fully functioned thereafter. A year later pro forma elections were held; but in February 1776, Tryon prorogued the body, and in April he dissolved it.

Meanwhile a kind of ad hoc government had been moving along a parallel track: government by unwieldy committees between May 1774 and May 1775, followed by a series of provincial congresses. The first was elected in April 1775, the second in November, the third in April 1776, and the last in June, consisting of 106 members. The latter finally convened on July 9, accepted the independence already declared by the Continental Congress, and a day later transformed itself into the Convention of Representatives of the State of New York.

The anomaly of having both a duly constituted government as well as a de facto rebel organization was piquantly brought home to New Yorkers on many occasions. On June 25, 1775, for example, the city had to stage simultaneously an official welcome for George Washington, who had recently been chosen commander in chief of the Continental Army and was passing through en route to Boston, as well as one for William Tryon, the royal governor who had just returned from England after more than a year's absence! Or, on August 24, 1775, a bizarre conference occurred upon Tryon's initiative: a joint meeting of his Council, the Corporation of the City of New York, members of the Provincial Congress, and the New York City Committee. Tryon, of course, was not supposed to acknowledge the existence of these last two bodies.

What made this even more complicated was the invisible line of sovereignty separating the Continental Congress and the patriot governments. Writing to George Washington on January 2, 1776, Charles Lee caught the quintessence of this curious situation rather well: "I conclude I shall receive the orders of the General Congress before, or immediately on my arrival, otherwise I should not venture to march into the Province, as by the late resolve every detachment of the Continental troops is to be under the direction of the Provincial Congress in which they are—a resolve, I must say . . . fraught with difficulties and evils—it is impossible, having two sovereigns, that any business should be carried on."*

The Livingston party, which had become closely identified with these extralegal agencies of rebellion, did not really want separation from Britain. They feared the destruction of upperclass control over provincial politics, and they desperately hoped that Whitehall would render a decision favorable to their extensive but disputed land investments in Vermont. Reluctantly they supported the war plans of the Continental Congress while

---

* On Feb. 14, 1776, a wonderfully symbolic conflict occurred. Tryon wanted to reconvene the Assembly in its proper chamber at City Hall, a room already preempted by the Provincial Congress. Two rival legislatures could not physically occupy the same room! What solution? The Congress walked one hundred feet and deliberated in the meeting room of the New York City Common Council.

resisting any measures aimed at outright independence. Thus John Jay kept hoping for some conciliatory resolution, and Robert Livingston expressed, on October 10, 1776, his fear of any new government created "without that influence that is derived from respect to old families, wealth, age, etc."

The issues of independence and the proper nature of any new government were the two major problems under discussion during the first half of 1776. As Jay wrote in April, "The first thing . . . to be done is to erect good and well ordered governments in all the colonies, and thereby exclude that anarchy which already too much prevails." By then Tryon had left the colony once again, the official Assembly had become defunct, the courts had ceased functioning (persons accused of crimes faced the prospect of indefinite imprisonment), and the threat of mob rule had to be taken seriously. Public opinion, at least on the patriot side, tended to run ahead of Whig leadership, though a turning point came in April when anti-British polemicists in the newspapers dropped their opposition to independence.*

Confusion caused by the transition to new governance was especially acute in the counties, where committees of correspondence had not fully supplanted traditional local government and yet steadily assumed many of its duties. Some of the judicial functions of local government simply stopped or else slowly dissolved. The physical loss of New York City to the British in September 1776, moreover, meant that thereafter all patriot political activity would shift to the rural towns and to Albany where the weapons of propaganda were less well developed and where the Livingstons enjoyed even more substantial influence. The British capture of Manhattan effectively shattered the extremist wing of the Whigs, gave the Livingstons domination of

---

* The fascinating story of the press in revolutionary New York deserves extended treatment. Rivington's *New York Gazetteer*, for example, was the largest and most influential Loyalist newspaper in America. After the British captured the city in Sept. 1776, Hugh Gaine sent one of his presses to Newark but continued publishing in New York as well. The very same newspaper was thereby able to publish simultaneously on both sides of the same questions!

the revolutionary movement in New York, and provided them with the opportunity to frame the state's first government at a convention held at Kingston early in 1777.

Beginning in mid-1775, meanwhile, military preparations and organization began to go forward in the colony. On June 28, New York authorized a recruiting campaign, and the five regiments that were raised participated in the disastrous siege of Quebec, under Arnold and Montgomery, in the winter of 1775–76. During 1776 the Provincial Congress altered the mode of selecting officers and organizing units. By December the procedure had been adopted of appointing officers and then assigning them recruiting districts in each county. Late in 1775 the provincial militia was also restructured, with various regiments combining to form the colony's six brigades, each one under the command of a major general. When the military situation required it, the government ordered some segment of the militia into the field for a specified period of time. These groups constituted the "levies." If there were too few volunteers to fill a quota, the counties resorted to a draft.

At the beginning of 1776, John Adams remarked to George Washington that New York seemed "a kind of key to the whole continent." For eight months past, in fact, and for as many more to come, New York's political and organizational deliberations had taken place under the guns of British warships—a chastening experience and a powerful inducement to moderation on the part of many. Late in August 1775, for example, a bombardment from H.M.S. *Asia* served as an admonition to the patriots to stop hauling cannon in order to fortify the town. Even when the ships did not fire—and they were, in fact, remarkably restrained—the fear persisted that they might put a stop to all outgoing shipping. In the summer of 1776, moreover, starting on July 2 when General Howe first landed troops at Staten Island, the British shifted their North American base from Boston to New York—a superior port with good access to the best lines of communication into the interior north and south.

Washington agreed with Adams's assessment of New York's strategic importance, and in March he decided to risk his army in order to make a stand there. "Should they get that Town and the Command of the North River," he wrote, "they can stop the intercourse between the northern and southern Colonies, upon which depends the Safety of America." Control of the Hudson River rapidly became a major consideration, and a great deal of time and expense was devoted to measures, such as gun emplacements and huge chains, that might prevent British warships from ascending the river.*

Meanwhile the drama of independence unfolded in New York amid shadows of uncertainty and foreboding. The Continental Congress had refused to lend New York 112,500 in Continental dollars, needed for immediate military expenses; therefore, the province would have to issue its own bills backed by future tax collections, a step the business community regarded as the beginning of financial chaos. Since exchange rates were so ambiguous, one ad hoc system of currency seemed sufficient. Alongside the Continental money, thirteen separate local currencies would only make a financial mess and drain off public confidence. Of necessity, though, New York emitted three hundred thousand pounds in currency in three stages during 1775–76; and in the years 1775–77 the Provincial Congress spent at least five hundred thousand pounds for all purposes, but especially for military supplies. To have raised and allocated such a sum, amid all that economic and political turmoil, remains an impressive achievement.

On July 9, 1776, exuberant patriots pulled down a huge equestrian statue of George III on the Bowling Green—one that

---

* The world's first underwater attack vessel, designed to submerge and secretly attach a mine to an enemy ship, was unsuccessfully deployed by the Americans in New York harbor during Aug. 1776. Called "The American Turtle," it contained a 30-minute supply of air for the one-man crew. Its intended victim was the 64-gun H.M.S. *Eagle*, flagship of Admiral Sir Richard Howe. Although the Turtle had performed flawlessly during test runs up and down Long Island Sound, its bit could not penetrate the *Eagle*'s newly copperplated bottom. British naval know-how saved Howe's vessel. But the world's first submarine had at least conducted a mission in New York in 1776.

had been erected in his honor by the Assembly in August 1770.* Part of the lead was used to make a mold from which Whig bullets would be cut, and some of the rest was melted down for actual bullets.

Three days later, however, Lord Howe landed nine thousand additional soldiers on Staten Island. Sir Henry Clinton arrived on August 1, and three weeks after that Howe brought fifteen thousand men and forty cannon to Gravesend, Long Island. Skirmishes occurred for four days; and then on the twenty-seventh, in the Battle of Long Island (or Brooklyn), the American defenders were defeated. Generals Sullivan and Stirling were captured, and Washington hastily withdrew his army to Manhattan. On September 11, a peace conference held on Staten Island between Lord Howe and a congressional committee failed to achieve reconciliation. Four days later the British began to occupy the city; but on the sixteenth, at the Battle of Harlem Heights, their invasion was temporarily repulsed. On September 21, the "trial" of Nathan Hale took place: he was brought before General William Howe at British headquarters in the Beekman mansion and executed the next day. Skirmishes occurred at Montresor's Island on September 24, at Throg's Neck on October 12, and at Mamaroneck on the twenty-first. By the eighteenth British troops had landed at Pell's Point, and on the twenty-third American forces abandoned Manhattan. They suffered a defeat at White Plains five days later; and on November 12, Washington crossed the Hudson to New Jersey. The British captured Forts Washington, Tryon, and Cock-Hill— all on November 16. From then until November 1783, the New York port area remained an impregnable British enclave.

Howe failed to follow up his victory at Long Island by vigorously seeking to destroy the rebel army, a decision that would one day come back to haunt him. But, ever the proper gentleman, he fought and conquered in elegant style. On November 30, 1776, he issued a proclamation of pardon at New

---

* More symbolism: much of the actual labor in pulling down the gilded tyrant was performed by the black slaves of freedom-loving patriots.

York. Loyalist refugees flooded into the city. Alongside the occupying soldiers and camp followers, they swelled the city's population to perhaps thirty-three thousand persons. Six months earlier, after most of the patriots had fled, the city's population may have dipped to as low as five thousand.

In 1777 the scene of action shifted upstate. On the military side, Burgoyne invaded New York from Quebec on June 1. A series of actions during July went largely in England's favor: the conquests of Ticonderoga, Skenesborough, and Fort Anne. The brutal murder of Jane McCrea by Burgoyne's Indian allies on July 27, however, did much to galvanize the Mohawk Valley farmers into action. General Schuyler found that recruiting became easier, and his army swelled in size. In August, though, Horatio Gates replaced the unpopular Schuyler as commander. For three weeks, from August 4 to 22, Colonel Barry St. Leger besieged the Americans in Fort Stanwix on the Mohawk River. On the sixth, a relief force of militia under General Nicholas Herkimer got caught at Oriskany in an ambush by Indians and Loyalists under the Mohawk chief Joseph Brant. Herkimer and his men held their ground bravely. A force led by Benedict Arnold soon arrived to support Colonel Gansevoort and Herkimer's militiamen, and St. Leger abandoned his siege.

By August Burgoyne's supply problem had become serious, but he decided to press on toward Albany anyway. On September 13, he crossed to the west side of the Hudson and engaged the entrenched position prepared by Horatio Gates at Bemis Heights. Six days later, Burgoyne was checked at Freeman's farm by General Daniel Morgan and Colonel Henry Dearborn. On October 3, General Clinton began to move up the Hudson in order to make contact with Burgoyne. He took Forts Clinton and Montgomery on the sixth, sent the fleet up to Kingston (which he burned on the thirteenth), but felt too insecure to continue on to Albany and beyond. Clinton returned to New York City for reinforcements and Burgoyne was lost. Between October 7 and 13 his substantial force of fifty-seven hundred men was repulsed at Bemis Heights, retreated to Saratoga, and was surrounded. On October 17, 1777, his army surrendered, pledged not to fight in the war again, and marched to Boston for return to England. Many historians regard this victory as the strategic turning point for the American cause during the War for Independence.

This phase marked a turning point for the Iroquois of New York as well. They had discovered at the outset of the war that neutrality was impossible because neither the Whigs nor the British would respect or permit it. When the Quebec Act of 1774 had placed former Indian territory under the jurisdiction of the governor of Canada, Whitehall insisted that this constituted yet another example of England's solicitude for the Indians. Royal officials argued in 1775 and 1776 that they, rather than the Americans, would defend Iroquois rights. Consequently most of the Indians sided with the crown; but, as one historian has commented, "in taking sides the Indians themselves divided over [Anglo-American] issues of which they had little understanding and over which they had no control." At the Battle of Oriskany in August 1777, Joseph Brant and most of the Iroquois, but not the Oneida, cast their lot with the British. Most of their military involvement would not occur until 1778–81; and when the war ended in 1783, the old Stanwix line as a restraining boundary for white settlers became hopelessly unenforceable. The effect of the war upon the Six Nations was to shatter the old unity of the League of the Long House. The impact of the peace would deprive the Iroquois of almost all their territorial inheritance. If the American Revolution helped to create a great nation, it also served to complete the destruction of another.

The completion of New York's *rite de passage* from colonial status to statehood came in April 1777, when the convention (at Kingston) voted and proclaimed the first constitution. Elections were held that spring and summer. On July 3, 1777, John Jay was appointed the first chief justice and Robert R. Livingston the chancellor. Six days later George Clinton officially defeated Philip Schuyler for the governorship, and on September 10 the State Legislature convened.

The committee that drafted this new constitution had deliberated for a protracted period, from October 1776 until the following March. A first draft required only two weeks to produce—and then another two months for revision and expansion. Why such a long delay? Many factors affected the process of creating a viable structure of government: the nearness of British forces and the precarious military situation, long absences by radical members serving military duty, and, most of all, the deliberate stalling of some moderate and conservative Whigs who felt that a more tranquil time might be more propitious for the formal birth of a new state.

In the drafting process, serious differences emerged between the two groups of Whigs. The outcome, predictably, was a compromise that slightly favored conservative Whigs. The governor's office would be weakened as compared with the strength of the erstwhile royal governor. He could have only a limited part in the legislative process. To qualify for the suffrage, a voter for Assembly candidates had to have either a freehold valued at twenty pounds beyond his debts, or he must rent land whose annual value was at least forty shillings, or he had to have been a freeman of Albany or have obtained freemanship in New York City before October 14, 1775. The convention thereby enlarged the size of the electorate for the Assembly (but may have reduced the suffrage among the "mechanics" of New York City). A secret ballot was provided, to go into effect after the end of the war.

Many of the necessary compromises resulted in elaborate expedients and complicated institutional mechanisms. The traditional governor's veto was converted into the Council of Revision consisting of the governor, chancellor, and judges of the Supreme Court. The bitterly controversial power of appointment led to creation of the Council of Appointment, consisting of the governor and four senators chosen by the Assembly. The State Senate emerged as a fairly strong institution, and the independent governor was elected directly by the people for a three-year term.

All in all, constitutional reformers outside of New York regarded this new document as a triumph for energetic and orderly government. The reactions of New Yorkers ranged across a broad but predictable spectrum of opinion. To some it seemed too democratic, to others too conservative. But most seemed to agree with Alexander Hamilton, writing to Gouverneur Morris on May 19, 1777, that "on the whole, though I think there are the defects intimated, I think your Government far the best that we have yet seen, and capable of giving long and substantial happiness to the people."

New York had emerged from a state of nature into statehood, had passed through a crisis of legitimacy despite the fragility of its historical tradition of diversity. By the autumn of 1777 the new polity was safeguarded and bolstered by the British defeat at Saratoga. Britain had lost its initiative in the north, and the state as well as the nation had gained confidence and a measure of stability. New York had shed its colonial status for certain. A colonial *heritage*, however, would long endure in ways both quaint and significant.

BIBLIOGRAPHY

One could well write a small book about the historiography and bibliographical history of colonial New York. Such a volume would begin with a lament over two tragic events: the loss of Dutch West India Company records (for the period 1623–36), sold as scrap paper at Amsterdam in 1821; and the fire that ravaged the New York State Library at Albany in 1911. It might then go on to treat a series of problems and misperceptions intrinsically interesting because they are virtually chapters in American cultural history: a quaint romanticization of the Dutch period; the popular caricatures by Washington Irving and the so-called literary offenses of James Fenimore Cooper; a certain defensiveness by New York antiquarians vis-à-vis the "achievements" of New England and Virginia; the linguistic barrier that existed until the later nineteenth century, by which time most of the early Dutch records had been translated; and, most of all, the foolish controversy concerning the "growth of democracy," especially whether the *greatest* credit belongs to the Dutch or the English heritage of "free institutions."

In lieu of that small book, the inquisitive reader might examine four essays: Milton M. Klein, "New York in the American Colonies: A New Look," in Jacob Judd and Irwin H. Polishook, eds., *Aspects of Early New York Society and Politics* (Tarrytown, 1974), 8–28; Patricia U. Bonomi, "The Middle Colonies: Embryo of the New Political Order," in Alden T. Vaughan and George A. Billias, eds., *Perspectives on Early American History: Essays in Honor of Richard B. Morris* (New York, 1973), 63–92; Frederick B. Tolles, "The Historians of the Middle Colonies," in Ray Allen Billington, ed., *The Reinterpretation of Early American History: Essays in Honor of John Edwin Pomfret* (San Marino, Calif., 1966), 65–79; and Douglas Campbell, *Historical Fallacies Regarding Colonial New York* (New York, 1879).

BIBLIOGRAPHICAL REFERENCES AND GUIDES

For information concerning archival materials, see Herbert L. Osgood, "Report on the Public Archives of New York," in *Annual Report of the American Historical*

376

Association for the Year 1900 (Washington, D.C., 1901), II, 67–250; Engel Sluiter, "The Dutch Archives and American Historical Research," *Pacific Historical Review*, VI (Mar. 1937), 21–35; and the *Guide to Public Vital Statistics Records in New York State*, 3 vols. (Albany, 1942). Access to the older sources, both primary and secondary, may be obtained through Charles A. Flagg and Judson T. Jennings, "Bibliography of New York Colonial History," *New York State Library Bulletin*, no. 56 (Feb. 1901), a 267-page compendium covering the period 1610–1776; James T. Dunn, "Masters' Theses and Doctoral Dissertations on New York History [1870–1954]," *New York History*, XXXIII (Apr. 1952), 232–36; (July 1952) 356–58; (Oct. 1952), 461–66; XXXVI (Apr. 1955), 233–51; and G. M. Asher, comp., *A Bibliographical and Historical Essay on the Dutch Books and Pamphlets Relating to New-Netherland and to the Dutch West-India Company and to Its Possessions in Brazil, Angola, etc. . . . .* (Amsterdam, 1854–67; reprinted 1960).

The journals of five organizations are invaluable mines of information: *Proceedings of the New York State Historical Association* (1900–, which includes the quarterly journal called *New York History* since Oct. 1919); *New-York Historical Society Quarterly* (1917–); *Journal of Long Island History* (1961–); *New York Genealogical and Biographical Record* (1870–); and *De Halve Maen* (1925–), published by the Holland Society of New York.

PRIMARY SOURCES

Certain reference works are indispensable as road maps through the major manuscript collections; among them are: Richard B. Morris and Evarts B. Greene, *A Guide to the Principal Sources for Early American History (1600–1800) in the City of New York* (New York, 1929; 2nd ed. 1953); Arthur J. Breton, *A Guide to the Manuscript Collections of the New-York Historical Society*, 2 vols. (Westport, Conn., 1972); Charles F. Gosnell, "Resources on Colonial History in the New York State Library," *New York History*, XL (Oct. 1959), 380–86; Robert W. Hill, "Resources on Colonial History in the New York Public Library," ibid., 387–413; and Walton H. Rawls, ed., *The Century Book of the Long Island Historical Society* (Tokyo, 1964), especially chaps. 6, 7, and 10.

The Historical Documents Collection at Queens College, Flushing, New York, has recently become a major repository of demographic and legal materials, notably: estate inventories (1662–1859); New York County will libri (1664–1879); New York County insolvency assignments; New York Court of Chancery decrees, papers, and minutes (1711–1847); and Letters of Administration for New York.

There are, of course, a great many other colleges and universities, local courthouses and historical societies, throughout the state with valuable source materials for the colonial period. In addition, significant collections will be found in institutions outside of New York, such as the minutes of the New York Commissioners of Indian Affairs (at the Public Archives of Canada in Ottawa), the Livingston family papers (at the Massachusetts Historical Society and Yale University Library), the Morris and Stevens family papers (at the New Jersey Historical Society), papers of Governor George Clinton (at the William Clements Library, Ann Arbor), and the pamphlets and rare books belonging to the McGregor Library (at the University of Virginia).

Edmund B. O'Callaghan did more, perhaps, than anyone else to bring the colonial records from their relatively inaccessible manuscript form to reasonably accurate printed versions. His major editorial projects include *Documents Relative to the Colonial History of the State of New-York*, 15 vols. (Albany, 1856–87); *The Documentary History of the State of New York*, 4 vols. (Albany, 1849–51); and *Calendar of New York Colonial Commissions, 1680–1770* (New York, 1929). Related volumes of importance are Edgar A. Werner, *Civil List and Constitutional History of the Colony and State of New York* (Albany, 1889); Charles Z. Lincoln, ed., *The Colonial Laws of New York from the Year 1664 to the Revolution*, 5 vols. (Albany, 1894); "Calendar of Council Minutes, 1668–1783," *New York State Library Bulletin*, no. 58 (Mar. 1902); *Journal of the Legislative Council of the Colony of New York, 1691–1775*, 2 vols. (Albany, 1861); *Journal of the Votes and Proceedings of the General Assembly of the Colony of New York . . . 1691 . . . 1765*, 2 vols. (New York, 1764–66); *Journal of the Votes and Proceedings of the General Assembly of the Colony of New York, from 1766 to 1776, Inclusive*, 9 vols. in 1 (Albany, 1820), actually beginning late in 1767; Lawrence H. Leder, ed., "The Missing New York Assembly Journal of April 1692," *New-York Historical Society Quarterly*, XLIX (Jan. 1965), 5–27; and Charles Z. Lincoln, ed., *State of New York: Messages from the Governors . . .* (Albany, 1909), I, covering 1683–1776.

Other published sources, pertaining to religion, society, and the economy, will be found in Hugh Hastings and Edward T. Corwin, comps., *Ecclesiastical Records: State of New York*, 7 vols. (Albany, 1901–16); William S. Pelletreau, comp., *Abstracts of Wills on File in the Surrogate's Office, City of New York, 1665–1801*, in *Collections of the New-York Historical Society for the Years 1892 to 1908*, 17 vols. (New York, 1893–1909); Julius M. Bloch, ed., "Wills of Colonial New York, 1736–1775," *National Genealogical Society Quarterly*, LIV (June 1966), 98–124; Leo Hershkowitz, ed., *Wills of Early New York Jews (1704–1799)* (New York, 1967); Berthold Fernow, ed., *Calendar of Wills on File and Recorded in the Offices of the Clerk of Appeals, of the County Clerk at Albany, and of the Secretary of State, 1626–1836* (New York, 1896); *The Calendar of New York Colonial Manuscripts: Indorsed Land Papers in the Office of the Secretary of State of New York, 1643–1836* (Albany, 1864); and Julius Bloch et al., eds., *An Account of Her Majesty's Revenue in the Province of New York, 1701–1709* (Upper Saddle River, N.J., 1966), comprising customs records of the port of New York. Herman M. Stoker compiled *Wholesale Prices for 213 Years, 1720 to 1932, Part II: Wholesale Prices at New York City, 1720 to 1800*, in *Cornell University Agricultural Experiment Station Memoir*, no. 142 (Nov. 1932), 201–22; and

Arthur H. Cole prepared *Wholesale Commodity Prices in the United States, 1700–1861* (Cambridge, Mass., 1938); 9–24 and 120–37 pertain to New York after 1720.

The reader seeking more personalized accounts of early New York should examine Roland Van Zandt, *Chronicles of the Hudson: Three Centuries of Travellers' Accounts* (New Brunswick, N.J., 1971); Cornell Jaray, ed., *Historic Chronicles of New Amsterdam, Colonial New York and Early Long Island*, 2 vols. (Port Washington, N.Y., 1968); *The Colden Letter Books* [1760–75], in *Collections of the New-York Historical Society, 1876–1877* (New York, 1877–78), and *The Letters and Papers of Cadwallader Colden*, in *Collections of the New-York Historical Society, 1917–1923 and 1934–1935*, 9 vols. (New York, 1918–37); and William H. W. Sabine, ed., *Historical Memoirs of William Smith, Historian of the Province of New York, Member of the Governor's Council and Last Chief Justice of that Province under the Crown, Chief Justice of Quebec* [1763–83], 3 vols. (New York, 1956–58, 1971).

Many of the local records were published during a burst of historical enthusiasm at the turn of the last century. Some of the more useful series include Berthold Fernow, ed., *The Records of New Amsterdam from 1653 to 1674*, 7 vols. (New York, 1897); Herbert L. Osgood, ed., *Minutes of the Common Council of the City of New York, 1675–1776*, 8 vols. (New York, 1905); Julius M. Bloch, et al., eds., "Seventeenth Century Dutch Records Relating to Long Island," *Journal of Long Island History*, III (Spring 1963, 1–18); IV (Fall, 1964), 16–39; Josephine C. Frost, ed., *Records of the Town of Jamaica, Long Island, 1658–1751*, 3 vols. (Brooklyn, 1914); Charles R. Street, ed., *Huntington Town Records, Including Babylon, Long Island*, 3 vols. (Huntington, N.Y., 1887–89); John Cox, ed., *Oyster Bay Town Records*, 8 vols. (New York, 1916–40); Benjamin D. Hicks, ed., *Records of the Towns of North and South Hempstead, Long Island*, 8 vols. (Jamaica, N.Y., 1896–1904); William S. Pelletreau, ed., *Records of the Town of Southampton . . .* , 3 vols. (Sag Harbor, N.Y., 1874–78); and see Douglas C. McMurtrie, *A Check List of Eighteenth Century Albany Imprints* (Albany, 1939).

SECONDARY SOURCES

GENERAL WORKS

The best one-volume history is by David M. Ellis, et al., *A Short History of New York State* (Ithaca, 1957; rev. ed. 1967); while the last single-volume treatment of the colonial era is Maud W. Goodwin's brief *Dutch and English on the Hudson: A Chronicle of Colonial New York* (New Haven, 1919). Mrs. Goodwin and several collaborators also edited a quaint set of essays, *Historic New York*, 2 vols. (New York, 1899). The best historical account by a colonial is William Smith, Jr., *The History of the Province of New-York*, edited by Michael Kammen, 2 vols. (Cambridge, Mass., 1972). It covers the period up to 1762. Ever since the Jacksonian days of John Yates, Joseph Moulton, and William Dunlap, there have been many multivolume histories of New York. The most detailed for the seventeenth century is John R. Brodhead, *History of the State of New York*, 2 vols. (New York, 1853–71); but the most comprehensive and scholarly overall is Alexander C. Flick, ed., *History of the State of New York*, 10 vols. (New York, 1933–37), the first three volumes of which treat the period from Indian origins until 1776.

Subjects of comprehensive scope and importance are covered in Berthold Fernow, "Coins and Currency of New York," in James G. Wilson, ed., *The Memorial History of the City of New York* . . . (New York, 1893), IV, 300–343; Patricia U. Bonomi, *A Factious People: Politics and Society in Colonial New York* (New York, 1971), an important work of research and synthesis; Milton M. Klein, *Politics of Diversity: Essays in the History of Colonial New York* (Port Washington, N.Y., 1974); Beverly McAnear, Politics in Provincial New York, 1689–1761 (unpubl. Ph.D. diss., Stanford University, 1935), an invaluable study, but one in which the author often reads more into the sources than they actually contain; Charles Hemstreet, *Literary New York: Its Landmarks and Associations* (New York, 1903); and Harold W. Thompson, *Body, Boots and Britches* (Philadelphia, 1940), the most comprehensive work on New York folklore.

For the best introduction to topography and physical survivals, see John H. Thompson, ed., *Geography of New York State* (Syracuse, 1966); *New York: A Guide to the Empire State* (New York, 1940), a product of the Writers' Program of the Works Projects Administration; Nicholas Zook, *Houses of New York Open to the Public* (Barre, Mass., 1969); Russell D. Bailey, *A Report on Historic Sites and Buildings in the Hudson River Valley* (Utica, N.Y., [1965]); John Reps, *The Making of Urban America* (Princeton, 1965), 147–54, 296–99, 331–39, 350–52, 456–58; and *The Magazine Antiques*, LX (July 1951), a Hudson River valley issue.

Important works concerning particular localities include Isaac Newton Phelps Stokes, *The Iconography of Manhattan Island*, 6 vols. (New York, 1915–28), which is a stunning visual treat; Bayrd Still, *Mirror for Gotham: New York as Seen by Contemporaries from Dutch Days to the Present* (New York, 1956); Theodore Roosevelt, *New York* [City] (New York, 1891), in which 10 of the 14 chapters concern the period before 1783; Henry R. Stiles, *A History of the City of Brooklyn* . . . , 3 vols. (Brooklyn, 1867–70); Benjamin F. Thompson, *History of Long Island*, 3 vols. (New York, 1918); J. Thomas Scharf, *History of Westchester County, New York* . . . , 2 vols. (Philadelphia, 1886); Robert Bolton, *History of the Several Towns, Manors, and Patents of the County of Westchester*, 2 vols. (New York, 1905); Alf Evers, *The Catskills: From Wilderness to Woodstock* (New York, 1972); Joel Munsell, comp., *The Annals of Albany*, 10 vols. (Albany, 1850–59); and Codman Hislop, *Albany: Dutch, English and American* (Albany, 1936).

TOPICAL READINGS

Each section corresponds to a chapter in the book.

CARRACKS AND CANOES

Anecdotal histories of the two major waterways are by Carl Carmer, *The Hudson* (New York, 1939); and Codman Hislop, *The Mohawk* (New York, 1948). Robert H. Boyle, *The Hudson River: A Natural and Unnatural History* (New York, 1969), contains some fascinating information along with historical material that is not always reliable. Benson J. Lossing, *The Hudson, from the Wilderness to the Sea* (Troy, N.Y., n.d.) has 306 charming engravings; and Edgar M. Bacon, *The Hudson River, from Ocean to Source* (New York, 1902), contains fascinating photographs taken of various sites during the 1890s. C. G. Hine walked up the east side of the Hudson and intermingled historical information with visual impressions in *The New York and Albany Post Road* (n.p., 1905). Paul Wilstach, *Hudson River Landings* (Indianapolis, 1933), is really a narrative of European settlement along the river.

William A. Ritchie wrote the most thorough *Introduction to Hudson Valley Prehistory* (Albany, 1958) and then expanded it into *The Archaeology of New York State* (New York, 1965; 2nd ed. 1969). These two works summarize research Ritchie has been doing since 1925. The best brief treatment will be found in Gordon Willey, *An Introduction to American Archaeology* (Englewood Cliffs, N.J., 1966), I, 247–83. For general background on the Indians of colonial New York, see Edward M. Ruttenber, *History of the Indian Tribes of Hudson's River* (Albany, 1872); and George E. Hyde, *Indians of the Woodlands from Prehistoric Times to 1725* (Norman, Okla., 1962). The classic older studies of the Iroquois include Lewis H. Morgan, *League of the Ho-Dé-No-Sau-Nee or Iroquois*, 2 vols. (New York, 1851); and W. M. Beauchamp, *A History of the New York Iroquois, Now Commonly Called the Six Nations* (New York, 1904). Mary E. Mathur, "The Iroquois in Ethnography . . . a Time-Space Concept," *The Indian Historian*, II (Fall 1969), 12–18, analyzes and compares some of these older works. Recent scholarship is exemplified by James A. Tuck, *Onondaga Iroquois Prehistory: A Study in Settlement Archaeology* (Syracuse, 1971); and Elisabeth Tooker, *The Iroquois Ceremonial of Midwinter* (Syracuse, 1970), an anthropological approach. The early period of Dutch-Indian contact is discussed in Allen W. Trelease, "Dutch Treatment of the American Indian, with Particular Reference to New Netherland," in Howard Peckham and Charles Gibson, eds., *Attitudes of Colonial Powers toward the American Indian* (Salt Lake City, 1969), 47–59; and Bruce G. Trigger, "The Mohawk-Mahican War (1624–28): The Establishment of a Pattern," *Canadian Historical Review*, LII (Sept. 1971), 276–86.

For general background on Dutch expansion overseas and colonization, see Pieter Geyl, *The Netherlands in the Seventeenth Century*, 2nd ed. (New York, 1961);

Violet Barbour, *Capitalism in Amsterdam in the Seventeenth Century* (Baltimore, 1950), an institutional and entrepreneurial approach; Charles R. Boxer, *The Dutch Seaborne Empire: 1600–1800* (New York, 1965); Charles Wilson, *The Dutch Republic and the Civilisation of the Seventeenth Century* (London, 1968), which is strong on economic and cultural aspects; and D. W. Davies, *A Primer of Dutch Seventeenth Century Overseas Trade* (The Hague, 1961).

For comparative perspective, see M. A. P. Meilink-Roelofsz, "Aspects of Dutch Colonial Development in Asia in the Seventeenth Century," in J. S. Bromley and E. H. Kossmann, eds., *Britain and the Netherlands in Europe and Asia* (New York, 1968), 56–82; and Cornelis C. Goslinga, *The Dutch in the Caribbean and on the Wild Coast, 1580–1680* (Gainesville, Fla., 1971).

The fascinating origin of New York place names is developed by Egbert Benson in *Collections of the New-York Historical Society*, 2d Ser. (New York, 1849), II, 77–148; and by George R. Stewart, *Names on the Land: A Historical Account of Place-Naming in the United States* (New York, 1945), especially 67–81.

COMMERCE AND COLONIZATION

The narrative of early exploration is treated succinctly in Milton W. Hamilton, *Henry Hudson and the Dutch in New York* (Albany, 1959), a 60-page booklet; and in W. M. Williamson, "Adriaen Block . . . 1611–14" (New York, 1959), a pamphlet. Philip Vail's *The Magnificent Adventures of Henry Hudson* (New York, 1965) is a popular account; and C. A. Weslager's *Dutch Explorers, Traders, and Settlers in the Delaware Valley* (Philadelphia, 1961) is scholarly as well as readable.

Dutch commerce and voyaging are handled by Simon Hart, the archivist of Amsterdam, in *The Prehistory of the New Netherland Company: Amsterdam Notarial Records of the First Dutch Voyages to the Hudson* (Amsterdam, 1959) and in "The Dutch and North America in the First Half of the Seventeenth Century," *De Halve Maen*, XLVI (Apr. 1971), 5–6, 15; (July 1971), 7–8, 10; (Jan. 1972), 11–12, 16; the latter article is especially useful for freight rates between the Netherlands and New Netherland. Two recent monographs examine the controversial topic of commerce and colonization: Thomas J. Condon, *New York Beginnings: The Commercial Origins of New Netherland* (New York, 1968); and Van Cleaf Bachman, *Peltries or Plantations: The Economic Policies of the Dutch West India Company in New Netherland, 1623–1639* (Baltimore, 1969). Interpretive problems are explored in three important essays: W. J. Hoboken, "The Dutch West India Company: the Political Background of Its Rise and Decline," in J. S. Bromley and E. H. Kossmann, eds., *Britain and the Netherlands* (London, 1960), 41–61; Thomas J. Condon, "New York's Dutch Period: An Interpretive Problem," *De Halve Maen*, XXXVI (Oct. 1961), 7–15; and Jan DeVries, "On the Modernity of the Dutch Republic," *The Journal of Economic History*, XXXIII (Mar. 1973), 191–202.

The relative importance of commerce and religion in Dutch colonization has also been controversial among historians. Jelle C. Riemersma emphasizes the secularization of economic behavior in *Religious Factors in Early Dutch Capitalism, 1550–1650* (The Hague, 1967), while George L. Smith stresses the conflicts attendant upon pluralism in *Religion and Trade in New Netherland: Dutch Origins and American Development* (Ithaca, 1973). Other aspects of the colony's early religious history are discussed in Albert Eekhof, *Jonas Michaëlius: Founder of the Church in New Netherland* (Leiden, 1926), which includes English translations of letters previously unknown; and Gerald F. De Jong, "The *Ziekentroosters* or Comforters of the Sick in New Netherland," *New-York Historical Society Quarterly*, LIV (Oct. 1970), 339–59.

For the genesis of New York City, see Victor H. Paltsits, "The Founding of New Amsterdam in 1626," *American Antiquarian Society Proceedings*, New Ser., XXXIV (1924), 39–65; the popular treatment by William Shepherd, *The Story of New Amsterdam* (New York, 1926); C. A. Weslager, "Did Minuit Buy Manhattan Island from the Indians?" *De Halve Maen*, XLIII (Oct. 1968), 5–6; and Arnold J. F. Van Laer, ed., *Documents Relating to New Netherland, 1624–1626, in the Henry E. Huntington Library* (San Marino, Calif., 1924), which contains an 18-page introduction, six lengthy documents, and explanatory notes.

Indian relations and economic problems during the 1630s and 1640s are discussed in Jean E. Murray, "The Early Fur Trade in New France and New Netherlands," *Canadian Historical Review*, XIX (Dec. 1938), 365–77, which utilizes French sources; Allen W. Trelease, *Indian Affairs in Colonial New York: The Seventeenth Century* (Ithaca, 1960); S. G. Nissenson, *The Patroon's Domain* (New York, 1937); Clarence W. Rife, "Land Tenure in New Netherland," *Essays in Colonial History Presented to Charles M. Andrews* (New Haven, 1931), 41–73; and Leo Hershkowitz, "The Troublesome Turk: An Illustration of Judicial Process in New Amsterdam," *New York History*, XLVI (Oct. 1965), 299–310.

The major source collections for the Dutch period are Edmund B. O'Callaghan, comp., *Laws and Ordinances of New Netherland, 1638–1674* (Albany, 1868), which has a marvelous 75-page index; Arnold J. F. Van Laer, trans., *New York Historical Manuscripts: Dutch*, 4 vols., edited by Kenneth Scott and Kenn Stryker-Rodda (Baltimore, 1974), comprising the register of the provincial secretary (1638–60) and the Council minutes (1638–49); J. Franklin Jameson, ed., *Narratives of New Netherland, 1609–1664* (New York, 1909); Arnold J. F. Van Laer, ed., "Letters of Wouter Van Twiller . . . 1636," *New York History*, XVIII (Oct. 1919), 44–50, and *Van Rensselaer Bowier Manuscripts: Being the Letters of Kiliaen Van Rensselaer, 1630–1643, and Other Documents Relating to the Colony of Rensselaerswyck* (Albany, 1908), in *State of New York, 90th Annual Report on the New York State Library*, II, a most extraordinary compilation of 849 pages, with documents actually spanning the period 1621–96.

THE STAMP OF PETER STUYVESANT

There is still no first-rate biography of Stuyvesant, but Henry H. Kessler and Eugene Rachlis, in *Peter Stuyvesant and His New York* (New York, 1959), have compiled a useful bibliography. Hendrik Van Loon's *Life and Times of Pieter Stuyvesant* (New York, 1928) is attractively written but sometimes misleading. Ellis Raesly's *Portrait of New Netherland* (New York, 1945) provides the best general treatment of this period. It is strangely organized and excessively whiggish but well researched and especially strong on social and literary history. For comparative insight, Raesly should be read alongside Paul Zumthor, *Daily Life in Rembrandt's Holland* (London, 1962). For attractive illustrations of period artifacts, see Maud E. Dilliard, *An Album of New Netherland* (New York, 1963).

The complex problem of religious toleration and church-state relations has been argued for a long time. The modern discussion begins with Frederick J. Zwierlein's *Religion in New Netherland: A History of the Development of the Religious Conditions in the Province of New Netherland, 1623–1664* (Rochester, 1910) and the same author's polemic "New Netherland Intolerance," *The Catholic Historical Review*, IV (1918), 186–216. More judicious treatment will be found in John Webb Pratt, *Religion, Politics, and Diversity: The Church-State Theme in New York History* (Ithaca, 1967); Gerald F. De Jong, "Dominie Johannes Megapolensis: Minister to New Netherland," *New-York Historical Society Quarterly*, LII (Jan. 1968), 7–47, and "The Dutch Reformed Church and Negro Slavery in Colonial America," *Church History*, XL (Dec. 1971), 423–36, a scrupulous examination of considerable evidence.

For commerce, immigration, and mobility in this period, see Pieter C. Emmer, "The History of the Dutch Slave Trade, A Bibliographical Survey," *Journal of Economic History*, XXXII (Sept. 1972), 728–47; Harold C. Syrett, "Private Enterprise in New Amsterdam," *William and Mary Quarterly*, 3d Ser., XI (Oct. 1954), 536–50; William T. Horton, *Jan Peeck, Tavern Keeper, Fur Trader and Land Owner* (Peekskill, N.Y., 1949); Morton Wagman, "The Rise of Pieter Claessen Wyckoff: Social Mobility on the Colonial Frontier," *New York History*, LIII (Jan. 1972), 5–24; and Bertus H. Wabeke, *Dutch Emigration to North America, 1624–1860* (Freeport, N.Y., 1944).

Problems of municipal government and judicial administration are treated in Philip L. White, "Municipal Government Comes to Manhattan," *New-York Historical Society Quarterly*, XXXVII (Apr. 1953), 146–57; W. Scott Van Alstyne, Jr., "The *Schout*: Precursor of Our District Attorney," *De Halve Maen*, XLII (Apr. 1967), 5–6, 15; (July 1967), 7–8; John E. O'Connor, "The Rattle Watch of New Amsterdam," ibid., XLIII (Apr. 1968), 11–12, 14; (July 1968), 9–12; (Oct. 1968), 13–14; Earle H. Houghtaling, Jr., "Administration of Justice in New Amsterdam," ibid., XLIII (Oct. 1968) 9–10, 15–16; (Jan. 1969), 17–19; Philip E. Mackey, "Capital Punishment in New Netherland," ibid., XLVII (July 1972), 7–8, 14; and Morton Wagman, The Struggle for Representative Government in New Netherland (unpubl. Ph.D. diss., Columbia University, 1969).

Communal life in the localities is superbly handled by Langdon G. Wright in

"Local Government and Central Authority in New Netherland," *The New-York Historical Society Quarterly*, LVII (Jan. 1973), 7–29, and Local Government in Colonial New York, 1640–1710 (unpubl. Ph.D. diss., Cornell University, 1974). Older studies include Irving Elting, *Dutch Village Communities on the Hudson River* (Baltimore, 1886); Augustus H. Van Buren, "Wiltwyck Under the Dutch," *Proceedings of the New York State Historical Association*, XI (Apr. 1912), 128–35; and Albert E. McKinley, "The English and Dutch Towns of New Netherland," *American Historical Review*, VI (Oct. 1900), 1–18, which is based upon outmoded assumptions about politics.

The Evolution of Long Island (New Haven, 1921), by Ralph H. Gabriel, has two useful chapters on the colonial period. Isabel M. Calder examines "The Earl of Stirling and the Colonization of Long Island" in *Essays in Colonial History Presented to Charles M. Andrews* (New Haven, 1931), 74–95; and Frederick W. Bogert concentrates upon Southold, Southampton, and East Hampton in "Long Island Settlements Prior to 1664," *De Halve Maen*, XXXVIII (Oct. 1963), 5–6, 15.

The diplomacy and decline of the Dutch period have recently been reexamined by Ronald D. Cohen, "The Hartford Treaty of 1650: Anglo-Dutch Cooperation in the Seventeenth Century," *New-York Historical Society Quarterly*, LIII (Oct. 1969), 311–32; and Kenneth Scott, ed., "*The Arms of Amsterdam*: An Extract from the Records of the General Court of Virginia, 1664," *Virginia Magazine of History and Biography*, LXXVII (Oct. 1969), 407–40. For an older account of "The Capture of New Amsterdam," see Henry L. Schoolcraft in the *English Historical Review*, XXII (Oct. 1907), 674–93, which concentrates on the diplomatic background.

Some of the most interesting source material for this period is found in Thomas F. O'Donnell, ed., *A Description of the New Netherlands by Adriaen Van der Donck* (Syracuse, 1968), written in 1652–53; Samuel Oppenheim, trans., "The Dutch Records of Kingston . . . 1658–1684," *Proceedings of the New York State Historical Association*, XI (1912), 1–171; Arnold J. F. Van Laer, ed., *Minutes of the Court of Rensselaerswyck, 1648–1652* (Albany, 1922), the only record of this court that has been preserved; and Berthold Fernow, ed., *Minutes of the Orphanmasters [Court] of New Amsterdam, 1655–1663* (New York, 1902), which is revealing about family life, social structure, and the transmission of property.

THE ANGLO-DUTCH PROPRIETARY

The single best study of this period is by Robert C. Ritchie, The Duke's Province: A Study of Proprietary New York, 1664–1685 (unpubl. Ph.D. diss., University of California at Los Angeles, 1972). It is especially valuable for information concerning taxation, economic issues, and population problems. See Ritchie's article "The Duke of York's Commission of Revenue," *New-York Historical Society Quarterly*, LVIII (July 1974), 177–87, a remarkable piece of research and reconstruction. For contrasting views on the problem of Anglo-

Dutch relations within the colony, see Steve J. Stern's "Knickerbockers Who Asserted and Insisted: The Dutch Interest in New York Politics, 1664–1691," ibid. (Apr. 1974), 113–38; and Albert E. McKinley, "The Transition from Dutch to English Rule in New York," *American Historical Review*, VI (July 1900), 693–724.

For the context of Anglo-Dutch diplomacy and cultural contacts during this period, see Charles H. Wilson, *Profit and Power: A Study of England and the Dutch Wars* (London, 1957); P. G. Rogers, *The Dutch in the Medway* (London, 1970), for the situation in 1667; Jan Kupp, "Aspects of New York-Dutch Trade under the English, 1670–1674," *New-York Historical Society Quarterly*, LVIII (Apr. 1974), 139–47; Ronald D. Cohen, "The New England Colonies and the Dutch Recapture of New York, 1673–1674," ibid., LVI (Jan. 1972), 54–78; D. W. Davies, *Dutch Influences on English Culture, 1558–1625* (Ithaca, 1964); and Charles A. Van Patten, "Dutch and English as Sister Languages," *De Halve Maen*, XLVI (Apr. 1971), 7–8.

Changes in the legal system and in the means of access to land in these years are discussed by Morton Pennypacker, *The Duke's Laws: Their Antecedents, Implications and Importance* (New York, 1944); S. G. Nissenson, "The Development of a Land Registration System in New York," *New York History*, XX (Jan. 1939), 16–42; Gerald F. Rooney, "Daniel Denton, Publicist of Colonial New York," *New-York Historical Society Quarterly*, LV (July 1971), 272–76; and Julius Goebel, *Some Legal and Political Aspects of the Manors in New York* (Baltimore, 1928), an important 22-page pamphlet.

A biographical approach to the political and administrative history of these years may be obtained through Montgomery Schuyler, *Richard Nicolls: First Governor of New York, 1664–1668* (New York, 1933); Kenneth Scott and Charles E. Baker, "Renewals of Governor Nicolls' Treaty of 1665 with the Esopus Indians," *New-York Historical Society Quarterly*, XXXVII (July 1953), 251–72; Jeanne G. Bloom, Sir Edmund Andros: A Study in Seventeenth-century Colonial Administration (unpubl. Ph.D. diss., Yale University, 1962), especially Pt. i, which concerns New York between 1674 and 1681; Elizur Y. Smith, "Captain Thomas Willett: First Mayor of New York," *New York History*, XXI (Oct. 1940), 404–17; and Bayrd Still, "New York's Mayoralty: The Formative Years," *New-York Historical Society Quarterly*, XLVII (July 1963), 239–55.

The social history of this period, especially changes in the colony's ethnic composition, emerges from such scattered treatments as Lawrence H. Leder, "The Unorthodox Domine: Nicholas Van Rensselaer," *New York History*, XXXV (Apr. 1954), 166–76; Kenneth E. Hasbrouck, "The 'Duzine' of New Paltz, New York," *De Halve Maen*, XXXVIII (Apr. 1963), 7–8; Matteo Spalletta, "Divorce in Colonial New York," *New-York Historical Society Quarterly*, XXXIX (Oct. 1955), 422–40; Peter Gouldesbrough, "An Attempted Scottish Voyage to New York in 1669," *Scottish Historical Review*, XL (Apr. 1961), 56–62; Henry Bayer, *The Belgians: First Settlers in New York and in the Middle States* (New

York, 1925); and John O. Evjen, *Scandinavian Immigrants in New York, 1630–1674* (Minneapolis, 1916), a biographical compendium.

A rich variety of sources, both public and private, has survived from this period. Among the most useful are Victor H. Paltsits, ed., *Minutes of the Executive Council of the Province of New York: Administration of Francis Lovelace, 1668–1673,* 2 vols. (Albany, 1910); "Transcription from the Records in the State Library from 1664 . . . to 1671," in Hugh Hastings, *Second Annual Report of the State Historian of the State of New York* (Albany, 1897), 135–369; "Transcription of the Records between the Years 1673 and 1675," in Hugh Hastings,*Third Annual Report of the State Historian of the State of New York, 1897* (Albany, 1898), 157–435; "Proceedings of the General Court of Assizes [1680–82]," *Collections of the New-York Historical Society for the Year 1912* (New York, 1913), 3–38; "Original Book of New York Deeds, 1673–1675," *Collections of the New-York Historical Society for the Year 1913* (New York, 1914), 3–62; and for the Albany area, Jonathan Pearson and Arnold J. F. Van Laer, trans. and eds., *Early Records of the City and County of Albany and Colony of Rensselaerswyck,* 4 vols. (Albany, 1869–1919) (I covers the period 1656–75, II the period 1678–1704, III the period 1660–96, and all are notarial papers; IV contains mortgages and wills for the periods 1658–60 and 1681–1765); and Arnold J. F. Van Laer, ed., *Minutes of the Court of Albany, Rensselaerswyck and Schenectady, 1668–1673, 1675–1680, 1680–1685,* 3 vols. (Albany, 1926–32).

On the more personal side, see Arnold J. F. Van Laer, ed., *Correspondence of Jeremias van Rensselaer, 1651–1674* (Albany, 1932) and *Correspondence of Maria van Rensselaer, 1669–1689* (Albany, 1935), letters revealing the business management of the patroonship and providing an intimate picture of daily life in the upriver community. We have three good accounts of the province between 1670 and 1680: Daniel Denton, *A Brief Description of New York* . . . (London, 1670; New York, 1845); Charles Wooley, *A Two Years Journal in New-York* . . . [1678–80] (London, 1701), reprinted in Cornell Jaray, ed., *Historic Chronicles,* I; and Bartlett B. James, ed., *Journal of Jasper Danckaerts, 1679–1680* (New York, 1913), a fine travel account by two Labadist visitors.

POLITICS AND THE PERILS OF INSTABILITY

The political economy of this period may be understood from Dorothy C. Barck, The Bolting Monopoly of New York City, 1680–1694 (unpubl. M.A. thesis, Cornell University, 1922), which emphasizes antagonisms between the metropolis and outlying rural communities; Helen Broshar, "The First Push Westward of the Albany Traders," *Mississippi Valley Historical Review,* VII (Dec. 1920), 228–41; Gary B. Nash, "The Quest for the Susquehanna Valley: New York, Pennsylvania, and the 17th-century Fur Trade," *New York History,* XLVIII (Jan. 1967), 3–27; and W. J. Eccles, *Canada under Louis XIV, 1663–1701* (New York, 1964), a scholarly and readable synthesis.

For war and diplomacy, Cadwallader Colden's *History of the Five Indian Nations*

Depending on the Province of New-York in America (London, 1727 and 1747; Ithaca, 1958) includes Indian speeches from the 1680s; George T. Hunt, *The Wars of the Iroquois: A Study in Intertribal Trade Relations* (Madison, Wis., 1940) is especially concerned with the Hurons and their neighbors; Robert A. Goldstein, *French-Iroquois Diplomatic and Military Relations, 1609–1701* (The Hague, 1969) has supplementary value; and Francis Jennings, "The Constitutional Evolution of the Covenant Chain," *Proceedings of the American Philosophical Society*, CXV (Apr. 1971), 88–96, opens up a fresh line of inquiry.

The most useful biographical approaches are Lawrence H. Leder, *Robert Livingston (1654–1728) and the Politics of Colonial New York* (Chapel Hill, 1961), in which there is the best available account of Leisler's Rebellion from the perspective of Albany; John H. Kennedy, *Thomas Dongan, Governor of New York (1682–1688)* (Washington, D.C., 1930); and Thomas P. Phelan, *Thomas Dongan, Colonial Governor of New York, 1683–1688* (New York, 1933). Arthur E. Peterson, *New York as an Eighteenth Century Municipality* (New York, 1917), contains a good deal of related information on the 1680s.

For the sociopolitical context of Leisler's Rebellion, see David S. Lovejoy, "Equality and Empire: The New York Charter of Libertyes, 1683," *William and Mary Quarterly*, 3d Ser., XXI (Oct. 1964), 493–515; Thomas J. Archdeacon, *New York City, 1664–1710: Conquest and Change* (Ithaca, 1975); and two extraordinary (but unpublished) papers by John M. Murrin: The Perils of Premature Anglicization: The Dutch, the English, and Leisler's Rebellion in New York (Oct. 1968) and English Rights as Ethnic Aggression: The English Conquest, the Charter of Liberties of 1683 and Leisler's Rebellion in New York (Dec. 1973).

For the rebellion itself, the best account is by David S. Lovejoy, *The Glorious Revolution in America* (New York, 1972), chaps. 14, 17, and 19. Also helpful are Charles H. McCormick, Leisler's Rebellion (unpubl. Ph.D. diss., American University, 1971); Bernard Mason, "Aspects of the New York Revolt of 1689," *New York History*, XXX (Apr. 1949), 165–80; and Jerome R. Reich, *Leisler's Rebellion: A Study of Democracy in New York, 1664–1720* (Chicago, 1953), which must be used with critical care.

For the documentary materials, see "Papers Relating to the Administration of Lieut. Gov. Leisler, 1689–1691," in O'Callaghan, ed., *Documentary History*, II, 1–438; "Documents Relating to the Administration of Leisler," *Collections of the New-York Historical Society for the Year 1868* (New York, 1868), 241–426; and three sets of sources edited by Lawrence H. Leder: " 'Like Madmen through the Streets': The New York City Riot of June 1690," *New-York Historical Society Quarterly*, XXXIX (Oct. 1955), 405–15; "Captain Kidd and the Leisler Rebellion," ibid., XXXVIII (Jan. 1954), 48–53; and "Records of the Trials of Jacob Leisler and His Associates," ibid., XXXVI (Oct. 1952), 431–57.

ANGLICIZATION AND SOCIAL CHANGE

The changing dimensions of Anglo-American politics after 1691 may be traced through a valuable series of articles: Lawrence H. Leder, "Dongan's New York and Fletcher's London: Personality and Politics," *New-York Historical Society Quarterly*, LV (Jan. 1971), 28–37; John C. Rainbolt, "The Creation of a Governor and Captain General for the Northern Colonies," ibid., LVII (Apr. 1973), 101–20, and "A 'great and usefull designe': Bellomont's Proposal for New York, 1698–1701," ibid., LIII (Oct. 1969), 333–51; John D. Runcie, "The Problem of Anglo-American Politics in Bellomont's New York," *William and Mary Quarterly*, 3d Ser., XXVI (Apr. 1969), 191–217; and G. M. Waller, "New York's Role in Queen Anne's War, 1702–1713," *New York History*, XXXIII (Jan. 1952), 40–53.

The leading men of these decades appear in James S. Leamon, War, Finance, and Faction in Colonial New York: The Administration of Governor Benjamin Fletcher, 1692–1698 (unpubl. Ph.D. diss., Brown University, 1961); Frederic De Peyster, *The Life and Administration of Richard, Earl of Bellomont . . . 1697 to 1701* (New York, 1879); Stanley H. Friedelbaum, Bellomont: Imperial Administrator—Studies in Colonial Administration during the 17th Century (unpubl. Ph.D. diss., Columbia University, 1955); Arthur D. Pierce, "A Governor in Skirts [Cornbury]," *Proceedings of the New Jersey Historical Society*, LXXXIII (Jan. 1965), 1–9; and the eminently readable Dixon Ryan Fox, *Caleb Heathcote, Gentleman Colonist: The Story of a Career in the Province of New York, 1692–1721* (New York, 1926).

Piracy and politics constitute the central theme of Willard H. Bonner, " 'Clamors and False Stories': The Reputation of Captain Kidd," *New England Quarterly*, XVII (June 1944), 179–208; Jacob Judd, "Lord Bellomont and Captain Kidd; A Footnote to an Entangled Alliance," *New-York Historical Society Quarterly*, XLVII (Jan. 1963), 66–74, and "Frederick Philipse and the Madagascar Trade," ibid., LV (Oct. 1971), 354–74.

Although we still have much to learn, there is a fair amount of literature on the emergence of an Anglo-American legal system after 1691: "Law in Colonial New York: The Legal System of 1691," *Harvard Law Review*, LXXX (1967), 1757–72; Herbert A. Johnson, "The Advent of Common Law in Colonial New York," in George A. Billias, ed., *Law and Authority in Colonial America* (Barre, Mass., 1965), 74–91, and "The Prerogative Court of New York, 1686–1776," *American Journal of Legal History*, XVII (Apr. 1973), 95–144, concerning the probate of wills; Albert P. Blaustein, "New York Bar Associations Prior to 1870," ibid., XII (Jan. 1968), 50–57; John R. Aiken, Utopianism and the Emergence of the Colonial Legal Profession: New York, 1664–1710, a Test Case (unpubl. Ph.D. diss., University of Rochester, 1967), an unusually interesting and original piece of work; Alden Chester and E. Melvin Williams, *Courts and Lawyers of New York: A History, 1609–1925*, 3 vols. (New York, 1925);

and a fascinating little monograph by Robert F. Seybolt, *The Colonial Citizen of New York City: A Comparative Study of Certain Aspects of Citizenship Practice in Fourteenth Century England and Colonial New York City* (Madison, Wis., 1918).

The denominational vicissitudes of these years have been explored by Thomas F. O'Connor, "Religious Toleration in New York, 1664-1700," *New York History*, XVII (Oct. 1936), 391-410; Gerald F. De Jong, "The Formative Years of the Dutch Reformed Church on Long Island," *Journal of Long Island History*, VIII (Summer-Fall 1968), 1-16; IX (Winter-Spring 1969), 1-20; and Boyd S. Schlenther, ed., *The Life and Writings of Francis Makemie* (Philadelphia, 1971), a valuable and interesting volume.

Alterations in family life may be perceived in Patricia J. Gordon, The Livingstons of New York, 1675-1860: Kinship and Class (unpubl. Ph.D. diss., Columbia University, 1959); Lawrence H. Leder, "Robert Livingston's Sons: Preparation for Futurity," *New York History*, L (July 1969), 234-49; John A. Krout, "Behind the Coat of Arms: A Phase of Prestige in Colonial New York," ibid., XVI (Jan. 1935), 45-52; and Mrs. John King Van Rensselaer, *The Goede Vrouw of Mana-ha-ta: At Home and in Society, 1609-1760* (New York, 1898).

Examples of architectural developments at this time occur in Peter W. Cook, "The Van Vechten House, Greene County, New York," *The Magazine Antiques*, CV (Feb. 1974), 392-97; Chase Viele, "The Knickerbockers of Upstate New York," *De Halve Maen*, XLVII (Oct. 1972), 5-6, 15-17; *Stone Houses of the Paltz Patentees* (New Paltz, N.Y., n.d.); and *Historical Sketch of the Old Dutch Church of Sleepy Hollow, Erected in 1685 and Organized in 1697* (North Tarrytown, N.Y., n.d.).

For some changes in the material conditions of life, see Wilberforce Eames, *The First Year of Printing in New York* [1693] (Chicago, 1928); George O. Zabriskie, "Calendars, Weights and Measures of Colonial Times," *De Halve Maen*, XLI (July 1966), 9-10, 17, which emphasizes the transition in 1703; George W. Roach, "Colonial Highways in the Upper Hudson Valley," *New York History*, XL (Apr. 1959), 93-116; and Donald E. Stanford, "The Giant Bones of Claverack, New York, 1705," ibid., XL (Jan. 1959), 47-61.

The primary sources available for this period are especially revealing about social conditions in New York City: "Ledger Number I, Chamberlain's Office, Corporation of the City of New York, May 11, 1691, to November 12, 1699," in *Collections of the New-York Historical Society for the Year 1909* (New York, 1910), 1-110, which shows the payments made by the city for various services; "Tax Lists of the City of New York, December 1695-July 1699," *Collections of the New-York Historical Society for the Years 1910-1911* (New York, 1911-12), 1-315, which contains marvelous data concerning the socioeconomic structure of the city's population; Rev. John Miller, *A Description of the Province and City of New-York . . . in the Year 1695* (London, 1843), written by the Anglican chaplain stationed there between 1693 and 1695; Wayne Andrews, ed., "A Glance at New York in 1697: The Travel Diary of Dr. Benjamin Bullivant," a 19-page pamphlet revised from the *New-York Historical Society Quarterly* (Jan. 1956); and

Malcolm Freiberg, ed., *The Journal of Madam* [Sarah Kemble] *Knight* (Boston, 1972).

For documentary evidence of anglicization in the administration of justice, see Paul M. Hamlin and Charles E. Baker, eds., *Supreme Court of Judicature of the Province of New York, 1691–1704*, in *Collections of the New-York Historical Society for the Years 1945–1947*, 3 vols. (New York, 1952–59); Kenneth Scott, comp., *Records of the Chancery Court, Province and State of New York: Guardianships, 1691–1815* (Middletown, N.Y., 1971), which actually covers the periods 1701–2, 1720–35, 1740–70, before independence; Dixon Ryan Fox, ed., *The Minutes of the Court of Sessions, 1657–1696, Westchester County, New York* (White Plains, N.Y., 1924), which is very poorly edited; and Lawrence H. Leder, ed., " 'Dam'me Don't Stir a Man': Trial of New York Mutineers in 1700," *New-York Historical Society Quarterly*, XLII (July 1958), 261–83.

ECONOMIC GROWTH AND PROBLEMS
OF INTERGROUP RELATIONS

New York's position in the Atlantic economy has now been illuminated by a cluster of monographs; among them are: two articles by Curtis P. Nettels, "The Economic Relations of Boston, Philadelphia, and New York, 1680–1715," *Journal of Economic and Business History*, III (Feb. 1931), 185–215, and "England's Trade with New England and New York, 1685–1720," *Publications of the Colonial Society of Massachusetts*, XXVIII (1935), 322–50; William I. Davisson and Lawrence J. Bradley, "New York Maritime Trade: Ship Voyage Patterns, 1715–1765," *New-York Historical Society Quarterly*, LV (Oct. 1971), 309–17; Glen Gabert, "The New York Tobacco Trade, 1716–1742," *Essex Institute Historical Collections*, CV (Apr. 1969), 103–27; Philip L. White, *The Beekmans of New York in Politics and Commerce, 1647–1877* (New York, 1956), a fine family history; William I. Roberts, "Samuel Storke: An Eighteenth Century London Merchant Trading to the American Colonies," *Business History Review*, XXXIX (Summer 1965), 147–70; and Lawrence J. Bradley, The London/Bristol Trade Rivalry: Conventional History and the Colonial Office 5 Records for the Port of New York (unpubl. Ph.D. diss., University of Notre Dame, 1971).

For the inland economy, see Thomas Elliot Norton, *The Fur Trade in Colonial New York, 1686–1776* (Madison, Wisconsin, 1974), which to some degree supplies the much needed sequel to Trelease, *Indian Affairs in Colonial New York*; Charles W. Spencer, "The Land System of Colonial New York," *Proceedings of the New York State Historical Association*, XVI (July 1917), 150–64, which is inadequate; and Armand S. LaPotin, The Minisink Patent: A Study in Colonial Landholding and the Problems of Settlement in 18th-century New York (unpubl. Ph.D. diss., University of Wisconsin, 1974).

The manors of colonial New York have not yet received comprehensive treatment. Some two dozen pamphlets concerning each of the manors were published privately by the Order of Colonial Lords of Manors in America (between 1913 and 1940), of which the one by Julius Goebel, *Legal and Political Aspects of the Manors in New York* (1928), is of exceptional importance. They may be supplemented by Harry C. Melick, *The Manor of Fordham and Its Founders* (New York, 1950); *Philipsburg Manor* (Tarrytown, N.Y., 1969), a 56-page booklet that is helpful on the Philipse family enterprises during the first half of the eighteenth century; and Charles H. Brown, *Van Cortlandt Manor* (Tarrytown, N.Y., 1965).

Some of the political and economic problems of land settlement are treated in George S. Pryde, "Scottish Colonization in the Province of New York," *Proceedings of the New York State Historical Association*, XXXIII (Apr. 1935), 138–57; Walter Allen Knittle, *Early Eighteenth Century Palatine Emigration* (Philadelphia, 1937); H. T. Dickinson, "The Poor Palatines and the Parties," *English Historical Review*, LXXXII (July 1967), 464–85; James E. Scanlon, A Life of Robert Hunter, 1666–1734 (unpubl. Ph.D. diss., University of Virginia, 1969), and "British Intrigue and the Governorship of Robert Hunter," *New-York Historical Society Quarterly*, LVII (July 1973), 199–211.

There are several fine studies of labor and the economy, notably Samuel McKee, Jr., *Labor in Colonial New York, 1664–1776* (New York, 1935); Richard B. Morris, *Government and Labor in Early America* (New York, 1946); Edgar J. McManus, *A History of Negro Slavery in New York* (Syracuse, 1966); David Kobrin, *The Black Minority in Early New York* (Albany, 1971); and Ralph R. Ireland, "Slavery on Long Island: A Study of Economic Motivation," *Journal of Long Island History*, VI (Spring 1966), 1–12.

The monetary history of provincial New York must be pieced together from Curtis P. Nettels, *The Money Supply of the American Colonies before 1720* (Madison, Wis., 1934); Richard A. Lester, "Currency Issues to Overcome Depressions in Delaware, New Jersey, New York, and Maryland, 1715–1737," *Journal of Political Economy*, XLVII (Apr. 1939), 182–217; Herbert A. Johnson, *The Law Merchant and Negotiable Instruments in Colonial New York, 1664–1730* (Chicago, 1963), a meticulous monograph; John H. Hickcox, *A History of the Bills of Credit or Paper Money Issued by New York, from 1709 to 1789* (Albany, 1866); and Samuel K. Anderson, Taxation in Colonial New York, 1691–1755 (unpubl. M.A. thesis, University of Washington, 1953).

Representative source materials for the economy during these decades would include Edward L. Towle, ed., "A New Baron de Lahontan Memoir on New York and the Great Lakes Basin," *New York History*, XLVI (July 1965), 212–29 (a document written between 1710 and 1713); "Indentures of Apprentices, 1718–1727," in *Collections of the New-York Historical Society for the Year 1909* (New York, 1910), 111–99 (wonderfully detailed indentures stating the terms of each contract); Dorothy C. Barck, ed., *Papers of the Lloyd Family of the Manor of Queens Village, Lloyd's Neck, Long Island, New York, 1654–1826*, in *Collections of the New-York Historical Society for the Years 1926–1927*, 2 vols. (New York, 1927); Edmund B.

O'Callaghan, ed., *Letters of Isaac Bobin, Esq., Private Secretary of Hon. George Clarke, Secretary of the Province of New York, 1718–1730* (Albany, 1872); and Edmund D. Daniel, ed., " 'Dialogue Concerning Trade': A Satirical View of New York in 1726," *New York History*, LV (Apr. 1974), 199–229.

POLITICAL CHANGES AND
CONSTITUTIONAL CHALLENGES

Indian relations shaped one dimension of New York politics and may be traced through a series of essays that are uneven in quality: Anthony F. C. Wallace, "Origins of Iroquois Neutrality: The Grand Settlement of 1701," *Pennsylvania History*, XXIV (July 1957), 223–35; Richmond P. Bond, *Queen Anne's American Kings* (Oxford, 1952); Arthur H. Buffinton, "The Policy of Albany and English Western Expansion," *Mississippi Valley Historical Review*, VIII (Mar. 1922), 327–66; Allen W. Trelease, "The Iroquois and the Western Fur Trade: A Problem in Interpretation," ibid., XLIX (June 1962), 32–51; Jean Lunn, "The Illegal Fur Trade Out of New France, 1713–1760," *Canadian Historical Association Report of the Annual Meeting Held at Montreal* (Toronto, 1939), 61–76, a superb piece of research. Pertinent source materials are found in Lawrence H. Leder, ed., *The Livingston Indian Records, 1666–1723* (Gettysburg, Pa., 1956), and Charles H. McIlwain, ed., *An Abridgment of the Indian Affairs . . . Transacted in the Colony of New York, from the Year 1678 to the Year 1751 by Peter Wraxall* (Cambridge, Mass., 1915; reprinted 1968).

The transatlantic nature of New York politics during the middle third of the eighteenth century has now been wonderfully documented by Stanley N. Katz in *Newcastle's New York: Anglo-American Politics, 1732–1753* (Cambridge, Mass., 1968), in "Newcastle's New York Governors: Imperial Patronage during the Era of 'Salutary Neglect,' " *New-York Historical Society Quarterly*, LI (Jan. 1967), 7–23, and in Katz, ed., "A New York Mission to England: the London Letters of Lewis Morris to James Alexander, 1735 to 1736," *William and Mary Quarterly*, 3d Ser., XXVIII (July 1971), 439–84, a fascinating correspondence that is handsomely edited.

The steady undermining of royal prerogative in New York has been thoroughly analyzed from several perspectives: by Rex M. Naylor, "The Royal Prerogative in New York, 1691–1775," *New York History*, V (July 1924), 221–55; by Carole Shammas, "Cadwallader Colden and the Role of the King's Prerogative," *New-York Historical Society Quarterly*, LIII (Apr. 1969), 103–26; by Beverly McAnear, *The Income of the Colonial Governors of British North America* (New York, 1967), which concentrates heavily upon New York; and by Eugene R. Sheridan, Politics in Colonial America: The Career of Lewis Morris, 1671–1746 (unpubl. Ph.D. diss., University of Wisconsin, 1972).

The political process in New York has also undergone close scrutiny: Patricia U. Bonomi, *A Factious People: Politics and Society in Colonial New York* (New York,

1971), which ranges comprehensively from the 1690s to the 1760s; Nicholas Varga, New York Government and Politics during the Mid-18th Century (unpubl. Ph.D. diss., Fordham University, 1960), an institutional approach, and "Election Procedures and Practices in Colonial New York," *New York History*, XLI (July 1960), 249–77; and two very important articles by Milton M. Klein, "Democracy and Politics in Colonial New York," ibid., XL (July 1959), 221–46, and "Politics and Personalities in Colonial New York," ibid., XLVII (Jan. 1966), 3–16.

The famous Zenger affair has received exhaustive treatment from Leonard W. Levy, *Legacy of Suppression: Freedom of Speech and Press in Early American History* (Cambridge, Mass., 1960), chap. 4; Stanley N. Katz, ed., *A Brief Narrative of the Case and Trial of John Peter Zenger . . . by James Alexander* (Cambridge, Mass., 1963); and less usefully from Henry N. MacCracken, *Prologue to Independence: The Trials of James Alexander, American, 1715–1756* (New York, 1964).

The problem of courts as a volatile political issue in these years has been explored by Joseph H. Smith and Leo Hershkowitz, "Courts of Equity in the Province of New York: The Cosby Controversy, 1732–1736," *American Journal of Legal History*, XVI (Jan. 1972), 1–50, which is much richer in documentation but lacks the contextual focus of Stanley N. Katz, "The Politics of Law in Colonial America: Controversies over Chancery Courts and Equity Law in the Eighteenth Century," in *Perspectives in American History*, V (Cambridge, Mass., 1971), 257–84; by Paul M. Hamlin, *The First Grievance Committee in New York* (New York, 1939), involving an episode in 1727–28; and two essays by Julius Goebel, Jr., "The Courts and the Law in Colonial New York" and "Law Enforcement in Colonial New York," in David H. Flaherty, ed., *Essays in the History of Early American Law* (Chapel Hill, 1969), 245–77, 367–91.

Richard B. Morris has written "Criminal Conspiracy and Early Labor Combinations in New York," *Political Science Quarterly*, LII (Mar. 1937), 51–85, and edited *Select Cases of the Mayor's Court of New York City, 1674–1784* (Washington, D.C., 1935). For a biography of the controversial Supreme Court justice, see Mary P. McManus, Daniel Horsmanden, Eighteenth-century New Yorker (unpubl. Ph.D. diss., Fordham University, 1960).

SECTS AND THE STATE
IN A SECULAR SOCIETY

Martin E. Lodge, The Great Awakening in the Middle Colonies (unpubl. Ph.D. diss., University of California at Berkeley, 1964), is an improvement upon Charles H. Maxson, *The Great Awakening in the Middle Colonies* (Chicago, 1920). J. J. Mol has written an interesting but unsubstantiated essay called *The Breaking of Traditions: Theological Convictions in Colonial America* (Berkeley, 1968), which concentrates upon the Dutch Reformed church and the German Lutherans. For an invaluable biographical guide to "The Colonial Clergy of the Middle Colonies . . . 1628–1776," by Frederick L. Weis, see *Proceedings of the American Antiquarian Society*, LXVI (1956), 167–351.

The problem of church and state is discussed in Pratt, *Religion, Politics and Diversity*, cited previously, as well as in Carl Bridenbaugh, *Mitre and Sceptre: Transatlantic Faiths, Ideas, Personalities, and Politics, 1689–1775* (New York, 1962); Edward J. Cody, Church and State in the Middle Colonies, 1689–1763 (unpubl. Ph.D. diss., Lehigh University, 1970); and Kenneth B. West, "Quakers and the State: The Controversy Over Oaths in the Colony of New York," *Michigan Academician*, II (Spring 1970), 95–105, who uses fresh sources: the minutes of the New York Yearly Meeting and the Flushing Monthly Meeting.

For the Anglicans in New York, see Jean P. Jordan, The Anglican Establishment in Colonial New York, 1693–1783 (unpubl. Ph.D. diss., Columbia University, 1971); Alison G. Olson, "Governor Robert Hunter and the Anglican Church in New York," in Anne Whiteman et al., eds., *Statesmen, Scholars and Merchants: Essays in Eighteenth-century History Presented to Dame Lucy Sutherland* (Oxford, 1973), 44–64, which unfortunately misquotes primary sources; and Nelson R. Burr, "The Episcopal Church and the Dutch in Colonial New York and New Jersey, 1664–1784," *Historical Magazine of the Protestant Episcopal Church*, XIX (June 1950), 90–111. Cultural activity by the Society for the Propagation of the Gospel is detailed in Frank J. Klingberg, *Anglican Humanitarianism in Colonial New York* (Philadelphia, 1940), which is rich with quotations from unpublished letters; John Calam, *Parsons and Pedagogues: The S.P.G. Adventure in American Education* (New York, 1971); and Sheldon S. Cohen, "Elias Neau, Instructor to New York's Slaves," *New-York Historical Society Quarterly*, LV (Jan. 1971), 7–27. The standard account of New York's oldest Anglican church is Morgan Dix, *A History of the Parish of Trinity Church in the City of New York*, 4 vols. (New York, 1898–1906).

For the transformation of the Dutch Reformed church during the eighteenth century, see Edward T. Corwin, *A History of the Reformed Church, Dutch, in the United States* (New York, 1894), and *A Manual of the Reformed Church in America, 1628–1902* (New York, 1902); as well as James Tanis, *Dutch Calvinistic Pietism in the Middle Colonies: A Study in the Life and Theology of Theodorus Jacobus Frelinghuysen* (The Hague, 1967); John P. Luidens, The Americanization of the Dutch Reformed Church (unpubl. Ph.D. diss., University of Oklahoma, 1969); Alexander J. Wall, "The Controversy in the Dutch Church in New York Concerning Preaching in English, 1754–1768," *New-York Historical Society Quarterly*, XII (July 1928), 39–58; and John J. Birch, *The Pioneering Church of the Mohawk Valley* (Schenectady, 1955), which tells the story of the first Reformed church at Schenectady, founded in 1680.

In addition to Harry J. Kreider's *Lutheranism in Colonial New York* (New York, 1942), there is unusually good material to be found in Arnold J. H. Van Laer, trans., *The Lutheran Church in New York, 1649–1772: Records in the Lutheran Church*

Archives at Amsterdam, Holland (New York, 1946); Simon Hart and H. J. Kreider, eds., *Protocol of the Lutheran Church in New York City, 1702–1750* (New York, 1958); John P. Dern, ed., *The Albany Protocol: Wilhelm Christoph Berkenmeyer's Chronicle of Lutheran Affairs in New York Colony, 1731–1750* (Ann Arbor, 1971), valuable for social and economic matters generally. T. G. Tappert and J. W. Doberstein have translated and edited one of the most revealing personal documents from all of American history: *The Journals of Henry Melchior Muhlenberg*, 3 vols. (Philadelphia, 1942–58).

Leonard J. Trinterud has written the best history of colonial Presbyterianism, *The Forming of an American Tradition: A Re-examination of Colonial Presbyterianism* (Philadelphia, 1949). It can be supplemented by Robert H. Nichols, "The First Synod of New York, 1745–1758, and Its Permanent Effects," *Church History*, XIV (Dec. 1945), 239–55; and Clifford K. Shipton, "Ebenezer Pemberton," *Sibley's Harvard Graduates*, VI (Boston, 1942), 535–46. Short histories of the *Reformed Church, German*, by J. H. Dubbs, and the *Moravian Church*, by J. T. Hamilton, will be found in *The American Church History* series, VIII (New York, 1895).

For the history of Jews and Judaism in colonial New York, see Jacob Rader Marcus, *The Colonial American Jew, 1492–1776* (Detroit, 1970), 305–12, 397–411, 863–73, and 890–92; Leo Hershkowitz and Isidore S. Meyer, eds., *Letters of the Franks Family (1733–1748)* (Waltham, Mass., 1968); and various unpublished histories by Samuel Oppenheim, housed in the Library of the American Jewish Historical Society, Waltham, Mass.

A UTILITARIAN CULTURE AND
THE USES OF LEISURE

Perhaps the best general introduction to this topic may be obtained from Milton M. Klein, "The Cultural Tyros of Colonial New York," *South Atlantic Quarterly*, LXVI (Spring 1967), 218–32; Esther Singleton, *Social New York under the Georges, 1714–1776* (New York, 1902), which relies heavily upon newspaper sources and concentrates upon the elite; and the quaint but informative *Colonial Days in Old New York* (New York, 1896) by Alice Morse Earle.

For the development of printing and literacy, see Charles R. Hildeburn, *Sketches of Printers and Printing in Colonial New York* (New York, 1895), an antiquarian but nonetheless useful book; Harry B. Weiss, "A Graphic Summary of the Growth of Newspapers in New York and Other States, 1704–1820," *Bulletin of the New York Public Library*, LII (Apr. 1948), 182–96, and "The Writing Masters and Ink Manufacturers of New York City, 1737–1820," ibid., LVI (Aug. 1952), 383–94; and John Z. C. Thomas, Printing in Colonial New York, 1693–1763 (unpubl. Ph.D. diss., University of Tennessee, 1974). Some examples of literary productivity will be found in Lawrence H. Leder, ed., "Robert Hunter's *Androboros*," *Bulletin of the New York Public Library*, LXVIII

(Mar. 1964), 153–90; Walter Klinefelter, *Lewis Evans and His Maps (Transactions of the American Philosophical Society)*, LXI (July 1971); and Oscar Wegelin, ed., *Jupiter Hammon, American Negro Poet: Selections from His Writings and a Bibliography* (New York, 1915; reprinted 1970).

For the development of two kinds of cultural institutions, consult Austin B. Keep, *History of the New York Society Library* (New York, 1908); Allston Brown, *A History of the New York Stage, from the First Performance in 1732 to 1901*, 3 vols. (New York, 1903); and Hugh F. Rankin, *The Theater in Colonial America* (Chapel Hill, 1965). The institutionalization of legal education is discussed by Paul M. Hamlin, *Legal Education in Colonial New York* (New York, 1939); and Milton M. Klein, "The Rise of the New York Bar: The Legal Career of William Livingston," *William and Mary Quarterly*, 3d Ser., XV (July 1958), 334–58.

Historians have found the development of King's College a significant means of understanding religious and political issues as well as cultural aspirations in the maturing colony. See David C. Humphrey, King's College in the City of New York, 1754–1776 (unpubl. Ph.D. diss., Northwestern University, 1968); Milton M. Klein, "Church, State, and Education: Testing the Issue in Colonial New York," *New York History*, XLV (Oct. 1964), 291–303, and the treatment of the controversy in Klein's introduction to *The Independent Reflector*; Herbert and Carol Schneider, eds., *Samuel Johnson, President of King's College: His Career and Writings*, 4 vols. (New York, 1929)—I contains letters from 1754–62, II contains philosophical correspondence with Colden from 1744 to 1753, and IV contains materials pertinent to the founding of the college, 1753–63; Joseph J. Ellis, *The New England Mind in Transition: Samuel Johnson of Connecticut, 1696–1772* (New Haven, 1973), chaps. 9–11; and Beverly McAnear, ed., "American Imprints Concerning King's College," *The Papers of the Bibliographical Society of America*, XLIV (4th quarter 1950), 301–39.

The best study of primary education is by Carl F. Kaestle, *The Evolution of an Urban School System, New York City, 1750–1850* (Cambridge, Mass., 1973); but it should be supplemented by Jean P. Waterbury, *A History of Collegiate School, 1638–1963* (New York, 1965); William W. Kemp, *The Support of Schools in Colonial New York by the Society for the Propagation of the Gospel in Foreign Parts* (New York, 1913); William H. Kilpatrick, *The Dutch Schools of Colonial New Netherland and New York* (Washington, D.C., 1912); and Daniel J. Pratt, *Annals of Public Education in the State of New York, from 1626 to 1746* (Albany, 1872), a collection of official acts and historical records. *Apprenticeship and Apprenticeship Education in Colonial New England and New York* (New York, 1917) is conveniently discussed and well documented by Robert F. Seybolt.

Other aspects of apprenticeship, artisan life, and craftsmanship emerge handsomely from the pages of Charles F. Hummel, *With Hammer in Hand: The Dominy Craftsmen of East Hampton, New York* (Charlottesville, 1968); Norman S. Rice, *New York Furniture before 1840* [in the Collection of the Albany Institute of History and Art] (Albany, 1962); V. Isabelle Miller, *Furniture by New York*

Cabinetmakers, 1650 to 1860 (New York, 1956); and Rita S. Gottesman, comp., *The Arts and Crafts in New York, 1726–1776: Advertisements and News Items from New York City Newspapers,* in *Collections of the New-York Historical Society for the Year 1936* (New York, 1938), a rich resource.

We do not have an up-to-date treatment of early New York architecture, but the following have been found very useful: Harold D. Eberlein, *Manors and Historic Homes of the Hudson Valley* (Philadelphia, 1924); Helen W. Reynolds, *Dutch Houses in the Hudson Valley before 1776* (New York, 1929); Rosalie F. Bailey, *Pre-Revolutionary Dutch Houses and Families in Northern New Jersey and Southern New York* (New York, 1936); Roderic H. Blackburn, "Restorations in the Dutch Settlement of Kinderhook," *The Magazine Antiques,* LII (Dec. 1972), 1068–72; and John Fitchen, *The New World Dutch Barn* (Syracuse, 1968), with examples ranging from the 1680s to the 1780s.

Early art is beginning to receive the treatment it so richly deserves. The most exciting recent works are by Mary C. Black, "Pieter Vanderlyn and Other Limners of the Upper Hudson," and Wayne Craven, "Painting in New York City, 1750–1775," both in Ian M. G. Quimby, ed., *American Painting to 1776: A Reappraisal* (Charlottesville, 1971), 217–49, 251–97; David H. Dickason, *William Williams: Novelist and Painter of Colonial America, 1727–1791* (Bloomington, Ind., 1971); and Jules D. Prown, *John Singleton Copley: In America, 1738–1774* (Cambridge, Mass., 1966). Older works, with many reproductions of the art itself, include G. C. Groce, Jr., "New York Painting before 1800," *New York History,* XIX (Jan. 1938), 44–57; Waldron P. Belknap, Jr., *American Colonial Painting: Materials for a History* (Cambridge, Mass., 1959), with a long section on New York artists and their patrons, 63–270; the Albany Institute, *Hudson Valley Paintings, 1700–1750* (Albany, 1959); and Hannah R. London, *Portraits of Jews by Gilbert Stuart and Other Early American Artists* (Rutland, Vt., 1927).

The story of science in colonial New York revolves very much around Cadwallader Colden. Particularly helpful is Brooke Hindle, "Cadwallader Colden's Extension of the Newtonian Principles," *William and Mary Quarterly,* 3d Ser., XIII (Oct. 1956), 459–75. Three unpublished dissertations are also illuminating: Alfred R. Hoermann, A Figure of the American Enlightenment: Cadwallader Colden (University of Toronto, 1970); John S. Martin, Social and Intellectual Patterns in the Thought of Cadwallader Colden (University of Wisconsin, 1965); and Jonathan Harris, The Rise of Medical Science in New York, 1720–1820 (New York University, 1971). For comprehensive treatment in a broader context, see Raymond P. Stearns, *Science in the British Colonies of America* (Urbana, Ill., 1970), especially 491–501 and 559–75.

Three primary documents are especially fascinating for the cultural life of the mid-eighteenth century: Milton M. Klein, ed., *The Independent Reflector . . . by William Livingston and Others* (Cambridge, Mass., 1963); Carl Bridenbaugh, ed., *Gentleman's Progress: The Itinerarium of Dr. Alexander Hamilton, 1744* (Chapel Hill, 1948), 49–96, a marvelous source because he traveled the length of the Hudson

Valley as well as Long Island; and Mrs. Anne M. Grant, *Memoirs of an American Lady* (London, 1808; 1901 ed., 2 vols.), for a childhood spent in the Albany area between 1758 and 1768.

EXPANSION, URBANIZATION, AND THE PROBLEM OF COMMUNITY

The population growth of this period may be traced through Evarts B. Greene and Virginia D. Harrington, *American Population before the Federal Census of 1790* (New York, 1932); Robert V. Wells, "The New York Census of 1731," *New-York Historical Society Quarterly*, LVII (July 1973), 255–59; Ira Rosenwaike, *Population History of New York City* (Syracuse, 1972); and Carl Abbott, "The Neighborhoods of New York, 1760–1775," *New York History*, LV (Jan. 1974), 35–54. A fascinating firsthand view of the native population arises from John Bartram, *Observations on the Inhabitants, Climate, Soil . . . and other matters worthy of Notice . . . in his Travels from Pensilvania to Onondago, Oswego and the Lake Ontario . . .* (London, 1751).

The growth of urban problems in New York City will be seen in the handling of public health, welfare, and police responsibilities. For the first, see Charles H. Weidner, *Water for a City: A History of New York City's Problem from the Beginning to the Delaware River System* (New Brunswick, N.J., 1974); and John Duffy, *A History of Public Health in New York City, 1625–1866* (New York, 1968). For the second, see David M. Schneider, *The History of Public Welfare in New York State, 1609–1866* (Chicago, 1938); Raymond A. Mohl, "Poverty in Early America, A Reappraisal: The Case of Eighteenth-century New York City," *New York History*, L (Jan. 1969), 5–28; and Kenneth Scott, "The Church Wardens and the Poor in New York City, 1693–1747," *New York Genealogical and Biographical Record*, IC–CII (July 1968–July 1971), passim. Problems of crime control and the administration of justice have been magnificently analyzed in Douglas S. Greenberg, "Persons of Evil Name and Fame": Crime and Law Enforcement in the Colony of New York, 1691–1776 (unpubl. Ph.D. diss., Cornell University, 1974); in Julius Goebel, Jr., and T. Raymond Naughton, *Law Enforcement in Colonial New York: A Study in Criminal Procedure (1664–1776)* (New York, 1944); in Leonard W. Levy and Lawrence H. Leder, " 'Exotic Fruit': The Right Against Compulsory Self-Incrimination in Colonial New York," *William and Mary Quarterly*, 3d Ser., XX (Jan. 1963), 3–32; and in James F. Richardson, *The New York Police: Colonial Times to 1901* (New York, 1970).

The social and legal circumstances of black people, particularly in relation to problems of social order, have been intensively discussed by Gerald F. De Jong, "The Dutch Reformed Church and Negro Slavery in Colonial America," *Church History*, XL (Dec. 1971), 423–36; Oscar R. Williams, Jr., Blacks and Colonial Legislation in the Middle Colonies (unpubl. Ph.D. diss., Ohio State University, 1969); and Edwin Olson, "The Slave Code in Colonial New York,"

Journal of Negro History, XXIX (Apr. 1944), 147–65. The two "revolts" still have not received their definitive treatment but are described in Kenneth Scott, "The Slave Insurrection in New York in 1712," *New-York Historical Society Quarterly*, XLV (Jan. 1961), 43–74; T. Wood Clarke, "The Negro Plot of 1741," *New York History*, XXV (Apr. 1944), 167–81; Ferenc M. Szasz, "The New York Slave Revolt of 1741: A Re-examination," ibid., XLVIII (July 1967), 215–30; Thomas J. Davis, ed., *The New York Conspiracy* [of 1741] *by Daniel Horsmanden* (1744; Boston, 1971); and also Leo Hershkowitz, ed., "Tom's Case: An Incident, 1741," *New York History*, LII (Jan. 1971), 62–71, a separate episode.

The political and administrative life of New York City during the middle third of the eighteenth century has been thoroughly described by George W. Edwards in *New York as an Eighteenth-Century Municipality, 1731–1776* (New York, 1917) and in "New York City Politics before the American Revolution," *Political Science Quarterly*, XXXVI (Dec. 1921), 586–602. See also Beverly McAnear, "The Place of the Freeman in Old New York," *New York History*, XXI (Oct. 1940), 418–30; Bruce M. Wilkenfeld, "The New York City Common Council, 1689–1800," ibid., LII (July 1971), 249–74; and Samuel K. Anderson, "Public Lotteries in Colonial New York," *New-York Historical Society Quarterly*, LVI (Apr. 1972), 133–46.

Episodes especially divisive in the community are related in David C. Humphrey, "Urban Manners and Rural Morals: The Controversy over the Location of King's College," *New York History*, LIV (Jan. 1973), 4–23; and Herbert L. Osgood, ed., "The Society of Dissenters Founded at New York in 1769," *American Historical Review*, VI (Apr. 1901), 498–507. The growth of community and an accompanying sense of responsibility appear with special clarity in Patricia Bonomi's pioneering study "Local Government in Colonial New York [Kingston, 1711–76]: A Base for Republicanism," in Judd and Polishook, eds., *Aspects of Early New York Society and Politics*, 29–50. Other community studies include Carl Nordstrom, *Frontier Elements in a Hudson River Village* [Nyack] (Port Washington, N.Y., 1973), which is conceptually interesting but flawed as a research model; Jessica K. Ehrlich, A Town Study in Colonial New York: Newtown, Queens County (1642–1790) (unpubl. Ph.D. diss., University of Michigan, 1974); James T. Adams, *History of the Town of Southampton* (Bridgehampton, N.Y., 1918), which is useful on the subjects of commerce and piracy in the eighteenth century; and Abigail F. Halsey, *In Old Southampton* (New York, 1940).

The most recent and fullest work on Albany will be found in two unpublished dissertations: Stephen E. Sale, Colonial Albany: Outpost of Empire (University of Southern California, 1973), which attempts to cover the entire story in too brief a space; and David A. Armour, The Merchants of Albany, New York: 1686–1760 (Northwestern University, 1965), which explores unused business records to good advantage. Alice Kenney has examined the social structure of colonial Albany more thoroughly than anyone else: in "Dutch Patricians in

Colonial Albany," *New York History*, XLIX (July 1968), 249–83, and in an important but neglected series in *De Halve Maen*, XLV–XLVI (Apr. 1970–Apr. 1971), entitled "Patricians and Plebeians in Colonial Albany," based especially upon a careful inquiry into church records.

Kenney has also given us the latest family study, *The Gansevoorts of Albany: Dutch Patricians in the Upper Hudson Valley* (Syracuse, 1969). Brooke Hindle's "A Colonial Governor's Family: The Coldens of Coldengham," *New-York Historical Society Quarterly*, XLV (July 1961), 233–50, is quite fascinating. E. B. Livingston's *The Livingstons of Livingston Manor* (New York, 1910) is invaluable as a source for that important New York family. Similarly, see George W. Schuyler, *Colonial New York: Philip Schuyler and His Family*, 2 vols. (New York, 1885). Charles E. Ironside, *The Family in Colonial New York* (New York, 1942), is totally inadequate and cries out to be redone.

Aspects of class structure and conflict, a controversial issue among historians of New York, are interpreted diversely in Irving Mark, *Agrarian Conflicts in Colonial New York, 1711–1775* (New York, 1940); Sung Bok Kim, "A New Look at the Great Landlords of Eighteenth-Century New York," *William and Mary Quarterly*, 3d Ser., XXVII (Oct. 1970), 581–614, an impressive piece of research, and The Manor of Cortlandt and Its Tenants, 1697–1783 (unpubl. Ph.D. diss., Michigan State University, 1966); Julian Gwyn, "Private Credit in Colonial New York: The Warren Portfolio, 1731–1795," *New York History*, LIV (July 1973), 268–93, a superlative and suggestive delineation of investments and the credit system; and Beverly McAnear, ed., "Mr. Robert R. Livingston's Reasons against a Land Tax," *The Journal of Political Economy*, XLVIII (Feb. 1940), 63–90.

Expansion, land speculation, and the political controversies they aroused have been written about at great length and with considerable skill by Ruth L. Higgins, *Expansion in New York, with Especial Reference to the Eighteenth Century* (Columbus, Ohio, 1931); Edith M. Fox, *Land Speculation in the Mohawk Country* (Ithaca, 1949); Julian Gwyn, "Prize Money and Rising Expectations: Admiral Warren's Personal Fortune," *Historie Sociale/Social History: A Canadian Review*, no. 8 (Nov. 1971), 84–101; Charles W. Spencer, "Sectional Aspects of New York Provincial Politics," *Political Science Quarterly*, XXX (Sept. 1915), 397–424; Oscar Handlin, "The Eastern Frontier of New York," *New York History*, XVIII (Jan. 1937), 50–75; Dixon Ryan Fox, *Yankees and Yorkers* (New York, 1940), a distinguished book of great charm, slight documentation, and some misleading generalizations; Ian C. C. Graham, *Colonists from Scotland: Emigration to North America, 1707–1783* (Ithaca, 1956); Philip J. Schwarz, New York's Provincial Boundaries: A Study of the Politics of Interest (unpubl. Ph.D. diss., Cornell University, 1973), which spans the full period 1664–1775; and Daniel J. Pratt, comp., *Report of the Regents of the University on the Boundaries of the State of New York*, 2 vols. (Albany, 1874–84), a rich documentary collection that covers the years 1614 to 1870.

WAR, TRADE, AND EMPIRE

General background on the colonial wars in New York may be obtained from Lawrence H. Gipson, *The British Empire before the American Revolution* (Caldwell, Idaho, and New York, 1936–70), especially III, V, VI, and VII; the ever readable Francis Parkman, *Montcalm and Wolfe*, 2 vols. (Boston, 1884); and Francis W. Halsey, *The Old New York Frontier: Its Wars with Indians and Tories, Its Missionary Schools, Pioneers and Land Titles, 1614–1800* (New York, 1901).

Anglo-American relations and an imperial perspective will be found in Edward P. Lilly, *The Colonial Agents of New York and New Jersey* (Washington, D.C., 1936); James R. Tootle, Anglo-Indian Relations in the Northern Theatre of the French and Indian War, 1748–1761 (unpubl. Ph.D. diss., Ohio State University, 1972); Alice Mapelsden Keys, *Cadwallader Colden: A Representative Eighteenth Century Official* (New York, 1906); Milton M. Klein, "Archibald Kennedy: Imperial Pamphleteer," in Lawrence H. Leder, ed., *The Colonial Legacy II: Some Eighteenth-Century Commentators* (New York, 1971), 75–105; Stanley N. Katz, "Between Scylla and Charybdis: James De Lancey and Anglo-American Politics in Early Eighteenth-Century New York," in A. G. Olson and R. M. Brown, eds., *Anglo-American Political Relations, 1675–1775* (New Brunswick, N.J., 1970), 92–108; and Stanley M. Pargellis, "The Four Independent Companies of New York," *Essays in Colonial History Presented to Charles M. Andrews* (New Haven, 1931), 96–123.

The Role of New York in King George's War, 1739–1748, is the subject of Robert E. Ziebarth's unpublished Ph.D. dissertation (New York University, 1972). James G. Lydon treats maritime aspects in *Pirates, Privateers, and Profits* (Upper Saddle River, N.J., 1970) and in "The Great Capture of 1744," *New-York Historical Society Quarterly*, LII (July 1968), 255–69. New York's position in intercolonial politics before the French and Indian War is described in Arthur H. Buffinton, "New York's Place in Intercolonial Politics," *New York State Historical Association Proceedings*, XVI (Jan. 1917), 51–62; John V. Jezierski, The Context of Union: The Origins, Provenience, and Failure of the Albany Plan of Union of 1754 (unpubl. Ph.D. diss., Indiana University, 1971); and John R. Alden, "The Albany Congress and the Creation of the Indian Superintendencies," *Mississippi Valley Historical Review*, XXVII (Sept. 1940), 193–210.

Until a worthy, full-scale biography of Sir William Johnson appears, we will have to be satisfied with Milton Hamilton's fine booklet, *Sir William Johnson and the Indians of New York* (Albany, n.d.), and his "Myths and Legends of Sir William Johnson," *New York History*, XXXIV (Jan. 1953), 3–26, along with James T. Flexner, *Mohawk Baronet: Sir William Johnson of New York* (New York, 1959); David S. McKeith, The Inadequacy of Men and Measures in English Imperial History: Sir William Johnson and the New York Politicians, A Case

Study (unpubl. Ph.D. diss., Syracuse University, 1971); and, best of all, *The Papers of Sir William Johnson*, 14 vols. (Albany, 1921–65).

The development of the French and Indian War from the Indians' perspective may be pieced together from John W. Lydekker, *The Faithful Mohawks* (New York, 1938), which emphasizes the political implications of S.P.G. activity; W. Vernon Kinietz, *The Indians of the Western Great Lakes, 1615–1760* (Ann Arbor, 1940); Georgianna C. Namack, *Fraud, Politics, and the Dispossession of the Indians: The Iroquois Land Frontier in the Colonial Period* (Norman, Okla., 1969); and Wilbur R. Jacobs, *Wilderness Politics and Indian Gifts: The Northern Colonial Frontier, 1748–1763* (Lincoln, Nebr., 1950). For the French vantage point, see W. J. Eccles, *The Canadian Frontier, 1534–1760* (New York, 1969), especially chaps. 7–8; John V. Jezierski, ed., "A 1751 Journal of Abbé François Picquet," *New-York Historical Society Quarterly*, LIV (Oct. 1970), 361–81; Guy Frégault, *Canada: The War of the Conquest* (Toronto, 1969); Edward P. Hamilton, ed., *Adventure in the Wilderness: The American Journals of Louis Antoine de Bougainville, 1756–1760* (Norman, Okla., 1964), the first English translation of the journals of Montcalm's aide-de-camp, who was in the Champlain Valley and at Fort William Henry in 1757; and Johnson G. Cooper, Oswego in the French-English Struggle in North America, 1720–1760 (unpubl. D.S.S. diss., Syracuse University, 1961).

General accounts of the war in New York may be obtained from Edward P. Hamilton, *The French and Indian Wars: The Story of Battles and Forts in the Wilderness* (New York, 1962), chaps. 12–16; Harrison Bird, *Battle for a Continent* (New York, 1965) and *Navies in the Mountains: The Battles on the Waters of Lake Champlain and Lake George, 1609–1814* (New York, 1962); and King L. Parker, Anglo-American Wilderness Campaigning, 1754–1764: Logistical and Tactical Developments (unpubl. Ph.D. diss., Columbia University, 1970). Important special studies include Stanley M. Pargellis, *Lord Loudoun in North America* (New Haven, 1933), for 1756–58; Theodore Thayer, "The Army Contractors for the Niagara Campaign, 1755–1756," *William and Mary Quarterly*, 3d Ser., XIV (Jan. 1957), 31–46; Wilbur R. Jacobs, "A Message to Fort William Henry: Drama of Siege and Indian Savagery," in Jacobs, *Dispossessing the American Indian: Indians and Whites on the Colonial Frontier* (New York, 1972), 68–74; and Robert C. Alberts, *The Most Extraordinary Adventures of Major Robert Stobo* (Boston, 1965).

Some of the political and constitutional implications of the war become clearer in Milton M. Klein, "William Livingston's *A Review of the Military Operations in North-America*," in Leder, ed., *The Colonial Legacy*, II, 107–40; James A. Rogers, Northern Colonial Opposition to British Imperial Authority during the French and Indian War (unpubl. Ph.D. diss., University of California at Santa Barbara, 1968); Charles W. Spencer, "Colonial Wars and Constitutional Development in New York," in *Addresses and Sermons Delivered before the Society of Colonial Wars in the State of New York, and Yearbook for 1914–1915* (n.p., 1915), 49–69; Mack Thompson, "Massachusetts and New York Stamp Acts," *William and Mary Quarterly*, 3d Ser., XXVI (Apr. 1969), 253–258; and Beverly McAnear, ed., "James Parker *versus* New York Province," *New York History*, XXII (July 1941), 321–30.

Some economic dimensions of these years emerge from William S. Sachs, "Interurban Correspondents and the Development of a National Economy before the Revolution: New York as a Case Study," ibid., XXXVI (July 1955), 320–35; William I. Roberts, "Ralph Carr: A Newcastle Merchant and the American Colonial Trade," *Business History Review*, XLII (Autumn 1968), 271–87; and Maxwell Whiteman, *Copper for America: The Hendricks Family and a National Industry, 1755–1939* (New Brunswick, N.J., 1971), 3–24. The war's sad consequences for Indian relations unfold in Nicholas B. Wainwright, *George Croghan, Wilderness Diplomat* (Chapel Hill, 1959); Irving Mark and Oscar Handlin, "Land Cases in Colonial New York, 1765–1767: The King v. William Prendergast," *New York University Law Quarterly Review*, XIX (1942), 165–94; John R. Sahli, "The Growth of British Influence among the Seneca to 1768," *Western Pennsylvania Historical Magazine*, XLIX (Apr. 1966), 127–39; and Peter Marshall, "Sir William Johnson and the Treaty of Fort Stanwix, 1768," *Journal of American Studies*, I (Oct. 1967), 149–79.

Some of the most revealing source materials for this period include Kenneth Scott, ed., *The Voyages and Travels of Francis Goelet, 1746–1758* (n.p., 1970); William S. Ewing, ed., "An Eyewitness Account by James Furnis of the Surrender of Fort William Henry, August 1757," *New York History*, XLII (July 1961), 307–16; Howard H. Peckham and Elias S. Wilentz, eds., *Journals of Major Robert Rogers* (New York, 1961), important for the theory and technique of "Indian fighting"; N. J. O'Conor, ed., *A Servant of the Crown in England and in North America, 1756–1761; Based upon the Papers of John Appy* . . . (New York, 1938); Hugh Hastings, ed., *Orderly Book and Journal of Major John Hawks on the Ticonderoga-Crown Point Campaign* . . . *1759–1760* (New York, 1911); Charles M. Hough, ed., *Reports of Cases in the Vice-Admiralty Court of the Province of New York* . . . *1715–1788* (New Haven, 1925); *Letter Book of John Watts, Merchant and Councillor of New York*, in *Collections of the New-York Historical Society for the Year 1928* (New York, 1928), covering 1762–65; and Oscar Handlin and Irving Mark, eds., "Chief Daniel Nimham v. Roger Morris, Beverly Robinson, and Philip Philipse—An Indian Land Case in Colonial New York, 1765–1767," *Ethnohistory*, XI (Summer 1964), 193–246.

"LIBERTY AND PROPERTY":
FROM RESISTANCE TO INDEPENDENCE

The advent of the American Revolution in New York has had a complex historiography and a vast bibliography. For the latter, see Milton M. Klein's comprehensive guide, *New York in the American Revolution: A Bibliography* (Albany, 1974). For the former, there is Bernard Mason, "The Heritage of Carl Becker:

The Historiography of the Revolution in New York," *New-York Historical Society Quarterly*, LIII (Apr. 1969), 127–47; and Milton M. Klein, "Detachment and the Writing of American History: The Dilemma of Carl Becker," in *Perspectives on Early American History: Essays in Honor of Richard B. Morris* (New York, 1973), 120–66. There are, essentially, three major issues about which historians still do not agree: whether the Revolution in New York was a dual event, a struggle for "home rule" but also to determine who would rule at home; whether *most* New Yorkers were indeed deeply conservative and reluctant to rebel (and if so, why?); and whether ideological considerations or matters of political economy played the more important role in determining attitudes and behavior during this period.

For a general treatment and detailed chronology, see Alexander C. Flick, *The American Revolution in New York: Its Political, Social and Economic Significance* (Albany, 1926); Evarts B. Greene, "New York and the Old Empire," *New York History*, VIII (Apr. 1927), 121–32; and Malcolm Decker, *Brink of Revolution: New York in Crisis, 1765–1776* (New York, 1964), which is poorly documented and overly dependent upon older interpretations, notably the seminal work by Carl L. Becker, *The History of Political Parties in the Province of New York, 1760–1776* (Madison, Wis., 1909). Three unpublished doctoral dissertations offer broad scope and newer emphases: Roger J. Champagne, The Sons of Liberty and the Aristocracy in New York Politics, 1765–1790 (University of Wisconsin, 1961); Keith W. Fitch, American Nationalism and the Revolution, 1763–1776: A Case Study of the Movement in the Colony of New York (Purdue University, 1972); and Jerome J. Gillen, Political Thought in Revolutionary New York, 1763–1789 (Lehigh University, 1972). Larry Gerlach has edited a documentary anthology that is equally broad in coverage, *The American Revolution: New York as a Case Study* (Belmont, Calif., 1972).

The judicial controversies that formed the backdrop to imperial conflict are discussed in Milton M. Klein, "Prelude to Revolution in New York: Jury Trials and Judicial Tenure," *William and Mary Quarterly*, 3d Ser., XVII (July 1960), 439–62; Herbert A. Johnson and David Syrett, "Some Nice Sharp Quillets of the Customs Law: The *New York* Affair, 1763–1767," ibid., XXV (July 1968), 432–51; Herbert A. Johnson, "George Harison's Protest: New Light on Forsey vs. Cunningham," *New York History*, L (Jan. 1969), 61–82, and (indirectly) "Civil Procedure in John Jay's New York," *American Journal of Legal History*, XI (Jan. 1967), 69–80.

For the intellectual and organizational development of radicalism in the colony, see Bernard Friedman, "The Shaping of the Radical Consciousness in Provincial New York," *Journal of American History*, LVI (Mar. 1970), 781–801; Herbert M. Morais, "The Sons of Liberty in New York," in Richard B. Morris, ed., *The Era of the American Revolution: Studies Inscribed to Evarts Boutell Greene* (New York, 1939), 269–89, an unfortunately simplistic essay; Roger J. Champagne, "Liberty Boys and Mechanics of New York City, 1764–1774," *Labor History*,

VIII (Spring 1967), 115–35, and "The Military Association of the Sons of Liberty," *New-York Historical Society Quarterly*, XLI (July 1957), 338–50; and Jesse Lemisch, Jack Tar vs. John Bull: The Role of New York's Seamen in Precipitating the Revolution (unpubl. Ph.D. diss., Yale University, 1962).

The Stamp Act Crisis: Prologue to Revolution (Chapel Hill, 1953) has been examined most thoroughly by Edmund S. and Helen M. Morgan. For related monographs, see Jesse Lemisch, "New York's Petitions and Resolves of December 1765: Liberals vs. Radicals," *New-York Historical Society Quarterly*, XLIX (Oct. 1965), 313–26; Neil R. Stout, "Captain Kennedy and the Stamp Act," *New York History*, XLV (Jan. 1964), 44–58; F. L. Engelman, "Cadwallader Colden and the New York Stamp Act Riots," *William and Mary Quarterly*, 3d Ser., X (Oct. 1953), 560–78; and Beverly McAnear, ed., "The Albany Stamp Act Riots," ibid., IV (Oct. 1947), 486–98.

The role of the press in prerevolutionary New York may be gleaned from Paul L. Ford, *The Journals of Hugh Gaine, Printer*, 2 vols. (New York, 1902); George F. Markham, An Analysis of the Treatment of George III in the New York City Newspapers, 1761–1776 (unpubl. Ph.D. diss., New York University, 1963); Michael D'Innocenzo and John J. Turner, Jr., "The Role of New York Newspapers in the Stamp Act Crisis, 1764–66," *New-York Historical Society Quarterly*, LI (July 1967), 215–31; (Oct. 1967), 345–65; Dwight L. Teeter, " 'King' Sears, the Mob and Freedom of the Press in New York, 1765–76," *Journalism Quarterly*, XLI (Autumn 1964), 539–44; Alfred L. Lorenz, *Hugh Gaine: A Colonial Printer-Editor's Odyssey to Loyalism* (Carbondale, Ill., 1972); and Beverly McAnear, "James Parker versus John Holt," *New Jersey Historical Society Proceedings*, LIX (Apr. 1941), 77–95; (July 1941), 198–212.

The presence of the British military as an irritant, and attendant problems, have been explored most thoroughly by John Shy, *Toward Lexington: The Role of the British Army in the Coming of the American Revolution* (Princeton, 1965); Nicholas Varga, "The New York Restraining Act: Its Passage and Some Effects, 1766–1768," *New York History*, XXXVII (July 1956), 233–58; Lee E. Olm, "The Mutiny Act for America: New York's Noncompliance," *New-York Historical Society Quarterly*, LVIII (July 1974), 188–214; and Lee R. Boyer, "Lobster Backs, Liberty Boys, and Laborers in the Streets: New York's Golden Hill and Nassau Street Riots," ibid., LVII (Oct. 1973), 281–308.

The Assembly elections of 1768 and 1769 received a rash of attention from Patricia U. Bonomi, "Political Patterns in Colonial New York City: The General Assembly Election of 1768," *Political Science Quarterly*, LXXXI (Sept. 1966), 432–47; Roger Champagne, "Family Politics versus Constitutional Principles: The New York Assembly Elections of 1768 and 1769," *William and Mary Quarterly*, 3d Ser., XX (Jan. 1963), 57–79; Bernard Friedman, "The New York Assembly Elections of 1768 and 1769: The Disruption of Family Politics," *New York History*, XLVI (Jan. 1965), 3–24; Lawrence H. Leder, "The New York Elections of 1769: An Assault on Privilege," *Mississippi Valley Historical Review*,

XLIX (Mar. 1963), 675–82; and James S. Olson, "The New York Assembly, the Politics of Religion, and the Origins of the American Revolution, 1768–1771," *Historical Magazine of the Protestant Episcopal Church*, XLIII (Mar. 1974), 21–28.

The economic situation during this period is best delineated by Joseph A. Ernst, *Money and Politics in America, 1755–1775: A Study in the Currency Act of 1764 and the Political Economy of Revolution* (Chapel Hill, 1973); Virginia D. Harrington, *The New York Merchant on the Eve of the Revolution* (New York, 1935); William M. Fowler, Jr., "A Yankee Peddler, Nonimportation, and the New York Merchants," *New-York Historical Society Quarterly*, LVI (Apr. 1972), 147–54; John A. Stevens, Jr., *Colonial New York: Sketches Biographical and Historical, 1768–1784* (New York, 1867); Irene D. Neu, "The Iron Plantations of Colonial New York," *New York History*, XXXIII (Jan. 1952), 3–24; and William I. Roberts, "American Potash Manufacture before the American Revolution," *Proceedings of the American Philosophical Society*, CXVI (Oct. 1972), 383–95.

Some of the most useful information and insights will be found in biographical studies, such as Dorothy R. Dillon, *The New York Triumvirate: A Study of the Legal and Political Careers of William Livingston, John Morin Scott, William Smith, Jr.* (New York, 1949); Milton M. Klein, The American Whig: William Livingston of New York (unpubl. Ph.D. diss., Columbia University, 1954); Harry M. Dunkak, John Morin Scott and Whig Politics in New York (1752–1769) (unpubl. Ph.D. diss., St. John's University, 1968); L. F. S. Upton, *The Loyal Whig: William Smith of New York and Quebec* (Toronto, 1969); Robert J. Christen, King Sears: Politician and Patriot in a Decade of Revolution (unpubl. Ph.D. diss., Columbia University, 1968; Isaac Q. Leake, *Memoir of the Life and Times of General John Lamb* (1850; New York, 1971); David F. Hawke, "Dr. Thomas Young—'Eternal Fisher in Troubled Waters': Notes for a Biography," *New-York Historical Society Quarterly*, LIV (Jan. 1970), 7–29. For the imperial side, see Catherine S. Crary, "The American Dream: John Tabor Kempe's Rise from Poverty to Riches," *William and Mary Quarterly*, 3d Ser., XIV (Apr. 1957), 176–95; Allan R. Raymond, The Political Career of Cadwallader Colden (unpubl. Ph.D. diss., Ohio State University, 1971); Solomon Henner, The Career of William Tryon as Governor of the Province of New York, 1771–1780 (unpubl. Ph.D. diss., New York University, 1968); and Milton W. Hamilton, "An American Knight in Britain; Sir John Johnson's Tour, 1765–1767," *New York History*, XLII (Apr. 1961), 119–44.

The difficult decision for or against independence is elucidated by Carl L. Becker, "John Jay and Peter Van Schaack," in *Everyman His Own Historian* (New York, 1935), 284–98; Edward P. Alexander, *A Revolutionary Conservative: James Duane of New York* (New York, 1938); Joseph Dorfman and Rexford Guy Tugwell, "John Jay: Revolutionary Conservative," in *Early American Policy: Six Columbia Contributors* (New York, 1960), 43–98; Bruce E. Steiner, *Samuel Seabury (1729–1796): A Study in the High Church Tradition* (Oberlin, Ohio, 1971); Leopold

S. Launitz-Schürer, "Whig-Loyalists: The De Lanceys of New York," *New-York Historical Society Quarterly*, LVI (July 1972), 179–98; and Don R. Gerlach, *Philip Schuyler and the American Revolution in New York, 1733-1777* (Lincoln, Nebr., 1964) and "Philip Schuyler and the 'Road to Glory': A Question of Loyalty and Competence," *New-York Historical Quarterly*, XLIX (Oct. 1965), 341–86.

The ultimate crisis has been treated from many perspectives: Bernard Mason, *The Road to Independence: The Revolutionary Movement in New York, 1773-1777* (Lexington, Ky., 1966); Staughton Lynd, "The Mechanics in New York Politics, 1774-1788," *Labor History*, V (Fall 1964), 225–46; Roger J. Champagne, "New York and the Intolerable Acts, 1774," *New-York Historical Society Quarterly*, XLV (Apr. 1961), 195–207, "New York Politics and Independence, 1776," ibid., XLVI (July 1962), 281–303, and "New York's Radicals and the Coming of Independence," *Journal of American History*, LI (June 1964), 21–40; Bruce Bliven, *Under the Guns: New York, 1775-1776* (New York, 1972); Milton M. Klein, "Failure of a Mission: The Drummond Peace Proposal of 1775," *Huntington Library Quarterly*, XXXV (Aug. 1972), 343–80; and Alice P. Kenney, "The Albany Dutch: Loyalists and Patriots," *New York History*, XLII (Oct. 1961), 331–50, a pioneering effort in political demography.

For frontier developments and Indian relations, see Eugene R. Fingerhut, Assimilation of Immigrants on the Frontier of New York, 1764–1776 (unpubl. Ph.D. diss., Columbia University, 1962); Charles R. Canedy, An Entrepreneurial History of the New York Frontier, 1739–1776 (unpubl. Ph.D. diss., Case Western Reserve University, 1967); Peter Marshall, "Colonial Protest and Imperial Retrenchment: Indian Policy, 1764-1768," *Journal of American Studies*, V (Apr. 1971), 1–17; Ralph T. Pastore, The Board of Commissioners for Indian Affairs in the Northern Department and the Iroquois Indians [1775-78] (unpubl. Ph.D. diss., University of Notre Dame, 1972); Barbara Graymont, *The Iroquois in the American Revolution* (Syracuse, 1972); and George F. G. Stanley, "The Six Nations and the American Revolution," *Ontario History*, LVI (Dec. 1964), 217–32.

The onset of fighting is described by Richard M. Ketchum in *The Winter Soldiers* (New York, 1973), which covers the hapless defense of New York in 1776–77; Thomas P. Robinson, "Some Notes on Major-General Richard Montgomery," *New York History*, XXXVII (Oct. 1956), 388–98; R. Arthur Bowler, "Sir Guy Carleton and the Campaign of 1776 in Canada," *Canadian Historical Review*, LV (June 1974), 131–40; Paul D. Nelson, "The Gates-Arnold Quarrel, September 1777," *New-York Historical Society Quarterly*, LV (July 1971), 235–52, and "Legacy of Controversy: Gates, Schuyler, and Arnold at Saratoga, 1777," *Military Affairs*, XXXVII (Apr. 1973), 41–47; and Don R. Gerlach, "After Saratoga: The General, His Lady, and 'Gentleman Johnny' Burgoyne," *New York History*, LII (Jan. 1971), 4–30.

For primary materials not previously mentioned, see John A. Stevens, ed., *Colonial Records of the New York Chamber of Commerce, 1768-1784* (New York, 1867);

G. D. Scull, ed., "The Montresor Journals," *Collections of the New-York Historical Society for the Year 1881* (New York, 1882), an important record of the years 1757–79 kept by two members of the British Corps of Engineers; Ross J. S. Hoffman, ed., *Edmund Burke, New York Agent; with His Letters to the New York Assembly* . . . (Philadelphia, 1956); Harold C. Syrett and Jacob E. Cooke, eds., *The Papers of Alexander Hamilton* (New York, 1961), I, covering 1768–78; *The Unpublished Correspondence of Robert R. Livingston* . . . (New York [American Art Association catalog], 1918); *Journals of the Provincial Congress, Provincial Convention, Committee of Safety and Council of Safety of the State of New York, 1775–1777,* 2 vols. (Albany, 1842); *Calendar of Historical Manuscripts, Relating to the War of the Revolution, in the Office of the Secretary of State, Albany, New York,* 2 vols. (Albany, 1868), covering 1775 to 1777. These volumes have no table of contents but a very fine index; many documents are reprinted in full or in part.

For the topography and physical remains of sites, see Richard Smith, *A Tour of Four Great Rivers: The Hudson, Mohawk, Susquehanna and Delaware in 1769, Being the Journal of Richard Smith of Burlington, New Jersey* (New York, 1906); New York State Historic Trust, *The Hudson Valley and the American Revolution* (Albany, 1968); Edward P. Hamilton, *The Champlain Valley in the American Revolution* (Albany, n.d.); and David C. Thurheimer, *Landmarks of the American Revolution in New York State* (Albany, 1972).